# Social Policy

## Theories, Concepts and Issues

THIRD EDITION

# Social Policy
## Theories, Concepts and Issues

THIRD EDITION

## Edited by Michael Lavalette and Alan Pratt

**SAGE Publications**

London • Thousand Oaks • New Delhi

Editorial arrangement and Chapters 1, 2, 3 and
    14 © Alan Pratt 2006
Editorial arrangement and Chapters 1, 4 and 16
    © Michael Lavalette 2006
Chapter 5 © Kath Woodward 2006
Chapters 6 and 13 © Laura Penketh 2006
Chapter 7 © Brian Lund 2006

Chapter 8 © Jonathan Pratt 2006
Chapter 9 © Beth Widdowson 2006
Chapter 10 © Iain Ferguson 2006
Chapter 11 © Stephen Cunningham and
    Jo Tomlinson 2006
Chapter 12 © Stephen Cunningham 2006
Chapter 15 © Gerry Mooney 2006

First edition published 2001
Second edition published 2006
Reprinted 2002, 2004, 2007

SAGE Publications Ltd
1 Oliver's Yard
55 City Road
London EC1Y 1SP

SAGE Publications Inc.
2455 Teller Road
Thousand Oaks, California 91320

SAGE Publications India Pvt Ltd
B-42, Panchsheel Enclave
Post Box 4109
New Delhi 110 017

**British Library Cataloguing in Publication data**

A catalogue record for this book is available
from the British Library

ISBN 978-1-4129-0170-3
ISBN 978-1-4129-0171-0 (pbk)

**Library of Congress Control Number: 2005926165**

Typeset by C&M Digitals (P) Ltd., Chennai, India
Printed on paper from sustainable resources
Printed in Great Britain by The Alden Press, Oxford

# Contents

# Contributors

**Stephen Cunningham**   is a Senior Lecturer in Social Policy at the University of Central Lancashire.

**Iain Ferguson**   is a Senior Lecturer in Social Work at the University of Stirling.

**Michael Lavalette**   is a Senior Lecturer in Social Policy at the University of Liverpool.

**Brian Lund**   is a Principal Lecturer in Social Policy at Manchester Metropolitan University.

**Gerry Mooney**   is a Senior Lecturer and Staff Tutor with the Open University in Scotland.

**Laura Penketh**   is a Lecturer in Social Work at Manchester University.

**Alan Pratt**   was formerly a Principal Lecturer in Social Policy at the University of Central Lancashire.

**Jonathan Pratt**   is a Lecturer in Social Policy at the University of Central Lancashire.

**Jo Tomlinson**   is a Principal Lecturer in Social Work at the University of Central Lancashire.

**Beth Widdowson**   is a Staff Tutor and Lecturer at the Open University.

**Kath Woodward**   is a Staff Tutor and Lecturer in Social Policy with the Open University.

# Acknowledgements

We would like to record our thanks to the contributors for their patience. We started putting the third edition together just as a computer virus struck one of our PC's, wiping chapters and causing a great deal of grief. The contributors simply re-sent their chapters and seemed to laugh off the inconvenience we had caused them!

At Sage there is a new team working with this edition but Zoë Elliott has been every bit as efficient as her predecessors. She has made working with Sage a pleasure.

Michael Lavalette
Alan Pratt
March 2005

# ONE
# Introduction
## *Michael Lavalette and Alan Pratt*

## Introduction

Many, perhaps most of you, will not be familiar with social policy as an academic discipline and the terrain it explores. Social policy, unlike English or politics or sociology, is not a subject that you will have covered in school, except perhaps as part of the history or citizenship curricula. As a result it is not surprising that many students are a little apprehensive when they first encounter the subject at university. What areas does it deal with? What skills will be needed? How does it relate to other subjects (like politics, history, sociology, economics or criminology)?

To help orientate you to the subject we start this book by trying to define social policy as a subject and outline the perspectives followed in the rest of the book. Our hope is that by the end of the book, you will be more aware of the contested nature of social policy debates and recognise the need to examine carefully all positions and statements on social welfare issues, no matter how painful the experience might be.

## What is Social Policy?

Richard Titmuss, who more than any other academic and teacher made the subject of social policy an accepted and 'respectable' academic discipline, wrote somewhat wearily of 'this tiresome business of defining social policy' (Titmuss, 1974: 28), and it is difficult not to sympathise with him.

One approach would be to follow the example of a multitude of books over the years and quote the opinions of the good and the great on the subject. Indeed, Titmuss himself adopted this policy on a number of occasions and it is a method adopted by David Gil (1973) in his now classic text *Unravelling Social Policy*. Although over 30 years old it can be argued that Gil's analysis remains one of the most authoritative and rigorous in the entire literature. He devotes considerable time to a review of then existing definitions of social policy as discipline and practice, and, in the end, rejects them all as being too limited; even Titmuss himself, though afforded due recognition for his sophistication and breadth, is regarded as being too narrow. For Gil, social policy's major focal concern is the analysis of access to life-enhancing and life-sustaining resources, and, as such, even foreign policy could legitimately be included within its domain. In contrast, Titmuss's observation seems rather too narrow, that basically:

> We are concerned with the study of a range of social needs and the functioning, in conditions of scarcity, of human organisation, traditionally called social services or social welfare systems, to meet those needs. This complex area of social life lies outside or on the fringes of the so-called free market, the mechanisms of price and tests of profitability. (Titmuss, 1976: 20)

Whatever its shortcomings for Gil, Titmuss's approach takes us to the heart of the matter and, in so doing, raises other problems which are as intractable as the definition of social policy itself and just as relevant. In essence Titmuss is concerned with the allocation of a limited range of resources to meet a range of social needs. In reality, although there have been variations between countries, these social needs are for health care, housing, education, income maintenance during periods of interruption or cessation of earnings, and that multiplicity of dependencies which in Britain are the concern of the personal social services. The market's role in meeting these needs should, according to Titmuss and the entire intellectual and political tradition he did so much to shape, be minimal. Consumption of these erstwhile commodities is far too important to be left to command over resources in markets. At this point it should be noted that there is no practical reason precluding the allocation of health care and the rest through unfettered private markets. An allocation of these experiences could be secured in this way and classical liberals in the past together with their neo-liberal counterparts today make exactly this point. The crux is whether such an allocation would be successful in meeting the population's needs.

Once again we are driven into the realm of definition. What constitutes need? Can anyone ever define need objectively? Is there a generally agreed definition of social need or must it be as open-ended as the definition of social policy itself. Thus we move from concept to concept, from definitional problem to definitional problem, and there is no easy way out, except perhaps to say, as the classical and neo-liberals do that the only 'things' whose allocation falls properly within the realm of public policy, and thus outside the market, are defence and law and order, the traditional functions of the night-watchman state. Otherwise, when we speak of social problems and social needs we are merely giving voice to our own particular prejudices, values and opinions. Such opinions may be more or less well-informed and clearly or ill articulated but if we move beyond the harsh and rigid logic of public goods theory we are left with little other than personal preference and tradition.

The tradition that the allocation of the experiences identified above is, in part at least, the proper responsibility of government is well-established throughout the industrial world, and rather than languish in a fog of relative values or be directed by the remorseless logic of perfect markets (which probably do not exist anyway), it might be both productive and sensible to proceed from this reality; and to take it as a 'given' in our analysis. For a variety of reasons, in a variety of methods, and with varying degrees of success all countries, to a greater or lesser extent, modify the operation of market forces in the allocation of health, housing, education, income maintenance and the personal social services. One of the continuing fascinations of social policy as a subject is the way in which debate about the propriety of state intervention itself and the relative merits of particular strategies and tactics of intervention has changed and developed over the years. Significant advances in conceptual and theoretical sophistication have been made over the last 50 years (many of them covered in this book) as the subject has grown and matured, but the objects of analysis remain much as Titmuss discussed them over 30 years ago. Thus:

1   The analysis and description of policy formation and its consequences, intended and unintended
2   The study of structure, function, organisation, planning and administrative processes of institutions and agencies, historical and comparative
3   The study of social needs and of problems of access to, utilisation, and patterns of outcome of services, transactions and transfers
4   The analysis of the nature, attributes and distribution of social costs and dis-welfares
5   The analysis of distributive and allocative patterns in command-over-resources-through-time and the particular impact of the social services
6   The study of the roles and functions of elected representatives, professional workers, administrators and interest groups in the operation and performance of social welfare institutions
7   The study of the social rights of the citizen as contributor, participant and user of social services
8   The study of the role of government (local and central) as an allocator of values and of rights to social property as expressed through social and administrative law and other rule-making channels

(Titmuss, 1976: 22–3)

Titmuss was, of course, as aware as anyone of the significance of occupational and fiscal welfare, indeed he pioneered their study (Titmuss, 1962), but the long quotation above is limited to the extent that it omits three areas of concern. First, there is no mention of the role of the market. To Titmuss and his colleagues market failure was both a historic fact and an article of faith. He shared with Myrdal (1972) the conviction that the long, post-war progress of the social democratic welfare state was an immutable reality. While the occasional tactical retreat might be necessary at times of transient political crisis, the strategic conquest of the market was secure. The history of industrial capitalism had demonstrated the market's unsuitability as an allocative agency for those resources essential to the experience of a full and complete life. Any possibility that a return to the market might be seriously advocated was minimal. Organisations like the Institute of Economic Affairs, founded in 1957, which canvassed such ideas were regarded as amusing, marginal irritants with nothing serious or substantial to contribute to the intellectual and political debate.

Second, there is a failure to recognise that social policies can be instruments of social control. Inherent to this Fabian complacency (although specifically rejected by Titmuss) was the idea that social policy would always tend to be beneficial, humanitarian and progressive. That in a world changed forever by the intellectual revolution personified by Keynes and Beveridge, discussions about the future of the welfare state would focus on points of administrative and technical detail rather than the institutional model of welfare itself. It was left to the theorists of the Marxist left and the neo-liberal right to point out the control and oppression of individuals and families present in relatively undemocratic and unaccountable welfare structures. The Fabian tradition of social administration, organised by and delivered to a relatively powerless population, was always susceptible to charges of paternalism. Authority and power did not rest with the citizen but with the bureaucracy which operated at several removes from those who received education, health care, housing and so on. It also became clear that much of the provision was structured on the lines of class, 'race' and gender. The terrain of social policy was an area of contention and struggle. On an altogether different plain, confirmation that social policy could be literally destructive and evil was to be found in the very recent example of Nazi Germany where the torture and murder and mass destruction of millions of Jews, homosexuals and gypsies, and the physically and mentally impaired was accomplished in the name of a clearly conceptualised and articulated social policy.

Finally, social policies are intimately bound to the societies in which they develop and reflect the priorities of these systems. Social democratic thinkers like Titmuss found this relatively unproblematic as we now lived in welfare societies where meeting the basic needs of the majority was paramount. But for other traditions in social theory this is not the case. For Marxists social policies exist within capitalist socio-economic systems and for neo-liberals within free market economies. In both these paradigms social policies are inherently problematic, reflecting, on the one hand, the contradictions of class divided societies and, on the other, the futility involved in attempts to control the free play of market forces.

These points emphasise that 'social policy' is in fact an intensely political – and contested – activity. It encapsulates an important arena of modern social life in which competing ideologies clash. In this regard it is worth bearing in mind that all writers on social policy 'have a politics' or a perspective on the world – and the authors in this collection are no different.

What unites the authors here is a rejection of the primacy afforded to the market as an institution of resource allocation by the major political parties in Britain. The authors occupy a variety of positions on the centre-left of politics and, indeed, disagree with each other at least as much as they do with the thrust of New Labour social policy. Given that one of our objectives is for you to understand the contested nature of the ideas and concepts dealt with in this book it is probably an advantage that it is a multi-authored text.

Reflecting the contested nature of the subject, this book is divided into three sections. In the first part we introduce different theoretical approaches to the study of social policy. Included are social democratic, neo-liberal, Marxist, feminist and anti-racist perspectives on the subject. In the second section we look at some conceptual debates. In particular we look at the questions of distributive justice, and of citizenship and a debate (in Chapters 9 and 10) over the merits (or otherwise) of 'postmodern' approaches within the discipline. Finally, we look at a number of issues and debates within social policy. It is impossible to cover all areas within the subject but the topics and issues selected give, we feel, an overview of important areas of ongoing public and social policy debate and, we hope, emphasise the importance of social policy as a subject discipline with relevance to people's lives.

# PART ONE
# Theoretical Approaches

In this first section we introduce the main theoretical approaches that have structured debate within the social sciences in general and social policy and social welfare studies in particular.

The first three chapters in this section deal with the 'grand theories' of neo-liberalism, social democracy and Marxism. Each of these approaches attempts to grasp the broad and general features of social life and attempts to provide holistic interpretations of the social world and of historical development. As such they are not primarily concerned with the specifics of social policy or developments in welfare provision but, nevertheless, each includes social welfare (its causes, developments and consequences) within its remit.

Central to these approaches is a focus on concepts like equality, justice, freedom and class. Yet, social theorists during the second half of the twentieth century noted the fact that such concepts ignored – or were 'blind' to – important inequalities and oppressions. Issues of gender and 'race' were often ignored in the writings of many 'grand theorists' and, as a result, feminist and anti-racist scholars have looked at the importance of these divisions and the ways in which gendered and anti-racist analyses can be included (or otherwise) within the three major approaches. The consequence is that 'theoretical approaches' to welfare that did not include feminist and anti-racist perspectives would be severely limited.

In Chapter 2 Alan Pratt examines those aspects of neo-liberal theory which have made such an important contribution to the explanatory power of the New Right ideology in general. After a discussion of the behavioural assumptions on which neo-liberal theory is predicated, he focuses on the claims of the free market as an allocative institution and the nature of politics in a mass democracy, and goes on to consider those characteristics which provide much of the clarity and edge of the entire perspective.

In Chapter 3 Alan Pratt examines the way in which social-democratic theorists have responded to the challenges and opportunities presented by the apparent development of a version of free-market capitalism. He discusses the extent to which this new social democracy has responded to the social and cultural changes present in modern society and whether or not this emergent political and social philosophy has succeeded in reflecting the traditional concerns of old social democracy, not least of which is the idea of a reciprocal approach to distributive justice.

In Chapter 4 Michael Lavalette looks at Marxism and welfare. Perhaps more than any other perspective Marxism produces most student apprehension. The concepts, terminology, ideas and language used by Marxists are 'new' to students and sometimes the language used by academic Marxists is unnecessarily complex. Nevertheless, Marxism remains a crucially important tradition with which students need to engage.

In Chapter 5 Kath Woodward introduces the feminist critique of welfare. She looks at the important role played by early social policy legislation in re-creating the family around the concept of the 'male breadwinner'. She then proceeds to look at the way the welfare state and social policies have developed to de-prioritise the concerns of women and to devalue women as secondary welfare citizens.

Finally in this section Laura Penketh looks at the assumptions of 'race' and the role of racism in shaping social welfare. She starts by challenging us to think about what is meant by 'race' and racism and then applies a committed anti-racist perspective to an analysis of the legislative framework and the operation of social welfare.

# TWO

# Neo-liberalism and Social Policy
*Alan Pratt*

---

**Outline Points**

- This chapter is devoted to an examination of one particular strand of liberal theory, that of possessive individualism and its role in the rise of free-market capitalism to a position where it is currently the dominant form of economic and social organisation across much of the globe.
- The growth in international economic instability following the collapse of fixed exchange rates and oil price increases in the 1970s.
- The significance of these changes for the nature and direction of economic and social policy.
- The crucial importance of the assumptions of methodological individualism, rationality and market supremacy for the generality of neo-liberal theory.
- The neo-liberal approach to liberty and its rejection of the concept of social justice.
- Public choice theory
- Neo-liberalism and the centre-left in British politics: towards a new consensus?

---

## Introduction

The purpose of this chapter is to consider one particular strand of Liberal theory, that of possessive individualism, and to attempt to judge its impact on British debates about economic and social policy. It develops a synthesis of the economic and political theories, and the behavioural assumptions on which they rest, and is located in the changed economic and social circumstances of the early 1970s which saw Western European governments fail to maintain the full employment and economic growth which underpinned the construction of post-1945 welfare states. It discusses the key individual components of neo-liberalism as an intellectual system, that is, rationality, the superiority of the market as an institution for optimal resource allocation, public choice theory, the public burden theory of welfare, government overload, and the supremacy of individual self-reliance and moral responsibility over the culture of dependence. After examining the coherence and consistency of these ideas the chapter concludes with an assessment of the extent to which this ideology has succeeded in creating a momentum towards a convergence of welfare systems based on a residual model of state welfare together with an enhanced role for voluntarism, the private market and occupational welfare in the new Europe that has emerged since the collapse of the Soviet empire.

## The Context

> Consensus policies became increasingly inappropriate to Britain's evolving needs. They had to be either reformed or replaced. In the mid-1970s they were, of course, to be replaced- ironically, by policies which closely resembled the very ones which had been perceived to fail in the 1930s. (Lowe, 1990: 182)

This extract from Lowe's essay on the historiography of the post-war consensus provides the basis of our agenda, which is about the replacement of one ruling set of ideas by another. Although significant, if unplanned, progress had been made in British social provision in the inter-war period, it was chronic, involuntary unemployment that was the major problem of economic and social policy. It dwarfed every other aspect of domestic politics, and, the work of revisionist historians of the period notwithstanding, unemployment remains the single most important image and memory of the age. The then dominant neo-classical Treasury view failed to provide any real solutions, and only slowly did a coherent and intellectually rigorous non-Marxist alternative appear, and even then it took the transforming experience of total war to force even the smallest crack in this orthodoxy.

At the heart of this new approach was Keynes's critique of a central assumption of neo-classical economic theory, that full employment was a general case. In *The General Theory of Employment, Interest and Money* (1936) Keynes demonstrated that equilibrium could exist at a less than full employment level of output and, because the system was in equilibrium, unless exogenous intervention occurred chronic, involuntary unemployment would persist. If governments had the desire they now, thanks to Keynes, had the tools to do the job. Whatever its equivocations and compromises might have been the 1944 White Paper on employment policy suggested that henceforth policy would be different. The commitment it contained to 'a high and stable level of employment' can be seen as the most important single event in the construction of the British welfare state achieved by successive British governments in the 1940s. Amongst other things it satisfied the most important of the three assumptions on which

Beveridge based his plans for social insurance and allied services. (The other two were the creation of a national health service and the introduction of a system of children's or family allowances.)

Just as the 1944 commitment to full employment signalled the dawn of a new collectivist age with an active interventionist government at its heart, so the abandonment of full employment, and the economic theories which had led to its achievement, by Callaghan and Healey after 1976 can be seen as the harbingers of a new-old world, a world shaped by exactly those theories which Keynes had seemingly dethroned 40 years earlier. In a very real sense the world had come full circle. Hayek, one of the twentieth century's most important classical liberal theorists, emerged from relative obscurity and became the single most important intellectual influence on the Conservative government which took office in 1979 armed with an agenda very different from the norm of the post-war period.

## The Collapse of Consensus

Ideas by themselves rarely change the direction of public policy: for them to have any lasting and real effect they must conspire with circumstances and in the 1970s the circumstances that had made possible the long post-war boom changed suddenly and dramatically. One of the most important achievements of international economic policy after 1945 was the creation of an ordered pattern of trading relationships between nations based on the system of fixed exchange rates that had emerged from the Bretton Woods conference. Cooperative and relatively free trade governed by institutions and structures such as the World Bank and GATT, designed to prevent the competitive devaluations and economic autarky that compounded the depression of the 1930s, was seen as the best hope for the capitalist world. However, this ordered system was unable to cope with the instabilities generated by the financial needs of an American government engaged in a shooting war in Southeast Asia and a war on poverty at home. The Smithsonian Agreement of December 1971 failed to contain the pressure and in 1973 a new system of floating exchange rates was introduced, one that provided the basis for the integrated world currency markets trading 24/7 we have become so familiar with today.

If, to these important changes in the capitalist world's financial system, we add the reality of profound technological change, an explosion in commodity prices (especially of oil) and the ending of the long post-war boom, the sudden collapse of the Keynesian system becomes more understandable. As a consequence a crisis in state authority developed throughout the advanced capitalist world and the search began for a new analysis and for policy prescriptions more in tune with this new world order. Britain, the weakest of the world's major economies, experienced this crisis earlier and more deeply than anywhere else. The failure of the corporatist attempts at modernisation in the 1960s and early

1970s meant that 'the existing policy regime was severely discredited by the dramatic worsening of performance on unemployment, inflation, economic growth and the balance of trade' (Gamble, 1987: 192).

## Neo-liberal Theory: the Substance

Although there are differences in emphasis and approach reflecting the predilections of individual writers, neo-liberal theory in general offers a coherent and consistent theory of how the world works and ought to work. The failures of the past can be quickly remedied if the old verities are reasserted and the proper relationships re-established between government and economy, state and individual, state and civil society, and between individuals themselves. Drawing especially on economics, politics and philosophy a powerful synthesis has been forged, one whose influence has been immense over the last thirty years as it has provided a new sense of direction to governments whose assumptions about the world have been changed by the events alluded to earlier. This set of ideas has led to a transformation of both the language and objectives of public policy throughout the world.

### Assumptions

Although detailed aspects of neo-liberal theory can be complex the totality is relatively clear and simple, resting as it does on a very particular set of assumptions about the nature of human behaviour and institutions. Of these assumptions the most important are methodological individualism, rationality and the supremacy of the free market.

### Methodological Individualism

Methodological individualism asserts that 'all phenomena are reducible to individual behaviour; organic entities such as "society" or the "state" are comprehensible only in terms of the activities of their constitutive individuals' (King, 1987: 94). In Margaret Thatcher's memorable phrase: there is no such thing as society. Free individuals go about their business within the general framework of the 'rule of law', knowing wherein their best interests lie, pursuing pleasure rather than pain. Embodied in contractual relationships these individual pursuits produce a set of collective outcomes which by themselves are neither good nor bad. They simply are. Others may take a moral position about these outcomes but methodological individualism would suggest that such positions are irrelevant. Discussion of them belongs to another realm.

### Rationality

The individual pursuit of self-interest only makes sense if individuals act rationally. So important is this assumption that without it the whole edifice of neo-liberal thought would be endangered. For, if individuals do not always behave in a rational fashion in all circumstances, what can we conclude about the outcomes of such behaviour? In this universe rationality is understood as the pursuit of perfectly informed self-interest. Any other kind of behaviour is inconceivable.

### Market Supremacy

The perfect location for the exchanges of these rational, perfectly informed self-interested individuals is the market. Markets are about exchange, and for neo-liberals market relationships are infinitely preferable to other forms of trans-action such as those of the political world. Although sometimes used as a syn-onym for capitalism, markets pre-date the capitalist mode of production. They have existed since the first act of trade took place and they are the best institu-tional setting for the conduct of economic affairs. We now turn to some of the most important of neo-liberalism's economic theories and begin with a more detailed examination of the market.

## Economics

### The Market

In essence neo-liberal economics differs little form the classical political econ-omy developed by the followers of Adam Smith from the late eighteenth cen-tury onwards, although it needs to be said that they detached Smith's preference for the market from his wider moral vision, one that includes a genuine sympa-thy for the poor. At the heart of classical political economy is a belief that the market is the best institution yet created by human activity for the conduct of economic matters.

Individuals bring their preferences to markets and the collective weight of these preferences represents a powerful set of signals that producers of goods and services would be foolish to ignore. It would not be a sensible business deci-sion to carry on producing commodities that consumers have shown through their actions they do not want. Failure to comply with the consumers' revealed preferences would guarantee the failure of any business to behave in this way. Given freedom of entry into the market other potential suppliers are always available who will recognise the facts of consumer sovereignty. These character-istics make markets efficient, sensitive and speedy signalling mechanisms, doing spontaneously that which is impossible or very difficult for governments or the former command economies of Eastern Europe.

Modern industrial societies are such complex entities that the idea of govern-ment taking responsibility for the myriad decisions necessarily involved in the optimal allocation of resources is foolish. It is beyond the capacity of govern-ments to do that which markets do naturally. Hayek (1944) derided the whole concept of government planning, and argued that any attempt to replace the market with a system of politically determined decision-making was bound to end in tyranny and disaster. The collapse of the economies in the former Soviet bloc, the emergence of a system of state-sponsored capitalism in the People's Republic of China and the retreat of managed economies everywhere all testify to this. Capitalism has triumphed and free market capitalism in particular.

In markets decision-making is delegated to the lowest possible level, that of the individual consumer and firm, and this de-centralisation of decision-making not only renders unnecessary the complex and over-staffed public bureaucracies of non-market economies (at a great saving to the public purse) but also produces outcomes that are autonomous, spontaneous and, because they represent the choices of free, perfectly informed and rational individuals, valid. In markets freedom of choice is guranteed and respected and, as Marquand notes, 'in the market liberal ideal, free men, freely exchanging goods and services without intervention by the state maximise the general interest by pursuing their own interests' (Marquand, 1987: 66). For neo-liberals the question is not so much what goods are allocated through the market but what goods must the state, and the state alone, provide. That is, it is concerned with the nature of true public goods. If we can establish the identity of these public goods, then it must follow, given the market's superiority as an institution for the allocation of scarce resources, that all other goods can and should be allocated through the market. Although there are differences of emphasis between individual neo-liberal theorists the general outlines of agreement are clear. Typical of them is Seldon, who argues that public goods have characteristics that clearly separate them from non-public goods. Thus, Seldon says that public goods are:

- Supplied collectively rather than separately to individuals or small groups;
- Provided by general agreement to pay jointly, 'that is, they require voluntary collective arrangements to coerce one another and also individuals who do not want the services at all but who cannot help benefiting from them' (Seldon, 1977: 17).
- Non-rival in the sense that until full capacity is reached they can be used by more and more people at no additional cost;
- For Seldon though, 'the essential characteristic of public goods is that they cannot be refused to people who refuse to pay, and who would otherwise have a "free" ride if they were not required to pay. Public goods, to be provided at all, cannot therefore be produced in response to individual specification in the market: they must be financed collectively by the method known as taxation' (Seldon, 1977: 18–19).

If we accept the validity of Seldon's characteristics of true public goods can we establish a list of those functions that the state alone can provide? It is not a lengthy list and comprises defence, a system of law and order, protection against contagious disease, and what he describes as 'a not obvious but important one: the production of knowledge and information' (Seldon, 1977: 19). Street lighting, lighthouses and externality problems such as pollution, together with provision to protect children and the mentally infirm are sometimes added to extend the list slightly.

The expansion of the state's role to include the provision of services other than true public goods is the hallmark of what has been termed the interventionist state. (Hall, 1984) This expansion, which normally includes education health care, housing, a variety of income maintenance programmes and the personal social services has led to a very large increase in public expenditure's share of national income in all OECD countries in the twentieth century, but especially since the end of the Second World War. The implications of this trend for public finances, and for the efficiency of the market economies within which this expansion has been located, is a particular concern of neo-liberal political economy.

### The Problem of Public Expenditure

In 1979 the first public expenditure statement of the incoming Conservative government asserted that excessive public expenditure lay at the heart of Britain's economic problems. In this it was no different from its predecessor led by Edward Heath in 1970 and the manifestos on which the Conservatives fought the elections of 1970 and 1979 share the same economic analysis and advocate the same prescriptions for recovery, with the exception that in 1970 monetarism had not yet established a significant presence on Britain's intellectual and political landscape, certainly nothing like the hold it was to have on Thatcher's administrations.

Public expenditure is invariably seen as a major problem, as a real and present danger to economic efficiency. Hence the popularity of the public burden theory of welfare with all neo-liberal theorists. As governments moved further and further away from their proper concern with the provision of public goods and took on responsibilities that ought to have remained with individuals in markets they inevitably found themselves in conflict with the private, productive sector of the economy for available resources. In this conflict there could only be one winner. Governments could offer a guaranteed rate of return on any borrowing they might need from the financial markets, a security that the private sector could not match. The public sector was also in competition for available supplies of labour, and even though government could not always match the salaries paid to educated and skilled labour in the private sector, job security and guaranteed, inflation-proof pensions could always sugar that particular pill. In brief, wealth creation in the private traded goods sector of the economy was in danger of being crowded out in this competition for resources (Bacon and Eltis, 1976). If this process was allowed to continue, negative-sum welfare-efficiency interactions were a certainty (Geiger, 1979). In other words, the productive ability of the economy would be compromised by the excessive demands of rising public expenditure.

The expansive and expensive welfare regimes of social democracies place a great strain on governments' revenue raising capacity. Impelled by the insatiable demands of greedy electorates and self-interested bureaucrats intent only on empire building, government has to tax more and borrow more. The level of direct taxation is of particular concern to neo-liberal economists and they take it as a given that if personal and company taxation is too high at the margin, work incentives and risk-taking will both be damaged. Why should employees work harder and take on more responsibility if they know that the value of the marginal pound earned by them is going to be significantly reduced by the government's depredations? The end result is bound to be that productivity will decline, output be reduced, and investment and risk-taking discouraged. In order to reverse this debilitating tendency it is essential that government reduce those taxes on companies and individuals that have led to the miserable situation described above. Do this and output and real incomes would both increase and Britain's long relative economic decline arrested.

For neo-liberals the dismal reality of a high tax, low growth economy is compounded by the possibility that if income in periods of non-earning is greater than income from employment, after taking into account such things as travel and other work-related expenses, there will be those who would prefer the leisure of unemployment to the demands of work. Traditionally the neo-liberal response to this has been not to raise employment income through devices such as the minimum wage and the expensive and wide-ranging system of tax credits favoured by the present government as part of its 'make work pay' strategy, but to widen the gap between earned income and benefit income by reducing benefits and making them more difficult to claim.

### The Labour Market

Labour is a commodity and, like any other commodity there is a market for it and that market can be cleared if the price of labour, i.e. wages, is determined by the normal market forces of supply and demand. If the market is left to its own devices and not distorted by government intervention (through initiatives such as a minimum wage) and the activities of powerful trades unions armed with significant legal immunities, the tendency would be towards little or no involuntary unemployment. There would always be frictional and structural unemployment of course, these are the desirable and natural features of any dynamic market economy as people changed jobs and employers in their search for better wages and conditions and as old industries decline and new ones emerge in response to new technologies and changing tastes. If involuntary unemployment does exist it is because of artificial rigidities in the labour market occasioned by the behaviour of organised labour. Neo-liberals' response to involuntary unemployment would always have an assault on the bargaining power of unions and whatever legal immunities they might enjoy at its heart. This would assist the necessary progress back towards a 'natural' rate of unemployment in a deregulated and more flexible labour market. Any other approach would be doomed to failure in the long run. Keynesian inspired attempts to reduce unemployment below its natural market-determined rate might have some temporary success but eventually these would lead to greater inflation as governments resorted to deficit financing to stimulate aggregate demand and, ultimately, higher unemployment. As Hayek said, 'unemployment has been made inevitable by past inflation; it has merely been *postponed* by accelerating inflation' (quoted in Marquand, 1987: 86). It is interesting to observe that since 1997 New Labour has done relatively little to restore unions' legal position to that they enjoyed before the Conservatives' succession of employment acts eroded their immunities and it has made no secret of its belief that the creation of significant labour market flexibility has been one important factor in Britain's much lower unemployment rate than the average for the European Union, not least in Germany where unemployment has recently reached five million.

## Inflation

The suppression of inflation is the key policy objective of neo-liberal economics. Secure this and a number of benefits will flow. Regular and sustainable increments to economic growth, low unemployment, rising disposable real incomes, and even improvements in the quality of justifiable public services can only be secured if inflation is conquered. If this meant some temporary hardship and misery for some as the toxin of Keynesianism was expelled then, as Norman Lamont said, unemployment was a price worth paying.

The precise nature of the relationship between excessive public expenditure and inflation has varied over time. All that neo-liberals are sure of is that there is such a relationship. If governments cannot raise all the revenue they need to fund their spending from taxation and charges then they will have to borrow. The government may be forced to a form of borrowing that would enable the banking system to increase its credit base and hence the supply of money in the economy. The theory was that after a time lag of around two years this increase in money supply would lead to an increase in the rate of inflation, thus demonstrating a mechanistic, causal relationship between the money supply and the general price level. In their earlier years the governments led by Margaret Thatcher were especially enamoured of this theory, an attachment that manifested itself in the Medium Term Financial Strategy(MTFS) which incorporated clear fixed targets for monetary growth, targets that were in line with expectations of growth rates in the real economy. While monetary aggregates are clearly important in macro-economic theory and obviously to the practical realities of economic life, for the neo-liberal approach to inflation they are critical. However, this aspect of the theory has proven to be most disappointing as it proved to be very difficult to reach an agreed definition of M (the money supply) that is so critical to monetarists' equations while in terms of economic policy it was difficult to control any definition of M at all. Eventually the MTFS was abandoned and with it went one of the central planks of monetarist theory. Although the control of inflation remains a major policy objective of neo-liberal theory the reduction of inflation experienced by most western economies in the last few years owes little to the application of monetarist ideas, with a rather more compelling reason being the pressure on the price of consumer goods being generated by rapidly expanding economies such as China and India together with the ability of industrial end commercial enterprises to relocate their operations to these and other new centres of capitalist enterprise. Only in those countries in the European Union that are bound by the strictures of the stability and growth pact does a semblance of theoretical monetarist orthodoxy exist and this has led to the European Union as a whole having a rate of economic growth far below that of the OECD in general. It is hardly surprising that France and Germany have both broken their obligations in this regard but are still experiencing unemployment levels far higher than the post-war average. It is likely that pressure from these two will force a major revision in the pact or even its de facto abandonment altogether. In Britain Gordon Brown gave operational independence for the management of monetary policy to the Bank of England with an obligation to meet an asymmetric inflation target of 2 per cent; any significant deviation from this requires the Governor to put his explanation in writing to the Chancellor. Britain's present institutional arrangements for the administration of monetary policy have general approval in the financial community and it is not without significance that the Conservative Party has abandoned its earlier opposition. The system could well become a blueprint for some badly needed changes in the European Union.

---

**Activity 1**

*In what ways do neo-liberals' behavioural assumptions affect their views on the economy?*

---

## Neo-liberalism: Aspects of Political Philosophy

The value premises of neo-liberalism are determined by its assumptions and methodological individualism, rationality and a preference for the free market are as important here as they are in its economics. Indeed economics and philosophy are part of that seamless whole that is neo-liberal political economy and: 'When properly presented, their arguments strike at the normative presumptions of the post-war welfare state' (Plant, 1990: 7). Plant's analysis of the normative content of neo-liberalism provides a coherent framework which we can use to develop a relatively complete account of its values and preferences.

### Liberty

For Hayek, liberty was the supreme virtue, far outweighing any other be it democracy or social justice or fraternity. The great tragedy of modern European civilisation was the gradual retreat from the understanding of liberty developed by British liberals from Locke onwards in face of the advance of the German tradition of an authoritarian, interventionist state possessed of a belief in its right to shape the economic and social destiny of its citizens. It posited a belief in the existence of a discernible 'national interest' which could be pursued and achieved through a range of specific programmes and instruments. For the classical and neo-liberal:

> Market relationships are freer, more spontaneous, in a strange way more authentic than political relationships: market power does not exist, while the state is, by definition, the realm of power and domination. (Marquand, 1987: 67)

Under the influence of this Germanic tradition Hayek argues that the tide turned against liberalism as planning and regulation became the new lodestones, deployed in the interest of a chimerical equality and social justice. As an émigré Austrian intellectual Hayek was well qualified to point out the dangers of authoritarian collectivism, especially in the conditions and social tensions generated by mass unemployment. His passion for liberty and suspicion of democracy are characteristics present in much neo-liberal literature and, as we shall see, they present neo-liberal theorists with some very real dilemmas. Hayek, though, had no doubt; liberty should triumph in every contest.

Since the emergence of liberal collectivist thought in Britain during the last quarter of the nineteenth century in the work of Green, Hobson, Hobhouse and Ritchie there had been an assumption about the relationship between liberty and welfare. Liberal collectivists moved beyond the formal, procedural notions of liberty central to classical liberalism such as those attached to civil, political and legal rights and asserted a positive as opposed to negative concept of liberty. In the twentieth century the idea has become associated with the notion of an equal worth of liberty (Plant, 1985). Thus, liberty is inextricably bound up with access to those experiences essential to the living of a full and civilised life, like education, health, housing and a guaranteed income. In fact those resources whose distribution is, perhaps, the most important feature of modern welfare states. Hayek recognised the significance of linking the freedom to act with the ability to act. It provided a powerful basis for arguing in favour of some vertical redistribution of resources since to do so would increase the worth of liberty enjoyed by those at the bottom of the scale of income distribution by enhancing their ability to act. This move to a more positive conception of liberty within the liberal tradition was an influential factor in the growth of the interventionist state in late nineteenth-century Britain, away from the hitherto dominant notion of the minimal state.

Neo-liberals reject the idea of positive liberalism, liberty as power and opportunity, and reaffirm their commitment to the older tradition. Their position has been well captured in the following statement: 'Liberty is liberty, not something else. And the slave is a slave: you do not set him free by feeding him' (Joseph and Sumption, 1979, quoted in Pope et al., 1986: 221). According to this negative liberty is the only valid approach. Liberty means the absence of coercion, and market outcomes are unforeseen. They are not the consequence of a deliberate political decision made by someone with the authority and power to determine such outcomes. The free market cannot restrict and impinge on liberty because market outcomes are the consequence of individual choices made by rational beings aiming to maximise individual satisfactions. The results of these outcomes may mean that some people get more than others, that there is inequality and real suffering but there is no compulsion; no political authority has intervened. As Hayek has observed, individuals are still free to try and improve their position by any means open to them provided that their actions are legal, do not coerce others and are consistent with the overarching 'general rule of law' that provides known, transparent and generally understood procedures. In market economies people are always free to try and try again using whatever energy and talents they possess. This is a hallmark of a free society.

### Social Justice

The positive liberty of liberal collectivism demands a rigorous, clearly articulated and generally accepted concept of social justice to serve as the basis on which resources can be allocated by non-market mechanisms. If market mechanisms are to be modified or dispensed with the least that is needed is a valid basis on which to intervene. Hayek was contemptuous of every attempt to develop an operational concept of social justice and dismissed them as self-indulgent posturing. (Hayek, 1944) Because market outcomes are not consciously intended they cannot be unjust since social injustice can only be caused by intentional acts. Consequently 'the moral demands of social justice evaporate' (Plant, 1990: 11). There are many possible criteria of social justice including need, merit, desert and so on, but in a free society there can be no general agreement about which criterion should be used as the operational basis of resource allocation. Therefore:

- Because of the absence of agreed criteria, allocation through non-market mechanisms will be arbitrary and discretionary. 'This will mean that at the very heart of the public policy of a welfare state will lie the arbitrary and discretionary power of welfare bureaucrats and experts charged with the impossible task of distributing resources according to intrinsically unspecific criteria' (Plant, 1990: 11).
- Because of the absence of known and agreed criteria there will be selfish and destructive competition by interest groups for resources. It is the relative power of interest groups that will be significant in the allocation of scarce resources. The powerful will win.

For all these reasons, neo-liberals contend that illusory ideas about social justice should be abandoned and the market liberated from government intervention. If some kind of welfare state had to remain it should be a residual one providing a minimal safety net for those who were not able to compete or operate in the market. Consistent libertarians would dispense with any kind of welfare state (Nozick, 1974).

## *Rights*

The idea that people possess welfare rights as a constitutive element of citizenship is essential to the liberal collectivist/social democratic view of the welfare state (Marshall, 1950). In contrast neo-liberals reject totally the idea that there are any such welfare rights. They see a clear and fundamental distinction between the legal and political rights at the core of classical liberalism and the putative claims of a right to welfare. These traditional rights which liberals have asserted and defended for centuries all imply duties of forbearance rather than the commitment of resources to substantiate them. The resource implications of accepting that citizens have rights to a certain level of education, health, income etc. are immense. On the other hand, civil rights are categorical and absolute. To claim that people have rights to welfare demands that we have a view of needs, and the probability is that such views will be open-ended with clear implications for governments trying to decide on the respective merits of these competing claims on scarce resources. Meeting one set of claims could well mean not meeting others. The lack of agreed criteria to enable us to distinguish between these claims must lead to anger and frustration and a possible erosion of faith in the political institutions of liberal democracy.

## *Poverty*

Neo-liberals have an absolute rather than relative concept of poverty and they conclude from this that there is very little, if any, poverty in modern Britain. A free market economy, liberated from the debilitating effects of government intervention, an institutional welfare state and the burden of high taxes is much the best mechanism for helping the poor; more precisely for helping the poor to help themselves. Market economies are by far the most effective means of wealth and job creation and their greater productivity will do more than anything else to improve the real living standards of the poor not least through the trickle-down effect. Poor people need the opportunity to work their way out of poverty and to break free from that culture of dependency which disfigures their humanity.

## *Culture and Values*

If the poor are to be weaned off welfare dependency and introduced to the world of enterprise risk and work, it is essential that the role of the free market is expanded and the values of the enterprise culture proselytised. The cause of poverty is not a dysfunctional economic system, nor a dysfunctional social system. Poverty is culturally determined by the values, attitudes, mores and lack of aspirations transmitted across generations. Therefore, if the policy objective is to improve the conditions of the poor, then the behaviour of the poor themselves must be changed. Welfare dependency saps initiative, autonomy, enterprise and the sense of being responsible for one's own destiny. If we remove the struc-tures that encourage dependency and restructure social policy so that people are moved off welfare and into the world of work then we can begin that process of cultural transformation essential to a genuine attack on poverty – genuine because it treats the causes and not the symptoms. Such a change might cause some initial discomfort but the prize of an economically dynamic and remoralised society is one worth securing.

## Public Choice Theory: the Apotheosis of the Rational Egoist

It has been argued that the novelty and real cutting edge of neo-liberalism is to be found not in its economic theory but in its view of politics. The promises of social democracy were based on the belief that government was inherently benign and inherently competent. 'The real originality of present day neo-liberalism lies in its attempt to turn that central presupposition on its head' (Marquand, 1987: 75).

The economic consequences of liberal democracies are determined by the nature of political activity in these societies, the major features of which are the existence of competitive party politics, mass electorates , and well-entrenched, well-organised interest groups. In this situation, market failure (a reason for government intervention in the first place) is less likely than government failure. There is an underlying theme of government 'overload'. The system cannot cope with the excessive demands generated by the politics of social democracy. As a consequence governments over-reach themselves:

> The result was a paradox. Big government turned out to be ineffective government. The more it tried to do, the more it failed. The more it failed, the more it lost authority. The more authority it lost, the more it failed. (Marquand, 1987: 73)

Public choice theory is a microcosm of neo-liberal political economy, resting as it does on the same behavioural assumptions. In King's words: 'The emphasis is on the micro-economic assumptions of actors (egoism, self interest) and context (a perfect political "market"), with utility maximisation and rational action by the parties also assumed' (1987: 100). The central assumption of all this is that political parties develop policies to win elections, not to consummate some vision of the public good.

Given the assumption of rational self-interest the sceptic can be forgiven for asking why individuals can be safely left to express their own wishes in the economic market place but not in the political one. They are after all the same people and rationality is a general assumption. The neo-liberal response is that there is a fundamental difference between the economic and political markets. In the former, consumers are constrained by an awareness of their own resource limitations and can be relied on to act with caution. In the latter they are under no such inhibitions since in a democracy the majority will prevail. Even if a voter prefers cheaper policies to expensive ones, she will have to pay her share of the expensive ones if this is what voters want.

This destructive pursuit of self-interest by individuals as voters creates a dilemma for public choice theorists. Liberty is the prime value and the free market is the institution to protect economic freedom. Similarly, democratic politics founded on universal suffrage, is, in one sense, synonymous with liberty: we choose our rulers in free elections and if they do not please us we can remove them. However, the selfish, if rational behaviour of individuals as voters is an important cause of system overload. How then can people be prevented from damaging that system, the free market economy, in which they can find the best opportunity of fulfilling themselves as individuals and which is also the best guarantor of that liberty which is the supreme political virtue?

In public choice theory bureaucrats cannot be expected to contain the excesses of democratic politics. After all, they share the same behavioural characteristics of all the other actors in the drama; voters, parties and interest groups. The idea of the disinterested public servant, impervious to any shred of self-interest, is a fiction. Bureaucrats are like the rest of us: greedy, vain, ambitious and keen to follow their own interests. They are more likely than not to judge their success by the size of the departmental budget and the number of people on the payroll. Many neo-liberal writers have proposed a series of institutional changes that would change the nature of political life in liberal democracies. These include constitutional amendments to enforce a balanced budget and the establishment of an independent commission to control the money supply. Hayek has made the most radical suggestion with his scheme to limit the vote to those aged 45 and over and excluding civil servants, old-age pensioners and the unemployed. The legislature elected on this basis would be in place for 15 years and would content itself with laying down the general rules for the conduct of business. Administration would be left to a subordinate assembly whose decisions would only be binding if they conformed to the general rules of the legislature. As Marquand notes, if 'the source of the problem is democracy, how can it be solved democratically' (1987: 81)?

---

### Activity 2

*After reading the last two sections:*

- *What services do you think a neo-liberal would argue should be the state's responsibility?*
- *What, in their view, should be the responsibility of the individual?*
- *How do they justify these allocations?*

## Neo-liberalism: Summary and Concluding Assessment

One of the most important features in the rise of neo-liberal ideas has been the influence of think tanks which have received a large amount of funding from business, and have been impelled not just by a desire to think critically about the character and consequences of social democracy but also by a determination to seek its political defeat. How successful has this well-funded activity been? Are neo-liberal ideas now the new common-sense and do intellectuals, policy makers, politicians and the public view the world in a different way than they did a generation ago? The answer to this question must be a qualified yes, although the extent to which this is a consequence of structural imperatives such as economic globalisation and the continuing revolution in technology must remain a matter of personal preference. As evidence of this sea change we need only to look at the way in which political parties of the left and centre-left, manifested in Britain by the Labour party's transformation from 'Old' Labour, with its formal ideology of social ownership, to 'New' Labour, which early in Blair's leadership jettisoned Clause 4 of the party's constitution that committed it to social ownership and, once in power, accepted the language of choice and the free market in a way that staggered many of its activists and voters. New Labour seems to have absorbed into its bloodstream neo-liberalism's belief in market mechanisms and its rejection of public enterprise. Some scholars believe that there has been a 'Thatcherisation' of the Labour party.

Having said that, this same Labour government has increased public expenditure's share of national income by a couple of percentage points to around 40 per cent of GNP and, after its self-denying ordinance in its first two years of office, has since delivered the biggest increase in real-term public expenditure in British peacetime history with levels of spending that are taking the country towards the European average after years of decline. Amidst all this there has been the largest amount of vertical income redistribution to the poorest 10 per cent of the population since 1945. All that we can say with certainty is that the picture of neo-liberalism's apparent success is full of conflicting messages. The Labour leadership uses the language of choice and markets as a matter of course and seems determined to extend the use of market mechanisms to more and more areas of public policy and there are complaints from trade union leaders that any attempt to discuss economic reform in anything other than neo-liberal terms is a waste of time. Yet this same leadership is proposing to press ahead with a massive expansion in the funding of child care provision across the whole nation in what seems to be a genuine attempt to help parents with dependent children achieve a more acceptable work–life balance.

## Further Reading

Kay, J. (2003) *The Truth About Markets: their Genius, their Limits, their Follies*, London: Allen Lane.

King, D.S. (1987) *The New Right: Politics, Markets and Citizenship.* London: Macmillan.

Marquand, D. (1987) *The Unprincipled Society.* London: Fontana.

Self, P. (1993) *Government by the Market? The Politics of Public Choice.* London: Macmillan.

# THREE
# Towards a 'New' Social Democracy
*Alan Pratt*

---

## Outline Points

- The transition to a deregulated global capitalism has led to major changes in Britain's occupational structure and a significant decline in the size and power of the manual working class that was so important in the rise of 'old' social democracy. This chapter examines the significance of these and other developments for the theory and practice of British social democracy.
- Rights, duties and the idea of civic responsibility.
- The place of the 'fair reciprocity' principle in distributive justice.
- Individual autonomy and social equality.
- The idea of the social investment state.
- The reconstruction of the relationship between the state and civil society.

---

## Introduction

In the first edition of this book which was published in April 1997, Kearns noted in his chapter on 'Social democratic perspectives' that the social democratic tradition was 'once again on the march and that its adherents no longer feel that they have lost the intellectual initiative' (Kearns, 1997: 27). Just a month later the British Labour Party ended 18 years of opposition by securing its largest ever victory in a general election, perhaps the most spectacular and symbolic event in a political revival of the centre-left which had begun with Bill Clinton's success in the US presidential campaign in 1992 and which, by the end of the century, had seen parties of the centre-left either in power by themselves, or as the major partners in governing coalitions, in a majority of the leading industrial nations of the OECD. Since the second edition appeared centre-left parties have not enjoyed the same degree of success in national and supra-national elections and in Germany the Schroeder government is in some trouble at both national and provincial levels because of very high levels of unemployment and cuts in the social budget. The intellectual self-confidence discussed by Kearns has waned somewhat but the work done in the recent past by social democratic theorists to create a 'new' social democracy, one more suited to a modern society allegedly characterised by economic globalisation, cultural and political diversity, the diminution of the importance of social class and greater individualism has a continuing relevance to the development of a coherent and effective challenge to neo-liberal political economy.

However, before we begin this task it is sensible to remind ourselves of the main characteristics and concerns of what might usefully be termed 'old' social democracy.

## Old Social Democracy: a Brief Review

Old or traditional visions of social democracy were rooted in the belief that significant degrees of autonomy and political power rested with national governments. They could, if they wished, take action to modify the operation of market forces and change the initial allocation and distribution of resources produced by market operations. In other words, politics mattered and could be used to achieve a variety of economic and social ends, including the creation of greater equality in the distribution of income and life-chances (for a definitive account of the possibilities of politics see Ringen, 1986). Armed with a range of more or less Keynesian policy instruments and intellectual insights, supported by a majority of electoral opinion (Fraser, 2000), and operating within a relatively stable international financial order based on the Bretton Woods agreement of 1944, national governments could run their economies in ways that would deliver economic growth, full employment, and tolerable levels of price inflation. For most Western industrial economies, including the UK, the result was the longest sustained period of economic growth in history. Although there is disagreement about the precise role of Keynesian demand management policies in securing this outcome, one undoubtedly made possible by the restocking and investment booms that sought to remedy the damage caused by the Second World War, there can be no doubt that, thanks to Keynes and his followers, governments now had the ability to iron out the worst excesses of the trade cycle.

The resources generated by this long boom in capitalist economies made it possible for governments to satisfy their populations' expectations of rising levels of real personal disposable income as well as their desire, expressed through the ballot box, for greater collective consumption in the form of high quality, decommodified health, education, housing, social welfare and income transfers in generally non-discriminatory and non-stigmatising ways.

This economic agenda was accompanied by an equivalent social philosophy which informed citizens' access to collective social consumption. It was a philosophy founded on notions of solidarity and citizenship, and Wolfe and Klausen (2000) have recently reminded us how important these two ideas were in the construction of the classic welfare state in the 1940s. Thus: 'a sense of solidarity creates a readiness to share with strangers, which in turn underpins a thriving welfare state' (Wolfe and Klausen, 2000: 28–9).

## Social Democracy in the New World Order

The decline, fall, and recrudescence of social democracy as philosophy and political practice are intimately bound up with the rise of neo-liberal orthodoxy as the ruling idea, together with the creation of a global economy driven by a quantum leap in technology, especially in information processing and communications. The real world now is a very different place from that in which traditional social democracy achieved its greatest triumph: that 'compromise between capitalism and socialism which was hammered out in Europe this century and which produced the actual product of the mixed economy and the welfare state' (Self, 2000: 281). This section of the chapter attempts a brief examination of the nature of the major changes in the external environment which transformed the modern world and demanded that social democracy itself change if it was to have a future as a political vision and programme.

### *Economic Globalisation and Neo-liberal Orthodoxy*

Since the dramatic collapse of the Soviet Union and its satellites in Central and Eastern Europe it has become part of conventional wisdom that there is now only one viable economic model, only 'one game in town'. That game is capitalism, and in the last decade of the twentieth century it has manifested itself as a triumphalist, free market doctrine which can simply ignore the attempts of individual nation states to articulate some vision of the national interest through political debate and action. Contrary to the beliefs of some adherents of globalisation this is not the first time in history that there has been a high degree of transnational economic power developed in the interests of a relatively small but hugely powerful group of corporations. Before the cataclysm of the First World War interrupted the process the world economy had acquired many of the characteristics of globalisation. The technology of the 'second wave of industrialization' had produced the means through which a new level of economic integration and dependency could be achieved, then as now, fuelled by an intellectual orthodoxy which preached the virtues of free trade (Atkinson and Elliott, 1999).

The difference between then and now is one of generality and speed. Undoubtedly there is now a greater degree of integration than there was in 1914. All of the leading contemporary international financial and trading organisations such as the International Monetary Fund, the World Bank, and World Trade Organization, are:

> strong supporters of the development and further expansion of the global economic system. They are naturally influenced by the strongest member states, especially the USA, and their financial contributions. They also are open to direct lobbying from major business and financial interests. This is particularly true of the World Trade Organization, whose network of advisory committees is dominated by the representatives of big corporations, and which is highly pro-active in spreading the gospel of freedom of trade and investment. (Self, 2000: 151)

Because these corporations control most of the world's investment decisions, national governments have felt obliged to compete with each other in an often unseemly scramble to attract the investment that would bring scarce jobs to declining regions and developing nations. The ability of these same corporations to damage communities and nations by transferring production across national boundaries to maximise profits and shareholder value is demonstrated now on what sometimes seems an almost weekly basis.

Another dimension of this particular version of liberal capitalism can be seen in the operations of the foreign exchange markets. Following the breakdown of the system of fixed exchange rates achieved at Bretton Woods in 1944, which provided the industrial world with the stability necessary to its expansion after 1945, there was a switch to floating exchange rates validated in the Smithsonian Agreement of 1971. Speculation has always been a feature of the world's financial markets, but since the Smithsonian Agreement the volume of such speculation has increased enormously, and instability has become a permanent feature. The amount of speculative capital flows across the world's financial markets has taken on a new dimension with the development of new technology. Trade in currency has become a twenty-four hours a day, seven days a week activity. There is always at least one major foreign exchange market open and decisions to trade currencies can be taken and transmitted instantaneously. These same financial markets have been completely liberated during the last thirty years as national governments have abandoned a whole range of controls over capital movements. The instability generated by these developments is obvious; as is the influence such markets can exercise on the decisions on economic and social policy taken by democratically elected governments. The threat to economic stability and the independence of national governments is profound.

This transition to a deregulated, global form of capitalism has led to major changes in the occupational structure and a significant decline in the manual working class. In Britain especially there has also been a sustained attack on the legal rights of trade unions, so serious in its consequences that British workers, regardless of occupation and skill, have fewer rights than any workforce in Europe. For social democracy as an ideology this decline in the size and potency of the manual working class has serious implications since it was this class which throughout the twentieth century had provided the heart and muscle of the movement; it was this class whose vulnerability in capitalist market economies social democracy was invented to remove. The protection and security afforded by a mixed economy, full employment, and the welfare state has been much reduced in the last two decades, a process led and informed by a new and confident neo-liberal orthodoxy, and the economic and political agenda in Britain is dominated by ideas and policies redolent of the heyday of classical liberalism in the nineteenth century. How has this occurred in a society with an advanced economy and a mature parliamentary democracy?

For Crouch the answer lies in 'the fate of class in British politics, and in particular the parabola of class politics during the course of the twentieth century which parallels and is a major cause of the parabola of policy' (Crouch, 1999: 71). At the beginning of the twentieth century the manual working class was the 'coming' class, the class of the political future. During the twentieth century, helped by the growth of new, Fordist forms of production and the development of Keynesian theory, it became a force that no government could afford to ignore. With greater economic prosperity and higher disposable real income, as a collectivity of individual consumers it also acquired a significant presence in the overall structure of demand for goods and services. In representative democracies political parties had to compete for the votes of this class, and its preferences inevitably found a presence in the programmes of all mainstream parties, especially in Europe. Below the surface of the mindset of the political and administrative elite (and in many cases, not far below the surface) was also a lurking fear that, if it were so minded, this class could overturn the whole system of capitalist social relations. Keynes's challenge to neo-classical political economy came at just the right time and made it possible to construct a more inclusive and regulated capitalism. In this new form of capitalism the interests of the manual working class were a vital consideration and in Britain all governments had the search for economic and political stability as their major strategic objective (Middlemas, 1980).

The decline in the size of the manual working class which Crouch refers to has meant that, 'it is a central mantra of the contemporary political elite that class no longer exists' (1999: 71). Its significance has been overtaken by 'new' concerns and cleavages such as ethnicity and gender, indeed to a general fixation with diversity, difference, and individualism. In this new world there is no place for a politics of class, especially a politics based on the interests of a class whose size and influence have been massively reduced by the creative destruction of technology-driven global capitalism.

We are constantly being told by members of the contemporary political elite, and by theorists of difference and diversity, that the concerns which led atomised workers in unstable capitalist market economies to seek a new ideology which would remove or modify their insecurities are now irrelevant. Currently existing capitalism is alleged to have produced a growing prosperity for all with an increase in individual opportunity. People see themselves as consumers not workers, as men or women or black or white or gay or straight or young or old or disabled; as anything in fact but members of a particular social class, least of all the working class. All this means that the need for a social democratic politics, certainly one characterised by social democracy's traditional concerns of equality, social justice, solidarity and citizenship, has disappeared. The decline of the traditional manual working class has been matched by an equivalent rise in the power of capital. Moreover, many of the jobs in the service sector industries which have replaced manufacturing jobs are insecure and filled by subordinate workers with little or nothing by way of effective trade union representation. The men and women who fill these jobs are working longer hours, and, as more and more women are drawn into the labour force, there are growing problems for the maintenance of stable family life. (See, for example, Hutton (1995).)

Thus, it could be suggested that this growth in insecurity means that ordinary people need more protection not less, that:

> . . . to argue objectively these needs no longer exist is quite specious. Needs for means to restrain the pressures of the market, including those of work, remain high on any objective political agenda, at least for any party stemming from the left. All that might have diminished is the capacity of those worried about such questions to place them on the political agenda. (Crouch, 1999: 72)

We now turn to a consideration of how the theory and practice of social democracy might respond to the changes and challenges discussed above, and the possibilities of constructing a political programme which represents a continuity with social democracy's traditional past and which resonates with an electorate whose dispositions and preferences have been influenced by neo-liberalism's nostrums.

---

**Activity 1**

- *What are the major economic, political and social changes to which social democracy has had to respond?*
- *Why has it been obliged to change?*

---

## Towards a New Social Democracy

Social democrats believe that the only valid means of securing political power is through electoral contest in representative democracies. Therefore the programmes which social democratic parties present to electorates must be sufficiently appealing that there is a chance that power can be achieved. The record of the British Labour Party in this regard has not been good in the twentieth century. Between 1945, when postwar general elections were resumed, and 1997 the Labour Party has only been in office for a total of 17 years: that is, from 1945–51, 1964–70, and 1974–9. Even during the halcyon days of the classic welfare state, Conservative governments were preferred at least as much as Labour.

From 1979 to 1997 the Labour Party had an even worse record, rejected by the electorate in four successive elections, those of 1979, 1983, 1987 and 1992. As in the 1950s the party engaged in a long and painful reappraisal of its purpose and programme, one that created much bitterness between competing factions. These self-evident splits intensified the electorate's distaste for Labour, although it must be noted that for a few years the Social Democratic Party, led by a core of Labour defectors such as Roy Jenkins, David Owen, Shirley Williams and Bill Rodgers, enjoyed a lot of public support. For the British Labour Party, the message was clear. The electorate had no fondness for disunity (as John Major was to discover so painfully in 1997), nor any liking for fundamentalist, left-wing agendas such as the one on which Labour lost so ignominiously in 1983. After 1983 the party was to write no more suicide notes as it began its attempt to reconnect with the electorate. Neil Kinnock and John Smith were to play key roles in this process but it was left to Tony Blair, who succeeded Smith after his untimely death in 1994, to complete a transformation which received its reward with a stunning victory in the 1997 general election.

Whatever one's views about the merits of the four successive Conservative governments which held office in the 18 years from 1979, there can be no denying their impact on national life and national politics in altering our perceptions of the relationship between the public and the private, between the state and the individual, between government and civil society. Perhaps their most remarkable success can be found in the revolution they achieved in the management and delivery of collective provision, a revolution which has been eagerly embraced by Blair's governments and, indeed, taken even further. All this is simply meant to say that social democracy is bound to have been influenced by this experience. Has there been a Thatcherisation of the centre-left or does contemporary social democracy offer an analysis of society and a set of prescriptions which are consistent with its long traditions? It is to these, and related questions, that we turn next.

## A Contemporary Social Democracy

Although we will have cause to make quite frequent references to the 'Third Way' and to *New* Labour it is not our intention to suggest that these terms are necessarily synonymous with the new social democracy. That they do, on occasion, overlap is certain but this should not constitute a major problem. The basic purpose of this chapter, it must be remembered, is to establish the contours of the new social democracy as political philosophy, as perhaps a new manifestation of the old social democratic impulse in very new times, and to see if there is any coherent policy agenda consistent with this vision.

The choice of the phrase 'new times' is not entirely accidental because it draws our attention to one of the major intellectual sources of Third Way politics. In a short but important article Finlayson (1999) sheds a great deal of light on the nature of Third Way theory and its relationship to both New Labour and the new social democracy. He notes that New Labour began to use the term 'Third Way' before Blair or Anthony Giddens had published their work on it. He writes that as a consequence of this lack of considered theory it (the Third Way):

> . . . could only appear vacuous or gratuitous, and that analysts were left considering not how useful or coherent it was, but what it might actually be. The only certainty seemed to be that 'old' models of social democracy and the conservative right had failed and something new was in need of development. (Finlayson, 1999: 271)

New Labour's position does not rest on 'a substantial moral claim about the nature of society and the distribution of its resources' (Finlayson, 1999: 271) but on a sociological claim about the real nature of modern society. While the world has been transformed by the economic, technological and cultural forces described above our political ideas about the world have not altered to the same extent. The Third Way is an attempt to provide this new political compass.

Finlayson argues that the Third Way has been shaped by two major intellectual influences: one associated with the analyses developed by Stuart Hall, Martin Jacques and others in the journal 'Marxism Today' in the 1980s, and the other in the sociology developed primarily by Anthony Giddens. The key ideas of what we might call the 'Marxism Today' perspective are to be found in Hall's analysis of Thatcherite neo-liberalism as a hegemonic project, and in the articulation of the concept of 'New Times'. The first of these is a theoretical critique in which Hall claims that political explanations and accounts derived from class analysis (the general approach adopted by Marxists and social democrats) were wrong theoretically and therefore the challenge for the left was to 'develop new strategies beyond a simple appeal to class allegiance that would generate a wide enough constituency for a hegemonic project of socialist renewal' (Finlayson, 1999: 273). The New Times strand was empirical rather than theoretical and argued simply that Marxism and social democracy were both 'empirically in error'. They did not correctly understand existing economic and social patterns. Post-Fordist flexibility created and required a new individualism and autonomy that should be enabled, not interfered with by the state' (Finlayson, 1999: 274). The left should respond by recognizing these new realities and develop a version of politics that could accommodate them.

Giddens's analysis demonstrates a similar general understanding of the nature of the new world created by contemporary capitalism, a world which has changed in unpredictable and surprising ways in which old ideas about Keynesianism and socialism are dead: one which is too 'complex, fluid and diverse to be managed by a central state' (Finlayson, 1999: 274). According to Finlayson, Giddens argues the need for a new 'life politics', one concerned with the emancipation of lifestyle, identity and choice, and his analysis of contemporary social relations ultimately provides: 'an alternative ethical basis to that of socialist anti-capitalism. This is a "philosophic conservatism", concerned with redeveloping and repairing social cohesion and solidarity' (Finlayson, 1999: 275).

## A Political Philosophy of 'New' Social Democracy

Whatever its strengths may be, Third Way theory is: 'not a political theory in a conventional sense but an attempt to think through the emerging social complexity of contemporary society' (Jayasuriya, 2000: 282). Given this lack of concern with political philosophy in Third Way writing, and in theories of diversity in general, where do we look for such a political philosophy? What attempts have been a made to recast social democracy in a way which is consistent with the complexity and diversity of modern societies? Is there, in fact, anything resembling a political philosophy (and political programme) of the new social democracy?

Clearly such a philosophy would need to bear in mind existing electoral preferences and traditional social democracy's history of defeat in the recent past. Although it must recognise these preferences it must also avoid the charge of being opportunistic and thus seen as simply a continuation of Thatcherite neo-liberalism by other means. It must also be able to demonstrate a genuine and strong sense of continuity with the traditional values and concerns of historical versions of the ideology. This presents an immediate and fundamental problem as Wolfe and Klausen (2000) have vividly demonstrated in an important article in the journal *Prospect*. They remind us that:

> For the 100 years, preceding the 1970s progressives in Europe and America pursued a politics of solidarity. The left demanded the creation and expansion of the welfare state. Public policy should redistribute income and subsidize, if not deliver directly, essential services such as education and health. The ideal was a society in which the inequalities associated with social class would fade away. (Wolfe and Klausen, 2000: 28)

Since the 1970s this ideal has been supplemented by the promotion of diversity: individuals and groups should not suffer because their gender, race, sexuality or physical status is different from that of the majority. As Wolfe and Klausen note:

> Herein lies the progressive dilemma of the twenty-first century. Solidarity and diversity are both desirable objectives. Unfortunately they can also conflict. A sense of solidarity creates a readiness to share with strangers, which in turn underpins a thriving welfare state. But it is easier to feel solidarity with those who broadly share your values and way of life. Modern progressives committed to diversity often fail to acknowledge this. (2000: 28)

A resolution of this dilemma has been suggested in the work of a number of thinkers writing in the general tradition of social democracy (e.g. White, 1999; Vandenbroucke, 1999; Coote, 1999; Jayasuriya, 2000).

White's essay seeks to establish the ideas of rights and responsibilities as central themes of the new social democracy. Together these constitute the doctrine of civic responsibility, a doctrine which Blair and his government have been most concerned to stress as a central element of their economic and social philosophy. The idea of civic responsibility is very controversial in centre-left politics. Some have argued that it conflicts with the traditional libertarian values of British social democracy, while others have claimed that: 'The commitment to balance rights and responsibilities expresses a conception of fairness and mutuality that has deep roots in the social democratic tradition' (White, 1999: 166). White's concern is to offer an interpretation and defence of civic responsibility from a specifically social democratic public philosophy, one defined by three core values: reciprocity, equal opportunity and autonomy. For White such a tradition is already present in broadly social democratic thought, specifically in the 'liberal socialism' of Hobhouse, Tawney and Crosland. Economic justice in this tradition is about a principle of reciprocity, 'according to which entitlements to income and wealth are properly linked to productive contributions' (White 1999: 166). As a theory of distributive justice it asserts that 'those who willingly share in the economic benefits of social cooperation have a corresponding obligation to make, if so able, a personal and relevantly proportional productive contribution to the community in return for those benefits' (1999: 168). Is the possibility that this obligation to contribute might be enforceable consistent with social democracy? White's answer is unequivocally 'Yes' and he cites writers as varied as Hobhouse, Tawney, Laski and Crosland to support him. He also makes the very important point that left-wing political culture might have moved too far away from this tradition in recent decades, perhaps because of a fear of blaming the victim. However he concludes by suggesting that this departure from an important principle of centre-left distributive justice might now have gone too far and that 'this is to be regretted, because the reciprocity principle does seem to capture a deep and widespread intuition about distributive justice' (White, 1999: 170). (For a full discussion of the wider concept of distributive justice see Brian Lund's chapter in this book.)

White's attempt to restore the idea of reciprocity to the heart of social democracy's renewed understanding of distributive justice is vital for reasons other than political theory. There can be little doubt that many of Labour's traditional core voters deserted during the 1980s because of their feeling that far too many 'free-riders' were battening on to the welfare state without making any contribution to the funding of that provision. The decline in the income tax threshold since the 1940s had drawn into the tax population millions of workers (and voters) who themselves were not particularly affluent, indeed, whose earned incomes were only a little, if at all, above benefit levels. Their resentment at what they felt was a gross injustice not only cost the Labour Party crucial votes but also resulted in significant damage to their attachment to a non-discriminatory, institutional model of welfare. Marquand (1996) has also noted the importance of reciprocity in old or traditional social democracy. In an important essay he has argued that the usual distinction between individualism and collectivism has been accompanied by a further distinction, one between two different conceptions of the good life. Thus:

> On the one side of the divide are those who see the Self as a static bundle of preferences and the good life as one in which individuals pursue their own preferences without interference from others. On the other are those for whom the Self is a growing and developing moral entity, and the good life is one in which individuals learn to adopt higher preferences in place of lower ones. (Marquand, 1996: 20)

The first of these are 'hedonist' or 'passive' and the latter 'moralist' or 'active'. This provides four possible groupings: hedonistic collectivists; moralistic collectivists; hedonistic individualists; and moralistic individualists. Since 1945 each of these has taken turns as the dominant influence on policy. What the centre-left forgot, or never knew, in the 1970s, 1980s and 1990s is the similarity between the moral collectivism of the Attlee government, a government which preached a doctrine of civic responsibility, and Thatcher's posture of moral individualism. By arguing for the return of reciprocity as a defining feature of a new social democracy, White is, in an important way, seeking a return to one of old social democracy's animating principles.

Notions of reciprocity do not exist in a void. They are conceptualised and articulated in real-world patterns of resource distribution and life chances. In this regard we should bear in mind that egalitarian and libertarian values are both important in liberal socialism. White's argument is that these egalitarian values demand that we look at the existing distribution of opportunity against which 'citizens' putative reciprocity-based obligations are enforced' (White, 1999: 167). Thus, the real concern for social democrats should be to ensure not just reciprocity but *fair reciprocity,* and fair reciprocity demanded the operationalisation of 'a robust principle of equal opportunity' (1999:171). Equal opportunity itself demanded some redistribution of initial market allocations and distribution of resources. If the state insisted on the application of an idea of reciprocity on the basis of unmodified market allocations, the chances are, as recent US experience demonstrates, that social policy would become entirely punitive. Thus:

> it is vitally important to stress that the reciprocity-based contract between citizens and community is a two-sided contract. that the community must do its bit by securing certain standard threshold distribution conditions, at the same time as the individual citizen is required to do his/her bit. (White, 1999: 171)

This might require that individuals have access to meaningful and non-stigmatising work for a decent, minimum income. It is interesting to note with regard to this latter point the extent to which the Blair government has become wedded to the idea of wage subsidisation through policy instruments such as the Working Families Tax Credit (since replaced by the Child Tax Credit and Working Tax Credit). That which was anathema to the Labour Party when the Family Income Supplement scheme was introduced in 1971 is now entirely consistent with its principles in the 'new age'. The introduction of a national minimum wage, major increases in Child Benefit and a serious attempt to provide decent and more generally available access to high quality child care demonstrate the strength of Labour's commitment to the idea and reality of work and, perhaps, to the idea of 'fair reciprocity'. Perhaps all that is required to secure the kind of background redistribution White demands as a pre-condition of fair reciprocity is for the state to act as 'employer of last resort' in areas with long standing and deeply rooted economic problems, together with vertically redistributive taxation of inheritances and other wealth transfers to preclude economic free-riding by the wealthy. A commitment to the creation and maintenance of full employment would also be useful.

White goes on to argue that his understanding of fair reciprocity is not the same as the 'New Paternalism' of American intellectuals such as Lawrence Mead who argue that the imposition of obligations is good for the moral well-being of recipients. By combining vertically redistributive taxation, a more equal opportunity to access decent income levels through work and/or benefits, and the obligations on citizens to make an acceptable, reciprocal contribution of some socially useful kind, White believes that social democracy can re-connect with the general public's instincts about distributive justice.

Autonomy is the third of White's core values and he is insistent that the idea of civic responsibility must be clearly separate and distinguished from 'a concern to promote or enforce a sectarian conception of personal morality' (1999: 167). A respect for individual autonomy would satisfy the libertarian impulses in social democracy which find their most powerful expression in the liberal tradition exemplified by John Stuart Mill. This tradition counsels us to refrain from activities that produce significant harm to our fellow citizens by, for example, avoiding intimidation, some forms of discrimination (such as gender, ethnicity, age etc.) and economic exploitation. Otherwise the state should leave people alone:

It must itself respect our spiritual integrity by giving us the autonomy to pursue our own good in our own way. We may refer to this idea as the autonomy principle. (White, 1999: 174)

In those instances when the state does act to define what we can or cannot do legally we need to be assured:

1  that this is indeed necessary to prevent a genuine harm;
2  that the gain in this respect is sufficiently large and sufficiently certain as to outweigh any damage to civil interests that may result from the state's new policy. (White, 1999: 174–5)

Jayasuriya (2000) has also recognised the need to recast the social democratic commitment to equality and freedom so that they reflect the complexity, diversity and plurality of modern society in his attempt to develop a normative rationale for new social democratic politics. Like White he bases his understanding of the new social democracy in 'a liberal conception of individual autonomy' and contends that: '. . . the key project . . . is to reconcile the social commitment to equality with a liberal emphasis on individual autonomy' (Jayasuriya, 2000: 283). He follows Sassoon (1996) in defining freedom as 'the material ability to make more choices. The role of the state is to ensure that everyone possesses such material ability' (Sassoon, 1996: 738). Thus for Jayasuriya, the key normative principle is *capability*. The enhancement of individual capability is viewed as central to the agenda of the Blair administration, specifically to the whole notion of social exclusion. He suggests that to think in terms of capability implies a notion of *complex equality* which is contrasted sharply with traditional egalitarian ideas of equality. Complex equality as an idea recognizes the need 'to take into account differences in circumstances and individual locations and the diverse ends of individuals' (Jayasuriya, 2000: 283). Capability therefore suggests a normative commitment 'to a notion of freedom defined in terms of the capability of people to make effective choices' (2000: 283). Jayasuriya draws on the work of Mark Latham (1998) as implying that at the heart of the new social democracy is an attempt to reconcile traditional egalitarianism with negative liberty and that 'it is this liberal socialism that is inherent in the new social democracy' (Jayasuriya, 2000: 284).

An important part of Jayasuriya's work is his critique of Giddens's approach to Third Way theory. Giddens, he argues, is preoccupied with redeveloping the welfare state in ways that respond to the new risks generated by a form of capitalism which has undermined the basis of traditional forms of welfare. In his analysis of the welfare state since the end of the Second World War Giddens distinguishes between negative welfare and positive welfare. Negative welfare is understood as action taken to compensate people for the costs and diswelfares they experience as a consequence of economic and social change. Positive welfare incorporates negative welfare but also attempts to develop 'the capacity for risk taking and integrating welfare institutions within the broader economic system' (Jayasuriya, 2000: 284).

This, in essence, is what Giddens means by the term 'social investment state'. The positive welfare state (and, by implication, the social investment state) are intensely concerned with the processes of inclusion and exclusion which facilitate or prevent individuals from taking part in economic activity, especially in labour market participation. A technology driven global economy creates the risk that certain groups such as the unskilled and the poorly educated may be permanently excluded from such activity. Traditional or negative forms of welfare, because they seek solely to compensate for diswelfares, may exacerbate social exclusion. Positive welfare, in sharp and marked contrast, would encourage capability and help prevent exclusion: inclusion would be a dominant objective of such a policy. This has clearly become the leitmotif of the Blair government, and for the government as well as Giddens, 'inclusion and exclusion have become important concepts for analysing and responding to inequality because of changes affecting the class structure of industrial countries' (Giddens, 1998: 103). The new global economy, obeying its technological imperatives, demands welfare policies structured to develop individual capability and the capacity to participate in the rapidly changing labour markets of contemporary capitalism. The old manufacturing industries with their largely male, full-time labour force have been replaced by industries and technology which thrive on flexible labour markets (helpfully de-regulated by government) demanding part-time or fixed-term or casual labour. The new welfare state according to Third Way theorists must reflect these changes and do all in its power to encourage labour market participation. As Jayasuriya observes: 'In the new global economy, employment is likely to be transitory, and therefore the new social welfare is designed to facilitate the re-inclusion of the unemployed into the economic mainstream' (Jayasuriya, 2000: 285).

How relevant are these ideas of negative and positive welfare states, social inclusion and social exclusion, and even Jayasuriya's concepts of capability and complex equality, to a new social politics that is genuinely in the social democratic tradition? There is nothing which is fundamentally problematic in Third Way theorists' identification of the implications of economic, cultural and social change for social democracy or the welfare state. It makes perfectly good sense to change the pattern of provision, perhaps even the nature of provision itself, in recognition of the significance of these contextual changes. What might be more difficult for a mainstream social democrat, one for whom ideas of reciprocity, equal opportunity and autonomy have genuine substance, is the nature of the analyses which have been made and the content of the policy suggestions. Contrary to the apparent assumptions and understanding of Third Way theory, insecurity is not a new phenomenon. People who exist by and through the sale of their labour in capitalist labour markets have their only access to the resources necessary to even an approximation of a full and civilised life determined by the nature of the bargains they can strike with potential employers. The vast majority of working people are still only a job loss away from poverty. It was an awareness of their inherent insecurity and vulnerability in capitalist economies that caused ordinary people to combine together in labour organisations and political parties so that they might possess a collective, countervailing power to deploy in their negotiations with employers and their dealings with politicians. There has been an objective change in capitalist economies and insecurity has increased, but that insecurity has increased because neo-liberalism has set the intellectual and policy agenda.It has been a politics which has clearly and deliberately sought to increase the power of capital vis-à-vis that of labour. The intent of much of the policy agenda suggested by Third Way theory has been to fit workers for capital's purposes: not to modify capital so that its consequences no longer initially and ultimately rest on the shoulders of those made poor, vulnerable, and unemployed by its operations. State action to shift the incidence of the costs of economic change from the poorest and most marginal members of society on to those more able to bear these costs was always a primary objective of the social democratic welfare state.

We may also add that concepts such as the social investment state, capability and capacity themselves are hardly new ideas. From this perspective:

> . . . welfare is viewed not as an end in itself, but as an investment by which people's capacity and choices can be enlarged; in other words this version of welfare places more emphasis on the positive role of welfare in helping individuals deal with risk, rather than playing a passive role as an instrument to provide security. (Jayasuriya, 2000: 285–6)

It is sometimes difficult to see why security should be regarded as 'passive.' It is not too outrageous to suggest that most people's lives are characterised in one way or another by a search for security. This is not surprising because with security comes confidence, optimism and, ironically, the willingness to take risks. In other words security is not such a debilitating condition after all. Perhaps those who have never known real insecurity find it difficult to understand the attraction it has for the majority of the population. It is appropriate to remind ourselves at this point of Michael Foot's note that one of Aneurin Bevan's favourite words in describing the power of the NHS was that it gave people a sense of 'serenity' at a time (illness) when they most needed it.

It would take a rather particular and perverse view of welfare practice in the UK to believe that, in general, the state has not been keen to secure people's re-attachment to the labour force. This has been done through a variety of policy instruments incorporating positive work incentives as well as strict disciplinary mechanisms. The problem for public policy has always been to secure an appropriate balance between compensating individuals and families for the diswelfares they experience through one or other contingency (unemployment, sickness etc.) and ensuring that everyone takes seriously her/his obligations and responsibilities to make a contribution, of whatever kind, to the public good. As White (1999) and Deacon (2000) have both suggested, in recent decades some on the left (Marquand's 'collective hedonists') have got this balance wrong, but the recognition that there is this form of reciprocal understanding has always been a central plank of social democratic philosophy. Thus, there is no real need to invent a 'Third Way' (Self, 2000).

It may well be that Third Way critics of traditional social democracy do not really understand it. On occasion they seem to misunderstand Keynesian theory, which was about far more than demand management, and they underestimate the capacity of national governments and regional or supra-national organisations to modify or challenge market triumphalism in the globalised economy. Theirs can be regarded as a defeatist politics, and, in this sense, not deserving of being included in a new and genuine social democracy. One is also left to wonder about the historical accuracy of assertions such as Jayasuriya's claim that:

> technological innovation, productivity and competitiveness have entered the lexicon of social democracy, taking pride of place over – if not replacing – the traditional Keynesian vocabulary of macro-economic management and distributive issues. (Jayasuriya, 2000: 286)

Social democrats, by the very nature of their analysis, have always argued that a competitive, innovative and high productivity capitalist economy was an essential pre-requisite for increasing levels of real personal disposable income and the creation of a comprehensive, generous institutional model of welfare. This is why social democratic intellectuals like Crosland took as their model the achievements and programmes of their counterparts in Sweden and the Federal Republic of Germany in the 1950s and 1960s. For them social democracy was essentially about the socialisation of consumption not the socialisation of production. The greater the volume of resources generated by a competitive and successful private sector economy, the greater would be the pool of resources the state could call on for its social agenda. On this agenda education and training had a very prominent place given their potential contribution as forms of economic and social investment. 'Education, education, education' was a social democratic mantra long before Tony Blair.

## What Kind of Programme?

So far our main concern has been to examine the ways in which the new social democracy has reacted to the changes associated with globalisation and advanced modernity at the level of normative values, of political philosophy, and we have noted the new emphasis given to ideas about fair reciprocity, autonomy, equal opportunity, complex equality and capacity. We now consider what economic and social policy agenda might best reflect this newly conceptualised social democracy.

Vandenbroucke (1999) argues that the second half of the 1990s witnessed a developing convergence in centre-left European literature on the welfare state. After making due allowance for national differences in circumstance and culture he suggests that this literature reflects a general agreement about a number of fixed points and focal concerns. Foremost amongst these is the conviction that employment policy is the key issue in welfare reform. Unlike the traditional concern with securing full employment for men, the social challenge today is full employment for men *and women*: 'It points to the need to rethink both certain aspects of the architecture of the welfare state and the distribution of work over households and individuals as it spontaneously emerges in the labour market' (Vandenbrouke, 1999: 37). The emerging welfare state should also cover new risks such as lack of skills and single parenthood, along with a recognition of new social needs, including the reconciliation of work, family life and education, and the negotiation of changes in both family and workplace over a person's 'entire life cycle' (Vandenbroucke, 1999: 37). An intelligent welfare state should respond to new needs and risks in an active and preventive way: it should be about social investment and not just the provision of compensatory social spending. Greater priority than hitherto should be given to active labour market policies tailored to individual needs and situations, policies which should seek to achieve a correct balance between incentives, opportunities and obligations. These policies should also try to avoid the poverty and unemployment traps associated with the dis-incentive effects of targeted taxes and benefits.

Perhaps the newest element of the converged policy agenda discussed by Vandenbroucke is the much greater importance given to the augmentation of low paid work through minimum wages and wage subsidisation. The apparent assumption that the state will continue to provide cash subsidies to low wages has attracted very little comment which is, perhaps, surprising given its intellectual and political significance. When this practice was first revived in 1970 in the form of the Family Income Supplements Act it attracted the wrath of the British Labour Party, then in opposition. One of Labour's concerns was the traditional one that it would subsidise bad and inefficient employers and, in effect, represent the institutionalised pauperisation of a significant proportion of the low paid. If Vandenbrouke is correct in his claims about the generality of wage subsidisation it surely represents a major departure for political parties of the centre-left: a genuine reflection of the triumph of pragmatism over principle. The market will always produce low-paid jobs and better these than no jobs at all: all the state should do is to raise the incomes of the low paid in ways which take account of the family demands on the low wage, through a combination of minimum wage legislation and wage-subsidisation. The continuing presence of these policies is again reflected in Vandenbroucke's observation that the new social democracy requires an economy which has not only a sector exposed to international competition, but also a private service sector not exposed to such competition in which the unskilled can find new jobs, probably subsidised by the state.

What is not so apparent at the moment in this revived and reconstructed social democracy is any general understanding of, and commitment to, the need for national governments, international economic organisations such as the IMF and the WTO, and regional agencies like the European Central Bank to respond to the normal fluctuations of the trade cycle. Notwithstanding the wishful thinking of the proselytisers of the 'new economics', the trade cycle has not been abolished. Unless there is collective and concerted action to respond to the decline in economic activity during cyclical downswings, unemployment will rise and there will be a reduction in the jobs available for the newly trained and re-moralised beneficiaries of active labour market policies. This is not a call for a return to the debased form of Keynesian demand management pursued by successive British governments during social democracy's earlier ascendancy, but a recognition that supply-side economics by itself is not enough. It is a call for social democratic politicians to recognise the validity of the claim that:

'The basis of Keynesian thinking is law, i.e. the one thing the Euro-left considers to be politically unimportant. It is about the intelligent application of the law and the adaptation of the legal framework to right the wrongs of the market. It is, above all, a recognition that the economy is a human creation, not a force of nature, and that what has been created can be adapted' (Atkinson and Elliott, 1999: 43–4).

Social democratic political leaders need to moderate their uncritical worship of the market as an institution and rediscover their commitment to the possibilities of politics for effecting significant changes in the distribution of resources and life-chances.

## What Kind of State?

A consistent theme in the new social democracy is a belief in the need to reconstruct the relationship between the state and civil society. It is argued that the traditional top-down approach typical of the Fabian strand in British social democracy, where the state decided what was good for people and then delivered it, resulted in a failure to meet the real needs and preferences of individuals and families. Similarly, neo-liberalism's attempts to break up public monopolies themselves led to a range of unacceptable consequences as service standards declined and inequalities spread. Thus a new set of mechanisms for service provision is required which avoid the failings of old social democracy and neo-liberalism, and which also reflects the growth of individualism and diversity. To use a current cliché: the state should 'steer more and row less'. As Coote says: 'One of the key features of a modern social democracy is that it has strong social objectives but a weak set of levers for achieving them' (Coote, 1999: 117). Techniques and approaches are required which will actively involve people more in programme development and delivery rather than resting content with their role as passive recipients of public policy. The image is of myriad possibilities of form and mechanisms in an expanded and genuine mixed economy of welfare, one in which the interests of consumers/users/citizens are paramount.

The idea that an over-mighty state might abuse and ignore individuals and families is not new in left politics and theory. It brings to mind the distinction between the 'mechanical' reformism of the Fabians, with their insistence on expert, scientific solutions, and the 'moral' reformism of liberal socialism which always insisted on the need to involve the active support and involvement of civil society. However it must be remembered that centralised, top-down solutions were, in part, chosen as policy instruments because of the gaps and deficiencies that existed in social provision before the creation of the institutional model of state welfare. If we move to a more pluralistic model of welfare provision, one which actively seeks to involve the community and other agents of civil society as partners in programme development and delivery, what happens then to the idea of territorial justice, the belief that people have the right to roughly the same standard of service regardless of where they live? Does this mean that government will take on greater responsibility for laying down national standards of service and become a very active regulator as it seeks to secure compliance with these standards? If so, what price then for local autonomy and responsibility?

Although one of the reasons for looking to self-activating individuals and groups is to use their physical and organisational resources, thus reducing demands on the public purse, it is inevitable that government will continue to contribute a major part of the income needed by local groups, voluntary bodies and community organisations. It is very likely that this will bring with it serious questions of accountability which cannot be ignored. How is this problem to be overcome? Moreover, there can be no guarantee that newly empowered local organisations will not use their authority to discriminate against one or other section of the population. It may also be the case that unpopular causes (mental impairment, lone parent families, for example) will find their needs ignored or marginalised.

If the concern of the new social democracy is to secure a much greater role for individual and group involvement, is the appropriate answer necessarily to be found in the resources and agencies of civil society? Might a more appropriate solution not be found in a re-energised and democratised form of local government, one given responsibility for all areas of social provision (health, education, housing, social care etc.) other than income maintenance? With coterminous spatial boundaries, and with a legal requirement to involve citizens and civil society at all levels of policy development and delivery, this revived local government may be a more effective mechanism for meeting the genuine interests and needs of local populations than anything else yet suggested. It could more easily guarantee territorial justice; meet the demands for a transparent accountability; involve citizens and groups as active participants in a genuinely democratic political process; and create a renaissance in civic life. With expanded power and greater and more democratic participation, there is every chance of increased voter activity and, with this, a greater legitimacy of the whole enterprise. British social democracy could secure a return to its old convictions that local solutions were the best solutions, especially if they had democratic legitimacy and authority.

## Conclusions

It is likely that the nature of the new social democracy outlined above will not be attractive to some, perhaps many, people who regard themselves as natural supporters of centre-left politics. With its emphasis on civic responsibility, earned rights, fair reciprocity and individual autonomy it will be criticised on the grounds that it concedes too much to the demands of global capitalism, and that it is imbued with a repressive moral authoritarianism. However, although these fears can be understood and recognised, the position adopted here is that it is possible and justifiable to claim that much of this new thinking is entirely consistent with the best traditions of social democracy.

Whether we like it or not the world has changed and social democrats are confronted by the realities of globalisation, new technology, diversity and individualism. What matters surely is the nature of the response developed by those on the left who would challenge prevailing orthodoxies. Third Way theory offers little in terms of normative political principles and is too accepting of the market's demands: it makes too many concessions to be regarded as properly social democratic, but the other ideas examined in this chapter point to a new vision of social democracy.

This is a vision which is sensitive to the realities of the modern world but combines this sensitivity with a continuing attachment to recognisably social democratic values. Through its newly regained focus on fair reciprocity as a defining approach to distributive justice it reconnects with the moral collectivism of the Attlee government of 1945–51 and resonates with the instinctive beliefs of a majority of the population. Combined with a reconstructed approach to the state's relationship with civic society and a willingness to delegate accountable powers to a renewed local democracy this is a vision of politics with rich potential in the twenty-first century.

## Further Reading

Gamble, A. and Wright, T. (1999) 'The new social democracy', supplement to the *Political Quarterly*. Oxford: Blackwell.

Giddens, A. (1998) *The Third Way: the Renewal of Social Democracy*. Oxford: Polity Press.

Wolfe, A. and Klausen, J. (2000) 'Other people', *Prospect*, December.

# FOUR
# Marxism and Welfarism
*Michael Lavalette*

---

### Outline Points

- Marxism is a philosophical system that treats the world, and the various social relations that shape it, as part of a 'unified whole' or totality.
- Thus the vast wealth created by capitalism cannot be separated from the immense inequalities that divide the world, or the swathes of poverty that capitalism creates.
- Welfare and social policy cannot be separated from the normal drives of capitalism.
- Welfare development will differ in different countries – the result of various socio-political factors.
- Following the historian John Saville, we can identify three key elements that shape welfare settlements within nation states: (1) the economic and social requirements of an increasingly complex industrial society; (2) the pressures which have come from the mass of the population as the perceptions of economic and social needs have gradually widened and become more explicit, and (3) the political calculations of the ruling groups.

---

## Introduction: A World of Vast Inequalities

In 1848 Karl Marx and Frederick Engels wrote the Communist Manifesto. In the Manifesto they wrote: 'The bourgeoisie, during its rule of scarce one hundred years, has created more massive and more colossal productive forces than have all preceding generations together' (1998: 15). The productive forces had been revolutionised, the system was dynamic and expansive, the potential for human fulfilment immense. And this was written in 1848! Today this quotation seems almost quaint. In 1848 capitalism existed in Britain, parts of Western Europe and the Eastern seaboard of America. In contrast, at the start of the twenty-first century, capitalism is a truly global system and the world is richer than it has ever been. As Susan George has noted: 'The world now produces in less than two weeks the equivalent of the entire physical output of the year 1900. Economic output doubles approximately every 25 to 30 years' (1999: 7). The wealth of the richest nations has recently been estimated at $30 trillion, the US alone at $12 trillion (Tran, 2005). A trillion is not a concept many of us can grasp easily. We 'know', in monetary terms, what a hundred or a thousand is, we may even have a vision of a million, *but a trillion?* To help let's write it out in full: the US economy is estimated at present to be worth $12,000,000,000,000.

Such wealth creates fantastic possibilities. We could easily feed the world's population several times over – thereby addressing the problem of the estimated 845 million people (about 14 per cent of the world's population) who are chronically or acutely malnourished (Sanchez and Swaminathan, 2005). We could ensure that every human being lives in a well-built home with access to running water and appropriate sanitation – solving the problem for the 2.8 billion people who lack access to basic sanitation and the estimated one billion people who live in slums (UNDP, 2003). We could immunise every child in the world against easily curable diseases like measles and provide cheap treatment for people with worm infestation and malaria – thereby dealing with one-quarter of the global burden of disease (Health Matters, 2000). As Professor Sachs, from the Earth Institute at Columbia University has noted: 'Every month, 150,000 children in Africa . . . are dying from the silent tsunami of malaria, a largely preventable and utterly treatable disease' (Tran, 2005).

We could use available technology to eradicate many killer diseases and make sure that all HIV and Aids sufferers across the globe have access to life sustaining drugs – and immediately address the HIV pandemic that is sweeping sub-Saharan Africa where, in 2004, two million people died of Aids, leaving 12 million children orphaned as a consequence (UNDP, 2003). We could make sure that all the world's children have access to primary and secondary education – thereby reversing the trend in 12 of the poorest countries in the world where primary school enrolment is in decline (UNDP, 2003). And we could ensure that all workers have reduced working hours and improved working conditions – thereby eradicating the scourge of cheap, sweated labour such as that imposed on 70 per cent of migrant garment workers in Los Angeles (Bas, 2004), address the problem of the 250 million child labourers across the globe (ICFTU, 2005) and eradicate the abomination of the estimated 27 million adult slaves (Vidal, 2005).

Yet the vast potential and wealth of society is not used to improve all our lives, the dominant social relations of capitalism mean that a small number of people enrich themselves at the expense of the vast majority and we live in a world of gross inequalities.

At the top of the pile there are the 'super-rich'. According to the *Sunday Times Rich List*, the wealth of the richest is staggering. The five wealthiest families or individuals in the world are (in order) the Walton family (owners of Walmart) whose wealth runs to £54.2bn, Bill Gates of Microsoft with £25.3bn, Warren Buffet with £23.3bn, the Albrecht family (from Germany) with £22.3bn and the Mars family (from the US) with £16.9bn (*Sunday Times*, 2004). The US magazine *Forbes* regularly produces a list of America's 'richest 400' and it notes that between 2003 and 2004 the individuals on their rich list *increased their wealth* by $45bn – in fact, even to get onto the *Forbes* list you must be 'worth' over $750 million (*Forbes*, 2004). The wealth of this tiny minority stands in stark contrast with 2.7 billion people that the World Bank estimates live on less than $2 a day and the 1.1 billion who live on less than $1 a day (World Bank, 2004).

The majority of the richest live in the affluent 'north' and the vast majority of the poorest live in the 'global south'. Economic inequalities between countries of the north and south have been widening steadily for 200 years – a situation that is made worse by the blight of 'Third World Debt' and since 1982, for example, the poorest countries in the world have paid $3,450bn in debt repayments to the countries and banks in the affluent north (Socialist Worker, 2005). But if we simply see the divisions of the world in geographical terms we miss the vast inequalities that divide nations.

So in the south, amongst the vast sea of poverty, there are islands of immense wealth. The sixth and tenth richest people in the world, according to the *Sunday Times* Rich List, both come from Saudi Arabia, King Falid (whose personal wealth is £13.5bn) and Prince Alwaleed (£10.8bn) – a country of vast inequalities and where 5 million working non-nationals have very few rights. Listed 22nd on the Rich List is the Mexican Carlos Slim Helu (£7.5bn) – a country where the minimum wage is $4 a day and millions remain trapped in subsistence farming in rural areas or live in shanty towns and are reliant on casual employment (New Internationalist, 2004).

Similarly in the 'rich' north there is poverty and increasing inequality. In Britain, for example, the level of inequality is at a 40 year high. The Institute of Fiscal Studies published a report in June 2004 that found that income inequality in Britain rose by 40 per cent between 1979 and 2001. The IFS found that the last 20 years of the twentieth century reversed the trend towards increasing equality that had continued since the First World War. The richest 1 per cent of individuals took 3 per cent of national income in 1979 but 8 per cent by 2000, representing a return to the position of the 1950s. (Elliot, 2004)

The trend towards growing inequality started in Britain under the Thatcher government in the 1980s but inequality in Britain has continued to increase since Labour came to power in 1997. According to the Office for National Statistics, the wealth of the super-rich has doubled since Tony Blair came to power. Nearly 600,000 individuals in the top 1 per cent of the UK wealth league owned assets worth £355bn in 1996, the last full year of Conservative rule; by 2002 that had increased to £797bn. (Carvel, 2004c)

How do we explain such vast inequalities? Is it because the rich work harder? Does Bill Gates, for example, work many millions of times harder than someone labouring long hours for $1 a day in the global south? Is it simply because of the greed and avarice of the fabulously wealthy? But Bill Gates has donated millions of dollars to medical charities; of course this still leaves him with billions, but an explanation simply based on notions of greed does not really fit.

The answer to this question, for Marxists, is that such inequalities are a direct consequence of the socio-economic system that we live in: capitalism.

---

**Activity 1**

*Think of the vast gulf in wealth between the very richest and the very poorest. Why might such inequalities exist? Are such inequalities 'natural' and inevitable?*

---

## Capitalism

Capitalism, as the quote from Marx and Engels that started this chapter emphasises, is a dynamic economic system. That dynamism arises from the pressure on manufacturers to try constantly to re-invest in production: to invest in new technology, to try and produce new goods, to try and sell more and more products. The problem is that whilst each company meticulously plans its productive activity, the system as a whole is unplanned. The system is one that lurches from periods of boom to periods of slump.

During booms companies are working flat out to produce as many commodities as possible. But this starts to lead to increased costs. As components, transport and labour become scarce (because all companies are expanding together the demand for these things increases across the system as a whole) the costs of production start to creep up. Further the more companies increase their output, the more difficult it is to sell all the commodities made. This is made worse because there is not one company making cars or tables or televisions but several – each increasing their output to try and sell more and more. Soon there comes a point where it is increasingly difficult to sell the goods that have been made, there is a general crisis of overproduction, and the system slides from a period of boom to one of slump where goods remain unsold and factories (and labour) is left redundant. The boom/slump cycle of capitalism is part of its very fabric.

Capitalism is also a system that is wracked by conflict. In particular two great divisions shape it. The first is a class division between the people who own and/or control the means of production (the offices, factories, machines and resources) needed to produce society's wealth (Marx called them the bourgeoisie) and the vast majority, the working class (Marx called them the proletariat) who have no means of survival beyond their ability to work for wages. The bourgeoisie and the working class are tied together in a relationship – the bourgeoisie can produce nothing without workers; workers, in turn, need paid employment in order to survive.

But this is not a relationship of equals. The wealth of modern society is created by the labour of workers but the commodities they produce generate vast profits for the bourgeoisie because there is no mechanism to force them to pay workers the monetary equivalent of the value their labour creates. To maintain their wealth the bourgeoisie must continuously try to make workers work longer, faster and for less money. For the working class, on the other hand, their interests are for higher wages, shorter hours, and longer holidays. The interests of workers and the bourgeoisie are, therefore, irreconcilable – they are tied together in a mutually antagonistic relationship of exploitation where the survival of the bourgeoisie as a class depends on the subjugation of the proletariat as a class.

The second great division within capitalism is one that separates the bourgeoisie into competing companies, organisations and 'capitals'. Marx termed the bourgeoisie a 'band of warring brothers', meaning they had a 'brotherly' interest in maintaining capitalism and the exploitation of the working class. This is their general class interest – the interest of *capital in general*. But they are warring brothers, competing with each other intensely with the aim of putting each other out of business and obtaining a greater share of the surplus product. Capitalism, then, is a system of *'many competing capitals'*. It is this competition between the competing units of capitals that drives each of them to invest resources in technology, to try and expand production and, at the same time, to attack workers' living conditions, to try and increase the rate of exploitation. The two structural divisions of capitalism therefore are intimately connected.

So where does welfarism fit into this picture? Is it not a set of provisions concerned with fulfilling human need rather than profit? Is it not an area of social life free from the dominant principles of market capitalism?

The ideological claims of welfare clearly suggest that it is a separate and distinct area of social life, geared to combating the worst manifestations of poverty and inequality, and structured by a general society-wide commitment to some shared humanitarian impulse. But this picture is misleading.

In his analysis of the capitalist mode of production Marx develops a distinction between the 'appearance' (or 'phenomenal forms') of the world as it represents itself in people's experience and the underlying 'essence' (or essential relations) which explain why the world appears as it does. Quoting Marx and Engels in *The German Ideology*, Sayer explains this distinction:

> phenomenal forms . . . merely suppose that at any given point there exists a constituted world whose phenomena have achieved . . . 'the stability of natural, self-understood forms of social life' . . . Unlike phenomenal forms . . . essential relations need not be transparent to direct experience. Phenomenal forms may be such as to mask or obscure the relations of which they are the forms of manifestation. (1983: 9)

To give an example, the capitalist market imposes itself on our daily life in myriad ways – work, leisure, family and social life are all shaped by the commodification of life and the ruinous operation of the market. Yet while it is a real social institution that affects all our lives, it is actually an external manifestation of the social relations of production (the exploitation of workers by capital) dominant in society, but disguised by the operation of the market itself. A similar recognition of the relationship and distinction between the 'appearance' of welfare in capitalist societies and its underlying 'essence' is necessary to fully comprehend the competing and conflicting roles of welfare provision. In other words it is necessary to delve beneath the surface appearance of welfare and its ideological claims and discover the competing and conflicting political, economic, social and ideological roles it performs.

Further, developing the distinction between 'capital in general' and 'many competing capitals' we can start to locate the various roles welfare performs within capitalism. The immediate economic interest of each unit of capital (whether it is a privately owned family firm, a joint stock company, a multinational corporation, a national state owned company, etc.) may be for cheap labour, with the social costs of reproduction borne by the worker and her family. But in the interests of 'capital in general' – for the system to survive, stabilise and for an appropriately trained, educated and healthy labour force to exist – the worker cannot be completely and unproblemmatically left to the whims of the market without threatening the very processes of accumulation upon which capitalism is built. This recognition may start to explain why capitalism needs welfarism – but at all times it is important to remember that 'capital in general' is an abstraction (although a legitimate and necessary one for analytical purposes) and that capitalism really comprises its many competing units and these have their own immediate interests which may clash with the long or short term interests of 'capital in general'. Thus, for example, while the representatives of any particular national capitalism may feel that their economy requires more highly trained graduates to enter the labour market many employers will be reluctant to pay any increased costs for this (through higher taxes, for instance) and some employers will be openly hostile to any such developments because they do not employ graduates but rely on cheap unskilled labour. Hence there is always room for conflict and disagreement over the direction, form and extent of welfare, its goals and purposes – welfarism is an inherently political activity.

## Analysing Welfare

Most accounts of welfare treat it as a separate sphere of social activity, something distinct from the general dynamic of capitalism. But for Marxists, although welfare cannot be simply reduced to the needs of economic production, it cannot be separated from the political and economic processes of capitalism.

The Marxist historian John Saville has suggested that we can identify three 'strands' which affect and shape welfare in different societies:

1 the economic and social requirements of an increasingly complex industrial society;
2 the pressures which have come from the mass of the population as the perceptions of economic and social needs have gradually widened and become more explicit;
3 the political calculations of the ruling groups. (1983: 11)

Let's look at these 'strands' in more detail.

### Economic and Social Requirements of an Increasingly Complex Industrial Society

In the earliest phases of capitalist expansion the basic problem for capitalism is to 'adapt' or 'mould' a free labour force to the requirements of industry, to break 'old' customs and traditions and to try and coerce people to work hard and participate in 'appropriate' and regulated social lives. There is a much greater emphasis on the state's controlling and regulating function.

Edward Thompson (1991), discusses a range of traditional practices which, in the eighteenth century, clashed with the new 'requirements of industry'. He notes how there was conflict over, for example, the attempt to move work activity from a 'task-orientated' to a 'time-measured' operation and the struggle to break what he terms the 'moral economy of the crowd' and establish market principles based around the 'laws' of supply and demand. Linebaugh (1991) in his study of crime, criminal justice and capitalism in the same period shows how increased regulation, criminalisation and judicial murder were used to enforce the new bourgeois moral and legal code on the developing working class.

Similarly, more obviously social legislation such as the Poor Laws in Britain were clearly shaped by the need to enforce 'moral responsibility' and the acceptance of wage labour by the poor and (certainly in the case of the 'new' Poor Law of 1834) to create a national labour market. As Pierson notes of the Poor Laws, their 'intent was clearly coercive' (1991: 53).

But poverty, hunger and repression are rather blunt weapons of class domination. For the capitalist system to stabilise there was a need, both politically and socially, to move beyond the more extreme manifestations of naked class rule. Further, as capitalism developed the very nature of the system means that, if it is to survive, a range of new economic, industrial and technological needs must be met. Welfare provision partially meets these demands. As Saville notes:

Industrial capitalism requires an increasing range of technical expertise; and that means an improving educational system. A labour force that suffers from a high incidence of disease – the result of dirt, poor housing, inadequate diet – is an inefficient labour force; and therefore the improvement of the physical environment in which working people live, the means of purchasing an adequate food supply, the availability of medical services in sufficient quantity and at a satisfactory level of competence, are all necessary if the industrial machine is to work at full stretch. (1983: 13)

Although welfare cannot be reduced to 'mere economics' it, nevertheless, fulfils certain basic economic needs for the system. For capitalism to exist and expand there is a requirement for certain activities to be performed and for certain services to be provided. Capitalism needs relatively healthy workers to labour efficiently in the offices and factories, it needs some sort of support mechanism for non-labouring individuals such as children, the elderly, the unemployed (and this may include basic financial provision) and new workers must be educated and trained in the skills they will utilise while at work (and hence increase their productivity). These provisions can be provided by individual capitalists (or groups of capitalists), be based on some form of 'insurance scheme' with payments being given to private companies to provide these services or they can be provided by the state.

Of course, it is not the case that without any of these systems or provisions capitalism would necessarily collapse – indeed there are sectors of the world economy where there is little in the way of health or educational provision, for example. But without these needs being met the system operates less efficiently, and given the competitive nature of capitalism, it results in units of capital (and indeed national economies) falling behind their international competitors.

Thus, the existence of basic welfare services reflects the recognition that while workers' labour may be commodified under capitalism, they cannot be abandoned completely to the market without potentially affecting present or future capital accumulation.

One central economic problem facing capitalism is related to the 'daily and intergenerational reproduction' of labour. This is the need to ensure that workers are (relatively) fit and healthy to be able to carry out their work, and that there are future generations of workers ready to enter paid labour. There is some evidence that the process of proletarianisation in the early to mid-nineteenth century was undermining the existence of the working class family (Engels, 1848/1978). The long hours of work, combined with shift patterns meant that in some districts 'family life' was completely disrupted. In these circumstances childrearing was problematic and domestic labour was left inadequately fulfilled. This created problems for both the bourgeoisie and the working class.

For the bourgeoisie it threatened the existence of a future workforce: while existing profits could be guaranteed on the basis of the cheap labour of men, women and children, the creation of surplus value in the future required the existence of a new generation of fit, healthy and disciplined workers. The break up of family life threatened all of this. From within the working class there were concerns that mass proletarianisation was having the effect of 'overstocking the labour market' and hence reducing wages. In these circumstances there were attempts from within both the bourgeoisie and working class to re-establish the family.

From the bourgeois perspective this matched their ideological commitment to the family while providing a network that would be responsible for childrearing, support for the elderly, sick and unemployed and would have a role in maintaining and supporting the existing workforce while socialising future generations of workers. From the working class perspective it was suggested that by establishing a 'family wage' (that is a wage earned by men and large enough to support an entire family) first children and then women could be withdrawn from the labour market. This would protect children from the worst horrors of the factory and allow women to engage in domestic labour to support the family. There was then a material reason why such a demand was raised and supported, although the family wage was rarely achieved in practice and represented a significant defeat for women, forcing them out of the labour market and into the home.

Nevertheless, the result was the growth of family related social policy. These were policies that initially restricted the hours of work and sectors of employment available to children and women but by the end of the nineteenth century such policies had become much more interventionist, attempting to structure and control working class family life. Today such concerns remain central to government policy strategies. Under both recent Conservative and New Labour governments family policy has taken on a vitally important ideological role (Lavalette and Mooney, 1999).

Here we can identify the linked 'social requirements' of developing capitalism mentioned by Saville. Capitalism must encourage workers to work hard, to be productive and committed to producing good quality work. But this is complicated by the fact that the system depersonalises and alienates individuals. Work is regimented, stressful and controlled, social life isolating and commodified. In these conditions if the system as a whole is to function it 'must encourage the general sentiment that the future will be better than the present or the past' (Saville, 1983: 13). Social policies have developed to give the working class the impression that they have a stake in the system. Welfare expansion (especially state welfare expansion) is part of the attempt to 'legitimise' capitalism, to win people politically to the system. Welfare provision seems to offer workers something for nothing, or it at least offers a collective benefit paid out of taxes for the care of the old, the sick or those unable to work. It seems to represent an arena where the market does not necessarily dominate and it apparently proves that the expansion of capitalism benefits us all – the 'appearance' is of a benign set of services constructed around some uniformly accepted set of values, the essential underlying relations are of a system which is in no small part constructed to meet some vital economic, social and political needs of the system as a whole.

The expansion of the various 'economic and social requirements' so far discussed does not mean that the state's 'social control' functions become any less important. As Novak notes: 'The maintenance of capitalism . . . require[s] a series of incentives and punishments' (1988: 30). Bruce Anderson, advisor to Conservative prime ministers in Britain during the 1980s and 1990s argued that post-war welfarism had: 'constructed slums full of layabouts and sluts whose progeny are two-legged beasts. We cannot cure this by family, religion and self-help. So we will have to rely on repression' (quoted in Jones, 1998: 16).

Within the criminal justice system in Britain there are continuing attempts to restrict and control accepted civil rights and liberties, including restrictions on the right to trial by jury, and there is a continuing, seemingly inexorable growth of the prison population – for both men and women (Jones, 1998, Williams, 2004, Kingston, 2004). According to Jones (1998) what we are witnessing is a brutalising turn within social policy in Britain where:

[The] increasing use of prisons and the ongoing onslaught on welfare entitlements are part and parcel of the new politics of repression and pessimism by which we are encouraged to understand the most impoverished and vulnerable as being beyond redemption and that their position in society is an accurate reflection of their worthlessness. (1998: 21)

As Pierson notes: 'There is a good deal of historical evidence to support the [Marxist] social control thesis' (1991: 53).

But social controls also operate, perhaps less spectacularly, within the daily functioning of welfare services and institutions. This includes attempts to control and regulate the behaviour of young people within schools (in part through what Bowles and Gittens (1976) have termed the 'hidden curriculum' of discipline and obedience to authority) or in their locality by implementing curfews and 'anti-social legislation' using a range of agencies such as the police, social services, school educational welfare services (truancy officers) and the wider juvenile 'justice' system (Jones and Novak, 1999; Lavalette and Mooney, 1999). It involves regulating and controlling family relationships or financial provision for children after relationship breakdown via, for example, the Child Support Agency or social work/services departments. Or ensuring that: 'the conditions that are placed on state benefits . . . are often orientated not to the meeting of recipients' needs but rather to the requirement not to undermine the dynamics of the labour market' (Pierson, 1991: 53).

Social policies also attempt to determine how we live our lives, what are appropriate childrearing practices, what are legitimate families, and how we should behave to qualify for benefits.

Recently, feminist, gay and lesbian and anti-racist histories have drawn attention to the ways in which social policies and welfare institutions attempt to control our lives by operating with a set of assumptions about how we live (or should live) our lives. In particular much welfare policy is based on familial assumptions. It assumes most women will be at home to raise children and provide domestic labour, that the family unit (of one adult male, one adult female and children) is the best site for childrearing, and hence that gay families are illegitimate (Wilson, 1997). It assumes that families have the responsibility to finance their children's higher education or provide care 'in a community setting' for elderly or sick relatives. It also reflects judgements about who should qualify for welfare benefits or services, invariably including a notion of 'citizenship' that questions the legitimacy of claims for benefits from 'outsiders' (Cohen et al., 2002).

Finally in this section, it is important to re-emphasise that welfare provision, its expansion and contraction, are intimately linked to the general process of accumulation. At certain periods the system has the ability to deliver certain reforms or forms of welfare provision. The long post-war boom (*circa*, 1948–1972) certainly eased the expansion of the various welfare systems in the advanced economies.

In contrast, during periods of economic crisis and slump there is a drive to reduce or cut government expenditure. Whether such cuts are achievable for the ruling class is a political question that depends, more than any other factor, on the collective response of the working class and the activities of the leadership of the labour and trade union movement. Politically, it is not an inevitable process but a potentially risky exercise that may provoke a collective working class response.

However, there are also limits beyond which cuts in service provision start to affect economic performance and the accumulation process. Thus capitalism 'needs' to invest in education and health systems, for example, to enhance their economic competitiveness, to legitimate the system, and to provide a degree of social control. At times of economic crisis they attempt to reduce social spending but such cuts are fraught with difficulties, which can lead to uncertainty and prevarication within the ruling class. To emphasise the point here, let's mention the social policy strategies of the two main international finance institutions, the IMF and the World Bank. In the 1980s both organisations were committed to Structural Adjustment Programmes (SAPs). Central to SAPs were demands that welfare and social provision should be cut. By the early 1990s, however, the World Bank started to change track, increasingly arguing that economic growth and expansion required investment in 'human capital' via, for instance, investment in education services, some basic forms of social provision and the amelioration of the worst manifestations of poverty. This is not to suggest that the World Bank is 'better' or even 'more progressive' than the IMF but it does indicate that welfare provides some basic needs for the system and hence cutting welfare can create problems for national capitals and their ability to continue with their competitive accumulation drive.

Thus welfare provision performs a number of roles in society. It meets economic needs, increases labour productivity and is an essential part of the process of generalised commodity production. It is part of a process of legitimating capitalism and creating an ideological veneer to cover the exploitative and oppressive structures of society. It is built upon, and reinforces, familial ideology, which reinforces women's oppression, and it attempts to structure, control and regulate our lives in numerous ways. But this is still only part of the picture. Welfarism can also be part of the 'social wage' and in this sense it can bring material benefits to workers. This being the case, it is perhaps not surprising that welfare provision is also directly affected by 'pressure from the masses'.

---

**Activity 2**

*What 'economic' needs or functions might state welfare fulfil?*
*In what way(s) do social welfare policies and institutions act to control the population?*

### Pressure from the Mass of the Population

The second general strand Saville noted was that welfarism is affected by the presence, demands and pressure of the masses. Once again it is necessary to unpack this somewhat, in particular to note that the pressure from the masses can be interpreted in two ways: through the politics of reformism and through the contentious politics of collective action.

### The Politics of Reformism

The organised presence of the working class movement has been central to the politics of reformism, social democracy or labourism – and within this tradition social welfare has been an important element of their goal to 'humanise' capitalism. Reformism has many roots and variations but central to most conceptions are the following claims. First, that capitalism has changed significantly since the nineteenth century. The capitalist class has increasingly lost its dominant position in society as it has been brought under control by the state and witnessed the nationalisation of core areas of economic activity. This is a consequence of the 'democratisation process' that reflects the expansion of the vote, the organised presence of a strong and centralised trade union movement and a social democratic political party able to reflect working class demands. Secondly, under conditions of sustained economic growth and enduring social democratic governmental incumbency, substantial welfare improvements can be achieved for the betterment of society as a whole. Thirdly, for these conditions to be met there should be strong class identification and correspondingly weak cleavages along religious, ethnic or linguistic lines (Pierson, 1991: 31). Under these conditions it is thought possible to transform capitalism towards socialism via the institutions of parliamentary democracy (see Chapter 3).

The presence of an organised working class, principally through a centralised trade union movement, gives the party (Labour or Social Democratic) the leverage to wrestle concessions out of capital. In the process it can further democratise society and create a 'decent society' along the lines of a social welfare state. Hence, in no small part, they are claiming that the growth and elaboration of various welfare systems is a direct result of social democratic parties' hold on government.

It would be ridiculous to deny that parliamentary politics matters and that social democratic or labourist parties have not affected state welfare provision in various countries. In Britain, for example, while a broad 'Keyenesian-Beveridgean' consensus was established between the major political parties in the post-war era, if the Conservative Party, rather than Labour, had been elected in 1945 the welfare state would have been significantly different in a number of key areas – most notably in terms of health care provision which would not have taken the form of a nationalised NHS. Nevertheless there are both theoretical and empirical issues that question the potential of reformist parties to deliver social reforms in all circumstances.

First, the theoretical problems. Central to the social democratic case is a claim that the basic drives and goals of the economy can be – or have been – tamed to some degree. One of the earliest 'reformist' writers was Eduard Bernstein. Bernstein (1909) wrote about developments in Germany at the end of the nineteenth century. He suggested that the development of cartels had overcome the boom/slump crisis tendency of capitalism. Anthony Crosland (1956) writing about Britain in the mid-1950s suggested nationalisation and state direction of the economy had established a sort of half-way house between capitalism and socialism. While today, theorists of the 'third way' like Anthony Giddens (1998) suggest that consumerism, the growth of information technology and economic globalisation have transformed the system out of all recognition. But while capitalism is constantly changing its organisational forms (from small family firms, to cartels, to multinationals for example) the basic social relations, and with it the horrors of inequality, oppression and exploitation, remain remarkably constant: the rich and powerful enrich themselves even more on the labour of the vast majority. Further, the basic contradictions of capitalism mean that the boom/ bust cycle with deepening economic crises has not been overcome, as the severe crises of the last decade in Japan, South Korea, Russia and various Latin American countries testifies.

Secondly, reformist parties may be elected to government, but this is not the same as control over the state which is much wider and includes many powerful, unelected interests (such as the police, army, judiciary, top civil service, the central banks). Further as Miliband (1972) emphasised in his history of the Labour Party the government does not control capital but is itself extremely vulnerable to pressure from capital to ensure it follows 'appropriate' pro-business policies.

Finally, the ideological commitment of social democratic parties is to the interests of both nation and class. On the one hand their goal is national efficiency, national economic improvement and success within the capitalist economic system and pursuing national interests both at home and abroad. On the other hand there is a set of values structured around overcoming the worst manifestations of poverty and inequality and expanding social benefits for all. Its aim is to re-direct some of the wealth created by an expanding capitalism to tackle some of the social problems capitalism creates. Of course during periods of economic expansion it is possible to pursue both these sets of goals, but at times of economic recession and slump both sets of values clash. During these periods social democratic governments have repeatedly pursued the interests of national capital and national economic efficiency at the expense of the interests of there own working class constituency who vote them into office. For example 'Old' Labour PM Harold Wilson faced with speculative pressure on the pound in 1964 revealed that while devaluation:

> would have given us a year or two breathing space . . . that would have enabled us to carry through our positive generous programmes of social reform . . . the national interest was one hundred per cent the other way . . . [further] there are many people overseas,

including governments, marketing boards, central banks and others, who left their money in the form of sterling balances, on the assumption that the value of sterling would be maintained. To have let them down would have been . . . a betrayal of trust. (Quoted in Miliband, 1972: 361/362)

Wilson was not the first nor was he the last to put the general interests of capital and of international financiers, governments and others above those of workers. More recently, in the 1980s and 1990s Socialist, Social Democratic and Labour governments in Greece, Spain, France, Sweden, Italy, Germany and Britain, for example, have all pursued welfare cutting, public expenditure reduction programmes in an attempt to appease the interests of national and international capital.

There are also empirical issues that question some of the assumptions of the social democratic perspective. For example, in most states welfare developments were initiated by conservative or liberal parties – rather than social democratic ones – and even at the high point of welfare state expansion conservative and liberal parties were not opposed to welfare settlements. Indeed in Britain, for example, more council houses were built in any four-year period by the Tories in the 1950s than there was by Labour and, perhaps even more surprisingly, more comprehensive schools were opened while Margaret Thatcher was Minister of Education than at any other period (Lowe, 1993).

Finally, in the post-war era the growth and domination of state policies structured around Keynesian economic management was central to the social democratic case that the state (or the government) could control and direct the economy utilising the wealth generated to develop and expand social welfare. But by the late 1970s Keynesianism increasingly went out of fashion as various forms of 'monetarism' became the dominant governmental economic paradigm. With this change government commitment to demand management of the economy and policies of full-employment were abandoned – seriously affecting social democracy's rationale and claims as the vehicle to deliver significant social improvement.

### Class Mobilisation

In his important comparative social policy text, Esping-Andersen (1990) discusses the concept of 'class mobilization' as a factor shaping welfare formation. In Esping-Anderson's book the concept is used to describe the political activity of the official trade union movement (or the trade union bureaucracy) and the dominant social democratic party and their chances of electoral success, it does not deal with the contentious political mobilisation of the working class; that is the various forms of collective action – strikes, marches, protests and demonstrations in favour of, or in defence of, welfare provision. But as Novak and Jones suggest: 'Welfare has always been at the heart of class struggle. . . . In the final analysis it is a concern for human welfare . . . that has fuelled the struggle for social transformation' (2000: 34). Class struggle and collective action affects welfare, occasionally this is in an obvious way but sometimes the relationship is less direct.

The general extent, nature and form of what we can call the 'class struggle' has an important impact on society in general, including welfarism. Charlton (2000) expands this theme by noting the way in which a growing and visible working class presence, combined with their increasing class combativity were central elements of the process of establishing more corporatist forms of welfare in Britain at the turn of the twentieth century. In this case, it is the nature and conflicts of class society that prompts welfarism. It is the potential of working class collective action (or fear of this potential) that motivates social policy. For example British Tory MP Quintin Hogg (later Lord Hailsham) claimed in 1944: 'if you do not give the people social reform, they are going to give you social revolution' (Hansard, 17 February 1943).

But sometimes, substantial waves of working class protest can affect social policy more directly and immediately. A few examples drawn from a variety of states will illustrate the point. In France the social welfare settlement was directly affected by working class collective protest and action which were part of the popular front struggles of 1936. In February of that year there were 1 million strikers in Paris, with mass factory occupations. As a direct consequence wages increased, the working week was restricted and paid holidays guaranteed (including the 'institutionalisation' of a summer holiday in August which remains in place today) (Danos and Gibelin, 1986).

In the late 1960s and early 1970s Italy was in the midst of a substantial wave of protest. As Ginsborg notes: 'As a result, the period from 1969 onwards saw the politicians mediate collective protest by a sudden increase in reform legislation . . . [these include] political reforms . . . [and] a number of social ones' (1990: 327). The list of social reforms includes an upgrading of pensions, legalisation of divorce and expansion of housing provision. In the US social legislation from the 'New Deal' era of the 1930s (including the Social Security Act 1935) were partially a response to the economic and political crisis of those years, the 'presence' of organised labour and substantial industrial conflict – by dockers, miners, teamsters, autoworkers, textile and mill workers and a range of factories where the 'sit-down' strike developed (Brecher, 1997). While in Japan, Gould suggests: 'it was only in response to the rice riots of 1918 that the government introduced the first genuine social security measure' (1993: 35/36). Although he fails to add that the various insurance and worker compensation acts of the immediate post-war years were instigated against the backdrop of what Halliday (1975) terms the 'post-surrender explosion' of the Japanese working class movement.

More directly, because certain forms of welfare delivery or social policies bring material or social benefits to the working class, social movements of the oppressed have often developed to defend particular welfare settlements or demand the expansion of various forms of provision. Again a few examples will illustrate the point.

One of the most notable examples in Britain arose as a consequence of the Rent Strikes which took place in Clydeside during the First World War. The move to a war economy meant that there was a rapid expansion of war related industries in Glasgow. Labour was sucked into the city to work in the shipyards, engineering factories and related industries and as a result there was a severe housing shortage. Landlords now had control of a valuable and scarce resource and put up their rents. The response from sections of the working class in Glasgow was to go on rent strike. These were led and organised by working class women and quickly gained the support of wide range of working class activists and trade unionists. When the strikers were pulled in front of the debtors courts there was a mass walk out from many workplaces on Clydeside, the women were released and the Government introduced the Rent Restriction Act which pegged rents to their pre-war level and prohibited landlords from increasing rents for the duration of the war (Dammer, 1980, 2000).

Clegg and Gough (2000) in their analysis of the various campaigns to defend abortion rights in both Britain and the US, argue that, in Britain, the joint action of working class women and men, from various socialist political parties, women's groups and trade unions have been vital to defend a woman's right to choose. Whereas in the US they suggest, the absence (or at least the weakness) of a generalised class response to the question or reproductive politics has led to significant retreat in this area. Whilst elsewhere Lavalette and Mooney (2000) have argued that the poll tax in Britain, implemented by the last Thatcher government between 1989 and 1992, met such a fierce response from working class communities because it was a clear generalised attack on workers' standard of living, on local authority welfare provision and on local government accountability. Thus attacks on welfare represent a potentially explosive source of grievance generating collective action by the oppressed and exploited.

Finally, a less documented area of working class pressure on welfare (at least by theorists of welfare and social policy in the academy) is the extent to which welfare workers can collectively shape welfare delivery. The expansion of welfare services has created a vast army of welfare workers – teachers, social workers, community workers, health care practitioners, benefit workers and a range of 'ancillary staff' throughout the various welfare systems – who are required to sell their labour power in order to survive and without whose work activity the various services would not be provided. The vast majority of these workers do not own or control the various tools they require to undertake their work tasks, and the vast majority of them find themselves subject to the authority of others while at work. What we have witnessed, especially in the post-Second World War era, is the 'proletarianisation' of vast numbers of welfare workers and linked to this, the growth of a range of trade unions representing welfare workers. For example, the largest trade union in Britain is Unison which represents workers in the National Health Service, local government (including social work and social service workers, workers in housing departments, welfare advice workers, community workers) and a range of workers in the voluntary and privatised welfare services.

Thus direct class mobilisations can have an important role in shaping and defending forms of welfare delivery and are an important part of the struggle of the oppressed to obtain a better world.

---

**Activity 3**

*If social policies merely bring economic benefits to capital or reinforce modes of 'social control', why do ordinary people continue to support state welfare systems and institutions like the NHS in Britain?*

---

### The Political Calculations of the Ruling Class

As we can see, there are a number of tendencies promoting and shaping social welfare. The precise form welfare takes, however, will also reflect the political calculations of, and divisions within, the ruling class – Saville's third strand affecting welfare development. As we have already emphasised the interests of 'capital in general' promotes some system-wide shared class interests on behalf of the bourgeoisie – for example, to maintain the profitability of the system, to maintain and increase the level of exploitation over the working class etc. But capitalism is a world of 'many competing capitals' – each with their own specific short-, mid- and long-term interests which create divisions over a range of political, social and economic questions within the ruling class. For example, when central banks meet to set interest rates within national economies it is not uncommon to hear groups in favour of interest rate cuts (e.g. to boost exports), those in favour of raising the interest rate (e.g. importers of components) and those advocating no change (e.g. to establish 'stability' on the financial markets). In Britain during the 1990s and early years of the twenty-first century there has been considerable division within the ruling class over the question of further European integration, the adoption of European social legislation and whether Britain should sign-up to the single European currency. As we noted earlier, there has been increasing divergence between the World Bank and the IMF over the appropriate strategies needed to stabilise and develop capitalism in a number of 'Third World' economies – in particular the appropriate social welfare strategies needed to encourage economic growth.

It may, in the abstract, be in the interests of 'capital in general' for certain welfare developments to take place, but in the real world of 'many competing capitals' different capitalists or sections of the ruling class may view their direct economic interests rather differently.

Finally, there are other divisions and aspects of 'ruling elite calculation' that can affect welfare. It is important to recognise that various interest groups within the ruling class can have an input on the political process and social policy development: the Catholic church in Italy or Ireland, both the openly pro-business parties in the US (the Democrats and the Republicans), for example. Occasionally the input of particular individuals within the state or the state bureaucracy is important: Chadwick, Beveridge and Bismark, for example, have had an important effect in shaping welfare delivery, and not just within their own countries. While, the form and intensity of the economic and political relationships and competition between states can also affect welfare choices: the effect of the US Marshall Plan on post-war Western European societies (including their welfare settlements) is clearly important, the state structures and welfare commitments of various countries in Latin America, Africa and South East Asia reflect their subordinate political, economic and military relationship with the US and various international financial institutions tied to the interests of the advanced capitalist economies. While, more benignly, states and state officials have often copied each other's models of economic and social policy delivery, in what is known as 'policy transfer'. For example, Japan after the Meiji Restoration (that is, according to Barrington-Moore (1973), Japan's 'bourgeois revolution from above') consciously attempted to follow the 'German model' of social and economic development (Gould, 1993). Or, more recently, the formation of various supra-national state bodies and organisations has brought with it increased pressures for policy transfer or harmonisation (for example, the various UN Conventions or EU Directives are a case in point).

Thus the political calculations of different sections of the ruling class (and often the conflict and competition between sections of that class) affect the general political process and within this the development, expansion and form of welfare delivery.

---

**Activity 4**

*Why might different sections or groups within 'ruling circles' find themselves in opposition to each other over questions of welfare retrenchment, or welfare expansion?*

---

## Conclusion

For Marxists, welfare developments are the outcome of a complex process of struggle and conflict which takes place within a context: the structural needs and requirements of capitalism and the uncertainties (economic, political and social) created by social life within capitalist society. In turn, policy developments will reflect the contradictions of capitalist society and the values of the bourgeoisie. Hence all such developments affect and structure our lives. They embody different 'proposed solutions' to any crisis but do so in a way which embodies ideological commitments: assumptions about how we live (or should live) our lives, about the causes of poverty and inequality, etc. Finally, whatever else they do, they cannot cure the ills of capitalism but at best paper over some of the cracks.

From our discussion we can identify a number of key elements which Marxist writers have identified as shaping welfare provision under capitalism. Welfare:

1 meets certain 'needs' that capitalism as a system generates;
2 is part of what has been termed the 'legitimation' process (that is of supporting the ideological veneer of capitalism, creating the appearance that capitalism brings us all benefits – rather than being a system based on exploitation);
3 is part of the attempt to control populations and determine how we should live;
4 reflects the demands of the oppressed and exploited to improve their lives materially;
5 service provision is often a profitable area of commodity production – some companies make vast profits out of providing welfare for users;
6 welfare services employ vast numbers of workers – social workers, health workers, those employed in benefits agencies, teachers, for example, – who often raise their own demands as workers over the conditions of their employment and the adequacies, or otherwise, of the resources and services available to them, and finally,
7 it is necessary to recognise that, economically, welfare provision can bring benefits to capitalism (for example by investing in education or skill training), while, at the same time, the general costs of welfare can drain resources that could otherwise be used for direct economic investment.

The pressures from each of these aspects of welfare do not all push in the same direction, some create demands for welfare expansion, others for welfare cuts; some are more easily combined with universalist forms of provision others with selective and stigmatising forms of delivery; some lead to increasing regulation of social life, others to deregulation and an imposed 'self-reliance'. It is in this sense that we can identify welfare as a deeply political activity reflecting the contradictions of capitalist societies.

The exact balance between these various elements is a historical, political question which is affected by various internal and external political and economic pressures. These contradictions can only be understood if we locate social policies and social welfare within the wider social totality. Social welfare is not a separate sphere of social activity but is intimately tied to the activities and functioning of modern capitalism as an integrated social system. Further, while social policies have developed in response to the problems generated by capitalism, the causes of such problems, their origins and their 'cures' are all contested issues. Thus we can delineate the various 'general welfare tendencies' that exist in all capitalist societies but need to combine this with a recognition of how these are actually developed in practice, a question requiring an analysis of the political developments of particular societies. It is this process which creates specific welfare settlements.

**Further Reading**

Ferguson, I., Lavalette, M. and Mooney, G. (2002) *Rethinking Welfare: a Critical Perspective*. London: Sage.

Lavalette, M. and Mooney, G. (eds) (2000) *Class Struggle and Social Welfare*. London: Routledge.

Saville, John (1954) 'The welfare state: an historical approach', in *The New Reasoner,* reprinted as 'The Origins of the Welfare State' in M. Loney, D. Boswell and J. Clarke (eds) (1983) *Social Policy and Social Welfare*. Milton Keynes: Open University Press.

# FIVE
# Feminist Critiques of Social Policy
*Kath Woodward*

---

**Outline Points**

Focusing largely on the UK, this chapter:

- Outlines the historical background to the development of feminist critiques of social policy;
- Explores some of the differences between feminist perspectives, such as liberal, Marxist/socialist, radical and black feminist approaches, which are manifest in their development over time and in more current concerns;
- Looks at what is distinctive about feminist critiques; picking out key concepts which form their theoretical framework, exploring the importance of gender, patriarchy, family, equality and difference, the public/private relationship and citizenship;
- Brings together analyses which show the articulation of gender, racialisation and class in addressing issues of gender inequality.

---

## Introduction

This chapter outlines feminist approaches to social policy, starting with some of the shared concerns of feminist critiques and moving on to an exploration of different perspectives within feminism. Feminist critiques are primarily concerned with two themes. First, the ways in which the gendered nature of social practices and institutions has been ignored and gender neutrality assumed within society and social policies, and secondly, the ways in which issues which are of particular relevance and importance to women have in the past been marginalised or excluded from the welfare agenda. In particular, feminists have drawn attention to the *patriarchal* structure of the welfare state and the different ways in which women and men have been incorporated into the role of citizens

(Pateman, 1988). More recently feminist concerns have developed understanding of the diverse concerns of different women and focused on *difference* as well as *equality* and what this means for citizenship in the twenty-first century.

Particular aspects which have been the focus of feminist critiques are discussed here in order to illustrate the impact of feminism and its different strands. The first of these is the *family*, which has been a major target of state intervention in the implementation of welfare policies and a key concern for feminist research and analysis (Segal, 1987, 1993). Linked to discussion of the family are the issues of domestic violence and sexual abuse, which have become major concerns in recent debates, having been put on the agenda as social, and not individual, problems by feminist activists and researchers with their insistence on listening to the voices of women within families and as survivors (Saraga, 1993). *Citizenship* is addressed as an example of an important concept in discussion of social policy, which feminists have argued is gendered and not universal or gender neutral (see also Chapter 10). The dilemma for contemporary feminist thinkers is to re-conceptualise gendered citizenship.

Thus, the main aims of this chapter are to provide an understanding of the major concerns of feminist analyses; to explore some of the differences between these analyses; to show how the different approaches focus on gender difference as a structuring principle in the provision of welfare; to suggest strategies for the analysis of social policy; and, by using the variety of feminist approaches, to develop a critical perspective on other theoretical positions.

## Historical Context

As Lewis (1992) argues, one of the key elements underpinning historical changes in welfare provision has been the shifting relationship between women, men, the family and the state. Women have long been the target of state intervention, often where concern with women as mothers was linked with state anxiety about children especially and family life in general. This can be traced back to the intervention of the state in the private arena of the family and notably to the development in European societies from the eighteenth century onwards of policies which were concerned with the body and health in a trend which Foucault called *biopolitics* (Foucault, 1987). The idea of state intervention into the family began to be taken for granted, with the notion that women were 'man's salvation, the privileged instrument for civilizing the working class' (Donzelot, 1980). So many of the ways in which people's lives are regulated and monitored by the state, which are assumed in the twenty-first century can be traced to specific interventions historically.

State intervention has been two-pronged. On the one hand it has been concerned with the regulation of sexual relations and in particular the enforcement of heterosexuality, and on the other it has focused on the 'family' and family-centred legislation, particularly targeting mothers and children. Let us look at each of these in turn.

### *Enforcing 'Appropriate' Sexual Relations*

The two main targets of state policy have been homosexuals and prostitutes, each seen as a danger to the 'British race', motherhood and the population, and with legislation structured by Victorian concerns about purity and pollution. Homosexuality was seen as a social threat, with the potential to affect the birth rate adversely and to undermine the patriarchal family and, by implication, the hierarchical social order and male authority. Debates about homosexuality in the nineteenth and into the twentieth century related to men, since women were defined by the state as asexual (Weeks, 1977), except as reproducers. The negative public image of the homosexual constructed, for example, by the trials of Oscar Wilde (Weeks, 1977) put pressure on men to marry and have children in order to be seen to be heterosexual, thereby creating a notion of 'normal' sexuality as heterosexual and taking place within the traditional family. This had repercussions for women even if lesbianism was not named in legislation. Lesbians have also been portrayed as a social threat, especially to the 'normal' family. Consequently, although motherhood is seen as women's 'natural' destiny and women are much more likely to be granted custody of their children in divorce cases, even when the woman has committed adultery, the lesbian mother is still less likely to be awarded custody (see Chapter 7). Such values also inform current access to new reproductive technologies where suitability is often defined in relation to a white, heterosexual, middle-class 'norm' (Woodward, 1999).

Explicit and direct attempts were made to categorise and control women's sexuality. This had a moral dimension, where the dichotomy of the 'good' (respectable) woman and the 'bad' (immoral) woman operated. The most obvious instances related to prostitution. The trigger to state intervention was fear about the spread of venereal disease among troops. This was clearly a serious health threat, although anxieties about physical well-being were conflated with those about moral degeneracy. Male sexuality was construed as an imperative which demanded relief. Unlike the situation for the civilian population, marriage was not the solution, as in the military population marriage was discouraged because the loyalty of soldiers was to their country and their command. However, the Contagious Diseases Acts of 1864, 1866 and 1869 put the entire onus of responsibility and blame for the spread of venereal disease on women (Walkowitz, 1980). Women identified as 'common prostitutes' by the police would then be subject to fortnightly examinations and would be interned in a 'lock hospital' if found to be suffering from venereal disease. There was less emphasis on medical treatment than on moral reform in the lock hospitals. As a result, lock hospitals subjected female inmates to a 'repressive moral regime' (Walkowitz, 1980: 61). The operation of these laws gave the police the right to stop and caution almost any women, thus allowing in particular for the regulation and control of working class, single women. Male protection through marriage and the 'respectability' thus afforded became even more pressing for women. Needless to say, the Contagious Diseases Acts had no positive impact on the spread of venereal disease, which actually increased between 1876 and 1882, because men were not inspected, and thus freely carried and spread the disease without any preventive or interventionist action by the state directed at them.

### Family Policy

Family policy, including the identification of women as mothers, with its underlying assumptions about what constitutes the 'normal' family – namely, the traditional, patriarchal, heterosexual family form, has been a particular focus of state intervention and welfare provision. The other main focus has been the idea of the *male breadwinner*. The 1834 Poor Law Amendment Act which reasserted the Elizabethan Poor Law was based on a major concern with labour and, in particular, the male worker. Women were on the whole considered to be dependants if they were married and non-workers if they were single. The main aim of legislation was to reduce unemployment and promote industry, the assumption being that much unemployment was voluntary. Men were divided into two categories, able-bodied and non-able-bodied, so that male, and hence family, entitlement to support depended on their capacity for work. Women's position was defined according to their marital status. This produced a three-fold categorisation, with the first and largest group being married women who were constructed as dependants of their husbands, the breadwinners. The second category included women without a man to support them, seen initially as a homogeneous category (Daly, 1994), to which the state was reluctant to give any support, but later subdivided intro the 'deserving' (such as widows) and the 'undeserving' (such as single mothers). Unmarried mothers, who were actually mentioned in the 1834 Report, were themselves to bear sole responsibility for their illegitimate children, although in 1844 it became possible for them to sue for an affiliation order against the father. In the nineteenth century it was women in this group who were more likely to be sent to the workhouse rather than granted outdoor relief, suggesting something of the contribution of moral discourse to the production of a female identity associated with shame and stigma. Single, childless women comprised the third category, which illustrates a division between women based on marital status that has echoes in British income maintenance to the present day. Such single women were regarded as having a duty to work, especially by 1869–70, when Poor Law administration was reviewed.

The notion of a male breadwinner is closely tied to the idea of the *family wage*. This concept is bound up with the historical development of the relationship between the family, social production, the modern labour market and industrial production. With the advent of protective legislation such as the Factory Acts of the 1840s, children were excluded from factories and from paid work outside the home. Women were increasingly employed in specifically female sectors of work and married women became less and less likely to be in full-time waged employment, becoming marginalised within the labour market (Barrett and McIntosh, 1980). The financial dependence of carers is implicit in the structure of a society in which responsibility for children and the elderly rests within the family and in which caring for children restricts access to paid work. The family wage assumes women's dependence on men. In the wage bargaining situation it gives men the authority to claim higher wages because of the needs of their dependants. Women do not need outside, paid employment because they have domestic responsibilities and because they are provided for by the male bread-winner; any income they provide is supplementary or 'pin-money'. The family wage undercut arguments for equality of pay and employment opportunities between women and men. Campbell and Charlton are quoted as saying, 'The Labour Movement has managed to combine a commitment to equal pay with a commitment to the family wage' but 'you can't have both' (in Barrett and McIntosh, 1980: 52).

Feminist critiques have not only pointed to the contradictions within the family wage demand, and its incompatibility with demands for equal pay, but they also question the extent to which 'male bread-winners' actually did earn an income sufficient to support a family (Barrett and McIntosh, 1980). Hence, not only did the concept not serve women's interests but neither did it provide the support for working-class families which it purported to do.

Although feminists have adopted different positions on the benefits or other-wise of the family wage, the notion still underpins the construction of the mod-ern family and women's place within it, for example through the high proportion of women in part time employment and women's overall lower earnings, still 80 per cent of men's on average (Social Trends 2004). Hartmann argues that the prin-ciple behind the family wage, of women's financial dependence on men, and men's rights to women's labour inside the home persists.

> Women's lower wages in the labour market (combined with the need for children to be reared by someone) assure the continued existence of the family as a necessary income-pooling unit. The family, supported by the family wage thus allows the control of women's labour by men both within and without the family. (Hartmann, 1979: 18–19)

State intervention developed throughout the nineteenth and into the twentieth century. Measures included giving Poor Law guardians the power to remove chil-dren from unsuitable, 'bad' mothers (the 1899 Poor Law Act), along with more positive initiatives such as the provision of school meals and campaigns for maternity insurance. Women were also to be educated in the art of mothering (Holdsworth, 1988; Sapsford and Abbott, 1988). The 1918 Maternity and Child Welfare Act which led to the provision of infant, and later ante-natal, clinics aimed to improve the quality of mothering. As Gittins points out, however, help was not given to the mothers themselves through this improvement in state support to children (Gittins, 1985). While trade union pressure led to more protection and security for men at times of illness or unemployment, mothers received virtually no support. The 1911 National Insurance Acts which introduced flat-rate subsistence benefits as of right on the basis of contributions in cases of unemployment, sickness, disability and workplace accidents did not cover married women (Gilbert, 1970), a demonstration of how, in the provision of welfare, women are identified primarily as mothers with little, if any, visible independent existence and identity.

After the end of the Second World War state policy sought to encourage women to leave the workforce and return to the home (Richardson, 1993). The Beveridge Report, although written in 1942 when women were actively participating in the public arena – for example, in the armed forces, in munitions factories and as land workers – assumed that in peacetime women would revert to traditional roles. Thus Beveridge stated: 'in the next thirty years housewives as mothers have vital work to do in ensuring the continuance of the British race' (Beveridge, 1942: para. 117).

Key notions about family life and women's place within that family, embodied in the Beveridge Report, are important in that they set the agenda for British welfare policies and underpin much of what follows. They are mentioned here in order to illustrate that agenda and the implicit assumptions which feminist analysis sought to reveal. Wicks summarises the assumptions of the Beveridge plan as being:

(a) that marriages are for life . . . the legal obligation to maintain persists until death or remarriage;
(b) that sexual activity and childbirth takes place, or at least should take place only within marriage;
(c) that married women normally do no paid work or negligible paid work;
(d) that women not men should do housework and rear children;
(e) that couples who live together with regular sexual relationships and shared expenses are always of the opposite sex. (Wicks, 1991: 93, citing Abel-Smith, 1982)

Berveridge makes quite explicit reference to the domestic, supporting role of women as mothers. Elsewhere, 'women' are subsumed as a category into 'the family', but while such universal categories appear to be gender-neutral, in reality they rest on assumptions regarding women's perceived position within society. Women are defined in familial terms as carers and nurturers, as in the Beveridge Report, or ignored and not mentioned specifically at all, as in discussion of citizenship as a universal category. One of the objectives of feminist research has been to show how 'Women are precisely defined, never general representatives of humanity or all people, but as specifically feminine, and frequently sexual, categories. . . . Being a man is an entitlement not to masculine attributes but to a non-gendered subjectivity' (Black and Coward, 1981: 83). This non-gendered subjectivity includes a notion of (male) universal citizenship and of particular kinds of citizens and does not permit the investigation of different gendered citizen subjects (Lewis et al., 2000).

**Activity 1**

*Look back over this section and try to establish:*

- *what was assumed about women's position in the family;*
- *the workplace;*
- *the nature of women's sexuality. How have women been defined by state intervention and what sort of divisions characterise women's and men's social positions?*

## Feminisms

One of the distinguishing features of the sexual division of labour and of women's social position has been the division between the public and the private arenas and a failure to identify the connections between the two. Demands of the private arena impact on women's participation, or lack of it, in the public arena for example. Women have been located within the private arena of the family, home and domesticity and men defined by their public role, especially in relation to the paid work from which women have often been excluded although this is changing. In the UK although their pay is still less than 80 per cent of men's women constitute 46 per cent of the labour market (Social Trends, 2004). This section looks specifically at the kind of questions which feminists raise in response to these issues, and suggests some of the conceptual tools which feminists have developed to explain how women's role has been constructed by state interventions.

Feminist perspectives locate gender as a structuring principle of social policy and the provision of welfare. Feminism puts gender first when defining social problems in explaining their causes or exploring appropriate levels of state or voluntary sector intervention. It contains different perspectives from which to address questions of gender, but what unites all feminist approaches is their concern with the question of how social policies affect women *in particular*. Initially, feminism can be seen as highlighting the differences and inequalities between women and men, focusing on the different experience of, for example, a social problem such as poverty. Poverty can be seen as a generic social problem, but feminist research demonstrates the different experience of women and men. For example, the use of the term 'family poverty' obscures gender differences and in particular the 'feminization of poverty' (Millar and Glendinning, 1987). Feminist research draws attention to the ways in which women and men view household income differently, with women tending to spend their earnings on domestic items and men retaining some income for their own purposes (Payne, 1991). In poor households women are more likely to deny themselves rather than any other family member (Graham, 1987). This illustrates how feminist approaches ask questions about the different experiences of women and men and challenge definitions of social problems, especially the notion of gender-neutral categories.

Another illustration of this is presented by the apparently gender-neutral concept of 'community care', which feminists have shown to be a euphemism for the unpaid work of women for their family members. 'Community care' is, on the whole, care by women (Finch, 1988). Such policies are based on the assumption that there is a gendered distinction between what Dalley has called 'caring for' and 'caring about' (1988). Whereas men are allowed to care about their families – that is, to feel an emotional bond, without having to care for them (that is, to undertake the practical work of caring) – women are expected to show that they care about family members by caring *for* them. Thus it is argued the conflation of 'caring about' and 'caring for' operates to ensure that women will continue to provide unpaid 'community care', with the added constraint of guilt which is experienced by those women who fail to fulfil their 'obligations'.

But feminist critiques are concerned about more than simply exposing the gendered nature of social policies and the definition of social problems with a particular emphasis on women. Feminism also involves some commitment to action to redress the inequalities which empirical enquiry reveals. In the above example of community care, Finch makes a plea for change, and argues, 'Women must have the right not to care and dependent people must have the right not to rely on their relatives' (Finch, 1988; 30). Thus, as well as drawing attention to gender differences and inequalities, through the deconstruction of categories and concepts and through empirical research which emphasises the need to listen to women's voices and women's accounts of their own experiences, feminism involves a call for change.

Challenging the assumption that it is 'natural' for women to serve and care for others would involve fundamental policy shifts in the provision of care for children, the sick, those with disabilities and the elderly as well as the care of the male workforce within the private arena of the home. It would also necessitate drastic alterations in employment practices. Finally, a further challenge linked to this commitment to action which feminism has presented is a questioning of the traditional orthodoxy of organisations and practices, notably of their hierarchical structures. Feminism has been associated with the collectivist, democratic, non-hierarchical forms of organisation of women's groups which reject traditional organisational practices and structures.

Notwithstanding the different approaches and emphases which exist within feminism, there are clearly a number of continuities and shared concerns which include:

1  giving gender a high priority;
2  asking questions about the position of women in particular in relation to the definition of social problems and levels of state intervention;

3  listening to women's voices;
4  drawing attention to gender differences and inequalities including inequalities among women;
5  having a political dimension which includes strategies for change; and
6  challenging hierarchical forms of organization.

---

### Activity 2

*Make a list of tasks generally assumed to be performed by men and those generally assumed to be performed by women.*

*What do you think would happen if it could no longer be assumed that women would provide the unpaid care on which community care depends?*

---

## Feminist Perspectives

Although feminists might agree about the existence of gender inequalities and seek to highlight women's experience, both empirically in their research methodology and in deconstructing 'gender neutral' categories, they do not agree on the causes of gender differences and inequalities, nor on the form which commitment to change and strategies for effecting change might take. The search for *explanation* is considered in what follows. This section outlines some of the differences between perspectives in what has been called 'second wave' feminism (Rendall, 1985), a category used to describe developments in the women's movement linking political activity and feminist theoretical work mainly in Europe and the United States, which began in the early 1960s. Some of these positions draw on the repertoires of the 'first wave' feminism of the nineteenth and early twentieth centuries, especially liberalism, and re-articulate conceptualisations drawn from mainstream – or what Daly (1978) has called 'malestream' – social theory. Others, especially those of Black feminism have developed in response to perceived limitations of 'second wave' feminism.

### Liberal Feminism

'First wave' feminists seized on the language of liberalism and demanded formal equality and equal rights to citizenship with men. In its campaigns, liberal feminism has sought to secure equal rights for women within the public domain, focusing on changing legislation. The concerns of this approach since the early 1960s have been about equality and civil rights, with the emphasis on the reform of existing institutions. Explanations of gender inequalities are located within the systems of social and political institutions which can be reformed through the actions of individuals. Organisations such as the National Organization of Women in the United States and the Equal Opportunities Commission in the United Kingdom are examples of this strand, with the policy paradigm based on the supposition that, given some reform of social institutions and practices, especially in employment and education, women could attain equality with men. Liberalism and neo-liberalism have set the agenda for much of the discussion of gender inclusion and may have led to recent claims that gender equality has been achieved and the contemporary situation is one of 'postfeminism'.

### Socialist/Marxist Feminism

Marxist and socialist feminisms have been more important in Britain than in the United States, possibly because of the stronger tradition of class-based politics. This perspective links the position of women to the dominant mode of production, and employs a Marxist analytical framework which presents a critique of *capitalism* (see Chapter 4), along with a feminist critique of *patriarchy*, as a form of power in which adult men oppress women through their authority and domination over everyone else, including boys and younger men (Rowbotham, 1969). Subsequent debates have engaged with the interrelationship between capitalism and patriarchy. This has involved focusing on women's 'dual role': first, their involvement in the reproduction, not only of the workforce, but also of social relations through their role in the private arena as they produce the next generation and care for the current labour force; and secondly, their activities in the public arena as a reserve army of labour, drawn in and out of the labour market to meet shortfalls in the labour supply (Rowbotham, 1974, 1989). This branch of feminism retains the Marxist emphasis on the unequal distribution of economic power, and thus class divisions within capitalist society, as a source of gender inequality, and stresses the interrelationship between public and private spheres of economic relations and those of gender, sexuality and domestic living.

### Radical Feminism

Whereas socialist and Marxist feminists stress class relationships and argue for a fusion of class analysis with an understanding of sex inequality, radical feminists argue that it is patriarchal relationships which provide the central division upon which other forms of oppression are based. The term 'sexual politics' (Millett, 1971) was used to describe unequal power relations between women and men, and patriarchy (that is, men's power), was seen as the source of women's oppression whether institutionally or personally. Radical feminism does not prioritise the economic structure and class relations as Marxists do but views the economy as one institution among many through which men exercise control over women. All social institutions, including the family, education, the law, the police and the military, as well as ideologies of romance (and, at the other extreme, representational systems such as pornography), are seen as part of these patriarchal relations. Some radical feminist positions developed out of what has been called the 'woman-centred' stage of second-wave feminism (Lerner, 1979), which gave priority to female experience as the focus of all study and the source of social and cultural values. Motherhood was a major concern of such approaches (Rich, 1977; Chodorow, 1978). While celebrating motherhood as an essentially female experience, accounts such as Rich's present extensive critiques of motherhood as a social institution under patriarchy which distorts women's experience. In the 1980s and 1990s radical feminist approaches extended Millett's focus on patriarchy to include heterosexuality as a social institution which oppresses women (Rich, 1980; Jeffreys, 1986), and in both, empirical research and political campaigns and practice have often focused on sexual violence and support for survivors (Kelly, 1988). The women-centred approaches of radical feminists have been important in establishing alternative 'self-help' welfare services outside the confines of the traditional welfare state. An example of this is the women's refuge movement, the establishment of safe homes for women victims of mental and physical abuse by men.

### Black Feminism

Boundaries between the different feminist approaches became blurred in the 1980s and 1990s, and other perspectives have developed from the theoretical positions outlined above. Most notably, feminism has had to take on board the critiques of black and minority ethnic women, many of whom have challenged the ethnocentricity of what has been seen as a predominantly white women's movement (Lorde, 1984; Aziz, 1992). For example early second-wave feminists' demand for free contraception and abortion on demand were challenged by black women denied the right to have children. What could be called black feminism has called for an interrogation of whiteness, the heterogeneity of which has also been highlighted, for example in relation to the multi-ethnicity which is a feature of the UK (Lewis and Phoenix, 2004). Recent work has also stressed the gendered operation of institutionalised racism by combining feminist approaches with those which focus upon diversity ( Lewis et al., 2000).

These approaches are briefly outlined here in order to indicate some of the differences between feminist positions. The main differences lie in the emphasis which is given to the factors contributing to gender inequality as well as in the tension between *equality* and *difference*. Should the policies advocated by feminists seek to promote equal treatment of women and men and equality as their goal, thereby assuming that there is a single category 'woman'? Or should such policies acknowledge both what is different about women (i.e. different from men) and the differences *among* women? Black feminists, for example have challenged the ahistoric, blanket category of patriarchy which was the focus of early radical feminism. Patricia Williams points to the weakness of race-blind versions of equality, which are defined by people who are white (1998).'Race' and ethnicity are not irrelevant; they are key components in making up identity. Also if equality involves gender neutrality, Anne Phillips suggests, that would appear to eliminate the possibility of affirmative, positive action, such as those which promote women's greater participation in public life (1999). Arguments which stress economic factors focus on the workplace and include the possibility of shared struggles between women and men, whereas the radical feminist position views men as the source of women's oppression. The liberal position is distinguished by its optimism about reform of the system, even of individuals negotiating their own more egalitarian relationships, without recourse to a revolutionary overthrow of existing social relations. All perspectives give some weight to the social and institutional sources of inequalities between women and men, which have often been used to confine women to the private arena of the home and to domestic, caring duties. This discussion also illustrates the close ties between feminist theory and social and political practice. It is through campaigns that feminists have put women and women's concerns on the public agenda, and the explanations which feminists offer for what their research and struggles reveal derive from listening to women's voices.

---

**Activity 3**

*What do you think are the causes of women's oppression according to:*

- *liberal feminists;*
- *Marxist/socialist feminists;*
- *Radical feminists;*
- *Black feminists?*

*What social policy initiatives and wider political solutions do you think each group would promote to secure women's greater independence and liberation?*

*Would these policies involve treating all women equally or recognising difference?*

---

## Feminism Turns to Culture

In the 1990s feminism could be seen to have taken a 'cultural turn' and to move from grand theory to local, cross-cultural studies of the complex interplay of sex, 'race' and class, from notions of a female identity to the instability of female identity and the active creation and recreation of women's needs. A new focus on discursively produced meanings about sexual and sexualised identities emerged. For some feminists their concerns became sexual difference and the creation of complex identities. As Michele Barrett and Anne Phillips have argued, 'in the past twenty years the founding principles of contemporary feminism have been dramatically changed, with previously shared assumptions and unquestioned orthodoxies relegated to history' (1992: 2). This 'turn to culture' has involved a concern with how meanings are produced, through language and practice and notably, following the work of Michel Foucault, through *discourse*. Women as the targets of social policies and as the recipients of welfare and constructed as 'good' or 'bad' mothers, as the 'dependent lone mother' through the language and practice of welfare provision (Woodward, 1997). This can also be seen as arising out of earlier political campaigns which have been called Identity Politics. Claiming an identity through membership of a marginalised group is the starting point for political activity. Identities of 'race', sexuality, disability are produced through how we see ourselves and how we are seen by others and social movements involved in identity politics have sought to reconstruct these identities through more positive representations and through the celebration of difference. Identities are given social meanings through the processes whereby they are represented. Culture and the production of meaning about who we are, are seen as very important. Thus the processes through which meanings are re-produced become key sites of investigation. Here the concern of some feminists is to deconstruct these processes, which appear to be fluid and changing, rather than fixed or static. An example of a changing identity, which has particular resonance for women is that of the 'working mother'. Recent shifts in government policy in the UK have reconstructed the association of paid work and lone motherhood into a notion of desirable independence. Women, including lone mothers are encouraged to achieve greater autonomy by engaging in paid work. No longer is paid work and motherhood construed as signifying irresponsibility and 'bad motherhood' it is seen as a desirable move away from dependency on the state. For example, as Ruth Levitas argues it is poor parenting, rather than parenting in poverty which has become the concern of the Blair governments in the UK (2005). Whilst feminists might have argued for the removal of women's dependency on men or on the state through access to paid work, such policies are based on the availability of that paid work and of affordable, appropriate child care.

Does this 'turn to culture' mean a retreat from economics and material inequality?

Lynne Segal, arguing from a socialist feminist position, says not. She suggests that the cultural and the material are not exclusive opposites and that feminists need both in their analyses (1999), which is a view supported by feminists like Skeggs, who deploy Pierre Bourdieu's concept of cultural capital to foreground class in their critiques (1997, 2004). Skeggs synthesises the insights of earlier feminist work with Bourdieu's model of power as cultural, symbolic capital and reinstates class into feminist analyses of inequality. As we have seen in different examples in women's lives, in the family, in relation to paid work and the state and sexual identity in this chapter, material circumstances shape experience and are themselves given meaning by cultural processes. However a focus on social exclusion and the diversity of identities may shift explanations from material inequalities which does not serve women's interests.

## Feminist Critiques of the Family

As should be clear by now, the family is a key social institution, a major focus of social policy, and of feminist research and analysis. Given the family's pivotal social position it is perhaps not surprising that feminists should see it as the key site for the exercise of male power and authority. As Millett notes, 'Patriarchy's chief institution is the family. It is both a mirror and a connection to the larger society' (1971: 55). However, although the family is changing, changes have often led to women being targeted as the source of social ills, ranging from boys' under-performance at school, to criminality and even marriage breakdown and the increase in teenage pregnancies.

The family has been the focus of many feminist critiques, moving from fierce criticism of the family – notably the patriarchal nuclear family – through powerful celebration of women's role as mothers, to diverse analyses reflecting positions which seek to address differences *among* women as well as those between women and men (Segal, 1993, Skeggs, 2004) and the diversity of family forms. What is important for analysis of social policy is the feminist questioning of dominant ideologies of family life and the focus on the patriarchal family as the source of women's oppression.

At the start of second-wave feminism, following the sustained attempt after 1945 to reconstruct and impose the traditional family, with women firmly positioned at its centre (as illustrated by the Beveridge Report), the main concern of feminists was to investigate that familial form, to challenge the view that the family was a safe haven, 'a little world immune from the vulgar cash nexus of modern society' (Barrett and McIntosh, 1985: 28). Friedan (1963) in the United States exposed the experience of the 'problem with no name' and the depression of housewives in the 1950s. Gavron (1966) described the feelings of frustration and isolation of housebound wives in Britain, and attention has been drawn to the despair, and even violence, experienced, by women within the family. The alienation and despair experienced by many women within the nuclear family and within marriage was well supported by empirical research – for example in the United States (Bart, 1971; Bernard, 1973) – and Britain (Oakley, 1974). Evidence was produced by listening to women's voices and by exploring those areas of the private arena, hitherto invisible and unquestioned, such as housework, previously not classified as work (Oakley, 1974).

Feminist research set the context for future methodological and conceptual debates as it fought to expose the gender-specific nature of apparently universal concepts like the family. The research challenged the assumptions of the Beveridge Report and, albeit less explicitly, of social policy initiatives such as community care which assume that the family can be conceptualised as a single unit. The internal organisation and functions of the family have to be investigated and the interconnections between the family and the wider social, political and economic context disentangled, exploring the interrelationship between the public and the private arenas.

The aims of many feminists in the early 1970s were to seek gender equality, through, for example, improving the conditions under which women experienced family life, because 'the socialization of housework, paid maternity leave, proper collective child care, publicly funded, and decent jobs with shorter working hours were the solutions advanced' (Wilson, 1989; 15). This could include more involvement by men in child care and domestic labour, stressing liberal notions of equality, where women and men should be able to participate in public life and in the labour market as well as being parents and carers.

The later 1970s saw the emphasis shift, with a move within feminism to revalue the female and celebrate uniquely female attributes and qualities, notably women's mothering. Rich makes a distinction between the repressive, patriarchal social institution of motherhood and women's mothering abilities. Chodorow explored the psychological effects of the fact that it is women who mother (Chodorow, 1978). Other feminists brought together these notions of a maternal identity, suggesting some universal characteristics of 'maternal thinking' and 'maternal practices' (Ruddick, 1980) and women's separate styles of moral reasoning (Gilligan, 1982). Such approaches have been more popular in the United States than in Britain, although some work using psychoanalytic theory, notably based on the Object Relations School, has informed more recent analysis of the mother–daughter relationship in psycho-social approaches which have developed out of earlier feminist psychoanalytic theories. For other writers this emphasis on motherhood was seen as reactionary and essentialist in its stress on a biological role and thus as colluding with a traditionalist view of women within the home (Segal, 1987).

This examination of the two facets of feminism in the 1960s and 1970s shows that it has ranged from critique to celebration of women's maternal role. However, both approaches include the need to explore the diversity of family forms, to challenge the notion that the nuclear family of 1950s ideology was universal and natural, and to argue for a deconstruction of the family as a natural unit and its reconstruction as a social unit (Rapp, 1979). Difference and diversity have increasingly become recognised following the critiques by black and Asian feminists of the ethnocentricity of white feminism's stress on the particular examples of white, middle-class women. Many black women might well have welcomed more leisure time at home freed from the demands of their low-paid work (hooks, 1984) and would not have experienced the boredom of Friedan's housewives. Others sought to secure their fertility rights against enforced sterilisation and contraception rather than struggling to obtain rights to abortion on demand as expressed in the demands of the Women's Liberation Movement (Aziz, 1992).

Feminist analyses have also had to engage with the realities of profound demographic and social change in a world the economics and politics of which have been transformed since the crises of the 1970s (see, for example, Chapters 3 and 4). Demographic change impacts upon domestic living with the growth of transformed family structures and relationships (Woodward, 2002). In Britain, as elsewhere in Europe, an increasing number of children were born to unmarried mothers. In 2002 41 per cent of babies were born to unmarried women. The number of children living with a lone parent rose from 7 per cent in 1972 to 23 per cent in 2003. Families are becoming smaller, and the average number of children among married and cohabiting couples in the United Kingdom is 1.7, with many more women choosing not to have a child at all. The OPCS estimates that nearly 25 per cent of women born in 1980 will not have any children. Britain has one of the highest divorce rates in Europe, estimated at 40 per cent of marriages in 2004, with three-quarters of all divorces instigated by women. More women, including mothers, are participating in the labour market, albeit often in low paid and part-time work with women constituting just under half of the workforce (Data from Social Trends, 2004). All of these factors create a very different pattern of domestic living for women from that represented by the familial ideologies of the 1950s. This changing climate coincided with the Thatcher years in Britain, when social policy involved a retreat from state welfare provision in favour of a market-led system, a retreat which created difficulties for many women, including the growing numbers of lone parent families, most of which are headed by women, living in poverty (Social Trends 2004, and also see Chapter 12). Feminist critiques of the family and social policy at this time stressed material factors as the major contributors to the problems of single mothers (Campbell, 1987) and have continued to focus upon the material conditions in which children are brought up in very diverse family forms, many of which remain unsupported by neo-liberal policies which present paid work as a panacea, without any understanding of the difficulties of child care and the discrimination which so many families experience.

---

**Activity 4**

*Consider the main features of the feminist critique of the family which have been discussed here. Which factors do such critiques take into account in analysing the family? What distinguishes feminist critiques?*

---

## Violence and the Family

In this section we explore two examples of violence within the family which have been 'rediscovered' in the last 20 years, and consider their implications for social policy.

### Domestic Violence

Feminism has contributed to the exposure of domestic violence and has challenged assumptions about the privacy of the home, showing that these assumptions are based on the idea that members of a family have a right to do as they please within that family, and that families should resolve their own problems if any occur and not appeal to outside, public agencies. Feminists have shown that such principles fail to address the unequal rights of different family members, and argue that the family structure reflects and reproduces men's power over women. Empirical investigation indicates that domestic violence committed by men against their female partners accounts for a quarter of all reported acts of violence and that 70 per cent of violence takes place within the home (Pahl, 1985). Feminist research has put this violence on the public agenda and has investigated women's perceptions of their experience.

Feminist explanations of the phenomenon vary, though in general radical feminist explanations see domestic violence as a feature of patriarchy and men's control over women: 'although there are many ways that men as a group maintain women in oppressed social positions, violence is the most overt and effective means of social control' (Yllö and Bograd, 1988). Such feminist approaches and studies of male violence, and especially feminist campaigns including the work of the Women's Aid Federation, have been very important in increasing awareness of gender inequalities, abuse and violence against women which had hitherto been concealed within the private arena of the family and personal relationships (Kelly, 1988). Women's campaigns have led to the establishment of refuges where the victims of violence can escape with their children and receive support and advice, and to increased recognition of the extent of domestic violence against women and the need for intervention – for example, by the police.

Socialist feminism sees domestic violence as resulting from class-related, economic factors, including poverty and material deprivation, which have been identified as significant contributory elements. The poverty which women and children experience is linked to the notion of the male breadwinner and to the construction of women's dependency. The lack of child care, and hence the difficulty experienced by single mothers in participating in the labour market, has ensured women's dependency on the state and on men. The gendered construction of income maintenance produces a system where men's eligibility depends on their labour market characteristics, such as age, invalidity and unemployment, and women's, in contrast, is determined by their marital and family situation. Unless women are single and childless, their access to income maintenance is determined by whether they are seen as having a man who could, or should, support them. Married women were encouraged to rely on derived insurance rights until the late 1970s and were barred from claiming means-tested Supplementary Benefit for the family until the early 1980s. The entitlement of mothers who are not married, or those who are separated or divorced, has been governed by moralistic directives over a period of time extending from the New Poor Law to Beveridge (Daly, 1994). Women's dependence on men or on the state, especially through non-contributory, means-tested provision rather than insurance provision in their own right, has tied women into social and familial relations which have often provided the site of their experience of domestic violence. Feminist perspectives challenge individualistic and psychological explanations of domestic violence and locate it within the broader social context.

### Child Abuse

The emergence of child abuse as a social problem in the last 20 years has attracted considerable media attention, sometimes leading to moral panics about the breakdown of family life, or perhaps more frequently, the scapegoating of social workers (MacLeod and Saraga, 1988). Feminist research in this area has again challenged existing assumptions about the privacy of the home, the responsibility of individuals, notably mothers, and the ideas of 'mother blaming'. Feminists have been concerned to explore the complexity of this phenomenon and to disentangle some of the assumptions about what constitutes child abuse, who is responsible and why it occurs.

In order to address these questions the distinction has been made between *physical* abuse and *sexual* abuse, and empirical research has been conducted which suggests that sexual abuse of children is mainly perpetrated by men, without specific characteristics of age, class or culture. Physical abuse is more frequently committed by women, although it has to be noted that women are much more likely than men to have responsibility for children (Saraga, 1993). Physical abuse is linked to cases of domestic violence (Finkelhor, 1983) and to class and poverty.

Feminist research raises questions about the definition of child abuse which reflects problems about what is considered normal and what abnormal, what is the boundary between the two, and who decides the location of this boundary. Feminist research has concentrated on the experiences of women and children as survivors of abuse, who had hitherto largely been excluded from research studies. This has raised questions about who should be investigated. Should it be victims or parents (for whom read 'mothers')? The last, and most important question is that of explanation, and it is in this area that the feminist contribution has been most significant. Feminists go beyond describing what happens and, in the case of domestic violence and child sexual abuse, ask questions about why men should seek to exercise power and control over women and children. Feminists do not see this violence as exceptional or deviant masculine behaviour, but rather as an extension of the social construction of male sexuality which is articulated through the language of power and domination (*Feminist Review*, 1988). Even though it can be argued that feminist critiques do not achieve full recognition, they have put domestic violence and child abuse on the public agenda where they have since been acknowledged as social problems. It is no longer possible to dismiss these issues as private concerns or even individual problems, although 'blaming the victim' and 'mother blaming' have not entirely disappeared from explanatory frameworks and interventions.

## Activity 5

*What behavioural traits would you characterise as (a) masculine, and (b) feminine?*

*Look at your list and think about which, if any, of these are: (a) biologically based or determined, and (b) which are socially constructed.*

*Has public policy been responsive to problems stemming from 'masculine identity'?*

## Gender and Citizenship

This section explores the concept of citizenship upon which the British welfare system is based. This widens the debate by focusing on the concept of citizenship which is accorded a significant role in some theoretical accounts of the welfare state and carries increasing weight in discussion of policies for social inclusion and cohesion. This section should be read in conjunction with Chapters 7 and 8.

Much writing on citizenship does not include the dimension of gender (Marshall, 1950; Mann, 1987; Turner, 1990). A great deal of debate about citizenship has been concerned with social class and draws on the work of T.H. Marshall, with its three components of civil, political and social citizenship (1950, 1975, 1981). Criticisms of Marshall have included discussion of his ethnocentricity and even of his failure to acknowledge the public/private dichotomy (Turner, 1990), but gender as a concept is significantly absent from these critiques. The fact that women did not achieve many of the features of either political or civil citizenship in Britain before 1928 might suggest that women have simply been slower to attain full citizenship status, but that it is still possible. In the liberal view, all that is required is the removal of legislative barriers and overt discrimination. A whole range of other civil rights has been won by women in western nation states: for example, access to education, the right to own property, to terminate a marriage and to professional employment (see Walby, 1988), some before suffrage rights and some in the years afterwards.

Feminist critiques of the second wave challenged the unified notion of citizenship as a model to which women can aspire on equal terms with men. They locate citizenship within the broader social context and stress the gender differences which a unified concept obscures. Although most theorists include class – and the key debate has been about the relationship between class and citizenship in a capitalist society – the structural factor of *patriarchy* has not been addressed. Feminists argue that 'democratic theorists fail to recognize the *patriarchal* structure of the welfare state; the very different way that women and men have been incorporated as citizens' (Pateman, 1992: 223). The structuring of the public and private spheres is crucial to the position of women and their citizenship status. 'The patriarchal division between public and private is also a sexual division. . . .

The public world of universal citizenship is an association of free and equal individuals . . . of men who interact as formally equal citizens' (Pateman, 1992: 226).

Walby argues that the patriarchal institution of the 'male-dominated household is incompatible with full citizenship' (Walby, 1994: 391) and that the solution to the exclusion of women from full citizenship rights is the socialisation of women's domestic role, just as other aspects of work in the domestic arena have been socialised – through schools, nurseries and hospitals, for example.

Feminists have shown how social citizenship depends largely on being a paid worker in order to obtain full rights. Women whose primary responsibilities lie with care of children, husbands and the elderly tend not to have access to the higher levels of income generated by occupational pensions. Overall, it is women's domestic and caring duties, part of the institution of patriarchy, which exclude them from full citizenship rights, making clear the gendered nature of the concept of citizenship. However, this also presents a dilemma for feminists. On the one hand it seems that to obtain full civil citizenship rights women should participate in the labour market and abandon the constraints of domestic duties, and on the other that women's caring roles should be recognised and supported. Lister argues that citizenship has to be re-gendered to embrace individual rights (such as social and reproductive rights) and political participation (2003).

As Pateman (1992) points out the oppositions between public and private and between men's independence and women's dependence are false dichotomies and it is essential to recognise the interrelationship between the public and private arenas. She argues for the construction of a welfare society instead of a welfare state to accommodate the changes which are taking place in employment and in patterns of domestic living. Lister argues for the creation of conditions in which women and men can combine paid work and caring responsibilities (2003). This challenge to mutually exclusive binary oppositions, such as male/female and public/private, upon which much of our understanding of gender has been based, is a feature of recent postmodernist feminist approaches which seek to address and understand difference and diversity.

---

### Activity 6

*What are the problems associated with policies which treat women as equal to men? Does this mean treating women and men the same?*

---

## Conclusion

This chapter has mapped out some of the shared concerns of feminist approaches as well as the different emphases of particular positions. It is no longer possible to talk of feminism, but only of 'feminisms'. However, all feminist approaches include a concern with gender and with asking questions about the position of women in relation to social policy. They go further than this and question the basis of universal categories such as citizenship and equality and of naturalistic concepts like the family, and in deconstructing these conceptualisations reveal their gendered dimensions. Often, as has been shown here, the universal category is largely male and women's exclusion has passed unobserved, until feminism drew attention to this. Feminist critiques have challenged traditional categories and oppositions such as the natural and the social, the material and the cultural and have engaged with the tension between equality and difference and the need to re-gender key concepts like citizenship. Challenging assumed binaries opens up the possibilities for diversity and participation. Feminist theories have developed out of political action and campaigning and are born of the interrelationship between theory and practice.

---

### Further Reading

Lewis, G., Gerwitz, S. and Clarke, J. (eds) (2000) *Rethinking Social Policy*. London: Sage/Open University.

Lister, R. (2003) *Citizenship Feminist Perspectives*. Basingstoke: Palgrave Macmillan.

Skeggs, B. (2004) *Class, Self and Culture*. London: Routledge.

# SIX

# Racism and Social Policy

*Laura Penketh*

---

### Outline Points

- Britain's black and Asian population continues to suffer from inequality and oppression; a whole range of social statistics emphasises the disadvantage faced by members of these communities.
- 'Race' is a social construction that developed with the rise of capitalism. It can be traced through distinct phases: the racism of slavery, of empire and of migration
- Racism is embedded within the social structure of modern societies.
- Within the welfare services racism is institutionalised.
- The Central Council for Education and Training in Social Work pioneered anti-racist developments in the early 1990s, emphasising the impact of institutional racism on service delivery.
- Stephen Lawrence's murder in 1993 brought institutional racism within the police force to the forefront of political and media debates.
- In both cases, the emphasis on institutional racism came under fundamental attack.

---

## Introduction

This chapter will explore the relationship between race and social policy, specifically analysing how racist assumptions and 'race-related' policies have influenced, and continue to influence the lives of Britain's black population.

Across the country on a daily basis, black people face violence and abuse against themselves, their families, their homes and their properties. Less conspicuous, is the manifestation of structural and institutional racism in society, which affects the representation and treatment of black people within a range of state institutions. Black people face systematic discrimination in the labour market, and the housing, education and health services (Solomos and Back, 1996). For example, the 1997/1998 Labour Force Survey revealed that:

> Unemployment rates were 6% for whites, 8% for Indians, 19% amongst the black community and 21% amongst Bangladeshis and Pakistanis [and that] . . . More than 40% of 16 to 17 year olds from ethnic-minority groups were unemployed compared to 18% of their white peers. (*Guardian*, 21 February, 2000)

In work the earnings of black people are likely to be lower than the wages of white workers in equivalent jobs. The Institute for Social and Economic Research found that, between 1985 and 1995, 'On average, Pakistani and Bangladeshi men earned just over half the salary of their white peers' (*Guardian*, 21 February, 2000). More recent figures, revealed in the 'Ethnic-Minority's Employment Task Force' published in 2004, show that Asian and black workers earn up to £7000 a year less than white people. The figures for some groups are starker than for others. For example, Bangladeshi salaries average £12,220 per year whilst the figure for white employees is £18,044. As well, black and Asian workers are still twice as likely as white workers to be unemployed (Hinscliff, 2004).

In terms of childhood poverty, 70 per cent of Bangladeshi/Pakistani children live in poverty, compared to 41 per cent of Afro-Caribbean children, and two and a half times the rate of white children (Bunting, 2004).

Black people are more likely to live in inferior housing in run-down areas (Ginsburg, 1992; Law, 1998), experience higher mortality and morbidity rates (Skellington, 1992; Blackburn Borough Council, 1996), worse health provision (Sivanandan, 1993), and are often subject to differential treatment in terms of educational provision (Troyna and Hatcher, 1992; Gore, 1998). For example, the Children's Society in 1999 revealed that Black children are six times more likely to be expelled from school than white children (*Guardian*, 21 February, 2000). These statistics were reinforced in the Macpherson report that published the findings of the Stephen Lawrence inquiry. Housing departments were seen to be too slow and bureaucratic in response to racist tenants, and in schools there was disturbing evidence of widespread racist attitudes amongst very young children, and a failure to implement anti-racist policies (*Guardian*, 25 February, 1999). While Statewatch noted that within the criminal justice system: 'Black people are between four and seven times more likely to be sentenced to prison terms, and nearly eight times more likely to be stopped and searched by the police' (*Guardian*, 21 February, 2000). For the first time, the particular social and economic disadvantage faced by Britain's Muslim community has been revealed in the Office for National Statistics' analysis of the religious dimension of the 2001 census (supplemented by data including the Labour Force Survey). It revealed that Muslims experience higher rates of unemployment than other religious groups, poorer health generally, and higher levels of disability. For example, rates of unemployment for Muslim men stand at 14 per cent compared to 4 per cent for Christians (Carvel, 2004a).

## 'Race' and the Origins of Racism

Following the Second World War scientists and social scientists were asked by the newly established United Nations to examine the question of whether 'racial' difference as expounded by the Nazis had any scientific foundation. They concluded that it had none. More recently the developing science of genetics has further confirmed this view by demonstrating that there is more statistically significant genetic diversity within population groups than between them. To geneticists, the physiological differences associated with 'race' have no more significance than hair or eye colour. Thus, 'race' is a social construct and not a scientifically valid reality. However, most people think that 'races' exist, institutions consciously and unconsciously discriminate against people on the grounds of 'race', and hence the concept motivates 'action', behaviour and discrimination, which we can understand as racism (Miles, 1984), which occurs: 'Where a group of people is discriminated against on the basis of characteristics which are held to be inherent in them as a group' (Callinicos, 1993: 17). In short, although biologically discrete races do not exist, racism certainly does, and millions of people's lives are blighted by racist discrimination. In order to understand why this is so, we need to critically explore and analyse how notions of racial superiority and inferiority developed historically.

At this juncture however, it is also important to note that we need to distinguish the term 'racism' from 'prejudice' and 'discrimination.' Prejudice means irrational attitudes and beliefs held by individuals, and discrimination concerns action on the basis of these beliefs. However, although visible minorities in society may suffer from the prejudiced views of individuals, which may result in unfair discrimination, racism is not merely the sum total of the actions of prejudiced individuals. As the following section reveals, any analysis of racism needs to go beyond individual and cultural prejudice to recognise the structural and institutional nature of racism. Structural analyses see notions of natural inferiority and superiority arising in the conditions of capitalism, and institutional racism describes the systematic discrimination that black people experience, in, for example, jobs, housing, and education. In short, racism is an institutional feature integrated into the history and social, economic, political and ideological fabric of British society (Sivanandan, 1982; Miles, 1989; Divine, 1991).

## The Roots of Racism

Racism is a relatively modern phenomenon that grew up with the development and expansion of capitalism (Miles, 1982; Fryer, 1984; Callinicos, 1993). According to Fryer (1984) it developed in three distinct phases that he terms, the 'racism of slavery', the 'racism of empire' and the 'racism of postwar migration'.

## The Racism of Slavery

The racism of slavery developed in the seventeenth and eighteenth centuries in order to justify the systematic use of African slave labour in the great plantations of the New World, when, during the eighteenth century alone, some twelve million African captives were transported to work on the plantations of North America and the West Indies (Blackburn, 1997). Racist ideologies were constructed based on the view that humankind was divided into races reflected in distinct biological characteristics, with white races being superior to black races. They constructed, promoted, and disseminated images of black populations as, for example, savage, unintelligent, dirty and licentious (Fryer, 1984). Edward Long, the son of a Jamaican planter, wrote in his 'Universal History' (1736–65) that Africans were:

> proud, lazy, treacherous, thievish, hot, and addicted to all kinds of lusts, and most ready to promote them in others . . . as . . . revengeful, devourers of human flesh, and quaffers of human blood . . . It is hardly possible to find in any African any quality but what is of the bad kind: they are inhuman, drunkards, deceitful, extremely covetous . . . (quoted in Fryer, 1984: 154)

Further, he stated that there was a continuous chain of intellectual gradation from monkeys through varieties of blacks, 'until we mark its utmost limit of perfection in the pure white' (quoted in Fryer, 1984: 159).

Notions of race and of biological superiority and inferiority were expanded upon during the mid-nineteenth century when there was the greatest migration of peoples in history, revealed in the mass migration of European immigrants to America, and to a lesser extent, Australia and South Africa (Hobsbawm, 1977). During this period, as a result of poverty, repression and famine in Ireland, there were high levels of Irish migration to Britain, when the Irish were described as, for example, 'human chimpanzees', charged with 'backwardness'. Notions of inferiority were based on the view that the Anglo-Saxon blood of the English was superior to the Celtic blood of the Irish (demonstrating that racism is not always an anti-black issue).

## The Racism of Empire

The racism of Empire can be traced through the expansion of colonial conquest at the end of the nineteenth century, and further reinforced inequalities within the social structure. By 1914 the British Empire covered 12,700,000 square miles, and had a population of 431 million, consisting of 370 million black people, but only 60 million of the white self-governing population. Britain's rulers therefore needed a racism more subtle and diversified, but just as aggressive, as that used to justify slavery (Fryer, 1988). As a result, from the 1840s to the 1940s, scientific theories reflecting notions of inferiority and superiority emerged to justify this exploitation. For example, phrenology, a pseudo-science that deduced people's characters from the shape of their skulls, was used to explain that the skulls of Africans clearly demonstrated their inferiority to humans. Anthropology was also used to demonstrate to the British that black people were closer to apes than to Europeans, and that they were intellectually inferior, and social Darwinism that black people, as a result of their inferior intellect, were doomed to extinction. As Anglo-Saxonism, racism claimed that God had fitted the British to rule over others – even though for most of human history Britain (and the North-West of Europe generally) remained a remote and backward place, far behind the advanced societies of the Mediterranean, Indian continent and China (Harman, 1999). In its popular version, the message that black people were savages, who could be rescued from heathenism by British rule, was transmitted through schools, newspapers, literature and popular entertainment. The main political function of all these theories was to justify British rule over black people (Fryer, 1988).

### The Racism of Post-war Migration

The third phase discussed by Fryer (1984) was the racism of post-war migration. In the post-war period Britain experienced an acute labour shortage, and politicians actively sought labour from Commonwealth countries. As a result, during the 1950s and 1960s, economic migrants from Britain's Commonwealth entered the country because of the demands of the job market, and as a result of poverty and lack of opportunity in their country of birth (due to the immiseration of the colonies under the British Empire). Workers were particularly needed in sections of the economy characterised by the poorest pay and conditions, such as textiles, catering and public transport, which white workers could afford to reject in an era of economic expansion and full employment. But precisely because of the history of racism and the way it was deeply embedded within British society, migrants arrived to face harrowing levels of discrimination and abuse. This is very important in understanding the position that the black population came to occupy both geographically and economically in Britain. The location of the black workforce within already overcrowded conurbations where they occupied the largely unskilled and low status jobs resulted in their also occupying very poor housing in inner-city areas. It also contributed to, and reinforced notions of white superiority, for racism offered white workers the comfort of believing themselves to be superior to black workers, and during economic crises enabled employers and politicians to scapegoat black workers and blame them when levels of unemployment rose (Husband, 1980).

---

### Activity 1

1  How can we explain the emergence of notions of white superiority and black inferiority during the seventeenth century?
2  In what ways have economic and political developments since then reinforced these ideas?

## The Racialisation of Politics

The growth of black migration to Britain in the immediate post-war period provoked a series of racist responses. First, prejudice was widespread and:

> More than two-thirds of Britain's white population . . . held a low opinion of black people or disapproved of them. They saw them as heathens . . . as uncivilised, backward people, inherently inferior to Europeans . . . and suffering from unpleasant diseases. They saw them as ignorant and illiterate . . . they believed that black men had stronger sexual urges than white men. (Fryer, 1984: 375)

The most prejudiced objected to mixed marriages, would not allow black people in their homes, and refused to work with them.

This prejudice led to many incidents of verbal abuse and physical violence which for many years, were treated with complacency by the government, state institutions and the population as a whole. In Nottingham and London, in 1958, there were anti-black race riots and disturbances, which led to black people being attacked with iron bars, sticks and knives, and gangs of white teenagers spoke of going out 'nigger hunting'. Yet the police, demonstrating their own hostility to the black population, offered no effective opposition to these groups and their activities.

However, discrimination can be direct and indirect, overt and covert, and during this same period, state social policy was imbued with racism. Labour and Conservative politicians, both fearful of losing votes and seats, progressively accommodated themselves to racism. They blamed the black population for 'race relations' problems, rather than the racism of the white population, and called for restrictions on black immigration. As a result, racism became institutionalised and legitimised, enshrined in the laws of the land, reflected in the development of state immigration controls whose aim was to limit black entry to Britain. An exploration of race-related legislation from the 1960s onwards demonstrates how the migration of labour to Britain became increasingly tangled up in the politics of race, and was mediated by the role played by politicians. For example, the Conservative politician Enoch Powell, who had encouraged black migration when there was a shortage of labour in the British economy, later warned the British population that as a result of increased immigration: '. . . their wives (were) unable to obtain hospital beds on childbirth, their children were unable to obtain school places, their homes and neighbourhoods were changed beyond recognition' (quoted in Sivanandan, 1981: 82).

In the post-war period racial discrimination was legal, and employers and other groups such as landlords could simply state that 'no coloureds' were wanted. In the mid-1960s in an atmosphere of increasing racist political activity, the government responded by adopting two related strategies: integration and restriction. Integration was to be achieved through a number of policies to promote appropriate relations between the 'races'. In 1965, the Race Relations Act made it unlawful to discriminate on the grounds of race, colour or ethnic or national origin in public places such as hotels, restaurants and swimming pools. The Act also set up the Race Relations Board to receive complaints of discrimination. Three years later, the Race Relations Act of 1968 made discrimination in the area of employment, housing and the provision of goods and services unlawful, and made it possible to bring cases of discrimination to court. The 1976 Race Relations Act replaced the 1968 Act, and for the first time the law was extended to cover indirect discrimination; that is, unlawful practices which, whatever their intentions, were shown to have a disproportionately adverse effect on the minority ethnic communities. The Commission for Racial Equality replaced the functions of the Race Relations Board at this juncture. Another piece of relevant legislation was the 1966 Local Government Act which provided funds for what became known as 'section 11' workers, who were employed to promote the integration of New Commonwealth immigrants into British society in areas such as education.

The second strand of government strategy was 'restriction' of black entry to Britain. The Conservative government in 1962 introduced the Commonwealth Immigrants Act which limited entry from the 'coloured' Commonwealth by making workers apply for different categories of work vouchers based on their occupational skills. Although the Labour party bitterly opposed this whilst in opposition, the degree of popular support for the measure caused serious problems for them during the 1964 election, and they reversed their position. Instead, they not only kept the Act on the statute books, but passed another such act in 1968 at the time of Enoch Powell's notorious speech on 'race' matters, and the crisis caused by the expulsion of British passport-holding Asians from Kenya (Penketh and Ali, 1997). In 1971 The Conservative government further tightened restriction on black migration by passing the Immigration Act, the consequence of which was British passport holders from the New Commonwealth were no longer guaranteed entry to Britain.

Since the 1980s, legislation associated with 'race' and immigration has become increasingly punitive as a result of economic recession, rising levels of unemployment, and the election of a right-wing Conservative government which reinforced notions that the black British presence was a threat to Englishness or Britishness. This was reflected in the 1981 British Nationality Act, and by Margaret Thatcher's positive references to Britain's history as an imperial power. For example, in 1978 she stated that:

> . . .you know, the British character has done so much for democracy, for law, and done so much throughout the world, that if there is a fear that it might be swamped, people are going to react and be rather hostile to those coming in. (cited in Miles, 1993: 76)

She and her government reinforced notions that the black British presence was a threat to Englishness or Britishness, reflected in the 1981 British Nationality Act, and by Margaret Thatcher's positive references to Britain's history as an imperial power.

These sentiments have been resurrected over the past decade in relation to the debate regarding asylum seekers and refugees, who face the same direct and indirect abuse that Asian and Afro-Caribbean migrants faced before them. They too are portrayed as 'economic migrants' seeking to abuse the hospitality of European states. Michael Howard, who was then Conservative Home Secretary, stated in the mid-1990s that: 'We are seen as a very attractive destination because of the ease with which people can gain access to jobs and benefits . . . only a tiny proportion [of asylum seekers] are genuine refugees' (cited in Cook, 1998: 152). As a result, legislation such as the Asylum and Immigration Act (1996), instead of focusing on the legal and welfare rights of immigrants, was increasingly involved in criminalising them. The Act included withdrawing asylum seeker's rights to income support, child benefits, and public housing, and anyone not satisfying entry clearance requirements was liable to detention. There have been scathing and vitriolic attacks on asylum seekers by politicians and sections of the press. For example, in the British press refugees were described as 'scum of the earth' and 'human sewage' (Marfleet, 1999: 75), and by the mid-1990s, a network of prison camps and holding establishments had been set up across the European Union, with the British state imprisoning asylum seekers at a rate of 10,000 a year (*The Independent*, 28 June, 1999). These debates failed to acknowledge that Britain was, in fact, a net exporter of people.

The *Observer* editorial (13 February, 2000) also expressed its disgust regarding the treatment of asylum seekers when it stated that: '. . . Britain has . . . the lowest rates of asylum seekers in the West . . . People need to be desperate to leave the country of their birth; most asylum-seekers are bona-fide applicants fleeing from oppression . . . The implicit racism [in the coverage of asylum seekers] expressed last week from the floor of the Commons . . . disgraced and belittled us all.'

The assault on asylum seekers remains unabated, with both major political parties attempting to outdo each other regarding the toughness of legislation. Amnesty International have warned of human rights violations as a result of the European Union drawing up a 'white list' of ten countries from which asylum applications will be presumed to be false by all European countries. Supposedly 'safe' countries include Chile, Costa Rica and a number of African states. (Travis, 2004). In Britain, David Davis, the shadow Home Secretary stated that: ' "Treasured" British values of tolerance were being threatened by "uncontrolled immigration"' (cited in *The Independent*, 7 October, 2004).

It is not only asylum seekers and refugees who are pilloried in Britain today. Particularly since the bombing of the twin towers in New York, the Muslim community has come under sustained political and media attack. A 2002 YouGov poll found that 84% of the public conceded that their suspicions of Muslims had grown since 9/11 (Saggar, 2004 in the *Guardian*, 9 November). There are other figures that reveal the alarming rise in the numbers of British Muslims experiencing discrimination over the past four years. The percentage of Muslims reporting discrimination because of their faith has doubled since 2000. This reveals that the build up of long term prejudice over many years has been exacerbated since 9/11 (al Yafai, 2004)

The media and politicians have been instrumental in perpetuating and reinforcing fears and discrimination associated with the Muslim community. The New Labour government has called for the speaking of English up to test standard as a prerequisite for British citizenship, as well as swearing an oath of allegiance to the queen. As Younge (2005) states:

> Today, Muslim identity has been singled out for particular interrogation in the West. Muslims have been asked to commit to patriotism, peace at home, war abroad, modernity, secularism, integration, anti-sexism, anti-homophobia, tolerance and monogamy . . . [They are] not being asked to sign up to them because they are good or bad, but as a precondition for belonging in the West at all. The fact that these values are still being contested in the rest of society, is, it seems, irrelevant. No other established community is having its right to live here challenged in a comparable way.

But, assimilation does not lessen racism, especially of the institutional type. If this were true, then, for example, black Caribbeans would be largely freed from the effects of racism. After all, they speak English as their first language, intermarry into the general population, their children mix with white children, and if they have a religion it is most likely to be a branch of Christianity (Mahamdallie, 2002).Yet, they still suffer disproportionate levels of poverty and disadvantage and still suffer institutional racism in the labour market and within state institutions.

---

**Activity 2**

1 *What do we mean by the 'racialisation of British politics'?*
2 *Since the 1950s, what form has direct and indirect discrimination taken in relation to Britain's black population?*

---

## Anti-discriminatory Perspectives

Since the 1950s there have been political attempts to address what are considered 'race-related concerns'. These have, in turn, been influenced by underlying assumptions regarding the black population, public anxiety, and the emergence of racial tensions, as described above. The 'race-related' perspectives that have emerged have produced various attempts to control or manage the situation. For some, this has been a problem of regulating relations between 'races'. Others have promoted social-democratic notions of multiculturalism, while a minority current has been motivated by anti-racism. It is to these competing perspectives that the chapter now turns.

### Assimilationist/Integrationist Perspectives

Assimilationist perspectives are based on the belief in the cultural and racial superiority of white society and the associated belief that black groups should be absorbed into the indigenous homogenous culture. That is, they are expected to adopt the British 'way of life' and not to undermine the social and ideological bases of the dominant culture. Integrationist perspectives also subscribe to assumptions of cultural superiority, and therefore place the responsibility on black communities to learn 'new customs' and ways of behaving in order to be accepted by the indigenous population.

However, they also believe that there has to be some attempt on the part of the 'host' community to understand the difficulties faced by black groups. Integration was described by Roy Jenkins in 1966 as 'equal opportunity accompanied by cultural diversity in an atmosphere of mutual tolerance' (quoted in Troyna, 1992: 68). However, both these 'race-related' perspectives, which still exert an influence today (as discussed above in relation to the Muslim community), tend to ignore the fact that most black people are British born and therefore quite competent in negotiating the dominant culture. For example, research carried out by the HMSO (1994) revealed that 75% of the British black population are UK born, and at least a quarter of a million are of 'mixed race'.

### Multiculturalism

During the 1970s and 1980s 'multiculturalism' was reflected in government initiatives associated with 'race'. Multicultural perspectives are based on the notion that learning about other peoples' cultures will reduce prejudice and discrimination in society, and are mainly about 'doing' things such as celebrating cultural diversity within a theoretical framework which is informed by integrationist perspectives. They incorporate the belief that contact with other cultural lifestyles will reduce the ignorance and prejudice of the white population. However, they can be criticised for focusing on individualistic and cultural analyses rather than structural analyses to explain the discrimination which black people experience in society. As such, they fail to explain how and why black groups are disadvantaged. As Sivanandan stated:

> There is nothing wrong about learning about other cultures, but it must be said that to learn about other cultures is not to learn about the racism of your own . . . unless you are mindful of the racial superiority inculcated in you by 500 years of colonisation and slavery, you cannot come to cultures objectively (1991: 41).

Analyses based on individuals and cultures led to the development of Racial Awareness Training (RAT) within state organisations, whose aim was to challenge racism by enabling professionals to 'discover' their personal racism. The implications of theorising racism as prejudice were criticised by Husband who stated that it 'reduces racism to human nature and individual fallibility, thus leaving the world of the state, the world of politics and major structural aspects of contemporary life out of focus' (1991: 50). The implementation of RAT, although representing a change in not seeking to pathologise black people, nevertheless reinforced the view that tackling individual prejudice was the major route to eliminating discrimination within professional institutions, and had a tendency to intensify the guilt and defensiveness of white professionals.

'Race-related' initiatives informed by cultural pluralism dominated the political agenda throughout the 1970s, until the election of Margaret Thatcher in 1979 who wanted to dismantle all 'race-relations' legislation and multicultural programmes. Despite the Conservative party's commitments however, as the 1980s progressed they utilised a range of 'race-related' initiatives. This was a result of uprisings in black communities in 1981 and 1985. Conservative politicians revived section 11 funding (specialist funding to support local government initiatives aimed at promoting the 'integration' of the black community) and promoted 'equal opportunities', often by putting black people in bureaucratic positions of power, which for some, led to their alienation from the black community. For example, Sivanandan stated: 'All the system did was make more room for the rising black petty-bourgeoisie – to get them into the media, the police force, local government, parliamentarise them – to deter extra-parliamentary protests' (1981: ii).

### Anti-racist Strategies

In the late 1970s and early 1980s anti-racist perspectives began to emerge, which in contrast to previous policies based on assimilationist/integrationist and multiculturalist perspectives, went beyond a concern with individual prejudice and culture in order to expose the structural and institutional nature of racism in society. This perspective was supported by a major survey published in 1984 by the Policy Studies Institute on the position of black people in Britain. It demonstrated that black people were still generally employed below their qualifications and skill levels, earned less than white workers in comparable jobs, and were still concentrated in the same industries as they were 25 years earlier (Brown, 1984). It also revealed discrimination in areas of welfare provision such as housing and education.

Anti-racist perspectives offer a much more radical interpretation of discrimination within society. They point to the ways in which racism is built into the structures and institutions of capitalist society. Thus, they are sceptical about the extent to which legislative reform alone can successfully challenge racism, or improve the lives of the black population. These doubts reflect a belief that the state is not neutral or independent, but is an expression of an economic, social and political system that benefits from racism by oppressing black people and dividing workers along racial lines – that it is a structural and institutional phenomenon within capitalist societies.

Consequently, strategies to tackle racism have involved external challenges by anti-racist organisations and coalitions within the communities, the workplace, and within state institutions. Some anti-racists, however, believe the fight against racism can only be carried out by the black community itself. Their argument is based on two premises. First, that the black population, as a result of their experiences, are particularly insightful regarding the roots and consequences of racism. Second, that the white population is inherently racist – their history, their culture and their social practices are built on racism, and therefore, no matter how well-meaning certain individuals may be, they can never eradicate all the vestiges of racism in their behaviour.

There are three possible counter-claims to these assertions. First, while it is certainly true that all black people in Britain experience racism and this has a detrimental impact on their life-chances, this does not necessarily mean that they have an inherent understanding of the institutional and structural nature of racism. There have been examples where different groups within the black community have come to see themselves as rivals competing for scarce resources, occasionally leading to violent conflict. In these circumstances division rather than 'racial unity' has been dominant within the black community. Thus there is nothing inevitable about a 'unified racial consciousness'.

Secondly, the black community constitutes a small minority of the British population as a whole, and simply looking towards the black community for political change would seem to limit the potential power and mobilising effects that anti-racist struggles can generate.

Finally, it is not the case that the black and white communities cannot stand together. Over the last 20 years in Britain, there have been a number of important examples of black and white groups standing together to defeat racist policies and practices, and to confront racist organisations. For example, in the mid-1970s the Grunwick's strike led by Asian (mainly women) workers became a central focus for the working class movement at the time. The predominantly Asian workforce was supported by a series of mass pickets of overwhelmingly white trade unionists, and the factory was 'blacked' by local post workers. (Ramdin, 1987). In the late 1970s 'Rock Against Racism' and the Anti-Nazi League were able to mobilise large numbers of black and white youth and various political activists in the struggle against both racism and the far-right (Jenkins, forthcoming). In a series of uprisings in the 1980s and 1990s, black, Asian and white youth fought together against poverty, deprivation and state policing (Hassan, 2000), while more recently, in 1999 at the Ford plant in Dagenham, an overwhelmingly white workforce went on strike against the racism meted out to black workers by supervisors, and the struggle of the Lawrence family was supported by various trade unionists such as firefighters, postal workers and council workers This led black writer, Darcus Howe to comment that there had been greater solidarity for the family from the white working class than the black middle class (Ferguson and Lavalette, 1999), leading us again to question the notion that all members of the black community understand each other's plight and that they will always stand together. These and similar events are often ignored or dismissed within the anti-racist literature, but they remain important occasions which demonstrate the possibility and potential of black and white unity in the anti-racist struggle.

---

**Activity 3**

*What are the dominant assumptions underlying assimilationist/integrationist, multicultural and anti-racist perspectives, and what strategies do they offer to deal with racism?*

---

## Tackling Institutional Racism within the Criminal Justice System and the Personal Social Services

Institutional racism is concerned with social structures and institutional practices rather than personal psychologies, and it focuses not upon the intentional acts of individuals but rather upon systematic outcomes of institutional systems and routine practices (Williams, 1985). It occurs when the routine practices of a profession or an institution produce outcomes which in their effect discriminate against members of the ethnic minority populations. Husband states that: 'It leads to the unhappy consequences that nice people can be accused of being culpable of participating in generating racist outcomes. It can be very disquieting for anyone to be told that independently of their own sense of personal agency they are perpetuating a form of racist practice' (1991: 53). In the last decade or so, two state institutions have both been confronted with evidence of the manifestation of institutional racism within their professions, and both have been forced to examine their race-related policies and practices. Developments within these two institutions, the Central Council for Education and Training in Social Work (CCETSW) and the criminal justice system, will now be critically explored.

### The Personal Social Services

During the 1980s, pressure to tackle institutional racism had become a major objective within the Personal Social Services, and CCETSW began to seriously address the issue. This led to the incorporation of anti-racist learning requirements into the Diploma in Social Work in the early 1990s. The aim was that eventually social workers in the field would be conscious of the nature of structural and institutional racism in British society, and would be able to support clients faced with such oppression. For the first time, a state institution had acknowledged institutional racism, and there was a concerted attempt to develop a more radical anti-racist approach. There was increasing recognition and concern that the black population was under-represented both as workers and clients in social work agencies (Cheetham, 1987), and that when they were represented, they were often pathologised using negative and damaging assumptions, endorsing the superiority of white culture over others.

The direction taken by CCETSW came about from discussions that took place amongst black and white sections of the social work academy and profession during the 1980s, in workshops, conferences and publications. As a result of these pressures and activities, in 1989 CCETSW introduced the 'Rules and Regulations for the Diploma in Social Work' (Paper 30), which made it a compulsory requirement for students undertaking social work training to address issues of 'race' and racism, and demonstrate competence in anti-racist practice. As a consequence, university courses and social work agencies were required to facilitate anti-racist training for students with the aim that, eventually, social workers in the field would be conscious of the nature of structural and institutional racism in British society, and would be able to support clients faced with such oppression.

In many ways this was a remarkable initiative, which represented a significant and important step forward. It emanated from a government agency and contained within its remit a recognition that Britain was an institutionally racist country, and that social work education and training should, as a consequence, be structured by anti-racist concerns and principles.

CCETSW, in 1988, formally adopted an anti-racist policy that stated:

CCETSW believes that racism is endemic in the values, attitudes and structures of British society, including that of social services and social work education. CCETSW recognises that the effects of racism on black people are incompatible with the values of social work and therefore seeks to combat racist practices in all areas of its responsibilities. (CCETSW, 1991: 6)

The Diploma in Social Work further stipulated learning requirements in relation to anti-racist social work which included:

Recognising the implications of political, economic, racial, social and cultural factors upon service delivery, financing services and resource delivery.

Demonstrating an awareness of both individual and institutional racism and ways to combat both through practice.

Developing an awareness of the inter-relationships of the processes of structural oppression, race, class and gender.

(CCETSW, 1991: 6)

Those providing courses (programme providers such as universities) were also expected to implement and monitor anti-racist policies and practices.

However, the successful implementation of CCETSW's anti-racist agenda was seriously impaired by a political, and in some cases, professional backlash, which denied the structural and institutional nature of racism, and accused CCETSW of being taken-over by groups of obsessed zealots whose major concern was to express rigid 'politically correct' values. Professor Robert Pinker, a prominent academic in the area of social work and social policy, was particularly vociferous in his condemnation of CCETSW's anti-racist developments, and his views reflect criticisms being articulated in other quarters. He stated: 'It was clear to some of us in the academic community that radical political elements had taken over the whole of the council's planning process' and that 'there would be no avenues of escape for either staff or students from this nightmare world of censorship and brainwashing'. He accused those involved in developing CCETSW's initiatives of believing that 'oppression and discrimination are everywhere to be found in British society, even when they seemed to be "invisible"' (Pinker, 1999: 18–19).

As a result of these criticisms, there were moves to undermine the relevance and importance of CCETSW's anti-racist recommendations. Jeffrey Greenwood, in taking over as chair of CCETSW in Autumn, 1993, defined himself as a supporter of equal opportunities, while publicly committing himself to 'rooting out politically correct nonsense' (quoted in *The Independent*, 28 August and 19 November, 1993). He then ordered a review of CCETSW's anti-discriminatory policies, and the Diploma in Social Work was published with the formal commitment to anti-racism dropped.

It is perhaps no surprise that, in the late 1990s, the MacPherson Report experienced a similar response from the Metropolitan police.

### The Criminal Justice System

It was the inquiry into the death of Stephen Lawrence, culminating in the MacPherson Report, that placed the issue of race and racism high on the political agenda in relation to the policing of Britain's black population. The report was significant in its acknowledgement that institutional racism had been a key factor in the police response to Stephen's murder, thereby moving away from an interpretation of racism based on personal prejudice.

Stephen Lawrence was murdered in 1993 by a group of white youths, and it was the endeavours of his parents, Neville and Doreen, who exposed the racism of the Metropolitan police in dealing with his death. In early 1997 a coroner's jury, after just 30 minutes of deliberation, returned a verdict of unlawful killing 'in a completely unprovoked and racist attack by five white youths' (*The Guardian*, 14 February, 1997), and in July, 1997, the then Home Secretary, Jack Straw, set up a judicial public inquiry into the case to be chaired by Sir William MacPherson.

The findings of the Macpherson Report were revealed in February, 1999, and concluded that racism exists in all organisations and institutions and is '. . . deeply ingrained. Radical thinking and sustained action are needed in order to tackle it head on . . . in all organisations and in particular in the fields of education and family life' (*The Guardian*, February 25, 1999).

During the inquiry, Michael Mansfield, QC, acting on behalf of the Lawrence family stated that:

> The magnitude of the failure in this case . . . cannot be explained by mere incompetence or a lack of direction by senior officers or a lack of execution and application by junior officers, nor by woeful under-resourcing. So much was missed by so many that deeper causes

and forces must be considered. We suggest that these forces relate to two main propositions. The first is that the victim was black and racism, both conscious and unconscious, permeated the investigation. Secondly, the fact is that the perpetrators were white and were expecting some form of protection. (Norton-Taylor, 1999: 22–23)

The conclusions of the MacPherson Report, that racism was institutionalised within British society were a radical departure from recommendations enshrined in the Scarman Report (1981), the last major investigation into police racism in Britain, commissioned after the Brixton riots of 1981. The Scarman Report denied the existence of institutional racism and instead defined racism as individual prejudice concluding that: 'The direction and policies of the Metropolitan Police are not racist. [I] totally and unequivocally reject the attack made upon the integrity and impartiality of the senior direction of the force' (Para 4.62, cited in Barker and Beezer, 1983: 110).

In short, the Scarman Report defined racism as individual prejudice. Not surprisingly, in contrast to the response to the MacPherson Report, it was well-received by superiors within the police force, reflecting their belief that the problem was one of a few 'rotten apples in the force' rather than a 'rotten barrel'. Furthermore, the police claimed that the behaviour of officers was itself occasioned by the street culture of black youth who:

'spending much of their lives on the streets . . . are bound to come into contact with criminals and the police'. Police 'misconduct' was then blown out of all proportion into a 'myth of brutality and racism' by the 'West Indian habit of rumour-mongering and their flair for endless discussion of . . . grievances'. (quoted in Sivanandan, 1981: ii)

During the course of the Lawrence inquiry, political commentators and the media were supportive of Neville and Doreen Lawrence, and were vociferous in their calls for justice. However, after the publication of the MacPherson Report their tone changed, and, like CCETSW's anti-racist initiative, the revelation of institutional racism within the police force was ridiculed and undermined.

However, despite this hostility, racism has been identified as a causal factor in other deaths during the 1990s. The deeply entrenched institutional nature of racism has been emphasised in the deaths, for example, of Ricky Reel, Michael Menson and Christopher Alder. In all these cases, the police were accused of behaving in a racist manner during the investigative process, demonstrating once again, how institutional racism is deeply embedded in the criminal justice system.

In both these cases, a similar pattern emerged. There was an increasing emphasis on racism within the two professions, which led to some attempts to challenge the dominant institutional culture and redirect practices and procedures. Yet, almost immediately, there was a backlash initiated by professional interests, politicians and the media. This emphasises the contentious nature of anti-racist initiatives and the fact that they challenge dominant political and cultural interests. However, these dominant interests are not passive in this process, but actively operate to reassert 'older values and assumptions'.

For example, in December 2000, William Hague gave a speech to the right-wing Centre for Policy Studies suggesting that, because of recommendations enshrined in the MacPherson Report black offenders are getting away with crimes because the police are not allowed to stop them, and pledging to overturn the tide of 'political correctness' which had brought the 'criminal justice system to its knees'. These comments were made despite research carried out by the Joseph Rowntree Foundation that found a range of agencies received almost 42,000 reports of racial harassment between April, 1999 and March, 2000, double the number of incidents recorded the previous year before the findings of the Stephen Lawrence Inquiry were published (*Guardian*, 22 November, 2000)

There are many other examples of instances, some high-profile, that demonstrate the racism enshrined in the criminal justice system. Black people remain the targets of police racism, and the number of violent black deaths in custody shows no sign of abating. Two prison officers were suspended in July, 2001 for allegedly intimidating black staff. A police raid on their home found a stash of Nazi memorabilia, neo-fascist literature and Ku Klux Klan material (Bright, 2004).

Although commentators, especially those close to the police, have argued that there is no racial bias in police stop and searches, even a Home Office study found, after examining the 2000 British Crime Survey that 'black people were more likely than any other group to be stopped by police while on foot or in a car' and that, 'after taking other demographic factors into account, being black still remained a predictor of this form of stop, as did being Pakistani or Bangladeshi' (cited in Mahmadallie, 2002: 15).

---

**Activity 4**

1  What role do state institutions play in reinforcing racism in British society?
2  What obstacles do they face when they attempt to challenge racism within their ranks?

---

## Conclusion

This chapter has emphasised the following points.

Although there is no scientific or genetic basis for the ideas of race, and it is a socially constructed term, it continues to have meaning in society, and racism has a negative and damaging impact on the lives and opportunities of Britain's black population. For example, they experience disproportionate levels of poverty and deprivation, and there is continuing evidence of the discrimination which they experience in the health service, the education system and in terms of housing provision.

Racism is a relatively modern phenomenon that emerged with the development of capitalism, and we can identify three major stages in its growth and expansion. First, there is the racism of slavery, second the racism of Empire, and third the racism of post-war migration.

In the post-war period, British politics became racialised. Relationships between the black and white communities were perceived as problematic by politicians. Both major parties pandered to racist sentiments in society, and there was a bi-partisan agreement which moved discussion on this issue towards the political right. As a result, 'race-related' legislation was introduced which pathologised and had a discriminatory impact on the black population.

From the 1950s onwards, different perspectives have been adopted in order to deal with racial tensions and improve the nature of race-relations in Britain. In the post-war period, assimilationist/integrationist perspectives were dominant. Multicultural approaches became popular in the 1970s, whereas from the 1980s onwards, a minority of activists and academics promoted an anti-racist perspective. All three perspectives continue to have varying degrees of influence in contemporary society, and should not be 'chronologically compartmentalised'.

Increasing evidence has emerged regarding the nature of institutional racism within state institutions which has been given a high political and public profile as a result of the inquiry into the murder of Stephen Lawrence and the attempts of CCETSW to introduce and implement anti-racist social work initiatives. Both examples provide evidence of the difficulties associated with such developments and their vulnerability to counter-attacks from political opponents.

Debates around 'race' and racism remain contentious in contemporary society, and the struggle for racial equality is ongoing.

---

**Further Reading**

Cohen, S., Humphries, B. and Mynott, E. (2002) *From Immigration Controls to Welfare Controls*. London: Routledge.

Visram, R. (2002) *Asians in Britain: 400 Years of History*. London: Pluto Press.

Fryer, P. (1984) *Staying Power: The History of Black People in Britain*. London: Pluto Press.

# PART TWO
# Conceptual Debates in Social Policy

At the heart of social policy debates is a series of 'contested concepts'. Concepts like freedom, equality, justice, rights, citizenship and community, for example. We may each have a vague idea of what we mean by these concepts but, if we stop for a minute, it is clear that we will have come across a usage that contrasts with our own.

Let's briefly take the concept equality and ask a few simple questions. Do we mean, for example, equality of opportunity or equality of outcome? Furthermore, as the theorist Amartya Sen (1992) notes, we need to consider the question 'equality of what?' Resources? Freedom? Welfare? And finally, we need to think about the potential 'clash' between different concepts. How can we combine equality with freedom? How do we 'manage' equality with difference?

These questions should alert us to the fact that writers and theorists from a variety of theoretical perspectives will often use the same concepts, but what they mean by them is often quite different. Understanding social policy, therefore, means at least having an awareness of these conceptual debates and their implications. This section aims to introduce some of these conceptual issues.

In Chapter 7 Brian Lund looks at questions of distributive justice – on what basis, if any, is it right for the state to distribute resources to individuals or groups within society and how should it be done? This is a highly charged area that has taxed various politicians and philosophers from different theoretical traditions. In a thorough review of debates on these questions, Lund looks at the answers provided by the New Liberals of the early twentieth century, Fabian socialists and New Labour politicians today. The chapter includes a review of the work of individual philosophers like Rawls, Hayek, Nozick, Walzer and Young.

In Chapter 8 Jonathan Pratt similarly unpicks the concept of 'citizenship'. Citizenship is one of the most significant and contested issues in social and political theory. For students of social policy and social welfare it is vital, wrapped up, as it is, with notions of welfare 'entitlement'. This chapter not only traces the historical genealogy of the concept, but also brings us up to date with a discussion of citizenship and globalisation.

Chapters 9 and 10 are slightly different. They introduce a debate over the 'validity' and relevance of postmodern and post-structuralist approaches to social policy analysis. In Chapter 9 Beth Widdowson introduces a strong defence of Faucaultian and cultural analyses of social welfare. While in Chapter 10 Iain Ferguson dismisses postmodern approaches and argues, instead, for an approach based on what he calls the 'radicalised enlightenment' to address the demands of the oppressed.

# SEVEN

# Distributive Justice and Social Policy
## *Brian Lund*

---

### Outline Points

- Distributive justice is concerned with principles used to allocate the social product between members of a particular society.
- In the late nineteenth century 'social liberals' and Fabian Socialists identified a 'social surplus' – the product of a harmonious and cooperative society – that was available for spending on social welfare.
- In *A Theory of Justice* (1971) Rawls claimed that inequalities are just if they produced the greatest gain for the least advantaged.
- Hayek, a major influence on the Thatcher government, argued that social justice is a 'mirage'. In a market economy patterns of income and wealth are the outcomes of a myriad of individual choices.
- New Labour has promoted social inclusion rather than social justice. Social inclusion is concerned with the 'human' and 'social' capital necessary to compete in a market economy whereas social justice is concerned with the fairness of such an economy.

---

## Introduction

'Justice' has many meanings. Here we will be concerned with distributive justice or 'how a society or group should allocate its scarce resources or product among individuals with competing needs or claims' (Roemer, 1996: 1). The terms 'social justice' and 'distributive justice' are broadly interchangeable but social justice has sometimes been given a wider meaning to encompass the equal worth of citizens as revealed in political processes and the respect given to different cultures. 'Distributive' justice has been chosen as the title of this chapter because, although the interaction between political processes, respect for culture and distributive outcomes is recognised, its focus is on the allocation of material resources.

Deliberation on distributive justice has a long lineage but, according to David Miller, 'theorizing about social justice became a major concern in the early years of the twentieth century' (Miller, 1999: 4). This awakened interest in the fair distribution of the national product was prompted by the attempts made by liberal philosophers to counter Karl Marx's claims that the owners of the means of production exploit the working class. Marx sought an end to capitalism and the creation of a new communist order that produced, and hence distributed, according to human needs. He believed 'social justice' to be a bourgeois concept constructed to try to harmonise the irreconcilable interests of the bourgeoisie and the proletariat. In contrast to Marx's desire to abolish class society the advocates of distributive justice wanted to reform the old order by modifying the established links between the acquisition and the distribution of resources. They sought to defend some existing property rights but gave the state a role in the redistribution of the 'social surplus' – the economic gains accruing from a co-operative, harmonious society.

## The 'New' Liberals and Social Justice

According to Blaug (1986: 84) Henry George's *Progress and Poverty* (1879) 'was the most widely read of all books on economics in the English-speaking world in the last quarter of the nineteenth century'. George asked why poverty persisted in societies where 'the introduction of improved processes and labour-saving machinery . . . has multiplied enormously the effectiveness of labour' (George, 1979[1879]: 4–5). He found the answer in the pattern of land ownership arguing that the price paid to use land, its 'rent') increased with expanding population and therefore 'rent' absorbed a large proportion of the increased productivity. Owners do not deserve the rewards accruing from land because it is the activities of an expanding population, not the efforts of landlords, that increases land values:

> The productive powers that density of population has attached to this land are equivalent to the multiplication of its original fertility by the hundredfold and the thousandfold. And rent, which measures the difference between this added productiveness and that of the least productive land in use, has increased accordingly. Our settler, or whoever has succeeded to his right to the land, is now a millionaire. Like another Rip Van Winkle, he may have lain down and slept; still he is rich – not from anything he has done, but from the increase of population.

> (George, 1979[1879]: 100)

George's ideal remedy for the 'undeserved' gains derived from land ownership was 'to substitute for the individual ownership of land a common ownership' (George, 1979[1879]: 128) but, as this would promote 'bitter antagonism', he promoted the taxing of all the excess rent gained from the special location of land. Such a tax would represent 'the taking by the community, for the use of the community, of the value that is the creation of the community' (George, 1979[1879]: 139).

The 'new' Liberals, anxious to halt the development of a politicised labour movement that might turn the Liberal Party into a 'mere cork on the Socialist tide' (Balfour, 1906 quoted in Pelling, 1993: 16), developed George's notion of a community created 'social surplus'. Leonard Hobhouse (1864–1929) and John Hobson (1858–1940), perhaps the most important 'new' Liberal theorists, worked within a paradigm known as 'organic' theory. According to the organic perspective society exists outside individuals and members of society have obligations to ensure that society functions in a harmonious and efficient manner. Both Hobhouse and Hobson identified a 'social surplus', generated by the progressive evolution of society, that could be taken from its existing owners for use in promoting the rights necessary to enable people to meet their duties. They recognised a right to work and a right to receive an adequate income for the fulfilment of the duties of fatherhood and motherhood (Page, 1996: 38). The resources to pay for this living wage would come from the redistribution of the 'undeserved' income derived from land and inheritance. 'We cannot afford to pay £500,000,000 a year', Hobhouse claimed, 'to a number of individuals for wealth that is due partly to nature and partly to efforts of their fathers' (Hobhouse, 1893: 78). Hobhouse also believed that, because the resources for a living wage were to be obtained from the collective social surplus, then the state had a right to enforce the obligations of citizenship. It could legitimately act as 'over-parent' to secure 'the physical, mental and moral care of children, partly by imposing definite responsibilities on the parents and punishing them for neglect, partly by elaborating a public system of education and hygiene' (Hobhouse, 1974[1911]: 25).

Thus, for the 'new' liberals, social justice consisted of taxing the undeserved social surplus for use in promoting the social rights necessary for everyone to contribute to a progressive society. However only 'undeserved' income was legitimately available to the state and the state should have no concern in guaranteeing a level of income above that necessary for the fulfilment of obligations. The 'new' liberals linked the notion of obligation to the idea of needs by identifying needs as the requirements necessary for individuals to fulfil societal obligations. In *Poverty: A Study of Town Life* (1901) Seebohm Rowntree used the notion of 'physical efficiency' to connect the needs of the individual to the need of society for an efficient labour force. He defined primary poverty as 'total earnings insufficient to obtain the minimum necessaries for merely physical efficiency' (Rowntree, 1901: 87). Because he wanted to protect his definition of poverty from any accusations of generosity Rowntree made no allowance for expenditure needful for the development of the mental, moral and social sides of human nature (Rowntree, 1901: 87). His calculation was related to 'the two chief uses of food', that is, 'heat to keep the body warm' and the 'muscular and other power for the work to be done'. Rowntree's clothing standard was based on working-class responses to the question: 'What in your opinion is the very lowest sum upon which a man can keep himself in clothing for a year? The clothing should be adequate to keep the man in health, and should not be so shabby as to injure his chances of obtaining *respectable* employment' (Rowntree,

1901: 107–108, emphasis added). By linking the need for national economic efficiency to the public role of the male worker Rowntree – 'throughout his life a "new" Liberal' (Briggs, 1969: 38) – moved the idea of need beyond the mere survival requirements recognised by the Poor Law.

'New' Liberal theory underpinned the financing of the Liberal reforms of 1906 to 1911. Lloyd George sought to pay for pensions, school meals and child welfare partly from the unmerited gains accruing from increases in land prices. He defended his 1908 budget, which included taxes on the development gain of land, by pointing out:

> land that not so many years ago was a 'sodden marsh' selling at £3 an acre was now, as a result of the commerce that comes through the docks and the consequent demand for accommodation, selling at £8,000 an acre. Who created those increments? Who made the golden swamp? Was it the landlord? Was it his energy? His brains? His forethought? No it was purely the combined efforts of all the people engaged in the trade and commerce of the Port of London – trader, merchant, shipowner, dock labourer, workmen – everybody except the landlord. (Lloyd George, 1909: 43)

## Fabian Socialism and Social Justice

The members of the Fabian Society, formed in 1884, expanded the notion of 'undeserved' income to include all forms of income from 'rent'. By 'rent' the Fabians meant 'the differential advantages of any factor of production over and above the worst in use' (Webb and Webb, 1913) such as the extra profit gained from the use of skilled rather than unskilled labour. Fabian economic theory meant more collectivist intervention than desired by the 'new' liberals but their insistence that the capitalist was entitled to some reward for investment (Macfarlane, 1998: 129) justified a more gradual approach to social change than demanded by Marx's followers. Nonetheless many Fabians believed that even when the 'social surplus' attributed to rent had been harvested, the inefficiency and waste of uncoordinated capitalist activity would remain (Thompson, 1996: 190). Accordingly they supported the common ownership of the means of production although more to promote efficiency than as a route to social justice. Other elements of the socialist movement upheld the common ownership of the means of production as the direct path to social justice irrespective of its merits in promoting national efficiency. The aim of Independent Labour Party, formed in 1893, was 'to secure the collective ownership of the means of production, distribution and exchange' and clause four of the Labour Party Constitution, agreed in 1917, stated that the party's objectives as:

> To secure for the workers by hand or by brain the full fruits of their industry and the most equitable distribution thereof that may be possible, upon the basis of the common ownership of the means of production, distribution, and exchange, and the best obtainable system of popular administration and control of each industry or service.

## Social Justice and State Welfare

According to Tomlinson (1997: 266) Labour's attitude to social services between 1945 and 1951 was conditioned by 'fear of insecurity . . . rather than equality' and the Labour Party, true to its constitution, regarded nationalisation as the main road to social justice. Labour's 1945 manifesto stated that 'The Labour Party is a Socialist Party and proud of it' and that 'there are basic industries that are ripe and over-ripe for public ownership and management in the direct service of the nation' (Labour Party, 1945: 6). In the 1960s, however, the de facto abandonment of nationalisation left 'tax and spend' as the only route to social justice deemed feasible (Crosland, 1956, 1974). In a section headed 'Social Justice', Labour's October 1974 manifesto stated that 'taxation must be used to achieve a major redistribution of wealth and income' (Labour Party, 1974: 9). It promised to introduce an annual tax on wealth as part of a more progressive tax structure that would provide additional finance for enhanced social security benefits and for spending on education, health care and public housing. Academic support for Labour's tax/benefits approach to social justice was provided by John Rawls' *A Theory of Justice* (1971), a book described by Blocker and Smith (1980: vii) as 'initiating a renaissance in social philosophy unparalleled in this century'.

## John Rawls' *A Theory of Justice*

According to Rawls social co-operation 'makes possible a better life for all than any would have if each were to live solely by his own efforts' (Rawls, 1971: 4) but there are potential conflicts about how fruits of social co-operation are to be shared. Thus 'a set of principles is required for choosing among the various social arrangements which determine this division of advantages' (Rawls, 1971: 4). These principles of social justice provide rules governing the appropriate distribution of the benefits and burdens of social co-operation.

### The Original Position

To establish the basic principles of justice Rawls invites us to imagine a situation in which we are considering the principles of a just society behind a 'veil of ignorance' where we have no information about our potential life-chances:

> It is assumed, then, that the parties do not know certain kinds of particular facts. First of all, no one knows his place in society, his class position or social status; nor does he know his fortune in the distribution of natural assets and abilities, his intelligence and strength, and the like.
>
> (Rawls, 1971: 137)

From this 'original position' potential participants in society construct principles of justice for the allocation of 'primary goods' – the goods that represent the necessary means for the pursuit of any plan of life whatever that plan may be.

They include rights and liberties, opportunities and powers, income and wealth and a sense of one's own worth (Plant, 1991: 99).

### Distributive Principles

The principles agreed by the participants in the discussion of the just society are, in priority order:

First Principle

each person is to have an equal right to the most extensive total system of equal basic liberties compatible with a similar system of liberty for all

Second Principle

Social and economic inequalities are to be arranged so that they are both:

(a) to the greatest benefit of the least advantaged . . . and

(b) attached to offices and positions open to all under conditions of fair equality of opportunity.

(Rawls, 1971: 102)

Rawls defends the agreement on the primacy of liberty with the argument that all individuals desire self-respect. Liberty is necessary to self-respect and equal liberty is necessary if human beings are to 'express their nature in free social union with others' (Rawls, 1971: 543). The second principle, known as the 'difference' principle, arises because, under the conditions of the 'original position' where people discuss the division of the social cake without knowing which slice they will obtain, participants will adopt a 'maximin' strategy. They will attempt to optimise the worst possible outcome because, in the real world, they might receive the smallest slice of the available resources. Rawls starts with the presumption that it will be agreed that all primary goods 'are to be distributed equally unless an unequal distribution of any or all of these goods is to the advantage of the least favoured' (Rawls, 1971: 101). Structuring a society to produce inequalities is legitimate only if such inequalities work to the advantage of the worst off. Thus an individual with natural talents – Rawls regarded natural talents as 'undeserved' – can utilise these abilities and become unequal but the 'maximin' principle provides insurance against the possibility that an individual may suffer because of luck or lack natural talents.

Rawls argues that in a well-ordered society 'it is necessary to set the social and economic process within the surroundings of suitable political and legal institutions' otherwise 'the outcome of the distributive process will not be just' (Rawls, 1971: 275). Accordingly he recommends four branches of government. An allocation branch would keep the price system workably competitive. A stabilisation branch would strive to bring about reasonably full employment. A transfer branch to be responsible for the social minimum and a distribution branch would have the task of 'preserving an approximate justice in distributive shares by means of taxation and the necessary adjustments in the rights of property' (Rawls, 1971: 276–277). Thus, using the established techniques of political theory such as the notion of a 'social contract', Rawls produced 'a philosophical apologia for an egalitarian brand of welfare-state capitalism' (Wolff, 1977: 195) – a system in evolution in most western industrial democracies since 1945 but, according to Rawls, without a systematic rationale.

---

**Activity 1**

*Explain what Rawls means by:*

- *The original position*
- *Primary goods*
- *maximin*

---

Labour's social programme of 1974 to 1976 certainly influenced income distribution to the benefit of the least advantaged. In 1975–76 government expenditure absorbed 48.7 per cent of Gross Domestic Product, the standard rate of income tax was 35 per cent and the highest rate of tax on unearned income was 83 per cent. In 1977 the Gini coefficient (a measure of overall inequality with 100 representing the extreme of inequality) reached a low post-war point of 22 (Johnson, 1999: 21). In the same year the poverty rate (measured as the proportion of the population below half the mean national income adjusted for family size) was 6 per cent – a reduction from 11 per cent in 1972 (Burgess and Propper 1999: 261). However, by 1976, the achievement of social justice via 'tax and spend' was under attack from both inside and outside the government. In February 1976 the Treasury declared that more resources were needed for exports and investment and that such resources could only be made available by restraining public expenditure. Moreover the Treasury asserted that, within total public expenditure, a high priority was to be given to expenditure 'designed to maintain or improve our industrial capacity, and to give us a better chance of success as the economy picks up' (Chancellor of the Exchequer, 1976: 1–2). Meanwhile, outside government, a powerful critique of the pursuit of social justice via taxation and state welfare was developing. Fredrich Hayek was the most important guru of an ideology that came to be labelled the 'New Right'.

## The Mirage of Social Justice

Hayek made a distinction between 'spontaneous' and 'made' orders. A 'spontaneous' order is governed by rules of conduct that provide a framework within which individuals pursue their own ends but no purpose for society is specified. In contrast a 'made' order has a specified purpose and 'order in society is seen as resting upon a relationship of command and obedience. It signifies a hierarchy in which a supreme authority instructs individuals as to how they must behave' (Gamble,1996: 36–37). Hayek regarded the market as a 'spontaneous' order and, in such an order, the idea of social justice is 'entirely empty and meaningless' (Hayek, 1976a: 11). In a market, there are no principles to apply to individual conduct which would produce a pattern of distribution that could be called just and therefore there is no possibility for the individual to know what he would have to do to secure the just remuneration of his fellows. So, says Hayek, although 'it has of course to be admitted that the manner in which the benefits and burdens are apportioned by the market mechanism would in many instances have to be regarded as very unjust if it were the result of a deliberate allocation to particular people. This is not the case' (Hayek, 1976b: 64).

If Hayek's notion of the market as a 'catallaxy' or spontaneous order, untouched by human design, is accepted then the idea of 'social' allocations, designed to alter the outcomes of market mechanisms in the direction of 'social justice', is at best misguided and at worst dangerous. 'It must lead to the extinction of all moral responsibility' (Hayek, 1976c: 129) and the very idea of social justice becomes a grave threat 'to most other values of a free civilisation' being 'the Trojan Horse through which totalitarianism has entered' (Hayek, 1976a: 66–67, 136). This is so because the achievement of social justice involves imposing a predetermined pattern on the unintended outcomes of market processes and the passing of laws affecting specific forms of behaviour. According to Hayek the only laws compatible with freedom are general, abstract laws concerned with procedures such as 'the rules of the law of property, tort and contract' (Hayek, 1976b: 109).

In Hayek's discourse the philosophical justification of redistribution via state welfare disintegrates. However as Espada (1996: 37) and Kley (1994: 24) have indicated, Hayek runs together the idea that social justice has no meaning in a market system with the notion that social justice is not a legitimate concept to apply to any type of society. Hayek assumes that the market order is the natural order but, because we know about the general outcomes of the market and, because we can construct alternative systems then there is no reason why we should accept such outcomes. We can choose between unfettered markets, regulated markets, a combination of a market with a welfare state or a communist system. Hayek's rejection of the idea of social justice creates what Hirsch has called the 'tyranny of small choices'. 'The core of the problem is that the market provides a full range of choice between alternative piecemeal, discrete, marginal adjustments but no facility for selection between alternative states' (Hirsch, 1977: 18)

---

**Activity 2**

*Which of the following laws would Hayek regard as legitimate?*

- *A law requiring all local authorities in London to reserve a proportion of their housing stock for homeless people.*
- *A law to ensure that contracts are enforced.*
- *A law imposing a special tax of 80 per cent on the increased value of land created by extra demand for houses generated by a movement of population from north to south.*

---

## Robert Nozick and Rectification

Robert Nozick (1974) has contributed a further objection to Hayek's insistence that social justice is a mirage. Nozick starts from a similar position to Hayek but reluctantly comes to recognise that historical injustices in acquisition negate the current legitimacy of market outcomes.

In *Anarchy, State and Utopia* (1974) Nozick maintained that: 'Individuals have rights, and there are things no person or group may do to them without violating their rights' (Nozick, 1974: ix). Nozick justified a minimal state 'limited to the narrow functions of protection against force, theft, fraud, enforcement of contracts, and so on', by constructing a plausible account how a minimal state limited to maintaining law and order may emerge without infringing individual rights (Nozick, 1974: 10–25). However he claimed that a more extensive state, involved in the redistribution of resources already acquired, violates individual rights. This is because current justice in distribution depends on the historical factors that created this distribution. If holdings were gained by creation, free exchange, or as a gift then they are legitimately the property of their current owner. Redistribution of acquisitions according to a 'patterned principle' such as 'equality' or 'social justice' violates the rights of the original holders – hence 'taxation of earnings from labour is on a par with forced labour' (Nozick, 1974: 169). This conclusion seemingly undermines the rationale of a redistributive welfare state and Nozick has been accused of 'proposing to starve or humiliate ten per cent or so of our fellow citizens' (Barry, 1975: 334). However Nozick was not a heartless libertarian. He recognised that market distributions 'seem arbitrary unless some acceptable initial set of holdings is specified, or unless it is held that the operation of the system over time washes out any significant effects from the initial set of holdings' (Nozick, 1974: 160). First there is the problem of how individuals can acquire rights to natural resources. Nozick tried hard to reconcile the outcomes of the market with established rights to natural resources but he could not find a response to conform to his entitlement theory. He was forced to the conclusion that one is entitled to a part of a natural resource if one leaves 'enough and as good' for others to have some use of it and if the position of others is not worsened by the initial act of appropriation. This concession opened the door to extensive state intervention in the distribution of resources for we must ask 'enough and as good' for what? Because if the primary purpose of the use of a natural resource is to satisfy basic needs then 'enough and as good' for needs satisfaction must be the answer to this question thereby giving the state a legitimate role in the redistribution of income and wealth.

Nozick was also concerned by the compounding impact of resources obtained in the past through force and, after much deliberation, he decided that reparations had to be made for historical injustices in acquisition:

> . . . a rough rule of thumb for rectifying injustices might seem to be the following: organise society so as to maximise the position of whatever group ends up least well-off in the society . . . Although to introduce socialism as a punishment for our sins would be to go too far, past injustices might be so great as to make necessary in the short run a more extensive state in order to rectify them. (Nozick, 1974: 152)

Thus, in contrast to Hayek, Nozick identified the problem of rectification and presented an argued case demonstrating why the establishment of free markets, without compensating mechanisms to rectify past injustices, produces unfair outcomes.

## Inequality and Social Justice

The application of Hayek's principles was the guiding canon of Conservative policy between 1979 and 1997 (Ranelagh, 1991: ix). The collective bargaining rights of trade unions were restricted, Wage Councils were abolished, assistance to regions reduced and industries were privatised. Income tax rates were cut in favour of increases in indirect taxation. The value of universal benefits was eroded and earnings related benefits were either scaled down or abolished. State services were brought to the market by privatisation and market principles were injected into state welfare via 'quasi-markets' (Bartlett et al., 1998). The outcomes of these policies are summarised in Table 7.1 and Table 7.2.

Of course an increase in inequality does not necessarily mean a contraction in social justice: remember Rawls argued that inequalities are just if they produce gains for the least advantaged. Nonetheless it is worth noting that the poorest decile of the population became worse off in *absolute* terms (after housing costs) between 1978 and 1996 (H.M. Treasury, 1999: 7) and it is difficult to argue that most of the gainers from the increase in inequality deserved their enlarged share of the gross national product. The increase in inequality did not enhance the absolute position of the least advantaged – a necessary condition for the justification of inequality under Rawls' conception of justice – and much of the increased inequality was derived from entrenched positions of advantage, not from entrepreneurial activity in global markets (Hobson, 1999).

**Table 7.1**  *Income of selected deciles as a percentage of the top decile: two adults with children 1978*

|  | Lowest decile | 2nd lowest | 3rd lowest | 4th lowest |
|---|---|---|---|---|
| Original income | 12 | 28 | 34 | 39 |
| Original income plus cash benefits | 24 | 30 | 36 | 40 |
| Disposable income | 31 | 35 | 39 | 44 |
| Income after indirect taxation | 29 | 34 | 37 | 41 |
| Final income (with value of 'in kind' service) | 39 | 40 | 43 | 46 |

*Source*: adapted from 'The effects of taxes and benefits on household income 1978', *Economic Trends*, 315, January: 1980, HMSO

**Table 7.2**  *Income of selected deciles as a percentage of the top decile: two adults with children 1996–7*

|  | Lowest decile | 2nd lowest | 3rd lowest | 4th lowest |
|---|---|---|---|---|
| Original income | 4 | 7 | 12 | 19 |
| Original income plus cash benefits | 12 | 16 | 20 | 25 |
| Disposable income | 14 | 20 | 23 | 28 |
| Income after indirect taxation | 11 | 17 | 19 | 25 |
| Final income (with value of 'in kind' service) | 25 | 29 | 30 | 34 |

*Source*: adapted from 'The effects of taxes and benefits on household income 1996–7', *Economic Trends*, 533, April 1998, Stationery Office

## Walzer's *Spheres of Justice*

In the 1980s conventional political philosophy was challenged by 'communitarians' who argued that, in its attempt to discover abstract, universal rules of distribution, mainstream political philosophy had ignored the social contexts in which all meaningful notions of social justice must evolve. Advocates of 'identity' and 'recognition' politics added the charge that 'liberal' political philosophy – obsessed by the individual as the basic unit of society – had neglected the institutional frameworks that generate social injustice.

Hayek and Nozick specified principles of distribution to be applied to all goods and services and, although Rawls made a distinction between 'primary' and other goods, his definition of primary goods was so broad that few domains remained in which to apply different principles from his basic tenets of justice. In *Spheres of Justice* (1983: 4–5) Michael Walzer asserted 'justice is a human construction' and 'there has never been a single criterion, or a single set of interconnected criteria, for all distributions'. Moreover he claimed that the recognition of the complexity of justice is essential to achieving equality. Egalitarianism, he says, has its origins in abolitionist politics; its aim has been to eliminate the experience of personal subordination and thereby create a society 'free from domination' (Walzer, 1983: xiii). Freedom from domination could be achieved by a full recognition that different spheres of life generate different principles of distribution through the shared meanings that come to be associated with varied goods and services. If each separate domain of life is allowed its particular principle of distribution then no single source of power (material wealth for example) can dominate society. Hence medical care, if thought of as a special 'needed good' 'cannot be left to the whim, or distributed in the interest, of some powerful group of owners and practitioners' (Walzer, 1983: 89). Other 'blocked exchanges' for money might include political office, military service in wars and freedom of speech.

So, against Hayek, Walzer made the point that, 'A radically laissez-faire economy would be like a totalitarian state, invading every other sphere, dominating every other distributive process. It would transform every social good into a commodity' (Walzer, 1983; 119–120). Walzer promoted the notion of 'need' as one of many principles of distribution but, like the 'new' Liberals he stressed that need had no objective status – other than in relationship to basic 'survival' needs – outside the 'shared meanings' that have become attached to different goods and services. In *A Theory of Human Need* (1991) Doyal and Gough took the opposite stance arguing that allocation according to need should be the principal criterion in assessing distributive justice. They were critical of notions of need as relative to cultural contexts or as constructed by discursive communities. Needs, they asserted, are universal in that everyone requires physical health and autonomy. They are the necessary conditions for participation in any form of life and for the achievement of any valued goal.

---

### Activity 3

*In what ways, if any, does health care carry 'shared meanings' that suggest it should be distributed in different ways from other goods and services?*

*Is it possible to specify the conditions necessary for individual autonomy that are not related to the specific society in which an individual lives?*

---

## Young and the Politics of Identity and Difference

In *Justice and the Politics of Difference* Iris Young (1990: 3) asked 'what are the implications for political philosophy of the claims of new group-based social movements associated with left politics – such movements as feminism, Black liberation, American Indian movements, and gay and lesbian liberation?' She argued that mainstream political philosophy had proved incapable of accommodating claims from these new social movements because it had attempted to construct a rational notion of social justice 'abstracting from the particular circumstances of social life that give rise to concrete claims of justice' (Young, 1990: 4). Moreover it had tended 'to focus thinking about social justice on the allocation of material goods and things, resources, income, and wealth, or on the distribution of social positions, especially jobs'. This restricted concern was inclined to ignore 'decision-making power and procedures, divisions of labour and culture' (Young, 1990: 15) that determine distributive outcomes as well as respect for difference and the self-respect of the members of minority communities.

Young insisted that the empowerment of oppressed groups was the issue. She defined oppression as 'the structural phenomena that immobilize or diminish a group' (Young, 1990: 42) and advocated the award of additional rights to certain groups because oppression had been generally applied to groups, not to individuals. Such enhanced group rights would extend the participation of the people historically excluded from the public sphere and thereby advance the practice of civic self-determination. Habermas puts the matter succinctly in relationship to the involvement of women in the public sphere. 'Rights can empower women to shape their own lives autonomously only to the extent that these rights also facilitate equal participation in the practice of civic self-determination, because only women themselves can clarify the "relevant aspects" that define equality and inequality in a given matter' (Habermas, 1996: 420). In *Multicultural Citizenship: A Liberal Theory of Minority Rights* (1994) Will Kymlicka supported the main thrust of Young's argument. He claimed that liberal theorists have had little to say about, for example, 'how the systematic devaluation of the roles of women can be removed' (Kymlicka, 1994: 89). The emphasis in liberalism on individual rights, he argued, does not automatically produce equal rights for minority cultures because the 'viability of their societal cultures may be undermined by economic and political decisions made by the majority. They could be outbid or outvoted on resources and policies that are crucial to the survival of their societal cultures' (Kymlicka, 1994: 109). Group differentiated rights can help to rectify this disadvantage.

---

### Activity 4

*Paul Kelly maintains that Iris Young does not adequately address the issue of the selection of the identity-conferring groups who will be allowed additional special representation. He argues that 'not all identities are due public recognition as many of these are the basis of coercive relationships and oppression . . . Young must employ a principle of inclusion which can discriminate among identity-groups but this raises the question of what principle of inclusion' (Kelly, 1998: 193).*

*Which groups, if any, do you think should be awarded extra representational rights?*

# New Labour, Social Justice and Social Exclusion

In 1996 Tony Blair declared that there was a 'limited but crucial role of government in a modern economy'. This role was to provide:

> A secure low-inflation environment and promote long-term investment; ensure that business has well-educated people to recruit into the workforce; ensure a properly functioning first-class infrastructure; work with business to promote regional development and small and growing firms; seek to open markets for our goods around the world; and create a strong and cohesive society which removes the drag on the economy of social costs. (Blair, 1996: 110)

Blair's endorsement of the market was modified by the promotion of a positive role for the state in promoting 'a strong and cohesive society'. This role was soon presented as meaning that concerted government action was necessary to tackle 'social exclusion' – a term embraced by New Labour in late 1997 when a social exclusion unit was set up in the Prime Minister's Office. The meaning 'social exclusion' is opaque but, as used by New Labour, the term:

- Directs attention to the interaction between the various factors involved in the *process* of becoming excluded rather than on the exclusionary outcome. Thus redistribution of income to the 'excluded' is not regarded by New Labour as a sufficient condition for social inclusion – the processes that lead to a low income must be addressed.
- Relates to the shortage of 'human' capital (the individual capacity to flourish in a capitalist-market economy) and a dearth of 'social' capital (the availability of support from family, friends, neighbours and voluntary organisations). Tony Blair has defined the 'social exclusion' 'as broadly covering those people who do not have the means, *material or otherwise*, to participate in social, economic, political and cultural life' (Blair, quoted in Scottish Office, 1998: 2, emphasis added).
- Differs from social justice in that it concentrates on the absence of the 'human' and 'social' capital necessary to compete for inclusion within the structures of a given society whereas social justice is concerned with the fairness of these structures.

Blair's contentment with the broad structures that determine distribution was revealed in a *Newsnight* television interview when he said: 'The issue isn't about whether the very richest person ends up becoming richer. The issue is whether the poorest person is given the chance that they don't otherwise have . . . the justice for me is concentrated on lifting incomes of those that don't have a decent income' (quoted in Bromley, 2003: 74).

The improvement of 'human' and 'social' capital has been pursued by New Labour through a variety of programmes. Welfare to work schemes supply incentives and assistance to enter paid labour because 'worklessness is the main cause of poverty and social exclusion' (Department of Social Security, 1999: 78). *Surestart, Health Action Zones* and *Education Action Zones* etc. aim at developing 'human' capital in deprived areas whereas *New Deal for Communities* is intended to foster 'social' capital. All these programmes are underpinned by the notion that rights must be

**Table 7.3**  *New Labour, poverty and inequality*

|  | 1996/7 | 2002/3 |
|---|---|---|
| % of children in relative[1] poverty after housing costs | 34 | 28 |
| % of children in absolute[2] poverty after housing costs | 34 | 17 |
| % of working age adults[1] in relative poverty after housing costs | 21 | 19 |
| % of working age adults in absolute[2] poverty after housing costs | 27 | 19 |
| % of pensioners in relative[1] poverty after housing costs | 27 | 21 |
| % of pensioners in absolute[2] poverty after housing costs | 27 | 9 |
| Gini coefficient | 34 | 34 |

[1]Less than 60% of the contemporary median income adjusted for household composition.
[2]Less than 60% of the median income adjusted for household composition at 1996/7 thresholds held constant in real terms.
*Sources*: Department of Work and Pensions (2004) *Households below average income 1994/5 to 2002/3*, http://www.dwp.gov.uk/asd/hbai/hbai2003/contents.asp.
National Statistics, *Income Inequality*, http://www.statistics.gov.uk/cci/nugget.asp?id=332

fastened to duties to enhance the social cohesion associated with such attachments. This approach was presented as a vital element of a 'Third Way' in politics. Advocates of the 'Third Way' maintained that market competitiveness is necessary for success in a global economy but that the state should promote opportunities for the socially excluded to participate in this global economy. The future of welfare was presented as 'investment in human capital wherever possible, rather than the direct provision of economic maintenance' (Giddens, 1998: 117). However, in 1999, the initial concentration on improvements in 'human' and 'social' capital was supplemented by an enhanced concern with direct income redistribution. At a lecture in memory of William Beveridge, Blair proclaimed a 'twenty year' mission' to 'end child poverty forever' (Blair, 1999: 7). A programme of direct income supplementation by a variety of 'tax credits', aimed at an interim target of reducing the proportion of children living in relative poverty by a quarter by 2004, followed Blair's announcement. The outcomes of the policies of promoting human and social capital plus direct distribution in favour of poorer children are summarised in Table 7.3.

New Labour's interpretation of a just society can be used to illustrate the theories of justice outlined earlier in this chapter. Blair's emphasis on the obligation of the individual, facilitated by the state, to take up opportunities is reminiscent of the 'new' Liberal stance. However the 'new' liberals qualified these obligations by the insistence that the 'undeserved' social surplus should be redistributed – an insistence almost absent from the New Labour's notion of distributive justice. So, according to Levitas:

Social inclusion now has nothing to do with distributional equality, but means lifting those poor over the boundary of a minimum standard – or to be more accurate, inducing those who are sufficiently sound in wind and limb to jump over it – while leaving untouched the overall pattern of inequality, especially the rich. (Levitas, 1998: 156)

Even Giddens, the guru of the 'third way' has recognised the link between equality of outcome and equality of opportunity and has endorsed Tobin's statement that 'one generation's inequality of outcome is the next generation's inequality of opportunity' (Giddens, 2000: 89).

There is a correspondence between New Labour's notion of distributive justice and that of John Rawls: New Labour's policies are clearly directed to improving the situation of the most disadvantaged members of society. However, Rawls starts from a presumption of equality arguing that a departure from an equal distribution can be justified only by demonstrating that such a departure will produce gains for the least advantaged above the share they might obtain from an equal distribution. In contrast New Labour's starting point is the legitimacy of the inequalities generated by a free market superimposed on the template of power and wealth forged in earlier times – a position similar to that of Hayek. Moreover, New Labour has not attempted to rectify past injustices in acquisition and thus its notion of distributive justice does not conform to that of Nozick.

Walzer demanded a pluralist society with different goods and services distributed according to principles generated by the 'shared meanings' that have come to be associated with different spheres of life. He was opposed to domination by a single distributive principle. New Labour's insistence that full citizenship can be obtained only through workforce participation appears to construct a model of 'citizen-worker' and to devalue other spheres of citizenship such as parenthood, voluntary activity and political participation (Phillips, 1999; Helm, 2000). Walzer might also be concerned about the reintroduction of market principles into the National Health Service via Foundation Hospitals and the Private Finance Initiative and the growing tendency for educational outcomes to replicate the existing patterns of income inequality (McKnight, Glennerster and Lupton, 2005: 66).

Certain dimensions of Young's conception of social justice are present in New Labour's stance. The term 'social exclusion' draws attention to the processes involved in distributive outcomes whereas 'poverty' can be interpreted as an outcome measure representative of the top down, cake-slicing approach of the past. Moreover, when in opposition, New Labour granted extra 'representational rights' to women in the form of women-only short lists in the selection process for Labour Party parliamentary candidates. Devolution and a new emphasis on pluralism has opened opportunities for representational politics but New Labour has not overtly promoted 'group' politics in public electoral systems, in appointments to public bodies or in the numerous managerial targets set by the Treasury in public service agreements (Spencer, 2000).

## Conclusion

We have seen that distributive justice is a contested concept. Disagreement has focused on four main dimensions of the idea. First, who are the 'subjects' of distributive justice – individuals or groups? Is Iris Young correct in asserting the priority of groups over individuals and, if so, on what grounds should we select the groups to be assigned special political and social rights? Second, what is the role of distribution according to need in a theory of justice? Is it possible to identify needs, above the requirements for survival, in an objective way so that a universal criterion of distribution is available? Third, can we apply the same distributive criteria to all goods and services? Are there not some goods and services that, because they embody special characteristics and shared meanings, should be distributed according to their intrinsic or indeed their socially created purposes? Finally, to what extent do the recipients of unequal shares 'deserve' their portions? Is justice 'historical' and related to the ways people acquire their resources or is it 'current' and thus related to the existing pattern of distribution regardless of how it came about?

---

**Further Reading**

Farrelly, C. (2004) *An Introduction to Contemporary Political Theory.* London: Sage.
Hills, J. and Stewart, K. (eds) (2005) *A More Equal Society? New Labour, Poverty, Inequality and Exclusion.* Bristol: Policy Press.
Swift, A. (2001) *Political Philosophy: a Beginners' Guide for Students and Politicians.* Cambridge: Polity Press.

# EIGHT
# Citizenship, Social Solidarity and Social Policy
## *Jonathan Pratt*

---

### Outline Points

- Social citizenship and social solidarity in the Beveridgean welfare state.
- Group rights and particularist approaches to social citizenship and welfare.
- The influence of globalisation in reshaping attitudes to social policy and welfare provision.
- Citizenship and conditionality: rebuilding support for state welfare?
- Citizenship based on residence in a community; 'cosmoplitan' citizenship: enhancing social citizenship?

---

## Introduction

In recent years, the contested concept of citizenship has risen once more to the forefront of academic and political debate. In addition to the continued expansion of academic research, we have seen the inclusion of citizenship as a taught subject within the national curriculum in 2002 and the establishment of 'citizenship ceremonies' for new UK citizens in 2004, which are just partial elements of the wider social policy agenda of Labour governments since 1997 which has been of huge significance in recasting the roles of state, individual and civil society with regard to the nature and extent of welfare provision. Thus, citizenship is of considerable political, social and academic currency, yet, the shifting sands of contemporary debate notwithstanding, the question of what exactly constitutes citizenship has proved to be an enduring one that has challenged societies throughout history, always latent, but often rising to prominence at times of marked social and economic change when the tensions and anxieties that so often accompany such developments are at their highest. A knowledge and understanding of the contested nature of citizenship, both historically and contemporarily, is obviously of particular importance to social policy given that as students and academics so much of our time is devoted to the analysis of arguments concerning the form and extent of entitlement to welfare provision.

The existing literature on citizenship comprises an enormous and complex body of knowledge incorporating different historical and political traditions, specialist strands of knowledge and particular debates that change according to time and place, fluctuating political imperatives, socio-economic circumstances and the fleeting tides of academic fashion. This being the case, it would be impossible for a chapter of this size to make any pretence of providing a representative overview of such complexity; rather, it has more limited and particular aims. In contrast to Chapter 9 of this book, this section will attempt to present a case for social policies and a sense of social citizenship based on notions of solidarity as the most effective means of fostering a more cohesive society faced, as all societies are, with the reality of scarce economic resources. Firstly, focus will be directed toward notions of solidarity in conjunction with the foundations of welfare states, particularly the UK; attention will then be drawn to important critiques of post-war welfare provision, followed by an assessment of some of the strengths and weaknesses of particularist approaches to welfare and citizenship, before concluding with discussion of some of the possible ways in which broad agreement and understanding on the nature of social citizenship might be forged anew on the basis of solidarity, given the enormous social changes that have taken place since the initial establishment of the welfare state.

## Solidarity, Social Citizenship and the 'Classic' Welfare State

The three decades after the Second World War are commonly referred to as the age of the 'classic' welfare state and the post-war welfare 'consensus'. Whilst such generalisations mask considerable complexities, particularly with regard to the reality of consensus (Fraser, 2000), they provide a convenient shorthand with which to describe a period in which the state intervened on an unprecedented scale to provide free (at the point of use) universal services in health and education alongside an expanding range of social security benefits. These developments were inextricably linked with particular conceptions of solidarity and social citizenship that this section will outline. Social citizenship was most famously defined by T.H. Marshall in *Citizenship and Social Class* (1950). Briefly, Marshall argued that citizenship had evolved through three phases: civil rights (freedom of speech, freedom of the person); political rights (freedom to vote and participate politically); and social rights (embodied in the institutions of the welfare state, such as health and education). In Marshall's view, it was social rights that rendered civil and political rights fully meaningful, and thus his conception of social citizenship had clear links with the ideas of 'positive liberty' espoused by New Liberals such as Hobson and Hobhouse. However, it is important not to exaggerate the extent or depth of this vision of social citizenship. Martin Powell (2002) has argued that Marshall's view of citizenship was vague and much more limited than is often supposed, aiming at equality of access to services rather than equalising incomes: 'the right to a modicum of welfare' (Marshall, in Powell, ibid.: 229). This minimalism was fully in keeping with the age, as we shall see shortly in analysis of Beveridge's vision of social security. As Field observed in the 1998 Beveridge Memorial Lecture: 'Beveridge wrote for an age when the vast majority of families were either very poor, or, at best, hovering only a few wage packets above the abyss' (Field, 1998: 2).

Ideas of solidarity obviously imply a sense of 'togetherness', reflecting the existence of common values, aims and beliefs: 'In its most general sense, the term solidarity represents the ties that unite individuals into a common moral community; a definition sometimes referred to as *social solidarity*' (Bergmark et al., 2000: 239, emphasis in original). This, of course can also be divisive: specific understandings of solidarity within any single organisation, group or institution (e.g. a trade union, political party, social movement or sector of the population) might not be shared by society as a whole. Thus, the difficult question is to what extent is it possible to establish and maintain solidarity at societal level – not motivated by any desire to discourage the disagreement, debate and dissent essential to any healthy democratic society, but by a hope to ensure that such debate can take place in a society in which the negative aspects of disagreement and dissent, such as violence, hatred and prejudice, are minimised – due, at least in part, to a broad social consensus on what it means to be a citizen. In terms of social policy, attempts to establish social solidarity have been most visibly expressed through the institutions of the welfare state.

The politics, philosophy and institutional forms of state welfare vary markedly from nation state to nation state and, according to Esping-Andersen (1990), can be grouped into broad patterns or types. Despite such differences, all welfare regimes attempt to bind people together in some way, in an attempt to establish some form of agreement on what it means to be a citizen: in terms of the organisation and delivery of welfare, this necessitates delineation of the respective roles, rights and responsibilities of both state and individual. In the age of the establishment of the modern welfare state in the UK, these vexed questions were addressed by the *Report of the Committee on Social Insurance and Allied Services* (1942), popularly known to history as the Beveridge Report, which served as the blueprint for post-war British society based upon a particular vision of citizenship and social solidarity that has shaped all subsequent debates. Within a broader context, it is interesting to note that similar conceptions of citizenship and solidarity were established contemporaneously elsewhere, albeit driven by different imperatives. In Canada for example, the Marsh Report on Social Security (1943), in strikingly similar terms to Beveridge, proclaimed that: 'Social insurance, as the commonly accepted way that modern industrial economies deal with social insecurity . . . has been justified by not only humanitarian and economic arguments but by the necessity of keeping the very political and social system intact' (cited in Brodie, 2002: 383). Brodie argues that the Canadian welfare state was created as part of a wider attempt at 'nation-building': state welfare, it was hoped, would establish greater solidarity amongst the diverse populations of Canada (English-speaking, French-speaking and native Canadian) and a greater sense of national unity in a relatively young nation state (ibid.). In the UK, by contrast, the Beveridge Report can be understood as an attempt at 'nation-rebuilding': as part of the process of post-war reconstruction, extending and deepening already existing forms of welfare provision in a far older nation state with a (at the time) comparatively homogeneous population. As has been extensively documented elsewhere (Timmins, 1996), the basis of solidarity in the Beveridgean welfare state was the two-parent, male breadwinner household which, during periods when earnings were interrupted, earned the right to social security benefits via the insurance contributions of the husband in full-time work. The plan for social insurance (national insurance; the means-tested safety net of national assistance; voluntary insurance) in conjunction with the assumptions that sensible post-war governments would introduce family allowances, some form of national health service and use economic policy to promote full employment would, it was believed, render 'want' in ordinary circumstances unnecessary. Married women were to be regarded as equal in status to their working husbands, with their own vital roles to play in rebuilding post-war society, an assumption that was to come under rigorous scrutiny both at the time and in future years.

As Jose Harris has argued, due to a complex variety of factors, it was by no means certain that the social insurance principle would form so central a basis of post-war welfare citizenship (in Marquand and Seldon, 1996). Despite hostility from Prime Minister Churchill, sceptical of what he regarded as its over-ambition, the Beveridge plan was enormously popular with the nation at large, selling about 600,000 copies. However, a model of solidarity based upon the principles and assumptions outlined above had as many weaknesses as strengths. By definition, insurance schemes are as exclusive as they are inclusive, and whilst the social insurance scheme was far more universal than pre-war levels of coverage, substantial sections of the population were either partially or wholly excluded. Such exclusion provided the basis for critiques of Beveridgean and Marshallian notions of citizenship and solidarity, most prominent of which have been feminist and anti-racist perspectives. Although, as noted above, the Beveridge plan was, to a large extent the toast of a nation in search of a 'New Jerusalem', the Report was nonetheless the object of contemporary feminist criticisms of considerable significance. In *The Woman Citizen and Social Security* (1943) Elizabeth Abbott and Katherine Bompass of the Women's Freedom League welcomed the Report in general, but took exception to Beveridge's view of the role of women in the national insurance scheme. In a highly detailed analysis, Abbott and Bompass were particularly critical of the loss of a woman's insurance rights on marriage, coupled with the fact that any future contributions by women would be voluntary rather than compulsory, and at a lower rate than those of their husbands. Beveridge's view that women's roles in society were different but of equal status came in for stinging criticism: 'The error – an error which lies in the moral rather than the economic sphere – lies in denying to the married woman, rich or poor, housewife or paid worker, an independent and personal status' (Abbott and Bompass, 1943: 3). In the decades that followed, such criticisms were built on by academics who argued that broad social changes in terms of the role of women, the inadequacy of social security benefits, large-scale post-war immigration and the breakdown of traditional family structures and the rise in divorce rates had rendered the Beveridgean conception of solidarity obsolete: women and ethnic minorities suffered major inequalities in terms of access to social security, housing and employment that equated to unequal citizenship, inequalities which, over sixty years later, are still present (Williams, 1989).

That critiques such as these are both valid and essential is not in doubt. However, for the purposes of the argument being developed in this chapter it is important to peer a little more closely at the complexities of history, whilst trying to avoid the Whiggish tendency to assume that the obsolescence of the Beveridge model was a historical inevitability. The viewpoints of Abbott and Bompass were not, of course, unanimously subscribed to by all women: as Harris notes, prominent campaigners such as Eleanor Rathbone and the Family Endowment Society and the National Council of Women shared many of Beveridge's views on the role of women in the home: 'not as private and politically disabling functions, but as a basis that was equal and in some respects superior to industrial employment in fostering civic virtue and capacity for public life' (in Marquand and Seldon, 1996: 128). Beveridge's belief in the two-parent, male breadwinner family unit as the basis of social solidarity was a widely held, mainstream political opinion and it is important that the social changes that he failed to foresee and which led to the undermining of his model should not obscure that fact. Blaming Beveridge for failing to anticipate the dramatic social changes in post-war Britain outlined above is, as Timmins has pithily observed 'a little like blaming medieval armourers for not foreseeing the effects of gunpowder' (1996: 57). Thus, the Beveridgean–Marshallian conception of citizenship and solidarity was undermined by both theoretical critiques and social change. Indeed, because of social, economic and political pressures, any incarnation of citizenship in any society based upon notions of solidarity is likely to lose currency and relevance to many members of that society as time progresses. That being the case, does it necessarily follow that any attempts to reach broad societal agreement on the nature of social citizenship and welfare should be abandoned in favour of particularist approaches that arguably represent a fairer and more accurate reflection of society as it is, rather than as normative approaches such as Beveridge's suggest that it should be? The next section will outline some of the strengths and weaknesses of particularist or identity based perspectives on citizenship and welfare which stress the importance of group, as well as individual rights.

**Activity 1**

*Do you think the Beveridgean model of social solidarity was inevitably doomed to failure?*

## Particularist Perspectives and Group Rights

In February 2004 David Goodhart, the editor of *Prospect* magazine, caused an outcry amongst a number of academics and journalists with his article 'Too diverse?' (see, e.g., Phillips, 2004). Goodhart argued that Britain's increasingly diverse society, whether in the form of variety of lifestyles or ethnicity, posed a significant challenge to supporters of both social solidarity and diversity. Increasing social diversity and the gradual decline of a 'common culture' illustrated, according to Goodhart:

> one of the central dilemmas of political life in developed societies: sharing and solidarity can conflict with diversity. This is an especially acute dilemma for progressives who want plenty of both solidarity – high social cohesion and generous welfare paid out of a progressive tax system – *and* diversity – equal respect for a wide range of peoples, values and ways of life. The tension between the two values is a reminder that serious politics is about trade-offs. (Goodhart, 2004: 30)

In many respects Goodhart's article echoed the views of Alan Wolfe and Jytte Klausen in an earlier *Prospect* article of December 2000. Wolfe and Klausen stressed the desirability of both solidarity and diversity, but stated the potential for conflict between these objectives, contending that an increasingly heterogeneous society was arguably associated with less willingness to share resources than was the case during the founding era of the welfare state: greater diversity increases the need for agreement on what makes us common members of a society, and thus attempts to create new forms of social solidarity are even more important now than in the time of Beveridge (Wolfe and Klausen, 2000). Are they right? To give an answer to this question necessitates an examination of conceptions of citizenship based on group rights.

As was noted in the first section, the Beveridgean conception of solidarity is a famous example of liberal citizenship based on individual rights. However, social citizenship in the heyday of the post-war welfare state was not experienced on an equal basis by all members of society. Proponents of group rights contend that notions of universal citizenship based on individual rights are naïve in that they fail to recognise that unequal power relationships in a plural society prevent many members of that society from enjoying the full benefits of citizenship because of particular aspects of identity such as race or gender (Faulks, 2000). Following the earlier example, the location of full citizenship in the social insurance-paying white male in full-time employment denied full citizenship to others. To counteract such inequalities it needs to be recognised that groups, as well as individuals, have conscious interests and rights in any just society. Such sentiments are expressed, for example, in the Runnymede Trust's *Report of the Commission on the Future of Multi-Ethnic Britain* (2000). In the introduction, the chair of the Commission, Bhikhu Parekh, stated that:

individuals have equal worth irrespective of their colour, gender, ethnicity, religion, age or sexual orientation and have equal claims to the opportunities they need to realise their potential and contribute to collective wellbeing. The principle of equal moral worth cannot take root and flourish within a structure of deep economic or social inequalities (ibid.: 2).

Britain is referred to as a 'community of citizens and a community of communities' where citizens who have different needs need to have full account taken of those differences: 'When equality ignores relevant differences and insists on uniformity of treatment, it leads to injustice and inequality . . . Equality must be defined in a culturally sensitive way and applied in a discriminating but not discriminatory manner' (ibid.).

It would be difficult to imagine how any progressive thinkers could dissent from many, if not all of these sentiments, but it does not necessarily follow that an understanding of citizenship centred on group rights and identity politics is the best way to minimise injustice and foster a more cohesive society. In a critique of the ideas of group-rights advocates such as Iris Young and Will Kymlicka, Keith Faulks (2000: 91–103) highlights a range of objections to group rights and a politics of difference; for example:

- How do societies decide which groups are legitimately entitled to be regarded as special cases and hence deserving of greater entitlements not available to all members of society? There is no non-arbitrary means of deciding which groups deserve special provision.
- Individuals have multiple identities and roles: to suppose that an individual's political position can be based upon a single aspect of their identity is to deny their complex individuality. Any single aspect of an individual's identity might be in a state of tension with another.
- A politics based on group rights would be more likely to lessen communication and understanding and increase tension between different social groups. If dominant social groups (e.g. white males) are unable to fully understand the problems of or empathise with members of oppressed groups, then what hope is there for social progress? For example, if 'men can never understand women's oppression, what incentive is there to encourage men to develop empathy and to adopt a critical stance towards their own behaviour?' (ibid.: 94)

Developing this last point within the wider context of critiques of new social movements, some writers on the left have questioned the efficacy of identity-based politics in achieving the aims of its supporters. Iain Ferguson, for example, in a case study of the mental health users' movement in Scotland, warns of the danger of regarding anyone from outside a particular oppressed group, in this case 'non-users', as 'the enemy'. Ferguson argued that service-user groups were far more effective in campaigning against cuts in services when they joined forces with 'outsider' groups such as public sector trade unions (in Lavalette and Mooney, 2000). Similarly, Ralph Miliband (1989), whilst acknowledging and welcoming the great progress achieved by the efforts of social movements, particularly feminist and anti-racist movements, nonetheless insisted from a Marxist perspective that the forces causing inequality and discrimination in society could only be more fully overcome if such movements worked together with labour movements, rather than regarding organisations such as trade unions as being irredeemably compliant with such oppression to preserve the social dominance of white males. However, the intention here is not to argue a Marxist case but merely to highlight some of the ways in which particularist and/or identity-based approaches to the politics of citizenship might be countered. As Faulks suggests:

> group rights risk freezing individuals into fragmented groups . . . and offer little hope for developing a common citizenship that aims not at *homogeneity* but *solidarity* . . . We should not make the mistake of assuming that because the ideas of liberalism are undermined by the context in which they operate, we must therefore reject these values altogether. (2000: 104, emphasis in original).

Diversity and difference are social realities that, as Goodhart, Wolfe and Klausen maintain, are to be valued and cherished. However, it has been contended here that an emphasis on group rights or particularist approaches is not the most desirable or effective means of protecting diversity and difference, nor is it the way to establish, extend and deepen social solidarity. If this line of argument is accepted, then to what extent is it possible to promote solidarity and agreement on the nature of social citizenship in the diverse, heterogeneous society of twenty-first century Britain?

---

**Activity 2**

*What are the merits and demerits of group rights and identity politics as bases of social citizenship?*

---

The following section will examine several themes in an attempt to address the question posed above. No firm answers are offered; rather, the analysis provides discussion of a number of possibilities focusing on the themes of social citizenship based on reciprocity, rights and responsibilities; on residence within a state or community; and on 'cosmopolitan' conceptions of citizenship. Before this, however, such issues need to be located within a wider context. All debates on social policy, welfare states and welfare provision have, in recent years, been overshadowed by the phenomena associated with globalisation. If we are to consider how social solidarity is to survive and prosper we must first ask whether state welfare, in the forms and to the extent that generations of citizens of many European states have experienced it, actually has a future?

## The End of State Welfare?

The reality or otherwise of a truly global, interdependent world market notwithstanding, a number of important trends in socio-economic, political and cultural development have been at the centre of academic debate; for example:

- The internationalisation of production.
- Liberalised capital and financial markets.
- The increasing dominance of transnational and supranational agencies.
- Internationalisation of culture. (Wilding, 1997)

Analysis of the trends listed above has led academics and policy makers to a variety of conclusions and, hence, there are competing perspectives on both the desirability and the reality of globalisation. Proponents of the 'strong' globalisation thesis, in close correspondence with neo-liberal political economy, welcome many of the implications of the four trends highlighted above. They argue that there has been increasing economic integration in world markets since the 1980s and that the growth in world trade, foreign direct investment (FDI) and financial markets has vastly outstripped average growth in GDP (Shin, 2000). Such developments are regarded as evidence of decreasing national controls over boundary-crossing transactions and thus expose producers to the rigours of increasing worldwide competition, wherein lies the road to rising prosperity for all. According to this view, the nation state is either dead or dying and individual nations are powerless in the face of the relentless and inevitable advance of global capital. Local and national loyalties will become increasingly irrelevant – in the eyes of Kenichi Ohmae, a champion of this worldview, 'Sony not soil' is a rallying call to arms (in Rodger, 2000: 167).

Does the above scenario signify the inevitable residualisation and decline of state welfare or have reports of the demise of the welfare state been greatly exaggerated? For a number of reasons, many scholars have argued that increased economic competition, principally from newly industrialised countries (NICs) poses a significant threat to the long-term survival of European welfare states. For example, the improved performance of NICs in world export markets has increased pressure on European industry and, consequently, Western European firms are transferring operations to nations in which labour costs, social costs and government regulations are less onerous (George, 1998; Palier and Sykes, 2001). Such pressures arguably lead to a 'race to the bottom', as states compete for increased foreign direct investment by reducing social costs by, for example, labour market deregulation and welfare retrenchment.

Thus, the long-term effects of such trends will be, it is argued, the undermining of the industrial base within advanced industrial nations which in turn weakens their ability to sustain levels of welfare provision to which the citizens of those countries have become accustomed. Such developments have been depicted by Peter Taylor-Gooby (2002) as the transition from the 'Golden Age' of the welfare state to a 'Silver Age'. Within the last decade, European states, regardless of the political character of different regimes, have undertaken similar types of reform. George (1998) itemises a range of factors that lend support to the aforementioned scenario:

- The promotion of private alternatives to state provision.
- Tougher eligibility criteria for social security benefits.
- Reduction in the generosity of benefits.
- Increasing use of charging for certain welfare services.
- Decline in relative value of pay and conditions for public employees.
- Privatisation programmes.
- Managerialism.

Of course, the precise nature of such reforms varies considerably across different regimes, but these developments are nonetheless indicative of a common trend. Just as the likes of Hirst and Thompson have questioned the reality of economic globalisation, other academics have adopted a similarly sceptical perspective in explaining recent changes in the character of state welfare regimes in advanced industrial nations. Paul Pierson, for example, has argued that the pressures on existing forms of state welfare provision are undoubtedly real, but are largely due to domestic, rather than exogenous forces. This position can be summarised as follows:

- In advanced economies, manufacturing has been supplanted by the service sector as the dominant form of economic activity: service sector associated with slower rates of economic growth than manufacturing.
- Welfare states have reached 'maturity', providing an ever-increasing range and depth of services: increasingly costly.
- Demographic change: an aging population and reduction in the fiscal base necessary to sustain welfare provision. (In Palier and Sykes, 2001)

Thus, it is not necessarily the pernicious influence of 'globalisation' that exerts pressure on state welfare provision, but domestic factors illustrative of welfare states and economies at a particular stage of development.

According to Taylor-Gooby (2002), despite the dominance of neo-liberal ideology on the world stage from the 1980s to the 1990s, the majority of western welfare states experienced increases in or maintenance of existing levels of social spending as a percentage of GDP. At face value, this evidence suggests that despite changes in the nature of the global economy, welfare regimes in advanced industrial nations have proved strongly resilient. However, the raw data do mask significant changes. Thus, whilst expenditure on state welfare has remained generally high, the reasons for and nature of that expenditure paint a less rosy picture. Much of the increase in welfare spending over the period covered by the data could be attributed to economic failure by paying, for example, higher levels of unemployment benefit – in the UK, during the deep economic recessions of the early 1980s and during 1989–92. Many of the trends identified by George listed above suggest that although welfare expenditure has generally increased, the character of provision has altered, with states favouring more restrictive, disciplinary forms of social policy. (See Shin (2000) for discussion of the widespread adoption of 'active' labour market measures.)

## Citizenship and Conditionality: Rebuilding Support for State Welfare?

Wherever the truth lies in the above debate, the importance of globalisation in shaping recent debates on the nature of social citizenship in the UK cannot be understated, since New Labour governments from 1997 have clearly and unashamedly set out to recast social citizenship in terms of the language of reciprocity, rights and responsibilities in order to meet the perceived challenges and pressures presented by globalisation. In what follows, attention will focus on the New Labour social policy agenda in an attempt to assess the extent to which it provides a basis for inclusion and social solidarity, drawing upon recent work by Dwyer (2002) and Lister et al. (2003) which has attempted to gauge the opinions of welfare-service users and citizens' own self-perceptions of their status in relation to a range of policy developments. New Labour's vision of citizenship centres on the idea of 'active citizens': simply expressed, this is a rejection of neo-liberals' expectation that people should be left to fend for themselves in the arena of the free-market economy, but also a rejection of the idea of a 'passive citizenry' – whilst welfare provision is viewed as a legitimate state activity, the government's version of the welfare contract requires citizens to do all they can to equip themselves with the necessary skills to enable them to meet the rapidly changing demands of a global economy.

In a speech in South Africa in October 1996, Blair expressed these values quite unambiguously:

> At the heart of everything New Labour stands for is the theme of rights and responsibilities. For every right we enjoy, we owe responsibilities . . . You can take but you can give too. That basic value informs New Labour policy. (In Deacon, 2000: 11)

At a more specific level, the summary to the Green Paper *New Ambitions for Our Country: A New Contract for Welfare* (DSS, 1998c) illustrates clearly the government's vision of the purpose of a reformed welfare state:

> We need a new 'contract' between citizen and state, with rights matched by responsibilities. We will rebuild the welfare state around the work ethic: work for those who can; security for those who cannot. (In Heron and Dwyer, 1999: 92)

The impact of this policy agenda and its ideological assumptions has proved to be a source of considerable controversy amongst academics, and forms part of a wider debate on whether or not New Labour can be genuinely considered to be a social democratic party (Freeden, 1999). Can social policies guided by such rhetoric form a basis for solidarity and inclusion? A common thread to much criticism of New Labour policy concerns its 'moralistic' approach to citizenship and welfare. The government has been criticised by both left and right in this regard: much left-wing angst centres upon social security policy and its allegedly punitive and harsh view of the poorest and most vulnerable groups in society (Jones and Novak, 1999). For example, the New Deal, home–school contracts, Probationary Tenancy Periods and Anti-Social Behaviour Orders have been cited as evidence of this. From the right, the neo-liberal rallying cry of 'nanny state' has in recent times begun to reassert itself, notably in relation to New Labour public health policy (Toynbee, 2004). There is a certain degree of disingenuousness to these lines of attack. By definition, all social policies have a moral basis of one sort or another – the creation of a welfare state in the 1940s was a moral decision, as was the sustained attack on the values and institutions of that welfare state in the 1980s; thus, it might be a useful idea in terms of the conduct of debate if academics, whatever their political preference, referred to policies as being ones which they disapprove of rather than imputing an inherently pejorative character to the term 'moralistic'.

Alan Deacon (2002) has argued that much left-wing criticism of New Labour is based upon a selective interpretation of the history of progressive thought, reflecting the dominance amongst social policy academics of what he calls the 'Titmuss paradigm'. This refers to the enormous influence on the development of social policy as an academic discipline by the late Professor Richard Titmuss: Titmuss, for most of his career was an avid supporter of unconditional forms of welfare provision and retained a passionate belief in the altruistic nature of human beings. Accordingly, if social policies were to have an integrative function and foster a sense of solidarity and community, they would have to be universal and non-judgemental in nature, available to all and not just targeted at the poorest members of society. Titmuss was a supporter of the great Christian socialist thinker R.H. Tawney and shared his belief in the importance of equality. However, according to Deacon, Titmuss avoided those aspects of Tawney's thought that ran counter to the values outlined above, principally his less optimistic view of the nature of humanity – people could be 'sinners' as well as 'saints' and hence had responsibilities and duties in addition to rights. Deacon suggests that the dominance of the Titmuss paradigm in social policy – the neglect of the importance of responsibilities, as well as rights – created an intellectual void on the left that presented a political gift to the right. Citing the theologian Ronald Preston, Deacon contends that Titmuss and the large cadre of academics that followed him were 'misled by the utopian element in Tawney's thought (without noting his qualifications). They often make the mistake of stressing only the dignity of man; they underplay his sinfulness. This . . . has the effect of presenting people of conservative disposition with an entirely unnecessary weapon' (Preston, 1979, cited in Deacon, 2002: 21–22).

The emphasis on responsibilities in New Labour rhetoric reflects the desire to avoid this alleged political error as a key part of the government's ambition to restore popular support for welfare and thus extend social solidarity. Leading figures in New Labour, not least Blair himself, contend that the electorate would be more willing to share scarce resources via tax-funded welfare programmes if it approves of the attitudes and behaviour of those who benefit from such programmes. Deacon claims that this is not simply a contractual relationship between state and individual – it illustrates Blair's belief that a good society needs to be founded on 'duty' and a sense of responsibility for the welfare of others (ibid.: 110–11). This returns us to the thesis of Wolfe and Klausen: that increasingly heterogeneous societies are arguably associated with less willingness to share resources than in the early days of the welfare state and that for a society to be more willing to extend solidarity is dependent upon the mutual responsibilities imposed by a citizenship constructed in the language of reciprocity. Further articulation of similar ideas can be found in the work of the former New Labour minister John Denham, who resigned from the government over the invasion of Iraq. In an analysis of research conducted in his own Southampton constituency, Denham coined the phrase 'the fairness code' as a means of summarising the expressed attitudes of a sample of his constituents towards welfare and citizenship. He defined this term as 'a simple assertion of an appropriate connection between effort and reward' (Denham, 2004: 29). In a clear rejection of the assumptions of the Titmuss paradigm, Denham asserts that: 'The left needs to regain confidence in the ability of public policy to change behaviour. We need to lose our fear of being "judgemental" . . . In principle, each interaction with public services should reinforce the idea of responsible use.' An overall approach to welfare constructed on these terms would foster a sense of 'earned citizenship' (ibid.: 32). How do such views correspond with other evidence on public perceptions of citizenship and solidarity? This is an important question to ask given that, according to Lister et al. (2003), there is little empirical knowledge of people's self-perception as citizens. Dwyer's (2002) investigation of the views of a range of welfare service users found considerable levels of support for conditional forms of welfare provision, though the level of this support tended to vary markedly from service to service, with conditionality being regarded as far less appropriate in determining access to health care than to housing. Lister et al. (2003) found that, from a complex range of responses, their survey group of young people demonstrated a greater awareness of responsibilities rather than of rights, suggesting that communitarian models of citizenship were the most commonly understood, and that when asked about 'good' and 'bad' notions of citizenship, expression of opinions on attitudes, values and behaviour were far more commonly articulated than aspects of 'good' citizenship relating to political participation. The extent to which such understandings are influenced by government policy and rhetoric or reflect already held beliefs is impossible to ascertain: the degree to which we are either encouraged or dismayed by the apparent prevalence of such conceptions of citizenship over others is entirely a matter of individual opinion and fuel for debate.

---

**Activity 3**

*'An increasing emphasis on conditionally based notions of reciprocity is the only means of securing long-term support for the welfare state.' Discuss the validity of this statement.*

---

## Citizenship as Membership of a Community: Extending Social Justice?

The New Labour emphasis on active citizenship and reciprocity, based on work for all who can, utilising the tax and benefits system to promote a vision of the 'good society', represents one important attempt to increase support for state welfare and social solidarity. How long this particular paradigm will retain political ascendancy is for time to determine and history to judge. So much space has been devoted to it in this section simply because of its current social and political importance. Before we conclude, there is space to briefly consider two other possible bases of social citizenship and solidarity. Firstly, rather than centring citizenship on normative models based on participation and reflecting prescribed attitudes, values and behaviour, another possibility lies in citizenship and solidarity being equated with membership of or residence in a state or community. Such approaches have been championed as a far more socially just and inclusionary means of enhancing citizenship and solidarity, based as they are on a single trigger criterion of residence, rather than work-based insurance contributions, as we shall see. However, it is important to recognise that allocation of citizenship rights according to residence in a community does not axiomatically mean a deepening of that citizenship. The classic example to cite in this regard is the 1834 Poor Law Amendment Act, which offered universal entitlement to relief to all persons with legal settlement in a parish or union of parishes. However, the deliberately stigmatising nature of a system of relief based upon less eligibility and the workhouse test conferred pauper status upon its recipients, singling them out as the feckless, work-shy or improvident who were unable or unwilling to sustain a 'respectable' independent existence. By contrast, proponents of more recent forms of residency-based entitlement have the opposite intention – the enhancement of citizenship. A prominent example of this is the concept of the citizens' (or basic) income, advocated in various forms by a number of academics (Faulks, 2000). Faulks explains this as a guaranteed sum paid to all adults, regardless of employment status, financed out of general and corporate taxation, which thus 'frees citizenship from market constraints' (ibid.: 119). Faulks's own favoured interpretation of a basic income would provide payment on the basis of community recognition of members' basic needs. Most variants on the citizens' income thus entail by definition a clear break with the contributory based model of solidarity established following the Beveridge Report, recognising and rewarding the efforts of those individuals without the contributions records to benefit from insurance-based provision, notably women who, as all evidence shows, tend to suffer more breaks in paid employment than men due, for example, to disproportionate time undertaking child care and social care responsibilities. In addition, it is argued, citizens' income would reduce the administrative complexity, cost and executive discretion associated with means-tested benefits.

On similar lines to the citizens' income, the debate over the long-term problems associated with pension reform have gained further impetus with the possibility of the government in future implementing some form of citizens' pension. This has been championed by Alan Johnson, the former Secretary of State for Work and Pensions, with residence, rather than national insurance contributions as the basis of entitlement. The proposals are supported by Age Concern England, whose Director-General Gordon Lishman stated that 'millions of women, carers, low-paid and part-time workers . . . are being failed by today's system . . . A citizens' pension, if paid at a higher level to the existing basic state pension, could be one way of doing this and is a welcome addition to the debate' (in Wintour and White, 2005). The attractions of both the citizens' income and citizens' pension in terms of their potential to enhance social citizenship are obvious, but they are not unproblematic concepts. The key questions here concern funding and work incentives. To become political realities, both ideas depend upon the generation of sufficient electoral support: can enough people be persuaded to extend solidarity on such an unconditional basis?

## 'Cosmopolitan' and 'Post-national' Citizenship: the Shape of Things to Come, or 'Nonsense on Stilts'?

'Citizenship has little meaning, conceptually or empirically, outside of the context of the modern national state' (Brodie, 2002: 379). As this statement suggests, citizenship rights have historically been conferred by individual nation states, but, as Murphy and Harty (2003: 181) point out, nation states have been increasingly affected by 'increased enforcement and monitoring of international and European human rights conventions' which enables, for example, labour migrants or refugees access to certain benefit or other citizenship rights. The range of theoretical approaches and arguments deployed in this field are immensely complex and involved, and space permits only passing reference to them here. However, for the purposes of this chapter we need to briefly consider the possibility that notions of 'cosmopolitan' or 'world citizenship' provide a possible means of extending social citizenship in individual nation states. Simply put, these theoretical positions emphasise the importance of citizenship based on our shared humanity, rather than a shared national identity (Murphy and Harty: ibid.). Critics of these perspectives provide arguments that suggest the need for caution amongst those potentially supportive of this position. In a critique of the ideas of cosmopolitans such as Martha Nussbaum, Brett Bowden (2003: 356–7) points out the hard truth that, whatever the appeal of, for example, the United Nations Declaration of Human Rights, 'it is still states that are invested with the primary responsibility for securing and maintaining those rights'. Whatever one's views on the association of citizenship with the nation state, the continuing reality of states as the providers (or withholders) of citizenship rights arguably renders conceptions of world citizenship meaningless: 'World citizenship is nonsense; active world citizenship is nonsense on stilts' (Heater, 1990, in Bowden, 2003: 352).

From a social policy perspective, the importance of this is particularly important to the recent debates over the treatment of asylum seekers and refugees in western democracies with advanced welfare states (see, e.g., Bloch and Schuster, 2002). The fact that the treatment of such people varies so much from state to state, and that their experience at the hands of welfare regimes is often discriminatory, offering welfare rights on an unequal basis to existing citizens, suggests that reliance on supra-national agencies or decrees provides no firm basis for the advance of citizenship. Indeed, the fact that many asylum seekers and refugees are effectively stateless only serves to exacerbate their vulnerability. As Hannah Arendt argued: 'The Rights of Man, supposedly inalienable, proved to be unenforceable . . . whenever people appeared who were no longer citizens of any sovereign state' (1967, in Bowden, 2003: 357).

---

**Activity 4**

*Assess the potential of notions of 'cosmopolitan' citizenship as a basis for enhancement of social citizenship rights. Is the increasing influence of supra-national bodies both inevitable and desirable, or, as Roger Scruton (2004) argues, a threat to liberty?*

---

# Conclusion

To summarise, this chapter has attempted to argue the case for approaches to social policy based on the primary objective of extending social solidarity as being the most effective means of promoting a more cohesive society. The Beveridgean interpretation of solidarity, despite its advantages compared to what had gone before, failed in the long run because major changes in post-war society meant that it came to be regarded as an inadequate basis of citizenship. This does not mean, however, that attempts to forge agreement and solidarity on the nature of welfare should be abandoned: all patterns of social provision and the ideas that govern them are creatures of their time and are likely to require revision as societies and attitudes change. Group rights are not the answer, since by definition they are arguably more likely to promote social division at the expense of solidarity. We have briefly examined New Labour's emphasis on active citizenship as a response to the perceived pressures of globalisation, followed by the less conditional vision of the citizen's income and the idea of cosmopolitan citizenship. In terms of enhancing social citizenship and building solidarity, all three approaches have their strengths and weaknesses which will have greater or lesser appeal depending on one's own political inclinations. As Lister et al. (2003) remind us, however, citizenship should not be thought of in terms of rigidly demarcated theoretical perspectives, since evidence suggests that in the real world people understand the concept in fluid terms, expressing opinions that apply across the spectrum of dry categories constructed by academics. To close, the opinion offered here is that within the context of the nation state, a sense of social citizenship based on commonly agreed (as far as that is possible) principles regarding the respective roles, rights and responsibilities of the individual and state is the most realistic means of preserving and extending support for state welfare in the long term.

---

### Further Reading

Deacon, A. (2002) *Perspectives on Welfare: Ideas, Ideologies and Policy Debates*. Buckingham: Open University Press.

Delanty, G. (2000) *Citizenship in a Global Age: Society, Culture, Politics*. Buckingham: Open University Press.

Faulks, K. (2000) *Citizenship*. London: Routledge.

# NINE

# Cultural Turns, Post-structuralism and Social Policy
*Beth Widdowson*

---

**Outline Points**

- The meaning of post-structural and cultural analysis.
- How the 'cultural turn' in the social sciences changes the way we see and understand social welfare.
- How key strands of Foucaultian post-structural analysis – power, knowledge and discourse – reveal the complex processes by which social policy is constituted.
- How and why cultural analysis works to expand the terrain of social policy.
- The challenges and tensions post-structuralism poses for social-policy analysts.

---

## Introduction

> The meaning of the welfare state is not a simple matter of definition. If it was we could short-circuit all [the] difficult arguments [about what the welfare state means] merely by imposing the superior – most rigorous, most consensual, most scientific definition . . . But the problem with meaning is that meanings are not fixed. On the contrary, they are changeable and contested. This is the profound sense of 'it depends what you mean by welfare states' since the meaning of the phrase 'welfare state' is neither stable nor uncontested. This is the point of entry to the cultural turn. (Clarke, 2004: 18)

This extract captures the chimeric quality of the welfare state. In it, Clarke challenges the idea that the welfare state is a fact 'in itself', and encourages us to think of it instead as something that is constructed through meaning and interpretation. This point may initially seem counter-intuitive or out of sync with our everyday experiences. These experiences are likely to be shaped by various kinds of contact and engagement with the welfare state, all of which seem to testify to its 'in fact' nature. But if we pause for a moment we can see that starting with the fact of the welfare state barely scratches the surface, as the fact we start with is only rendered meaningful through interpretation or knowledge. For instance, the way in which we see the welfare state is likely to be shaped by aspects of our personal identity and experience. Disabled people may therefore see the welfare state differently to those who are defined as able-bodied. Likewise, ethnic minority groups may see it differently from ethnic majority groups. Being young, old, homosexual, heterosexual, male or female may also shape the way in which we see and interpret the welfare state.

Likewise, viewed from some perspectives, the welfare state is about class. For example, when seen through a Marxist lens, the welfare state is about class inequality and class conflict. This contrasts sharply with the welfare state we see when we look though a liberal lens, and the emphasis it places on notions of the individual and the market.

---

**Activity 1**

*Take a moment to think about how liberal and Marxist analyses see the welfare state. What social relations do they emphasise?*

---

During the last thirty years or so, social sciences have taken a cultural turn. Though relatively late in taking this turn compared to academic disciplines like sociology, cultural analysis is now becoming an established part of the academic discipline of social policy. This turn to matters cultural has worked to illuminate the complexity of meanings that are attached to the welfare state, and the complicated interplay that exists between social difference and social inequality. Encompassing a wide range of theoretical influences, ranging from cultural or revisionist forms of Marxism (e.g. Gramscian and Althusserian) and feminism, through to postmodernism, post-structuralism, phenomenology and symbolic interationism, the cultural turn in its simplest sense means taking culture seriously. Emphasising how it involves an expansive engagement with the ideological, Clarke offers a more comprehensive and precise definition, and argues that the cultural turn involves:

> Diverse sources of interest in the cultural, ideological, discursive or symbolic features of social welfare . . . There has always been work within social policy around the topic of ideology. However, this has tended to be in the form of ideology conceived as a relatively systematic body of politically oriented ideas which have – to a greater or lesser extent – influenced the development of social welfare. By contrast, the cultural turn in social policy has treated the realm of ideology in a more expansive way – as involving the implicit assumptions as well as explicit ideological conceptions that have informed the social character of welfare . . . It

enables an approach that moves beyond treating 'society' as a backdrop or passive context against which welfare states are studied . . . From a 'cultural' standpoint, contexts are active and productive: they shape and constitute what is possible, imaginable, knowable and desirable because they embody (contested) imaginaries. (2004: 47–8)

The cultural turn, therefore, challenges the notion that the welfare state is a 'fact' in itself. It engages with ideological matters but does so in a way that explores the everyday meanings that shape the way we see welfare. Also, and related, it pushes against the boundaries that conventionally define the welfare state. It does this by challenging the notion that the welfare state is somehow divorced from society: that a clear line divides the two. Instead, it sees the two as being mutually constitutive and looks at how social relations shape the welfare state and how the welfare state shapes social relations.

This chapter looks at how the cultural turn transforms and expands how we see welfare. The second section briefly explores some of the movements underlying the cultural turn, looking in particular at how social policy and the post-Second World War consensus around the welfare state became unsettled through the mobilisations of different social movements and conflicting political ideologies. Section three very briefly notes how post-structuralism differs from other theories of social welfare. Moving on to a more detailed exploration of the work and ideas of Michel Foucault, I look in particular at the way in which the 'cultural' is illuminated through the concept of discourse. The final section offers a brief summary and makes some concluding comments about the tensions and challenges a Foucauldian analysis suggests for social policy.

## Movements towards the Cultural Turn

During the 1970s, radical social policy and Marxist analyses were virtually synonymous. Offering compelling insights into how the welfare state worked to reproduce rather than combat class inequality, Marxist analyses argued that the real meaning of the welfare state turned on class – that it was about class control, class conflict and class inequality (Gough, 1979). In doing so it offered a sharp contrast to, and critique of, orthodox social policy analysis and its social administration foundations which were constituted initially in preparing people to work in welfare professions like social work; a feature which engendered an eclectic and empiricist theoretical base (Brown, 1983). Rooted in social-reformist political ideologies, this orthodoxy tended to see the welfare state as a 'good deed in a naughty world – a charitable, non-productive burden borne on the back of the 'normal' productive institutions of the economy (Donnison, 1962, cited in Brown, 1983: 95).

Marxist analyses offer a far less sanguine vision of what the welfare state means than that offered by orthodox analysts. The two perspectives nonetheless share important common ground, and are each firmly rooted in the foundation ideas of Enlightenment thought, which turn on progress, justice, equality, reason

(O'Brien and Penna, 1998). Both perspectives are predicated on the idea that history has a clear, overarching story-line or narrative. They also agree that the story-line involves progressive movements forwards, even though they radically diverge on what constitutes progress. In addition, the assumption that there is such a thing as a 'rational universal subject', and that this subject or subjects constitute the drivers or agents of historical progress – is shared by both.

By the end of the 1970s this shared ground became less certain. Social policy – both in the sense of government policies and the academic discipline – found itself standing on increasingly 'shaky ground' (Clarke, 2004: 11). Orthodox ways of seeing the welfare state which had become sedimented or settled in the post-Second World War period became unsettled (Lewis, 1998). Rather than seeing the welfare state as an essentially 'good deed in a naughty world', commentators on the right inverted this post-war social policy sensibility and argued instead that it represented a burdensome 'bad deed' in a market-driven world. On the left, the (re-)emergence of various social movements – feminist, anti-racist, gay, lesbian and disability – added to, and in some cases simultaneously critiqued, Marxist perspectives. Like Marxist analyses, these were highly critical of the welfare state. Working to show the social and cultural differences though which welfare was both constituted, and constitutive of, these different movements demonstrated how this involved processes of subordination, marginalisation and exclusion.

Feminist movements emphasised the patriarchal roots and practices of welfare and linked these to patriarchal relations in other social domains like the family. Emphasising how the composition of the welfare state was informed by patriarchal processes and assumptions, the feminist movement demonstrated how it was implicated in the (re)production of women's inequality in society through education, social security and so on. In concern with parallel mobilisations around sexuality, (dis)ability and ethnicity, these movements collectively emphasised that the meaning of the welfare state could not simply and only be seen in class terms (Taylor, 1996). This politicisation and revelation of diverse and intersecting power relationships worked to open up and expand the boundaries of social policy. Traditionally conceptualising the relationship between public and private in terms of the state and the market/private sector, the emphasis feminism places on the family as a site of welfare thus reconfigured notions of the 'private' to include the private, domestic sphere (Pascall, 1986; Lister, 2000).

The meaning of the welfare state – where it began and ended, whether it was a good or bad thing, if it was about class and/or patriarchal and/or other forms of control mapped around (dis)ability, ethnicity, sexuality and other forms of difference – therefore become contested and unstable. Intersections between different social divisions further underlined this process. Emphasising the plurality and complexity of identity, this worked to challenge the idea that one source of identity – being working class, being a woman and so on – could be privileged as the primary locus of difference. So, for instance, if we take gender as our focus and the unity category of 'woman' more specifically, it becomes apparent that this division is cross-cut by other differences. Thus disabled women within the feminist movement argued that it, and its academic analogue, valorised the experiences of able-bodied women and marginalised those of disabled women (Morris, 1991). Likewise, black feminists asserted that some of the movement's key concepts and demands privileged the experiences and concerns of white women (Carby, 1982). These various divisions around difference made the meaning of the welfare state even more complicated, as it became apparent that the meaning of welfare was not only about gender and/or class but also about differences of (dis)ability, ethnicity and so on. This point, and the challenge it suggests for developing a fully inclusive social policy, is noted by Lister:

> Whatever the area of social policy, an undifferentiated gender analysis obscures the concerns of different groups of women in the same way that an undifferentiated class analysis has ignored gender and other social divisions . . . Thus, for example, so long as a gendered analysis of community care focused on women as carers, it elided the sometimes different perspectives of disabled and older women. Likewise, a heterosexist norm serves to write lesbians out of the welfare picture. (Lister, 2000: 33)

Placing the 'politics of difference' firmly on the agenda of social policy, these developments also raised important questions about the nature and operation of power. Thus grand or 'big picture' theories like Marxism or liberalism pose political questions almost exclusively in terms of the state (O'Brien and Penna, 1998). This, as feminist analyses suggest, places other important domains of power like the family, and the intersections that exist between it and the state, on the margins. Such grand or 'big picture' theories also tend to turn on economistic and top-down accounts of how power works. When applied to the study of the welfare state this has the effect of privileging the economic over the cultural and tends to suggest that the 'proper' subject of social policy investigation should centre on the redistributive function of welfare (Clarke, 2004). There are two problems with such a formulation. First, while the economic is clearly crucial in terms of social inclusion and well-being, it is not the only factor (Hillyard and Watson, 1994). Second, and perhaps more fundamentally, economic or material questions around redistribution are necessarily filtered and made meaningful through cultural processes and practices. So, even if redistribution is accepted as the proper focus of social policy, in order to comprehensively engage with this we need to take cultural matters fully into account (Clarke, 2004). Such a comprehensive engagement makes us attentive to the complex interplay between difference and inequality. It therefore illuminates the way in which poverty and inequality are unevenly distributed according to gender, (dis)ability, ethnicity and other forms of difference.

## Foucault and Post-structuralism

In a rich and expansive body of work that spans explorations of sexuality, madness, crime, punishment and the development of medical expertise, Foucault investigates both private and public domains. In common with other post-structuralists like Derrida and Barthes, his work is concerned with language and how language constructs meaning. It therefore clearly foregrounds the cultural. Further, while the economic is present in the analysis he develops, Foucault's approach suggests this is only rendered meaningful through the cultural.

Rather than starting with the notion of a rational meaningful subject, and seeing language as a simple reflection and expression of meaning, post-structural analysis inverts this logic and its Enlightenment roots. For post-structuralists, language and the various ways in which it is evidenced – spoken, written and so on – is instead seen to provide the medium through which the subject and 'social reality' is constituted (Hall, 2001). Moreover, because language is fluid, ever changing and both historically and culturally relative, the emphasis post-structuralism places on language means that it also takes issue with other key Enlightenment ideas.

Thus if language constitutes 'reality', and language is relative rather than universal, this suggests a rejection of the idea that history can be read as an evolving 'big story'.

Such overarching accounts – termed meta-narratives by post-structuralists – are thus firmly rejected. It also means that power is seen as disperse and fluid in its operation and is no longer understood as a quality primarily associated with the state or class. Rather power is a quality that through language is enacted and mediated through a variety of different institutions, apparatuses and process. When seen through a post-structural lens, the welfare state is therefore less certain and fixed. It is not a fact in itself, but is instead constitutive of, and constituted by, a variety of different competing interests, meanings and power relations.

### Foucault: Power, Knowledge and Discourse

Foucault's work reveals the pervasive nature of power. He explores how it permeates and shapes all social relations: from teacher and student, social worker and client, doctor and patient through to parent and child. As noted above, orthodox and Marxist analyses see power as operating in a top-down and negative fashion. Rather than seeing power as something that 'excludes', 'represses', 'conceals', Foucault, in contrast, sees it as productive and creative. Power, in his eyes, therefore 'produces reality' (Foucault, 1977: 194). Arguing against top-down conceptualisations, where power is seen as a property or possession, he suggests power should be regarded as a strategy. Elaborating on what he terms the 'micro-physics' of power, he argues that power and knowledge are intimately connected and intertwined:

> (P)ower is exercised rather than possessed; it is not the privilege, acquired or preserved, of the dominant class, but the overall effect of its strategic positions . . . Furthermore this power is not exercised simply as an obligation of prohibition on those who 'do not have it'; it invests them, is transmitted by them and through them, just as they themselves, in their struggles against it, resist the grip it has on them. This means that these relations go

right down into the depth of society, that they are not localised in the relations between the state and its citizens or on the frontier between class . . . [P]ower produces knowledge . . . power and knowledge directly imply one another; that there is no power relation without the correlative constitution of a field of knowledge, nor any knowledge that does not presuppose and constitute at the same time power relations. (Foucault, 1977: 26–7)

The power–knowledge nexus is therefore key from a Foucauldian perspective, and it is through discourse 'that power and knowledge are joined together' (Foucault, 1978: 100). Further, while discourse starts with language, it is about more than the simply linguistic, as Livia and Hall note:

> By discourse, Foucault meant 'a group of statements which provide a language for talking about a particular topic at a particular historical moment' . . . Discourse is about the production of knowledge through language. But . . . since all social practices entail meaning, and meanings shape and influence what we do – our conduct – all practices have a discursive aspect (Hall, 1992, p. 291). It is important to note that the concept of discourse in this usage is not purely a 'linguistic' concept. It is about language and practice . . . Discourse, Foucault argues, constructs the topic. It defines and produces the objects of our knowledge. It governs the way that a topic can be meaningfully talked about and reasoned about. It influences how ideas are put into practice and used to regulate the practice of others. Just as a discourse 'rules' in certain ways of talking about a topic, defining an acceptable and intelligible way to talk, write, or conduct oneself, or also, by definition, it 'rules out', limits and restricts other[s] . . . Foucault does not deny that things have a real, material existence in the world. What he does argue is that 'nothing has any meaning outside of discourse . . . [And that] things meant something and were true . . . only within a specific historical context'. (1997: 44–6)

Discourses are therefore about more than language. The way in which discourses construct meaning through the knowledge–power nexus makes language count. It shapes how we see welfare, defines what is and is not possible and regulates policy and practice. Actions and consequences flow from language. Social policy – as government policy – constitutes welfare subjects as 'lone parents', 'job seekers', 'cared-for children', 'service users' and so on and this process of constitution has real consequences for the lives of those constructed in this fashion. For example, Parton's (1996) exploration of social work discourses reveals how notions of surveillance and control are embedded within this. The study explores how this translates into a professional practice that involves regulating rather than challenging social inequality. Likewise, Lee-Tweweek's (1998) exploration of discourses of care in a nursing home for older people demonstrates how this resulted in the objectification of the older people, who were seen as something to be managed rather than as sentient, feeling and rounded individuals.

Further, discourses are not hermetically sealed. They are not based on simple, static, binary divisions whereby one discourse is subordinate to and in the power of another dominant discourse. Rather, discourses (re)animate and speak to each other. Foucault clearlys explores and illustrates this point in *The History of Sexuality* (1978, Arguing against essentialist notions of sexuality, where sexuality is seen as a fact that is fixed through different and intersecting discourses of sexuality. In doing so, emphasis is placed on how discourses speak to each other, and constitute sites of both repression and resistance. Citing the example of homosexuality, he thus argues:

> We must not imagine a world divided between accepted discourse and excluded discourse, or between the dominant discourse and the dominated one; but as a multiplicity of discursive elements that can come into play in various strategies ... We must make allowance for the complex and unstable process whereby discourse can be both an instrument and an effect of power, but also a stumbling block, a point of resistance and a starting point for an opposing strategy. Discourse transmits and produces power, it reinforces it, but also undermines and exposes it, renders it fragile and makes it possible to thwart ... [T]he appearance in nineteenth century psychiatry, jurisprudence, and literature of a whole series of discourses on the species and sub-species of homosexuality, inversion, pederasty and 'psychic hermaphrodism' made possible a strong advance of social controls into this area of 'perversity', but it also made possible the formation of a 'reverse' discourse; homosexuality began to speak in its own behalf, to demand that its legitimacy or 'naturality' be acknowledged, often in the same vocabulary, using the same categories by which it was medically disqualified. (1978: 100–1)

The feature of discourse makes it possible to explore the criss-crossing and multi-dimensional quality of social difference and inequalities. So, for example, Phoenix (2000) looks at the intersections between discourses of masculinity and racialised discourses in her study around the educational 'under-performance' of boys. In doing so, she offers an expansive engagement with the ideological. Looking at how everyday meanings have real-life consequences, she explores the different intersections between racialised discourses, discourses of masculinity and the discourse of educational achievement. Indicating the way in which hegemonic forms of masculinity in part turned on a resistance to teachers and education, Phoenix notes how these features were particularly ascribed to, and unevenly mobilised by, black boys of African-Caribbean descent, and how these intersections operated to constitute their educational 'under-performance'.

Likewise, Lee-Tweweek's (1998) study of care in a nursing home, cited above, explores the way in which the various control and distancing strategies used by female nursing auxiliaries in part involved a resistance to gendered discourses of care, which turn on notions of femininity, nurture and compassion. She argues that auxiliaries saw their paid care work as having little to do with caring as it is generally conceived in the social imagination. She graphically evidences how resistance to such hegemonic discourses of care – and the localised strategies of power they express – involved the women care workers in a series of practices which constructed the bodies of those from whom they 'cared' as bodies to be managed and controlled.

### Bio-power and Disciplinary Power: Making Bodies Visible

Foucault identifies two kinds of power: disciplinary and bio-power. Both are mapped around the body and indeed much of the work in social policy is concerned with body work in one form or another; a feature which has only very recently begun to be noted in the academic discipline of social policy (Twigg, 2002). Thus 'disabled bodies "ethnic" bodies, children's bodies, sexualised bodies, old bodies, bodies in need, bodies in danger, bodies at risk are all well at the heart of the social' (Lewis, cited in Twigg, 2000: 37). Both forms of power turn on making bodies visible.

In the case of bio-power, this process of making visible is exercised at the level of population. Populations are monitored, differentiated and divided up – dates of birth, death, marriage and so on are recorded and registered. Rather than existing as an undifferentiated category, population becomes demography and something to be recorded and managed. Declining or increasing birth rates are monitored, putative imbalances between older and younger populations are revealed. Rendered meaningful through different discourses, these construct different and conflicting interpretations and policy prescriptions. So, for example, information on birth-rates may be mobilised with eugenic discourses. Likewise, forecasts of a demographic 'time-bomb', turning on a putative 'imbalance' between young and older workers, are wielded. These forecasts translate into contested policy prescriptions around migration and pension policies. For instance, certain kinds of immigration are encouraged to address skill shortages: a feature that has knock-on and negative implications for the countries from which such high-skilled labour, in areas like medicine, is 'recruited'. In the case of pensions, workers are made increasingly responsible for funding their own retirement. Such processes of responsibilisation in part turn on discouraging and enforcing the point that workers should not rely on the diminishing national 'pot' of state contributions (argued to result from a declining working-age population and increased levels of longevity) to fund their retirement.

---

**Activity 2**

*List some of the various ways populations are differentiated by demographic analysis:*

- *Select one of these and think about what kinds of meaning are attached or associated with this social difference. For example, what meanings are attached to being young, or older, or middle-aged, or to a one- or two-parent family?*
- *What kinds of different policy responses are evoked or associated?*

---

Disciplinary power is most systematically explored by Foucault in *Discipline and Punish* (1977). Charting the birth of the prison, it begins with a description of a 'public execution and a timetable' (1977: 7). The account of a public torture and execution in 1757 is graphic, the torture described sadistic in the extreme.

This is contrasted with a description of the punishment meted out in a juvenile prison less than a century later; a punishment which at first sight seems more humane in the sense that no death or physical torture is involved. Instead the punishment turns on the timetable and what this symbolises: the constant management, control, monitoring and surveillance of the prisoners' day-to-day life. Influential contemporaries in the field of criminology tended to conceive this shift as involving a progressive historical movement towards a more humane society, a view consistent with Enlightenment thought.

In contrast, Foucault interpreted the move from bloody, spectacular public tortures and executions to imprisonment as simply evidencing a different, equally present if less visible form of power and control. Suggesting that the end of the eighteenth century witnessed the eclipse of overtly physical punishments mediated through the sovereign power and rule of the king, he argues subtler and more pervasive forms of control developed in its wake. It is in making this case that he develops the concept of disciplinary power. In contrast to traditional, sovereign forms of power which turn on power that is seen, something that is physically and forcefully apparent, Foucault defines disciplinary power as a power that is exercised:

> through its invisibility; at the same time it imposes on those whom its subjects a principle of compulsory visibility. In discipline (power) it is the subjects who have to be seen. Their visibility assures the hold of the power that is exercised over them. It is the fact of constantly being seen, of being able always to be seen, that maintains the disciplined individual in his (or her) subjection . . . In a disciplinary regime . . . individualisation is 'descending': as power became more anonymous and more functional, those on whom it is exercised tend to be more strongly individualised; it is exercised by surveillance . . . by observation . . . by comparative measures that have the 'norm' as reference . . . In a system of discipline, the child is more individualised than the adult, the patient more than the healthy man (or woman), the madman (or madwoman) and the delinquent more than the normal and non-delinquent. (1977: 187–93)

Foucault regarded the panopticon as the model means of exercising disciplinary power. Involving a prison design by the social reformer Jeremy Bentham, the plan provided an exemplar of the features Foucault associated with the operation of disciplinary power. So, for example, the design specified that prisoners should be segregated from the rest of the society and isolated from each other, that they were to be subject to surveillance, that their daily routine was to be imposed and controlled, and that their activities should be constantly examined, monitored and recorded. Although the design was not executed it was very influential in the construction of prisons during the nineteenth century. Moreover, Foucault does not limit his analysis of disciplinary power in prisons – as the extract above indicates. He charts how various social institutions – the family, schools, hospitals, asylums, factories, workhouses – were implicated in the creation of what was defined as normal (and by association, what was defined as abnormal or deviant). For example, he noted the way in which processes of examination operated to divide up, monitor and sub-divide populations in areas like education and how these strategies of power were linked to expert knowledge. For Foucault, the 'judges' of normality are present everywhere, as he asserts we live in a 'society of the teacher–judge, the doctor–judge, the educator–judge, the social–worker–judge; it is on them that the . . . reign of the normative is based' (1977: 304).

---

**Activity 3**

*Think about the notion of examination and how this is applied within the expert fields of education and/or medicine:*

- *Identify the various ways people are subject to educational and/or medical examination, and the consequences this has for their lived experiences.*
- *Now try to identify some of the ways in which these processes of examination and the educational and/or medical discourses in which they are rooted are cross-cut by other discourses, organised around hegemonic notions of class, femininity, masculinity and so on.*

---

For example, in *Madness and Civilisation* (2001), Foucault argues against Enlightenment ideas that Reason (and conversely, Unreason or madness) are facts in themselves. Instead, he suggests that both are historically specific, mutually defining and socially constructed, and he explores the role of experts in constituting 'madness'. Noting the way in which different populations were divided up through the strategies of bio-power. Foucault demonstrated how an essentially undifferentiated population in the eighteenth century became translated into a plurality of populations from the later part of the century (sane/insane, able-bodied/disabled, employed/unemployed and so on). So, for instance, the 'mad' were separated from the 'bad' who were in turn separated from the 'sick'. Each were allocated their own institutional space, respectively the asylum prison and hospital. Exploring the interplay between the segregation of the 'mad' and the development of the science of (in)sanity (psychiatry, psychology, psychoanalysis) Foucault shows how the discourses of these different sciences of (in)sanity created, defined and elaborated on the category and experience of madness. So in this case, the expert or 'judge' of normality becomes the psychiatrist, psychologist or psychoanalyst.

Further, and underlining its pervasive quality, power is described as entering the body in the sense that disciplinary power also becomes a means by which we regulate ourselves. So, for instance, the 'humane' self-regulatory strategies emerging around the management of 'madness' in the nineteenth century, when compared with earlier strategies involving various forms of physical restraint and punishment, were seen by Foucault to signal 'madness mastered' rather than liberated. This observation has clear and apparent contemporary resonance if we think about the various ways in which we are increasingly being made responsible for our own well-being through various health campaigns. Such processes of responsibilisation turn on positioning us within various types of expert discourse. If we take the advice, we become involved in a process of self-regulation. If we do not, we may at some level feel that we should take the advice and/or mobilise alternative, counter discourses to render our position of resistance meaningful. Anti-smoking and various other health and social welfare policies are obvious examples here. For example, we are increasingly being encouraged and coerced into taking ever greater responsibility for securing our pension futures in older age. Expert knowledge, filtered through economic and political discourses that privilege the market, therefore constructs us as 'pension stakeholders' and place the onus of responsibility on us for saving for our older age (Widdowson, 2004). In some cases, such processes of responsibilisation may turn on making us an expert of ourselves. For instance, an expert patient becomes responsible for managing his or her own chronic illness. Alternatively, we may turn our own self-knowledge into expertise by struggling against dominant discourses or forms of knowledge. The disability movement offers a good example of this, in that it has very effectively mobilised self-knowledge through its development of the social model of disability. In doing so it has struggled against and challenged reductive, essentialist and hegemonic medical models of disability.

---

### Activity 4

*Identify a health or other public-welfare campaign targeted at changing behaviour:*

- *What kind of expert knowledge did it involve?*
- *What form of self-regulation did the campaign advocate and how was this encouraged through the language and images of the campaign?*
- *How did the campaign construct the target population and was the target population appealed to differently according to age, class, ethnicity, gender and other social divisions?*

---

## Conclusion

Post-structuralist perspectives look beyond and beneath the 'fact' of the welfare state, and in doing so challenge the idea that the welfare state can be seen as a 'fact' in itself. Viewed through a post-structuralist lens, the welfare state is instead seen as being both constituted by, and constitutive of, diverse, competing and conflicting meanings. From a Foucauldian perspective, discourses are the medium of constitution, and it is through explorations and engagements with discourse that the different meanings of welfare are illuminated. The concept of discourse is therefore crucial to a Foucauldian analysis, and it is important to note that the power–knowledge nexus on which discourse turns makes language matter in the sense that it is not just about linguistics but is also about action. Discourses thus have real and important consequences – they define, limit and constrain. But they also constitute points of resistance, 'stumbling blocks' against which to react and shape alternative strategies through counter-discourses.

Further, and related, because discourses are inherently plural and criss-crossing, the concept promotes and facilitates an engagement with diversity and complexity. Thus, not only can class be seen, so also can (dis)ability, gender ethnicity, sexuality and other social divisions, by exploring the various discourses that construct these difference, and the intersections that exist between them. Cultural analysis does not therefore deny the importance of class, or indeed challenge its objective reality any more than it does any other aspect of the social. Rather, it refuses to privilege it as the only or dominant focus of analysis (Clarke, 2000). Moreover, the fluid and disperse model of power on which the concept of discourse in part hinges, shifts the focus of analysis towards the everyday of social relations and enables horizontal and vertical ladders of meaning to be traced and explored. Thus, on the one hand, the concept enables us to move away:

> from the sublime ideas of the intellectual elite and towards the mundane discourses of disciplinary institutions that more directly affect the everyday life of the masses. Ideology is [therefore] no longer seen as the airy dialogue of great minds, but as the prosaic encounter of the criminal and criminologist, neurotic and therapist, child and parent, unemployed worker and welfare agency. (Poster, cited in Watson 2000: 70)

On the other hand, it makes it possible for us to look at how these local ladders of meaning connect with those which have a broader reach.

Foucauldian perspectives therefore clearly have much to add to how we see welfare. The concept of discourse, the nuance and fluid conceptualisation of power and the interconnections between this and forms of knowledge, facilitates an engagement with the cultural in its fullest sense. Nevertheless, it does raise important, difficult and challenging questions. In some sense, these all turn on the relativist position that lies at the heart of post-structuralist ways of seeing welfare and, related to this, the weight it gives to the social and social construction more specifically. Regarded as involving an 'over-socialised' account, it is argued that Foucauldian approaches simply involve replacing one form of determinism with another (Shilling, cited in Twigg, 2000). So, rather than being determined by 'real', material factors like class, social discourses become the medium through which welfare is determined. This point, and the questions it raises about the relationship between the social and the material (defined in terms of the body rather than the economic) is beginning to open up very fascinating lines of investigation within the discipline of social policy. And these investigations are particularly important because – as noted above – welfare work largely turns on body work, in one form or another (Twigg, 2002).

The relativist position of post-structuralist approaches to welfare generates further questions and tensions. These questions are not specific to social policy. Indeed they have spawned much debate within the philosophy of both the social and natural sciences. Nonetheless, the empirical and practitioner roots of ortho-dox social policy, and more specifically its commitment to social justice and equality – a commitment which is shared by both orthodox and radical perspec-tives – arguably makes these questions particularly difficult for the academic dis-cipline of social policy to come to terms with. Thus if we reject the idea of object reality or suggest that it may exist but it is beyond our comprehension, the idea that universals of truth, justice and equality exist is also rejected. Along with this rejection goes the idea that such universals can be used as a yardstick against which to measure a better or worse society or approach to welfare. This clearly generates tensions for the discipline of social policy and may explain why it was so late in taking the cultural turn and why its foothold continues to be less cer-tain than that gained in other disciplines. It might also explain the continuing and considerable forms of criticism, resistance and opposition that have been reg-istered against it from within the discipline itself; criticisms that have included accusations that post-structural theories act as an 'ideological smokescreen' and conceal pervasive patterns of social inequality (Taylor-Gooby, 1994: 385).

Marxist analyses have been particularly critical of post-structuralist approaches to welfare on account of the way they deny the objective reality of class relations and inequality (Mooney, 2000), and these resonate with those expressed around gender and class. For example, Skeggs (1997) argues that post-structuralist engage-ments with gender difference marginalise the relationship between class and gender, and the experiences of working-class women in particular. While these critiques are compelling and persuasive in emphasising the importance of both gender and class, the extent to which a Foucauldian perspective necessarily inhibits an engagement with these and other divisions is nonetheless contentious, as noted above. Thus, while it may deny the objective reality of class – in the sense that class, like other aspects of the social – is seen to be rendered meaningful only through discourse, this does not render class (or other social divisions) meaning-less. It simply means that it is not constructed as the primary or only significant site of difference and social inequality. In short, although looking at welfare through a post-structuralist lens means that no one form of social difference is constituted as 'the difference', this does not mean that differences of class, gender and other social differences are denied. Consequently, as long as these differences, and the intersections that exist between them, constitute 'differences that make a difference' (Hallett, cited in Lister, 2000: 33), they will, or should, continue to con-stitute important and vital fields of social policy investigation – irrespective of the analytic lens which is applied. And post-structuralist approaches, together with those more widely mapped around the cultural turn, for all the reasons outlined above, offer important, interesting and expansive ways of approaching such investigations. So, though not without contention, such approaches enrich our understanding of social policy in all its complexity.

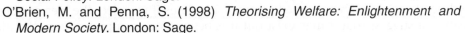

### Further reading

Clarke, J. (2004) *Changing Welfare, Changing Welfare States: New Directions in Social Policy.* London: Sage.
O'Brien, M. and Penna, S. (1998) *Theorising Welfare: Enlightenment and Modern Society.* London: Sage.
Taylor, D. (ed.) (1997) *Critical Social Policy.* London: Sage.

# TEN
# Living in a Material World
# Postmodernism and Social Policy
*Iain Ferguson*

---

### Outline Points

- Postmodern perspectives in social policy represent a break with the traditional *material* and *normative* concerns of the discipline.
- Postmodernism is a 'contrast' concept, challenging three aspects of modernism: modernisation, modernism (literary and artistic) and modernity.
- 'Incredulity towards metanarratives' is the central tenet of postmodernism.
- Within social policy, postmodern approaches have sought both to explain current societal transformations and also to provide a basis for more critical approaches within social welfare.
- There are strong historical, philosophical and political objections to postmodernism as both explanatory framework and basis for emancipatory practice. The concept of the 'radicalised Enlightenment' offers an alternative way of understanding and addressing the claims of oppressed groups within society.

## Introduction

Since its origins in the late nineteenth century, the discipline of social policy (or social administration, as it was known for much of that time) has been distinguished both by its overriding concern with the *material* conditions in which people live (particularly the 'problem' of poverty) and with ways of *improving* these conditions and/or *controlling* the behaviour of poor people. Its focus, in other words, has traditionally been both *material* and *normative*. Within traditional social administration approaches, that focus on people's material conditions often led to an atheoretical empiricism, a preoccupation with collating 'facts' (about poverty levels, for example) or evaluating existing policies with limited critical analysis of the wider political and economic framework in which these policies were developed. Similarly, the normative concern with improving people's living conditions was often underpinned by a naïve and uncritical notion of 'progress' which failed to recognise the role of welfare as a tool of social control and of the ways in which social policies often actively contributed to the oppression of large sectors of the population, such as unemployed people, women and black people (Williams, 1989). The development of a critical social policy in the 1970s and 1980s was a much-needed response to these limitations in traditional approaches. That said, even with these limitations, traditional social administration approaches produced much that was valuable in both uncovering and challenging the extent of inequality within contemporary capitalism (with Townsend's work on poverty being an obvious example – see, e.g., Townsend et al., 1988).

Postmodernism, the worldview with which this chapter is concerned, is based on a rejection of both material and normative approaches to understanding social life. In its underlying assumptions about the nature of the world – its *ontology* – it starts from the premise that language and appearances are all there is; there is no 'objective' reality or 'objective truth' outside of language, only different 'discourses' or 'narratives', different ways of making sense of the world, none more 'valid' than any other. In terms of its normative outlook, postmodernism's starting point is an 'incredulity towards metanarratives', a rejection of eighteenth-century Enlightenment notions of progress and, more particularly, of theories (known as 'metanarratives' or 'grand narratives') which seek to make sense of the world as a whole or *totality*. Such 'totalising' worldviews are seen as both misguided (since there is no single objective 'Truth', only many local 'truths') and also dangerous, since they may lead (and, postmodernists argue, have led) to the suppression of difference and diversity. Hence, insofar as postmodernism is concerned with social change at all, then at best, it is with small, local changes.

Not surprisingly perhaps, given the traditional emphases of social policy, postmodernism has had less impact on social policy than on other, less applied, academic disciplines (Taylor-Gooby, 1994). Paradoxically, however, given that a significant section of critical academic opinion sees postmodernism as a thoroughly reactionary philosophy which leads people *away from*, rather than *towards*, social change, its greatest impact within social policy (and even more so, social work) has been amongst those writers seeking to develop a theoretical foundation for a *critical* social policy and social work practice. The particular form of postmodernism to which these writers subscribe is usually referred to as 'weak' or 'affirmative' postmodernism, which seeks to combine elements of postmodernism with elements of structural social work and critical social policy. Pease and Fook, for example, argue that: 'We believe that a weak form of postmodernism informed by critical theory can contribute effectively to the construction of an emancipatory politics concerned with political action and social justice' (1999: 12). In an influential text, Leonard, a leading figure in critical social work and social policy in the 1970s, similarly argues that 'postmodernism provides a now essential ingredient in a revitalised Marxism' (Leonard, 1997: xiii).

The claim that postmodernism can provide the basis for a critical social policy and an emancipatory social work practice will be critically evaluated later in this chapter. Before then, however, it is necessary to attempt to define exactly what postmodernism is.

## What is Postmodernism?

Postmodernism is essentially a 'contrast' concept; it takes its meaning as much from what it claims to supersede or replace as from the positive elements of its definition (Kumar, 1995) Any discussion of postmodernism therefore has to start with a brief discussion of modernism and its related concept, modernity.

Like postmodernism, modernism is subject to many, wide-ranging definitions. In his definitive study, the late Marshal Berman made a useful distinction between three key terms associated with modernism. Firstly, *modernisation*, which refers to the economic, social and technological developments which emerged alongside capitalist society. Secondly, *modernism*, in the form of experimental movements in the arts from the futurists at the beginning of the twentieth century through to various tendencies in modern art in the 1960s. Finally, Berman refers to *modernity* as the radically transformed character of life under capitalism which began as a philosophical challenge (the Enlightenment) to traditionalism in the eighteenth century but reached its zenith in the major European and American cities of the late nineteenth and early twentieth centuries (Berman, 1982, 1999).

The major changes proclaimed by postmodernism mirror these three areas. In relation to economic and social development, adherents of postmodernism argue that capitalism has undergone a fundamental change, in one version from 'organised' to 'disorganised' capitalism (Lash and Urry, 1987), in another from a *Fordist* society, based on mass production involving the standardisation of products, Taylorist 'scientific management' of labour and assembly-line techniques, to *post-Fordism*, based on small-scale 'niche' production, the use of new computer-based technologies and with design and 'branding' a major selling-point (Burrows and Loader, 1994). The next section will consider the ways in which these ideas have been applied to welfare systems.

---

### Activity 1

*What objections might there be to the claim that capitalism has undergone a fundamental transformation in recent years?*

---

In relation to the second claim, postmodern art claims to have broken with modernist art movements and to be based on notions of eclecticism, pluralism and pastiche, the mixing of radically different elements and styles form different historical periods and different cultural traditions. As an example, postmodernists point to 1980s architecture, which often drew on old and new types of glass and brick, based around styles of architecture often centuries apart.

It is, however, for the philosophical challenge which it poses to modernism that postmodernism is most notorious. The nature of that challenge is summed up concisely (if in typically convoluted fashion) by one of postmodernism's leading thinkers:

> I define postmodern as incredulity toward metanarratives . . . The narrative function is losing . . . its great hero, its great dangers, its great voyages, its great goal. It is being dispersed in clouds of narrative language elements . . .
>
> Thus the society of the future falls . . . within the province of a . . . pragmatics of language particles. There are many different language games – a heterogeneity of elements. They only give rise to institutions in patches – local determinism.
>
> The decision-makers, however, attempt to manage these clouds of sociality according to input/output matrices. (Lyotard, 1984: xxiv)

'Incredulity towards metanarratives' is the central tenet of postmodernism. 'Metanarratives' are attempts to make sense of the world as an interconnected whole or *totality*. Examples would include Marxism and feminism. For Lyotard, Baudrillard and followers, such attempts are misplaced for two reasons. First, they are based on the modernist or Enlightenment assumption that it is possible to discover objective 'scientific' truth about the world in which we live. Following post-structuralist thinkers like Foucault and Derrida, however, postmodernists argue that there is no 'objective reality' outside of language to be discovered; only language games, each presenting their own version of 'truth' – there is no Truth with a capital 'T'. Postmodernism, then, is an extreme form of *social constructionism* (Burr, 2003) or *anti-realism*, in which there are only different social constructions or local narratives, each one as valid as the other.

A second reason for rejecting metanarratives, postmodernists argue, is that the notion of a single Truth usually involves the suppression of other 'truths'. Metanarratives, in other words, lead to oppression and totalitarianism. The conclusion is that attempts to make sense of the world as an interconnected whole are not only misguided but dangerous. Instead, we should recognise that there are many voices or narratives, all with equal validity, and celebrate this diversity (including uncovering these voices which have previously been suppressed by dominant narratives).

The attractions of this perspective for a radical social work and a critical social policy are not hard to see. The history of welfare is a history of the suppression of the voices of service users and of their oppression by services geared to containment and control rather than to meeting human need, even when conducted in the language of care and concern. One need only think, for example, of the ways in which biomedical understandings of mental ill-health have usually involved the suppression of service users' perspectives and experience (Rogers et al., 1993). In the next part of this chapter, the extent to which post-modernism can provide a firm theoretical basis for challenging such oppression will be considered in detail. First, however, it is necessary to consider some of the more general objections that have been made to postmodern theorising. These may be grouped under three headings: historical/sociological; philosophical; and ethical/political.

### Historical/Sociological Objections

As noted above, postmodernism is essentially a contrast concept. It implies that a particular historical period – modernity – is now over and has been replaced by a new period – postmodernity – characterised by different forms of social and industrial organisation, different forms of art and literature. These claims, however, have been challenged both on the grounds of their historical accuracy and also on their interpretation of the changes that have taken place. In terms of literature and art, for example, Callinicos has argued that many of the features supposedly associated with postmodern art – the juxtaposition of different styles, often from different historical periods, the use of montage, and so on – are in fact defining features of *modernism*, typical of the work of early twentieth-century writers such as Eliot and Joyce (Callinicos, 1989: 14–15). Similarly, in terms of the changes that have taken place in modes of production and industrial organisation, it has been argued that characterising capitalism in the late twentieth century as 'post-Fordist' both exaggerates the nature of the changes that have taken place (since capitalism has always been a dynamic system, constantly revolutionising its methods of production and distribution) and also underestimates the extent to which to which 'Fordist' modes of organisation have actually increased both socially (in terms of white-collar work, for example, in typing pools or call centres) and geographically (in countries such as Brazil, India and China) (Taylor-Gooby, 1997). No one would deny that real changes have taken place in the organisation of economic, social and cultural life in the late twentieth century. What many do dispute, however, is the way in which adherents of post-modernism interpret these changes (with one of the most important critics of postmodernism, for example, the German philosopher Jurgen Habermas, preferring to describe the current period as 'High Modernity' – Habermas, 1987).

### Philosophical Objections

A second set of objections concerns the anti-realist basis of postmodernism, the notion that there are no firm foundations to social life but only language games. While the philosophical basis of this view has been extensively challenged elsewhere (see, e.g., Norris, 2000), in this chapter our main concern is with the implications of such a view. As Pilgrim has noted in a paper critiquing the uses of postmodernism within family therapy (Pilgrim, 2000), postmodernists are far from being the only people to see the value of narrative approaches, or to recognise the socially constructed nature of the world in which we live, or to celebrate diversity. However, the extreme social constructionism and anti-realism of postmodernism raises huge difficulties for those concerned with change, whether at an individual therapeutic level or at a wider structural level. He gives the example of a family where incestuous relationships were reported to have occurred down generations. While a *realist* approach would want to know whether the abuse had actually happened, by contrast, workers adopting an *anti-realist* stance would only be interested in the narratives which family members gave, since the 'truth' can never be established. Yet, as Pilgrim argues, clearly whether or not the abuse did actually happen would have important legal and therapeutic implications.

The point carries even greater weight in relation to social and structural issues. How do we know that any of the Gulf Wars actually happened (notoriously, the leading French postmodernist Baudrillard argued that the first one didn't but was a media spectacle) or the Holocaust for that matter, or the rape of thousands of women during the wars in Yugoslavia in the 1990s? Or in terms of social policy, how can we establish a relationship between class and mental ill-health, or gender and depression, if the social 'facts' on which we rely to do so have no objective reality? In its denial of the existence of anything outside language, postmodernism denies us any access to these areas of life and consequently to the possibility of social change. As Pilgrim comments: 'postmodernism, by querying the relevance and reality of structures, actively resists the legitimacy of explanation. Postmodernism does not get its hands dirty with empirical investigations of reality. Instead it stands on the sidelines generating unending discourses about discourses' (2000: 13).

---

**Activity 2**

*In what respects might postmodernism itself be described as a 'grand narrative'?*

---

### Ethical/Political Objections

The third set of objections to postmodernism relate to its ethical/political claims. The starting point for postmodernism (and for post-structuralism) is the rejection of the legacy of the Enlightenment. The Enlightenment refers to that group of mainly French and Scottish eighteenth-century intellectuals, including Adam Smith and David Hume in Scotland, Diderot and Voltaire in France, and Kant in Germany, whose ideas represented a radical break with previous ways of understanding social and moral life (Broadie, 1997; Callinicos, 1999; Herman, 2001). Callinicos suggests that these thinkers had two decisive features in common: first, a model of rationality derived from Newtonian physics; second, an attempt to extend this scientific understanding to the whole of society (Callinicos, 1999: 15–16). In practice, this meant that human reason, not tradition or religion, should form the basis of society. In addition, it involved an attempt to understand society as an interconnected whole, often linked to optimistic notions of historical progress, in which one mode of society was replaced by another more advanced one (a notion most fully developed in the writings of the nineteenth-century German philosopher Hegel).

All of these assertions are rejected by postmodernists. First, rather than seeing history as progress, they follow the nineteenth-century German philosopher Friederich Nietzsche and his twentieth-century disciple Michel Foucault in seeing the 'will to power' as the driving force of human society. Notions of progress, evolution, democracy, reason are so many shibboleths which simply mask the reality of oppression. Social life, like nature, is an endless struggle for domination. The conclusions which Nietzsche drew from this were essentially aristocratic, anti-democratic ones: only the strong individual, the 'Superman', could drag humanity forward. Following Nietzsche, Foucault similarly rejected Enlightenment notions of progress and much of his work, beginning with his history of madness (Foucault, 1967), was concerned with uncovering and exploring the *discourses* (forms of power/knowledge) through which domination was exercised. Unlike Nietzsche, however, Foucault also saw the possibility for resistance: 'where there is power, there is resistance' (Foucault, 1981: 95). As power is everywhere, so too is resistance, hence the potential for localised struggles against oppression and domination (which in Foucault's own case meant supporting campaigns for prisoners' rights and for the rights of people with HIV/AIDS).

Second, whereas Enlightenment thinkers (and Hegel and Marx after them) sought to develop theories which made sense of society as an interconnected whole, postmodernists reject such 'grand narratives', such overarching explanations, both on epistemological grounds (as we saw above, there are only language games) but also because such attempts to 'privilege' one discourse over another (the discourse of class or gender, for example) are essentially attempts at domination which can only succeed at the price of the suppression of other discourses (such as blacks or gays). Therefore all discourses are equally valid.

Space does not permit a full consideration of these postmodern claims but three brief points can be made. First, the recognition of the 'dark' side of modernity (or more specifically capitalism), including, for example, its failure to address the oppression of woman and blacks, and its potential for oppression is far from new. The 'two-sided' nature of this new society – capitalism – and its potential to exploit and oppress as well as to create the material basis for freedom from hunger and want was at the heart of Marx's critique of capitalism, while the oppressive potential of capitalist rationality informed both the writings of the German sociologist Max Weber and, even more so, the writings of the Marxist

Frankfurt School (Stirk, 2000). (Foucault expressed regrets in later life that he had not encountered the writings of the Frankfurt School much earlier.) Rather than seeing the way out as involving the rejection of reason *per se*, however (which, incidentally, creates problems for postmodernism as a philosophy based on rational argument), other solutions are possible, including the notion of the 'radicalised Enlightenment', to be discussed in the final part of the chapter.

Second, if as Foucault and others argue, power is everywhere and if all discourses are equally valid, then the *ethical* basis for choosing one discourse over another, or for siding with the oppressed against the oppressor (as Foucault did), is not clear. In fact, as another leading post-structuralist thinker Jacques Derrida admitted, 'I try *to act* where I can to act politically while recognizing that such action remains incommensurate with my intellectual project of deconstruction' (cited in Stirk, 2000: 59). In other words, the decision to challenge oppression or social inequality is a personal whim, no more and no less valid than the decision to participate in the oppression and exploitation of others. Some of the implications of this viewpoint for social work will be considered more fully in the next section.

Finally, the notion that any attempt to understand society as a whole (let alone bring about large-scale social change) will end in tyranny is also far from new. It is in essence the position of conservative thinkers from Edmund Burke in the 1790s through to the philosopher Karl Popper who, in his Cold War diatribes against Marx and Hegel, reached the conclusion that only 'piecemeal social engineering' was either possible or desirable, a conclusion that bears many similarities to the postmodern view that local struggles and local changes are the best we can hope for (Popper, 1945/2002). It is a profoundly conservative notion. If any attempt to bring about real change is likely to make things worse, then passivity and quietism become political virtues. In essence, we live in the best of all possible worlds.

Callinicos has argued that the historical roots of postmodernism's pessimism and passivity are to be found in the failure of the great social upheavals of the late 1960s to overthrow the bastions of capitalism and in the 'discovery' by erstwhile Marxists of the true extent of repression and brutality in so-called 'socialist' regimes in places like Kampuchea and China. It is the resulting disillusionment, he argues, rather than any intrinsic intellectual coherence or worth, that has made postmodernism so attractive to many of those 'children of '68' who have given up any hope of bringing about large-scale societal change (Callinicos, 1989). As noted above, however, within social policy and social work postmodernism has also had an influence on people who clearly do want to fight oppression and injustice. The extent to which postmodernism can provide a firm, theoretical basis for that struggle will be the subject for the remainder of this chapter.

## Postmodern Welfare?

Postmodern perspectives have been applied in two main areas of social welfare. Firstly, it has been argued that they are valuable in helping to make sense of the changes that have taken place in the organisation and delivery of welfare services since the late 1980s (Williams, 1992; Parton, 1996; Thompson and Hoggett, 1996; O'Brien and Penna, 1998). Secondly, as noted in the introduction to this chapter, some theorists have argued that postmodern perspectives, at least in their 'weaker' (Pease and Fook, 1999) or 'affirmative' (Rosenau, 1992: Parton and Marshall, 1998) form, can provide a basis for critical or emancipatory practice in social welfare, more radical and thoroughgoing than earlier 'grand narratives' of liberation, particularly Marxism (Leonard, 1997; O'Brien and Penna, 1998; Pease and Fook, 1999). Each of these areas will be discussed in turn.

### The Restructuring of Welfare

The question became . . . 'is there a Thatcherite way we can improve the quality of the welfare state services without the public having to pay for them?' The answer was internal competition. Once you say 'we want the good features of competition, with independent bodies competing, in a service that remains publicly funded', then the internal market just falls out as the conclusion . . . for us 1988, with the Education Reform Act, the NHS Review, the Griffiths report and the Housing Act, was the annus mirabilis of social policy. (David Willetts, interview, cited in Timmins, 1996: 433)

The 1980s and 1990s were a period of considerable change in the organisation and delivery of welfare services in the UK. While different writers have emphasised different aspects of these changes, the four areas identified by Clarke provide a useful starting point for exploring this issue (Clarke, 1996: 45–6). These are:

1 *Marketisation.* By this Clarke is referring to the introduction of competition between welfare providers and to the deliberate creation of 'internal' or 'quasi' markets which are alleged to mimic real markets.
2 *The introduction of 'mixed economies of welfare'.* Alongside the introduction of competition went a conscious attempt, enshrined in law and policy guidance, to shift the balance of provision away from the state towards the 'independent' (i.e. voluntary and private) sector.
3 *The shift in responsibilities from formal to informal care – to 'care by the community'.* There is now a substantial literature on the 'familialisation' of social welfare since Griffiths, and in particular its implications for women carers. As Clarke notes, the blurring of the link between the public and private spheres entailed in this redrawing of welfare boundaries also has major implications for the regulation and surveillance of families, implications which have become more, not less, pronounced under New Labour with increasing responsibilities being placed on parents (Jones and Novak, 1999).
4 *Managerialisation.* This refers to the processes and mechanisms involved in the implementation of the above changes, specifically the key role accorded to management in bringing about change. It includes both the principles on which welfare organisations are constructed and also the regimes of power and control existing within such organisations. Again, the issue of managerialisation in the restructuring of welfare services has been the subject of considerable discussion and analysis (Clarke, et al., 1994; Clarke and Newman, 1997).

As a description of the major changes that have taken place in welfare in recent years, few theorists of whatever ideological persuasion would disagree with Clarke's summary. In terms of the focus of this chapter, however, what is important is the way that writers sympathetic to postmodernism seek to make sense of these changes. For, as Clarke himself has argued in a paper critical of postmodern perspectives on welfare, the concern is 'not about whether "something is going on" but that the ways in which changes are being appropriated theoretically are flawed' (1996: 44).

That appropriation by what O'Brien and Penna describe as 'the postmodernisation thesis' involves seeing the changes identified above as involving a qualitative break with previous forms of welfare characteristic of 'the modern' (O'Brien and Penna, 1998). The problems in periodising social change and development in this way have already been discussed in the first part of this chapter. In respect of welfare provision, the core of the thesis is that:

> it is possible to detect in the contemporary world patterns of social organisation, control and experience that differ both quantitatively and qualitatively from those of the recent past . . . The patterns of change are understood as conforming to emergent trends through which every dimension of social life is being reconfigured. Of particular note are trends towards political-economic decentralisation, localisation, fragmentation and desocialisation. (O'Brien and Penna, 1998: 193)

*Desocialisation* or *desocietalisation* in the sense of the decline of the nation state and the growth of international forms of communication and trade is discussed in detail elsewhere in this text, while *localisation* and *fragmentation* in the sense of a new politics concerned primarily with local issues and based on a politics of identity rather than a wider political programme will be discussed in the next section. Decentralisation refers to the tendency of bureaucratic organisations to devolve power down to more local units of organisation but more generally might be seen to include the areas identified by Clarke above. As an example of such decentralisation, O'Brien and Penna cite Parton's discussion of the shift within social work from the ethos and practice of genericism to the administrative specialism of care management (Parton, 1994).

There are two major problems with the postmodernisation thesis as a way of making sense of this shift. Firstly, in seeking to demonstrate the break with what has gone before, proponents of the thesis tend to *overstate* the extent of the changes that are taking place and *understate* the degree of continuity with what existed previously. In terms of welfare policy, elements of continuity might include: a focus on the poor (with nine out of ten clients of social services, for example, in receipt of state benefits (Becker, 1997)); an emphasis on the rationing of welfare services, with care management a mechanism for means-testing (Harris, 2003); a focus on disciplining and regulating the behaviour of the poor (no less pronounced under New Labour governments than under previous Conservative governments (Jones and Novak, 1999)); and resistance by the poor and the organised working class to the attempts of governments to cut the welfare budget and reduce the social wage (Clarke, 1996; Lavalette and Mooney, 2000).

Oliver and Barnes also draw attention to the continuities in welfare policy in their discussion of the application of postmodern perspectives to disability issues:

> We are not convinced that modernity can be dismissed or that postmodernity should be embraced in the ways that are now fashionable. We do not see where we are now as somewhere different from where we were 50 or 20 years ago; rather we are confronted with the same issues that we have always been confronted with, even if the circumstances in which we confront them have changed and are changing. For us capitalism continues to rule OK! Even if it is now global rather than based on the nation state. (Oliver and Barnes, 1998: 4)

A second criticism of the postmodernisation thesis is that it is quite possible to explain the changes in the form of welfare provision discussed above without resort to the perspectives of postmodernism. The quote from the leading Thatcherite theoretician David Willetts which introduces this section, for example, suggests that these changes might be more convincingly explained in terms of the neo-liberal and neo-conservative agendas which informed the later Thatcher governments (Clarke, 1998: 17). Smith and White (1997), in their critique of the application of postmodern perspectives to social work practice, provide a good example of just what such an analysis might involve. 'New Right' agendas undoubtedly did represent a break with the so-called social-democratic, Butskellite consensus which broadly characterised the welfare programmes of both Labour and Conservative governments from the end of the Second World War to the mid-1970s. That 'break', however, is more fruitfully seen as part of an attempt by ruling classes in Britain and elsewhere to rethink welfare strategy in the wake of the re-emergence of economic crisis in the 1970s than as signifying the 'end of modernity'. In that respect, Clarke's suggestion that a focus on what he calls '*an expanded repertoire of strategies for capital accumulation*' is likely to be more productive than a focus on post-Fordism/flexible accumulation strategies is one which we would share.

---

### Activity 3

*What are the main limitations of portraying changes in welfare regimes in recent decades as involving a transition from modernity to postmodernity?*

---

### Postmodernism – Basis of Emancipatory Critique?

It is now common to distinguish between postmodernism as a means of 'characterising the present' (Browning et al., 2000) – the 'postmodernisation thesis' discussed above – and what O'Brien and Penna refer to as 'social postmodernism' (1998: 195), meaning postmodernism as the basis for a new politics. The main elements of this second aspect of postmodernism were outlined in the first part of this chapter. As we saw there, at the heart of such a postmodern politics is a 'radical perspectivism':

> It implies that since there is no factual ground on which to base theory and practice – in other words, there are no factual grounds on which to base true and false interpretations – then all knowledges of the world, including scientific and religious knowledges, are equally ungrounded interpretations of it. Poverty, disability, discrimination, it seems are not facts but interpretations and combating them is the expression of a value based on interpretation rather than a theory based on fact. (O'Brien and Penna, 1998: 196)

It is in the postmodern challenge to those 'knowledges' or 'grand narratives' that seek to make sense of the world as a totality – which in the field of welfare, tends to mean structuralist theories such as Marxism or feminism – that some writers have seen the possibility of a new 'emancipatory' politics of welfare ( Leonard, 1997; Wilson, 1997; Pease and Fook, 1999).

The charge against these overarching theories in the sphere of welfare is two-fold. Firstly, it is argued, they are reductionist. In seeking to make sense of the whole, they 'flatten' difference and diversity, in the process reducing and distorting whole areas of social experience. In a critique of class-based explanations in sociology, for example, Bradley argues that:

> The recognition that social inequalities and divisions could not be subsumed under one monolithic theory, that of class, led to a growing appreciation of the complexity of social differentiation in multi-cultural, post-colonial societies, where many sources of difference – class, gender, ethnicity, 'race', age, region, dis/ability, sexual orientation – intertwined to produce multi-faceted and intricate forms of social hierarchy. (2000: 478)

While in the first instance, this critique of Marxist approaches came in the 1980s from feminist and black nationalist writers wishing to stress the 'autonomy' of gender and 'race', it converged neatly with emerging postmodern perspectives which 'saw society in terms of a multitude of social groupings which formed around different potential sources of identity and had their own distinctive cultures, lifestyles and consumption patterns' (ibid.).

A second criticism of the operation of 'grand narratives' in the area of social welfare is that they distort, deny, silence the experience of minorities and, consequently, whatever the intentions of their adherents, they function as part of an apparatus of power and oppression which serves the interest of specific privileged groups. Those who wish to develop 'emancipatory practice' on the basis of postmodern perspectives, therefore, would see their role as being to 'give a voice' to those whose voices have historically been ignored or silenced within dominant discourses, including those discourses which portray themselves as discourses of emancipation. The link between such a politics and the wider theoretical premises of postmodernism is summarised by Leonard as follows:

Because meaning is continually slipping away from us, there can be no essential, certain meanings, only different meanings emerging from different experiences, especially the experiences of those who have been excluded from discourses, whose voices and whose writing have been silenced. In the Western culture of modernity, this has meant especially the excluded voices of women, non-white populations, gays and lesbians and the working classes in general. (Leonard, 1997: 10–11)

The main implication of this approach for the formulation of social policy is an emphasis on 'particularism' as opposed to the 'false universalism' of the post-war welfare state, with its assumption of the white, able-bodied heterosexual male as the norm, an assumption which in practice was used to deny the needs of certain groups, including women and black people. Thompson and Hoggett summarise the postmodernist case in the area of social policy as follows:

[I]n the name of particularism, diversity and difference, such policy should not be formulated within a guiding framework that is universalist in character; it may even question the desirability of incorporating *any* significant element of universalism into social policy. (1996: 23)

That many groups in society, including people with disabilities and people with mental health problems, as well as working-class women and members of ethnic minorities, have experienced aspects of the operation of the welfare state as disempowering and oppressive is well documented. The extent to which a policy based on particularism and informed by postmodern perspectives would challenge that oppression, however, is much less clear. Three particular aspects of postmodern thought must give cause for serious doubt: its individualism; its rejection of structural explanations of poverty and inequality; and its moral relativism.

## A Postmodern Social Policy?

First, let us consider individualism. In a sense the very idea of a postmodern *social* policy is a contradiction since at the heart of postmodernism is a radical individualism. Postmodernism goes beyond identity politics in rejecting not only class as a basis of common interest and action but *all* bases of collective identity – whether gender, disability or 'race' – since they are all premised on a wider narrative about how the world works. One might assume that that would disqualify postmodernism from making any contribution to debates about social policy. In fact postmodernism's individualism and emphasis on individual consumption make it quite compatible with social policies which are very far from being radical or emancipatory. As one writer sympathetic to postmodern perspectives has commented: 'In practical policy terms, postmodernism can be seen to fit all too well with a government that denies the existence of society and prioritises individual expenditure over public welfare' (Wilson, 1997: 349).

While Wilson is mainly referring to the social policies of the British Conservative governments of the 1990s, her comments also have relevance for the policies of governments in Britain and elsewhere based on 'Third Way' notions. For as Jones and Novak note, under New Labour:

> As in contemporary theories of postmodernism, people are identified not by their collective experiences – as workers, as women or black people – but as individuals. It is not the same individualism as that of the new right, although it draws many parallels, not least with the 'active citizens' that fleetingly formed part of John Major's agenda in the early 1990s. The new right's individualism was of the sink or swim variety. New Labour's individualism is much more actively promoted. (1999: 179)

In fact, core postmodernist themes – the celebration of 'ephemerality, fragmentation, discontinuity'; the rejection of structural explanations of poverty and inequality; adoration of all that is new and 'modern', coupled with an ironic disdain for 'old-fashioned' notions of commitment and solidarity – chime in very well with current 'Third Way' notions of welfare with their stress on the 'end of ideology'.

Secondly, consistent with the individualist emphasis noted above, there is the postmodern rejection of *structural* explanations of poverty and inequality. In contrast to Marxist approaches, which are primarily concerned with the ways in which one class (comprising a very small number of people) is able to use its economic, political and ideological power to exploit and oppress another class or classes (comprising a very large number of people), postmodern theorists, and their post-structuralist predecessors like Foucault, see power as *omnipresent*, as everywhere (and one might argue, nowhere):

> When I think of the mechanics of power, I think of its capillary forms of existence, of the extent to which power seeps into the very grain of individuals, reaches right into their bodies, permeates their gestures, their position, what they say, how they learn to live and work with other people. (Foucault, cited in Watson, 2000: 68)

As Watson correctly comments on this passage: 'Such a view stands in clear opposition to the notion that the state or capital as a concentrated site of power needs to be overthrown or dismantled for socialism or universal social justice to be achieved' (ibid.).

In fact, the implications for social policy potentially go much further than a rejection of the revolutionary socialist case for the overthrow of capitalism. Postmodernism's view of power and resistance as essentially localised and located in the micro-relations between men and women, black and white, and so on is at best likely to lead to a focus on local issues, small-scale studies. Since large-scale societal transformation is neither possible nor desirable, the best that can be hoped for is reform at a local or individual level. Thus, even quite limited reform programmes which require a degree of national structural change, such as those proposed in respect of health inequalities by the Black Committee and more recently the Acheson Committee, are likely to be seen as problematic. Not surprisingly then, as Wilson has noted, 'The unwillingness of the postmodernists to conceptualise structured power relations in a traditional way presents problems for those who work with or study disadvantaged groups' (ibid.). In fact, there are indications that the influence of postmodern ideas in welfare thinking is already starting to have a negative impact in this area. In an early critique, Taylor-Gooby expressed the fear that a growth in influence of postmodern perspectives within social policy would lead to a neglect of issues concerning poverty and inequality:

> The implications for social policy are that an interest in postmodernism may cloak developments of considerable importance. Trends towards increased inequality in living standards, the privatisation of state welfare services and the stricter regulation of the lives of some of the poorest groups may fail to attract the appropriate attention if the key themes of policy are seen as difference, diversity and choice. (1994: 403)

Since then, a number of writers have noted the paradox that at a time when the gap between rich and poor has been shown by numerous studies to be greater than it has ever been (and, according to recent research, in the UK context has continued to grow under a New Labour government), the lack of interest amongst social science academics in exploring class and material inequalities has never been greater (Bradley, 2000; Mooney, 2000). While it would be misleading to attribute the neglect of these issues solely to the growth of postmodernism, not least since this neglect goes back to the 1980s (Becker, 1997), it is nevertheless arguable that the Foucauldian emphasis on the 'the specific, the local and the particular' (Watson, 2000: 76) reinforces and legitimises that neglect.

Finally, there is postmodernism's oft-noted moral relativism. In a previous paper, I have considered some of the implications of that relativism for anti-oppressive social work practice (Ferguson and Lavalette, 1999). Suffice it to say that a metanarrative (for of course, as several critics have noted, postmodernism is itself a metanarrative) which refuses to 'privilege' any discourse over any other scarcely provides a firm foundation for a critical social policy. As Crook has noted:

> When radical social theory loses its accountability, when it can no longer give reasons, something has gone very wrong. But this is precisely what happens to postmodern social theory, and it seems very appropriate to use the over-stretched term 'nihilism' as a label for this degeneration. The nihilism of postmodernism shows itself in two symptoms: an inability to specify mechanisms of change, and an inability to state why change is better than no change. (1990: 59)

It would be ironic indeed if social policy as an academic discipline, having finally shaken off the phoney neutrality of the tradition of empiricist social administration, should now opt for the even more pernicious 'ironic detachment' of postmodernism. That said, the willingness of more than 50 leading social policy academics to write an open letter to the national press in 1999 protesting against the implications of New Labour's 'welfare reform' for the poorest sections of society and arguing for increases in universal benefits suggests that notions of solidarity and a commitment to social justice are still stronger than the scepticism and nihilism encouraged by postmodernism.

---

**Activity 4**

*How valid is postmodernism's claim to provide a more radical basis for an eman-cipatory welfare than Marxism?*

---

## Conclusion: the Alternative to Particularism – the Radicalised Enlightenment

In the light of the above discussion, it may seem strange that postmodernism should hold any attractions for social policy theorists, particularly those committed to what Leonard has dubbed 'emancipatory welfare' (Leonard, 1997). It is nevertheless true that many of those who are drawn towards the ideas of post-structuralism and postmodernism see these ideas as *more* radical than the traditional alternative of Marxism. In explaining that attraction, two factors seem of particular significance. On the one hand, there is a widespread disillusionment with the version of Marxism associated with the Communist Parties internationally, reinforced by the collapse of what are usually (and misleadingly) referred to as the 'state socialist regimes' of the former USSR and Eastern Europe. I have argued elsewhere that Stalinism in theory and practice, not least in its influential Althusserian incarnation, is the antithesis of the genuine Marxist tradition and, rather than repeat these arguments here, would refer readers to previous publications (Ferguson and Lavalette, 1999; Ferguson et al., 2002). On the other hand, there has been a growing scepticism regarding the 'false universalism' of welfare policy, partly in response to the growth of movements such as the disability movement. It is this latter point which I shall briefly address here.

It is worth noting that the 'false universalism' not simply of the welfare state but more generally of the Enlightenment, is not a new theme. As Callinicos has noted:

> Ever since Marx and Nietzsche in their different ways subjected the Enlightenment to crit-ical scrutiny, the very ideas of universality and rationality have been under suspicion for secreting within themselves hidden particularisms . . . the universal rights and happiness promised by the French and the American revolutions tacitly excluded, among others, slaves, the poor and women. (1999: 310)

As he goes on to argue, there are really only two ways to respond to these limitations of the Enlightenment's promise of universal emancipation. One is to conclude that every universalism is a masked particularism and then decide which particularism (or coalition of particularisms) one prefers – the postmodern option. In terms of welfare policy, the dangers of such a strategy, particularly during a period of welfare retrenchment, are obvious. At best, it can allow governments, whose overriding concern is limiting welfare expenditure, to play off one group against another as they squabble over the limited resources on offer. At worst, it can contribute to a backlash against oppressed groups whose legitimate demands for affirmative action or positive discrimination can be portrayed as being at the expense of the basic welfare needs of the majority – one factor used in the undermining of the policies of left-wing Labour councils in the 1980s and seen in recent attacks on 'political correctness' (Smith, 1994; Penketh, 2000).

Alternatively, Callinicos argues, one can respond to the failures of the Enlightenment project by seeking a *genuine* universality, a social and political order from which no one is excluded. A powerful plea for this latter position from the perspective of the disability movement is provided by Oliver and Barnes when they argue that:

> Although versions of the good society vary, for us it is a world in which all human beings, regardless of impairment, age, gender, social class or minority ethnic status can co-exist as equal members of the community, secure in the knowledge that their needs will be met and that their views will be recognised and valued . . . for us, disabled people have no choice but to attempt to build a better world because it is impossible to have a vision of inclusionary capitalism; we all need a world where impairment is valued and celebrated and all disabling barriers are eradicated. Such a world would be inclusionary for all. (1998: 102)

In contrast to the pessimism of postmodernism, this view implies the possibility of successful collective action on the basis of opposition to a common enemy – global capitalism – an enemy which, *pace* postmodernism, can be both understood and changed.

Significantly, the end of the twentieth century saw the emergence of just such collective action, around the meeting of the World Trade Organization in Seattle in 1999 (Charlton, 2000). Since then, despite having been written off on a regular basis by sceptical media commentators, the anti-capitalist (or global justice) movement that emerged at Seattle has survived the backlash following the bombing of the World Trade Center on September 11, 2001; gone on to stage much bigger mobilisations at Genoa, Florence and many other sites; has organised huge gatherings at World Social Forums in Sao Paulo, Cairo and Mumbai, as well as European Social Forums at Florence, Paris and London; and has played a central role in building the biggest anti-war movement the world has ever seen (Bircham and Charlton, 2001; Callinicos, 2003a) It is the hope offered by that movement, as well as the coherence of its intellectual critique (recognised by system 'insiders' such as Joseph Stiglitz, former chief economist at the World Bank – Stiglitz, 2002), which continues to offer the most effective response not only to the dominance of neo-liberal globalisation but also to the nihilism of postmodernism.

## Further Reading

Ferguson, I., Lavalette, M. and Mooney, G. (2002) *Rethinking Welfare: a Critical Perspective*. London: Sage.
Leonard, P. (1997) *Postmodern Welfare: Reconstructing an Emancipatory Project*. London: Sage.
Noble, C. (2004) 'Postmodern thinking: where is it taking social work?' *Journal of Social Work*, 4 (3): 1–16.

# PART THREE
## Some Contemporary Social Policy Issues

Any selection of a range of issues deemed to be worthy of inclusion in an undergraduate text of this nature is bound to be arbitrary to some extent. In this section we look at some pressing social policy issues (Chapter 12 looks at the 'pensions crisis' and Chapter 13 the question of food policy that is developing as a major social problem); we look at questions of age-related social policy and welfare (Chapter 12 on pensions and Chapter 11 on children and young people); the impact of 'neo-liberal' policy within Britain (Chapter 15 on the management of welfare) and internationally (Chapter 16 on globalisation), and look at a very traditional form of benefit which has come back to the fore in recent years – wage-supplementation benefits.

In these chapters we feel we provide a range of topics that emphasises the scope of social policy both as an academic discipline and as a form of government activity. These chapters also see our authors utilising the theories and concepts developed in Parts One and Two to develop an analysis of these current social policy issues.

In Chapter 11 Steve Cunningham and Jo Tomlinson look at the relationship between the state and child-related social policy. Exploring the conflict at the heart of the 'care/control' dichotomy they produce an historical overview of the development of the juvenile justice system and the more recent response of the state to child refugees.

In Chapter 12 Steve Cunningham looks at perhaps the most pressing social policy problem in Britain (and Europe) at the present period – the 'pensions crisis'. In Britain the value of state pensions has been undermined and pensions privatised. Yet this process has brought huge problems for retired people and for future pensioners. The government suggests that the problem is a demographic one: that we are living much longer than before, and that, as a result, the retirement age should be increased. But is there an alternative solution to the problem?

In Chapter 13 Laura Penketh looks at another increasingly high-profile and contested area of social policy and political debate: food policy. In recent years food regulation has not been viewed as a central part of the social policy field. However, as Britons become heavier and more sedentary, as food becomes more refined and processed and as the quality of school meals served to children declines, it is clear that food policy and regulation of the food industry are becoming 'hot topics'. We hope that this chapter will show that food policy is relevant to social policy as a subject and, we hope, encourage further research and interest in this topic.

Historically one way of passing benefits to the poor has been through paying a supplement to wages. Obviously to qualify for such a benefit the recipient has to be in work; indeed, so advocates would suggest, it is an inducement to work. Under New Labour, wage supplementation has come back to the fore within social policy. But does wage supplementation not also provide a benefit to low paying employers? In Chapter 14 Alan Pratt looks at these issues in an historical overview of the development of wage supplementation in Britain from the Poor Law to the present.

One of the key elements in New Labour welfare reform has been the use of 'partnerships' and markets in the delivery of welfare services. In Chapter 15 Gerry Mooney looks at this process and its consequences on service users.

Finally, social policy and the welfare state are today said to operate in a radically different climate – an era of globalisation. The suggestion is that social policy developments and the welfare state are shaped by economic factors beyond the control of nation states. In Chapter 16 Michael Lavalette introduces a discussion on globalisation and social policy. He starts off by asking us to think about what 'globalisation' means (or may mean) and tries to locate the use of 'globalisation discourse' within a particular socio-political context at the beginning of the 1990s. He suggests that while there have been significant international socio-economic developments in recent years these do not mean that states can no longer shape social policies nor that the 'era of the welfare state' has come to an end. Rather, he suggests that wrapped up in talk about 'globalisation' is a political project to re-shape the world according to neo-liberal principles – which emphasise that politics remains vital to social policy discussion and leads us back to the first section of the book and the contested theoretical interpretations of the modern world and the position of social welfare within it.

# ELEVEN

# Children, Social Policy and the State
## *The Dichotomy of Care and Control*
## *Steve Cunningham and Jo Tomlinson*

---

**Outline Points**

- Children and the state, over three centuries.
- Juvenile justice, trends and provisions.
- Refugee children, policy and control.
- The dichotomy of care and control.

---

## Introduction

Over the last twenty-five years or so politicians, journalists and various social commentators have seemingly come to the conclusion that 'childhood is in crisis' (Scraton, 1997).

On the one hand, this crisis reflects the fact that large numbers of children in Britain are being brought up in the most desperate circumstances. In the final quarter of the twentieth century child poverty had increased more in Britain than in almost any other developed society and in 2002/3, at the beginning of the Labour government's second term in office, some 3.6 million children (28 per cent of all children) were living in poverty. This compares with 1.9 million (14 per cent of all children) in 1979 (Child Poverty Action Group, 2004: 2). The 'childhood' these children endure is significantly detached from the 'ideal' many of us hold on to.

On the other hand, children are increasingly portrayed as unruly, uncontrollable, amoral and even 'evil'. As Bob Franklin notes:

> Ideologically, children have become the focus of a moral panic . . . [P]resentations of children have metamorphosed them from . . . innocent 'sugar and spice' angels . . . into

inherently evil demons who, typifying Britain's declining moral standards, seem incapable of distinguishing right from wrong. (1995: 4–5)

Yet despite the growing problem of child poverty, it is this latter issue that is increasingly dominant within political debates. Decades of 'liberal' criminal justice policies, introduced at the behest of 'sentimentalists' and do-gooders', have, we are told, fostered the creation of a culture of disrespect. Core 'British' values of civility, reasonableness and an unquestioning respect for authority and the law have been progressively undermined. Unlike in the past, children of the 'underclass' now run amok without fear of punishment:

> At every level, society has simply stopped setting boundaries between appropriate and inappropriate behaviour. Delinquent children are treated as if they were adults with rights. Teachers or social workers can't restrain them without falling foul of some rights-based law. The police have abandoned the streets to the child gangs. (Phillips, 2002: 10)

For Phillips (2002) the descent into 'lawlessness' has been a relatively rapid one. A combination of 'feckless', irresponsible parents (particularly lone parents) and a policy of being 'soft' on young criminals are, she argues, responsible for the rise of a new breed of 'mindless' bullyboys, vandals, muggers and teenage tearaways. Child criminals are 'coddled', parents have abandoned their responsibilities, and as a result there has been a violent shift away from respect for authority and discipline. Her solution is quite straightforward: introduce stringent criminal-justice policies that will deter delinquent behaviour, and reinforce parental responsibility.

Hardly a day goes past, therefore, without some commentator or politician discussing the decline in the public morals of today's youth, contrasting our current 'ominous' predicament with a previous 'golden age' of harmony and respect. As Pearson (1983) notes, this view of British history as one founded on stability and decency is deeply ingrained in the self-understanding of the British people. In the past, the 'accumulated traditions of our national culture' were sufficient to guarantee order and security, whereas nowadays we need the iron fist of policing in order to ensure we might sleep soundly in our beds.

Our intention in this chapter is to show how this conception of the past, whilst a daily feature of contemporary debates, is inaccurate. Concerns about the disruptive behaviour of hoards of 'feckless', uncontrollable working-class youths are, as we will show, not particularly novel. Nor, as we shall see, are individualised explanations for juvenile offending, which locate its causes with a breakdown in young people's respect for authority and in an absence of parental control, unique to contemporary Britain. The chapter is divided into two broad sections. The first section shows how the notion that 'deviant', badly brought-up working-class youths posed a threat to public order, and needed to be subjected to strict, coercive methods of control, remained an important influence on the state's response to childhood right throughout the nineteenth and twentieth centuries. The final section is devoted to a critical analysis of New Labour's claims to be pursuing a more progressive, welfare-orientated approach towards children, based on the principle that 'every child matters'. Here we consider whether the government's policies towards children in two areas – juvenile justice and asylum – have been influenced by a 'controlling' or 'caring' agenda.

## The State and the Treatment of Child Offenders in the Nineteenth Century

Despite our perception of the nineteenth century as being a golden age for childhood, for much of that century 'childhood' was considered to be a brief, relatively unimportant stage of life. For the most part, children were treated as 'little adults' and exposed to the responsibilities and demands of adulthood at a very early age. 'Childhood' simply did not exist for the vast majority of children, and it was not until the latter third of the nineteenth century that state legislation began to recognise their 'special' and distinct physical, social and psychological needs.

Regarding juvenile justice, at the beginning of the nineteenth century, Britain's legal system granted few concessions to age and, invariably, the full range and force of criminal sanctions was applied to adults and children equally. In the case of child offenders aged over fourteen there was no question of leniency; they were simply deemed to be able to discern between good and evil and faced the same forms of trial and punishment as adults. Those aged between seven and fourteen were, theoretically, held to be in *doli incopax*; that is, they were presumed innocent unless strong evidence of 'mischievous discretion' could be proven (May, 1973: 9). However, 'proof' that children had acted with malicious intent was frequently forthcoming and in such cases their behaviour was seen to be the result of a conscious devotion to 'vicious' habits. Thus, it was felt that child offenders needed to be held wholly accountable for the consequences of their actions. As one judge explained after condemning a 10-year-old boy to death for stealing letters at Chelmsford Post Office, there was a need to avoid the 'infinite danger' of it 'going abroad into the world that a child might commit . . . a crime with impunity, when it was clear that he knew what he was doing' (cited in Hammond and Hammond, 1941: 13).

Children could be – and on frequent occasions were – sentenced to death for what were, even by contemporary standards, relatively minor offences. For example, at the Old Bailey, in 1814, on one day alone, five children under 14 were condemned to death after being found guilty of theft and burglary (Pinchbeck and Hewitt, 1973: 352). In all, 103 children under 14 received capital sentences at the Old Bailey between 1801 and 1836. Nor were children spared other forms of 'adult' punishment. For instance, between 1812 and 1817, 780 males and 136 females under the age of 21 were transported to Australia (May, 1973: 9). The following extract, taken from the Registers of Stafford Prison for 1834, provides an illustration of the sort of 'crimes' that were deemed to warrant such a penalty:

William Biglen: Aged 14, for stealing one silk handkerchief – sentenced to transportation for seven years . . . Matilda Seymour: Aged 10, for stealing one shawl and one petticoat – sentenced to transportation for seven years . . . Thomas Bell: Aged 11, for stealing two silk handkerchiefs – also sentenced to transportation for seven years. (Pinchbeck and Hewitt 1973: 352)

Transportation was often portrayed by its advocates as a 'reformative' punishment for children, because, it was argued, it extracted them from their immoral surroundings, and gave them a 'new start' in life. However, the regimes that greeted juveniles dispatched to the colonies stood in stark contrast to these claims. Child convicts were seen primarily by their 'guardians' or 'masters' as an economic resource and the 'apprenticeships' into which they were bound constituted little more than a system of convict slave labour. Children were compelled to undertake hard, physical work for little or no reward, and at the same time were forced to endure savage disciplinary regimes where floggings and other forms of physical (and sexual) abuse were administered routinely. Of course, the severity of the experience of transportation was not entirely incidental. On the contrary, ill treatment was tolerated, and even encouraged, in order to appease contemporaries such as Lord Ellenborough (Chief Justice of the King's Bench), who were concerned that the prospect of 'a summer's excursion, in an easy migration, to a happier and better climate' might act as an inducement for juveniles and others to commit crime (Radzinowicz and Hood, 1986: 474).

Child offenders given custodial sentences within Britain often fared no better than those who were transported. Prior to the introduction of the first penal institution for juveniles, offenders of all ages and types were herded together, detained and subjected to the same forms of restraint and discipline. The establishment of a specialist 'boys prison' at Parkhurst in 1838 did little to mitigate the fate awaiting juvenile offenders. The authorities, influenced by the Poor Law principle of less eligibility, feared that humane and reformative conditions would place a premium on the commission of crime and encourage parents to succumb to the temptation to allow their children to be supported, educated and reformed at the public's expense. The Parkhurst regime was shaped by a determination to ensure that the position of the juvenile offender was not made 'more eligible' than that of the honest law-abiding child. Thus, boys were forced to wear manacles, the diet provided to inmates was sparse and a code of silence was enforced.

It was not until the 1850s that the state came under sustained pressure to alter the way it treated juvenile offenders. Foremost among those campaigning for change was the social reformer Mary Carpenter. Her 1853 book *Juvenile Delinquents: Their Conditions and Treatment* attacked the regime at Parkhurst boys, prison, accusing it of attempting 'to fashion children into machines through iron discipline, instead of self-acting human beings'. She called for the introduction of educational, 'home-like' reformatory schools, the principal aim of which would not be to punish, but to restore the child offender to its 'true position of childhood' (cited in Muncie, 1984: 36). Within a year after the publication of Carpenter's book, the Youthful Offenders Act (1854) empowered judges and magistrates to sentence offenders under 16 to separate voluntary-run juvenile Reformatory Schools. This went some way towards acknowledging that child offenders had specific mental and physical needs, and should not necessarily be dealt with in the same manner as adult prisoners. However, the architects of the 1854 Act, and those subsequently responsible for implementing its provisions, were as concerned to preserve elements of control, deterrence and less eligibility as they were with child-welfare considerations.

Once in Reformatory Schools, children found the conditions uniformly harsh and strict. School managers adhered unswervingly to the Reverend Sydney Turner's suggestion that the daily regime should consist of 'exposure to weather and cold', a diet that was 'studiously plain', and a system of 'manly training in obedience, regularity, industry and self-control' (cited in Weiner, 1994: 138). The hard, gruelling labour children were required to perform in the schools could rarely be regarded in any sense as 'training', and in most cases was determined by the economic exigencies of the institutions and the desire of their managers to make a profit. Indeed, in many cases 'economically productive' children were detained longer than necessary because they were seen by those responsible for the institutions as a positive asset (Muncie, 1984: 39).

By the 1880s, leading politicians began to express disillusionment over the severity and effectiveness of the punishments meted out to young offenders. For instance, in 1884, the Liberal Home Secretary, Vernon Harcourt, condemned the inappropriate detention of children in Reformatory Schools. The managers of these schools, he argued, regarded themselves 'as a sort of earthly providence' and thought that the more children they could 'get and keep from the parents the better' (cited in Hurt, 1984: 55). In a surprisingly frank private letter to a colleague, he acknowledged the profoundly unjust – and class bias – nature of the juvenile justice system over which he presided:

> Many if not most of the cases in these schools are now those of children who for some petty act of naughtiness (such our own children commit every day) are seized upon, hauled off by the Police before the Magistrate, who without inquiry into the character of the home of the parents commits them to Prison and takes them away from good or happy homes for seven or eight years. (Cited in Wiener, 1994: 290)

In the years following Harcourt's criticisms, a number of reforms were introduced, the effect of which was to gradually set in motion a process of differentiation between the treatment of child and adult offenders. The Liberal government finally established the principle that juvenile offenders should be tried and punished separately from adults in 1908, when its Children Act set up a system of specialist juvenile courts and abolished the imprisonment of children under the age of 14. Herbert Samuel, the Minister who introduced the Children Bill into Parliament, insisted the courts 'should be agencies for the rescue as well as the punishment of children', and child offenders 'should receive at the hands of the law a treatment differentiated to suit his special needs' (Hansard, Vol. 183, c. 1436).

What concerns motivated those responsible for initiating reform of the juvenile justice system at the turn of the nineteenth century? Herbert Samuel claimed that its provisions were 'saturated with the rising spirit of humanitarianism' (Radzinowicz and Hood, 1986: 633). Some historians share this view today. For example, in their seminal analysis of the evolution of childhood, Pinchbeck and Hewitt (1973: 612) claim that the second half of the nineteenth century was characterised by 'a general awakening, a "quickening" of social . . . conscience over neglect and cruelty of all kinds'. For authors such as these, then, altruism and 'intolerability' were the master cards. This was an age when philanthropists, such as Mary Carpenter, and campaigning organisations, such as the Howard Association, discovered a 'new and barbarous world', and the Christian consciences of the general public and politicians of all political shades were touched by the excesses exposed (Roberts, 1969: 318).

In fact as Muncie (1984) argues, the trend towards treating child offenders separately and differently from their adult counterparts was influenced by far less altruistic concerns. In part, it represented an attempt to reduce the populations of expensive, notoriously overcrowded jails. More importantly, though, it reflected growing evidence that suggested that the experience of imprisonment neither deterred nor rehabilitated. On the one hand, prisons exposed children to the promiscuous, contaminating influences of hardened adult criminals. On the other, they 'scarred the young with a life-long stigma which prevented respectable, honest employment and forced children back into criminal life' (May, 1973: 12). The improvement of conditions in Reformatory Schools also owed less to humanitarian sentiment and more to the realisation that the harsh, penal regimes found in them were inhibiting rehabilitation.

---

**Activity 1**

*Talk to your parents and grandparents and ask them how children and young people were portrayed in their era.*

- *What examples could they give regarding the 'problem of young people' in their day?*
- *Has anything changed?*
- *Do you think a 'golden era' has ever truly existed for children and young people?*

*Write a definition of the term 'moral panic'.*

*List some examples of recent moral panics relating to children and young people.*

---

## Care and Control – Legislation in the Twentieth Century

Most analyses of the development of social policy at the turn of the twentieth century focus on the state's increased willingness to assume greater responsibility for children's welfare. However, a desire on the part of the state to exert greater control over the behaviour of working-class children and their families shaped, and has continued to shape, the state's regulation of childhood. Despite frequent allusions to 'children's rights', the notion that 'deviant', poorly socialised, working-class youths posed a threat to public order, and needed to be subjected to strict, coercive methods of control, remained an important influence on juvenile justice policy right throughout the twentieth century.

In some respects, the failure of a number of commentators on twentieth-century social policy to acknowledge the influence of social control concerns on child-related legislation is understandable. Punitive policies have frequently been introduced alongside 'progressive' measures, and when this has occurred, the rhetorical emphasis politicians have placed on 'positive', 'caring' proposals has had the effect of 'cloaking' retributive policies in a discourse of liberal reform (Muncie, 1990a). It is perhaps for this reason that Pinchbeck and Hewitt's suggestion, that the twentieth century heralded the emergence of 'more generous and liberal provisions for children in all walks of life', has rarely been challenged in 'mainstream' social policy texts. Such interpretations of history have, however, not remained entirely uncontested. Muncie (1998: 178), for example, has drawn attention to the extent to which social control concerns influenced the shape of child-related legislation introduced during the first two decades of the twentieth century. He points out that the 1908 Children Act, ostensibly seen by social policy historians as a progressive piece of legislation, removed a child's right to trial by jury and to legal representation. He also highlights the fact that it empowered the courts and the state to act upon not only the delinquent, but also the 'neglected' child. The legal definition of the latter category was left deliberately vague, so that it encompassed children found begging and those whose parents were deemed to be 'incapable', 'unworthy' or 'immoral'. Because the conditions constituting neglect were so broad, the Act effectively enabled the state (in the name of 'welfare') to intervene and control working-class family life to a much greater extent than was ever before possible.

The attention subsequently devoted to the assumed 'progressive' effects of early twentieth-century child-related legislation has also served to divert attention away from the simultaneous introduction of coercive, punitive legislation. For example, the Prevention of Crime Act, passed in the same year as the 1908 Children Act, was directly influenced by social control concerns, providing, as it did, for the setting up of Borstal institutions for young offenders. Despite official claims that these were designed to foster 'training' and 'reformation', the Borstal regime was influenced primarily by a desire to deter and control 'inappropriate' modes of behaviour among working-class youths. It was based on 'stern and exact discipline' and the sentences of those committed to the institutions were indeterminate (up to a period of three years). Youthful offenders, it was argued, needed to be removed from the 'demoralising' influences of their families and communities for a significant period (Newburn, 1995: 130).

It is worth noting here the continued emphasis contemporary policy makers placed on what they felt were the moral causes of crime. As was the case in the nineteenth century, delinquency was seen to be the result of selfish 'criminal tendencies' and/or immorality, bad parenting and poor socialisation within working-class families. The possibility that certain relatively minor misdemeanours – for example, the stealing of coal, food and items of clothing – may have been prompted and, indeed, justified by extreme poverty and the struggle for survival was ignored. In fact, as Pearson (1981: 153) points out, this type of offence – 'simple and minor larceny' – constituted the single most important category of juvenile crime during this period. Juvenile crime was often merely a symptom of wider structural problems such as worklessness, deprivation and inadequate social support. However, the juvenile justice system continued to be shaped by the belief that delinquency was due primarily to contaminating, immoral surroundings and/or intrinsically egotistical anti-social behaviour.

There can, then, be little doubt that social control considerations were a significant influence on early twentieth-century child-related social policy. To what extent, though, did such concerns continue to influence policy as the century progressed? The immediate post-Second World War period is often seen as marking a watershed, in that it is said to have heralded a further movement towards an explicitly welfare-orientated approach on the part of the state towards children. Pinchbeck and Hewitt (1973) point out that the 1944 Education Act raised the school-leaving age from 14 to 15 and established the principle of secondary education for all. They also draw attention to the introduction of family allowances and the 1948 Children Act, which provided for the setting up of specialist local-authority Children's Departments. Certainly, the rhetoric that surrounded the introduction of these policies was uniformly positive and 'reformist'.

More recently, however, historians have drawn attention to the gap between the progressive rhetoric that accompanied these measures and their failure to deliver the promised 'New Jerusalem' for children. And as was the case at the beginning of the twentieth century, the emphasis that was placed on the 'reformist' motives underpinning post-war child-related reforms served to disguise the simultaneous introduction of measures designed to control and regulate the behaviour of working-class children more stringently. For example, whilst most 'mainstream' social policy texts applaud the introduction of the 1945–51 Labour government's 'care-orientated' 1948 Children's Act, its Criminal Justices Act that was passed in the same year is rarely mentioned. Influenced by the perceived success of the 'glass house' during wartime, this latter measure allowed courts to sentence children aged 14 and above to a 'short, sharp punishment' in purpose-built detention centres (Muncie, 1990a: 53). Despite being presented as experimental, and as a humane alternative to prison, the detention centres that eventually emerged proved to be neither temporary nor reformative. In fact, the 'experiment' lasted some 40 years, and, throughout this period, its rehabilitative record was extremely poor. For instance, a 1959 study found that 45 per cent of junior inmates (14–16) and 56 per cent of seniors (17–21) reconvicted within two years of leaving. Despite this, the 1961 Criminal Justices Act paved the way for an expansion of the system. The number of children and young persons detained subsequently increased from 2000 at the end of the

1950s to 6000 by the mid-1960s. By 1974, when over 10,000 passed through detention centres, the futility of the 'experiment' – vividly illustrated by a 73 per cent reconviction rate for junior inmates – was clearly evident to criminal-justice professionals. However, failure was not allowed to stand in the way of what was proving to be a populist political initiative. Indeed, a series of largely unjustified moral panics about juvenile delinquency, mugging and football hooliganism in the late 1970s served to reinforce the arguments of those calling for juvenile miscreants to be subjected to harsher, more retributive modes of punishment. What followed, argues Muncie (1990a: 60), was 'a new onslaught on the rehabilitative ideal and a shift towards an ideology based on punishment and an obsession with vindictiveness'.

## Criminal Justice under the Conservatives

At its 1978 annual conference, the then opposition Conservative Party engaged in a passionate, full-throated debate on the apparent rise in juvenile crime and the breakdown of law and order. Amidst calls to 'bring back the birch and to inaugurate "Saturday Night Floggings" for soccer hooligans', William Whitelaw, the Shadow Home Secretary, reaffirmed his pledge to toughen up the law by introducing a new regime of short-sharp-shock detention centres. These would be 'modelled on the Army glass house system of physical drill and unrelenting discipline' (Pearson, 1983: 12). It came as no surprise then when in October 1979, William Whitelaw, the newly appointed Conservative Home Secretary, announced that the detention centre 'experiment' would be extended and that its regime would be tightened still further:

> [Life] . . . will be conducted at a brisk tempo. Much greater emphasis will be put on hard and constructive activities, on discipline and tidiness, on self-respect and respect for those in authority . . . These will be no holiday camps and those who attend them will not ever want to go back. (Cited in Muncie, 1990a: 60)

How successful was this new, tougher regime? In 1984 government-sponsored research found that it 'had no discernible effect on the rate at which trainees were reconvicted'. Even the right-wing Conservative group the Monday Club dismissed the policy as 'gimmickery', arguing that little could be achieved with young offenders 'by shouting at them, giving them meaningless tasks and trying to make them feel as humiliated, isolated and worthless as possible'. However, it was perhaps the human consequences of the new, 'tougher' approach that were most disturbing. Records show that there were 175 known cases of deliberate self-injury between 1979 and April 1988 and at least two suicides in detention centres. Faced with opposition from the Prison Reform Trust, the Prison Officers' Association, NACRO and the Howard League, detention centres were formally abolished in 1988, and thereafter the numbers of children given custodial sentences fell significantly (Muncie, 1990a: 63–64 and 1993: 176). However, as in the late nineteenth century, the gradual movement away from a retributive approach was not driven by altruism or humanitarian sentiment. Rather, it represented a long overdue acknowledgement of the failure of custodial sentences to rehabilitate young offenders (in 1989, the Children's Society calculated that 84 per cent of those sent into youth custody re-offended within two years). The shift was also influenced by concerns over the costs of juvenile detention. For instance, studies showed that a three-week custodial sentence was more expensive than a year of supervision or community service (Muncie, 1999: 196, 197). To a government as ideologically committed to cutting public expenditure as Margaret Thatcher's neo-liberal administration (see Chapter 3), the fiscal attraction of a shift to non-custodial modes of dealing with child offenders must have been considerable.

At the same time, though, it is important to acknowledge that the late 1980s were a period when 'children's rights' were being placed firmly at the forefront of the national and international political agenda. On the domestic front, the Conservative government passed a Children Act in 1989, which, it claimed, extended children's rights in a number of areas. The overarching aim of the 1989 Children Act was to provide far-reaching reform of child-care legislation, and bring together private and public law relating to children. The welfare of the child was deemed to be paramount and this, it was stipulated, should be considered first and foremost in all proceedings under the Act. Embodied within the ethos of the Act was a requirement for courts, and by definition social workers working with children, to ascertain the wishes and feelings of the child, and to apply the child-centred principles of the 'welfare checklist'. There is a focus on children's rights throughout the Act, with an emphasis on children having a say on all decisions affecting them. In the international sphere, the United Nations adopted a Convention on the Rights of the Child in 1989, and, subject to certain reservations, it was ratified by Britain in 1991. For many academics, child-welfare organizations and child-care professionals the British Conservative government's apparent willingness to acknowledge certain basic minimum rights for children was a welcome, but long overdue development. It was hoped that the 1990s would see a new 'settlement' for children, not just in relation to juvenile justice, but also in welfare provision generally.

At a rhetorical level then, the political climate certainly appeared to have changed. And it did seem that in one area at least – juvenile justice – a new 'welfarist' approach was subsequently pursued. As Rutherford (1999: 47) notes, the futility of retributive forms of punishment for child and young offenders *was* increasingly acknowledged, and 'concerted efforts were made at the level of both policy and practice to fashion an approach to youth justice that was rational, reflective and humane'. Consequently, much greater use was made of 'diversionary' measures such as informal warnings and cautions, and the result was a dramatic fall in the number of children and young persons given custodial sentences – between 1983 and 1992 the number of males aged 14–18 sentenced to immediate custody declined from 13,500 to 3300 (Goldson, 2000). This new approach seemed to have much in common with the emerging 'children's rights agenda'. However, it soon became evident that the government was less committed to the extension of children's 'rights' than its rhetoric implied. Within the space of no more than two years the Conservative Government had dismantled most of the progressive juvenile justice reforms it had implemented.

The *volte face* on juvenile justice policy occurred between 1992 and 1993, after a series of high-profile crimes involving children led to a ferocious backlash against rehabilitative methods of dealing with young offenders. Paradoxically, the blame for the apparent breakdown in youth discipline and morality was placed on the 'diversionary' strategies of 1980s and early 1990s that had, in fact, been extremely successful in curbing juvenile crime – between 1983 and 1994, the period when children were increasingly diverted away from custodial sentences, the numbers of young people aged 17 or under convicted or cautioned declined by 34 per cent (Muncie, 1998: 195, 206). However, influential right-wing commentators such as Charles Murray (1994) continued to insist that the cause of the apparent upsurge in juvenile crime lay in the 'coddling' of habitual young criminals. In the moral panic that ensued, the achievements of the 'welfarist' approach were ignored, and politicians and lurid media coverage portrayed 'informal warnings' and cautioning as an unacceptably lenient means of dealing with 'yobs' (Goldson, 2000: 36). This, in turn, led to pressure for harsher sentences to be imposed on juvenile miscreants. Some, such as Lord Justice Woolf, sought to draw attention to the emphatic failure of custodial sentences to rehabilitate. However, encouraged by sensational populist journalism, right-wing elements in his own party, and an opposition Labour Party seeking to make political capital out of the emergence of a 'yob culture', Kenneth Clarke, the Conservative Home Secretary, announced his intention to introduce new powers to lock up 'really persistent nasty little juveniles' (Moore, 2000: 116).

The 1994 Criminal Justice and Public Order Act, with its creation of new, harsher penalties for child offenders, represented the pinnacle of this policy reversal. As Bandalli (2000: 81) argues, it 'systematically eroded much of the "special status" of childhood in criminal law and produced a matrix of provisions to facilitate and increase the criminalisation of children'. Consequently, the number of young offenders under 21 in prison increased by 30 per cent between June 1993 and June 1996 (Moore, 2000: 118). As for the conditions found in the institutions in which children were detained, the government's own Chief Inspector of Prisons, Sir David Ramsbotham, was appalled at what he discovered in 1997. It seemed to him that the 'majority of establishments holding children and young adults' were operating 'as human warehouses rather than reforming institutions', and that 'criminal attitudes, rather than being challenged', were 'in too many cases being reinforced'. He concluded that the conditions were 'in many cases . . . far below the minimum conditions . . . required by the Children Act 1989 and the UN Convention on the Rights of the Child'. Once again, it was the human consequences of the denial of basic fundamental rights that were most disturbing – between 1994 and 1997 there were 41 suicides and 4112 reported cases of self-harm among young inmates (Home Office, 1997a). Clearly, the acknowledgement of children's 'rights' in the juvenile justice arena proved to be a temporary, short-lived experiment.

## New Labour: Does 'Every Child Matter'?

To a large extent, the Labour Party's May 1997 General Election victory represented a popular rejection of the neo-liberal ideas and philosophies that had, in the words of Robin Cook, then a senior Shadow Minister, created a society in which 'so many children begin their lives in families excluded from the stimulus, the security, the pleasures of life that the rest of society takes for granted' (Shrimsley, 1996). To what extent, though, did May 1997 represent the beginning of a new, more progressive, rights based agenda for children? Certainly, during its time in opposition the Labour Party condemned the detrimental impact of Conservative policies, including juvenile justice policies, on the nation's children. Here, for example, is Tony Blair commenting upon the Conservative government's retributive, 'control'-orientated approach towards juvenile justice policy:

> Let us be clear. No one . . . but a Tory would deny the influence that . . . social conditions can have on the way in which our young people develop. That is why we need to remedy not just the faults of the criminal justice system but the culture of despair, hopelessness, drugs, violence, instability, poor education and poor job prospects that characterise elements of our young people today. To achieve that, we do not need or want lectures from Ministers on the responsibilities of everyone else but themselves. (Commons Hansard, 11/1/94, c. 41)

Hence, those interested in child welfare welcomed the landslide General Election victory of New Labour in May 1997, and looked forward to the adoption of a more constructive approach in relation to both juvenile justice and child welfare generally.

In government, New Labour's rhetoric on children rights has been welcomed as being much more inclusive and progressive than that of previous Conservative governments. The current government, for example, accepts that child poverty is a significant problem in the UK, and it has committed itself to achieving explicit child poverty reduction targets. It has also introduced a range of child-centred initiatives – for example, the National Childcare Strategy, Connexions, Sure Start, Educational Action Zones, and Children's Trusts – all, apparently, with children's interests and welfare at their heart. More recently, in 2003, the government published a Green Paper entitled *Every Child Matters*, which committed it to putting all children's needs at the heart of everything it did. The introduction to the Green Paper, written by the Treasury Minister, Paul Boateng, emphasised the 'importance' the government places on children's welfare and rights:

> Children are precious. The world they must learn to inhabit is one in which they will face hazards and obstacles alongside real and growing opportunities. They are entitled not just

to the sentiment of adults but a strategy that safeguards them as children and realizes their potential to the very best of our ability. (Department for Education and Skills (DfES), 2003: 4).

The principles enshrined in *Every Child Matters* formed part of the Children Act, which received its Royal Assent in November 2004. 'The Act', according to the government, 'provides a legislative spine for the wider strategy for improving children's lives. This covers the *universal* services which *every child* accesses, and more targeted services for those with additional needs' (DfES, 2005: 1, our emphases). One of the main features of the Act (based on the principle that 'every child matters') is its insistence that 'key agencies who work with children put in place arrangements to make sure that they take account of the need to safeguard and promote the welfare of children when doing their jobs' (DfES, 2004: 1). Also included in the Children Act are provisions for the creation of a Children's Commissioner, whose job it will be to raise awareness of the best interests of children and young people, to ensure children's rights form a key component in public policy and to report annually to Parliament, through the Secretary of State, on its findings.

The rhetoric underpinning *Every Child Matters* and the Children Act is certainly 'progressive' and universalistic in nature. Both the Green Paper and the Act identify the unmet needs of a number of hitherto hidden and marginalised groups. However, reference to the welfare needs of specific groups of children was omitted from both *Every Child Matters* and the Children Act, undermining the government's otherwise 'universalistic' rhetoric. Our case studies below examine the impact of recent policies on two such categories of 'unmentioned' children, youth offenders and children of families seeking asylum. We will argue that the government's failure to acknowledge the needs of these two groups of children in policy documents and legislation is not inadvertent, and relates to the wider 'controlling' agenda, which forms a key plank of New Labour's public policy. In short, we will argue that the trajectories of both youth justice and immigration policy under this government suggest that a controlling agenda is still very much in evident and that 'every child does not matter'.

## Juvenile Justice

Although *Every Child Matters* failed to consider the needs of juvenile offenders, a short, separate Home Office document, *Youth Justice: Next Steps*, examined the measures deemed necessary 'to tackle effectively the problems caused by, and the needs of, those young people who do become involved in crime' (Home Office, 2003b: 4). However, the 'needs' of youth offenders were barely mentioned in the document. Overwhelming emphasis was placed on 'the problems caused by' youth offenders, and the necessity for effective measures to deter offending, including custody. The document's failure to consider the welfare of youth offenders, led the Local Government Association (LGA, 2004: 8), and others, to inform the government of their 'grave concerns that the primacy of the welfare of the child would be undermined and . . . severely weakened' in its youth justice strategy. As Hilton Dawson (2004), a Labour backbench MP and former social worker argued, the government appeared to be setting out 'the prevention of offending as its single main purpose without mentioning the best interests of children'.

Despite these anxieties, some of New Labour's initiatives do appear to contain elements of the reformist principles enshrined in *Every Child Matters*. Many (for example, the national Childcare Strategy, Children's Trusts and Educational Action Zones) form part of the government's much vaunted 'joined up' strategy for combating social exclusion, and, it could be argued, reflect Labour's traditional emphasis on the need to address the 'social causes' of juvenile crime. However, as Smith (2003: 57) states, the ostensibly 'reformist', 'progressive' measures introduced by New Labour comprise but one component of its youth crime strategy. Another, more coercive element, shifts the agenda away from 'welfare' (hence the absence of any substantive consideration of this in *Next Steps*) and focuses on the perceived need to address anti-social pre-criminal behaviour 'by imposing a range of control measures on "problem" children and their families'. These include Anti-Social Behaviour Orders, Child Safety Orders, Curfew Orders and Parenting Orders. The rationale used to justify these initiatives said little about the 'social causes' of crime (or the 'rights' of youth offenders), locating its origins instead in the 'fecklessness' and 'irresponsibility' of children and parents. The following comments, made by the then Home Secretary, Jack Straw, encapsulate the emphasis now placed on 'moral culpability' rather than structural inequality:

> Today's young offenders can too easily become tomorrow's hardened criminals. For too long we have assumed they will grow out of their offending behaviour if left to themselves . . . an excuse culture has developed within the youth justice system . . . it excuses itself for its inefficiency and too often excuses young offenders who come before it, allowing them to go on wasting their own and wrecking other people's lives . . . offenders are rarely asked to account for themselves . . . Parents are not confronted with their responsibilities. Victims have no role and the public is excluded. (Cited in Muncie, 1999: 148)

As Brownlee (1998: 316) argues, Labour's 'continuing tendency to locate the causes of crime at the level of individual failure in a range of pronouncements makes it clear that the punitive discourse which was so much a feature of the previous administration has survived the dramatic demise of the Conservative government'. With Parenting Orders, for example, the blame for crime is placed on uncaring, 'dysfunctional' parenting, and the solution therefore is not structural reform, but to reinforce parental responsibility. Thus, parents can now be forced by the courts to attend counselling or guidance sessions; they can be required to see that their children get to school every day, and to ensure that they are home by a certain time at night (Home Office, 1997b). Unsurprisingly, such initiatives are not without their critics. For Drakeford and McCarthy (2000: 102) and Smith

(2003) these 'solutions' conveniently mask the extent to which juvenile crime and 'ineffective parenting' are themselves merely 'a symptom of more fundamental problems and pressures, including poverty, social exclusion and structural inequality'. Working-class parents (particularly mothers) and their children have, according to Drakeford and McCarthy, become convenient political scapegoats, and the government's own responsibility for ensuring families have access to adequate housing, worthwhile educational provision and a decent income have been sidestepped. Similar criticisms have been made about another such initiative, Youth Inclusion and Support Panels (YISPs). Launched in 2000, YISPs have been given the remit of identifying potentially 'problematic' children prior to any offending taking place by using a complex statistical formula of 'at risk' indicators. However, as Goldson argues, there are dangers in premising intervention on what children 'might' do rather than what they have done:

> Increasingly guilt is no longer the founding principle of formal intervention, which can now be triggered without an offence being committed. Instead, intervention is now premised upon a 'condition', a 'character', or a 'mode of life', which is assessed as 'failing' or posing a risk . . . Children will be judged not only on the basis of what they have done, but what they might do, who they are, or who they are thought to be . . . In the final analysis . . . terms such as 'potential offender', 'at risk', 'pre-delinquent', 'crime prone' . . . all mean the same thing in criminal law – they actually mean innocent! (2003: 4)

The problem with YISPs and other such initiatives is that the welfare 'needs' of vulnerable children become sidelined, and the overarching focus of policy instead becomes their potential 'misdeeds'. In practice, this generates very real tensions for social workers working with children who offend, who have been trained in accordance with the welfare principle enshrined in the Children Act 1989. These social workers increasingly find their practice underpinned by a controlling rather than a caring ethos. Indeed, as Smith (2003) suggests the very name of the new Youth Offending Teams, and the fact that they are distinct and separate from child and family social work signals a concern with children's offending behaviour first and foremost, at the expense of a concern with their welfare. The consequent loss of the primacy of welfare for this group of children would seem to contravene the spirit of both the Children Act 1989 and the UN Convention on the Rights of the Child.

Consequently, interventions are based less around the welfare requirements of children, and more around the desire to control them. Ironically, the early 'identification' and labelling of such 'problem' children poses risks which may serve to generate a self-fulfilling prophecy, increasing rather than decreasing the likelihood of future offending behaviour. Meanwhile, the real, structural causes of youth offending remain unresolved. Rarely now does the government seek to link criminal actions to structural inequality. Indeed, academics, criminal justice groups and child-welfare organisations that do seek to establish such a connection are often accused by the government of promoting a culture that 'too often excuses the young offender . . . implying that they cannot help their behaviour because of their social circumstances' (Home Office, 1997b: 2). Critics of these initiatives argue that the solution to juvenile crime lies not in the harassment and stigmatisation of those already living on the margins of society, but in the eradication of the deep structural inequality generated by two decades of neo-liberal government.

---

**Activity 2**

*Have a look at a selection of local and national newspapers – can you find any examples of children who are involved in the criminal justice system (e.g. on children who are the subject of ASBOs)?*

- *How are these children portrayed in the media?*
- *What are the possible implications of this?*

---

Another major component of the government's juvenile justice strategy focuses on even more coercive initiatives, designed to deter and punish children who have committed crimes through custodial sentencing. Whilst some commentators had become alarmed at the tone of the law and order rhetoric emanating from Labour in opposition, it was hoped that the Labour government would distance itself from custodial methods of dealing with juvenile offenders (Moore, 2000: 121). These hopes have been dashed. As the following comments, made by the then Home Secretary David Blunkett in 2002, illustrate, custodial sentences for children have constituted a key component of Labour's 'strategy of deterrence':

> One of the biggest challenges we now face is how to deal with young offenders who believe that their age makes them untouchable, who flout the law, laugh at the police and leave court on bail free to offend again. The public are sick and tired of their behaviour and expect the criminal justice system to keep them off the streets. (Cited in Smith, 2003: 67)

In the name of 'deterrence', then, child offenders have continued to face imprisonment 'despite the fact that the treatment they will receive is likely to harm them further and compound their problems' (Moore, 2000: 125). In fact, the numbers of children in prison have doubled since 1993, and the figures continue to rise. In August 2004, 2637 under-18s were in secure detention, compared with 1769 in November 2003. Overall, 5400 children received custodial sentences in 2003/04 (Anonymous, 2004).

A 2004 report by HM Prison Inspectorate, *Juveniles in Custody*, has provided a damning indictment of the conditions experienced by these children in detention. It shows that few, if any, improvements have been made in the treatment of child prisoners since the publication of Sir David Ramsbotham's findings in 1997. The picture that emerges is one of a harsh, punitive, humiliating régime that offers children few opportunities of rehabilitation. Certainly, children in youth-offending institutions are not treated with dignity and respect, a key requirement of the UNCRC and the Children Act. First, the locations of institutions make it extremely difficult for children to maintain contact with parents. Up to a quarter had not had one visit from anybody, mainly due to the long distances children were held away from their home and families. The physical environments of the institutions housing juveniles were also found to be inappropriately harsh. Only 18 per cent of children were offered the opportunity of daily outdoor exercise and only half of all boys had access to a daily shower (in some girls' institutions, only 20 per cent of inmates had the opportunity to take a daily shower). Personal safety was also found to be a major concern. Just over a third of boys and girls felt unsafe and anxious about bullying-related behaviour from other inmates. In all, 41 per cent of boys and 27 per cent of girls had experienced bullying, or insulting remarks from fellow inmates, whilst 24 per cent of boys and 12 per cent of girls said that they had been kicked or physically assaulted by peers whilst in custody. In some cases, this bullying was racially motivated. 9 per cent of all boys and 4 per cent of girls said that they had been picked on because of their race or ethnic background (in some institutions up to 17 per cent of inmates had been the subject of racist abuse). Worse still, *Juveniles in Custody* found that bullying and harassment by staff was a significant problem. Twenty-two per cent of boys said that they had had insulting remarks made about them by members of staff. Even more alarmingly, 9 per cent of boys and 3 per cent of girls reported that they had been kicked or physically assaulted by a member of staff during their periods in custody (HM Inspectorate of Prisons, 2004).

These findings suggest that the basic human rights and welfare needs of children in detention clearly 'do not matter' as much as those of other, 'law-abiding' children. On this specific point, the government has faced criticism from the UN Committee on the Rights of the Child. Jaap Doek, the Chairman of the UN Committee, argues that the UK stands alone in Europe in terms of its unnecessary jailing of juveniles:

> Urgent action is required to remedy the plight of children in custody . . . many children are officially classed as too vulnerable for prison service custody, and there are continuing and grave concerns about children's access to education, health care and protection . . . My committee recommended in 2002 that detention should only be used as a last resort, yet the UK still locks up more children than most other industrialised countries. Why is this tolerated? (Cited in Carvel, 2004b: 1)

Once again, it is the tragic human consequences of the isolation, fear, bullying and harassment of children in custody that are most disturbing. Since 1998 14 children have killed themselves whilst incarcerated (Anonymous, 2004: 4). One of these children, 14–year-old Adam Rickwood, became the youngest person in

British penal history to die in custody when he was found hanging in his cell in Hassockfield secure training centre in August 2004. The death soon after of another child in custody, 16-year-old Joseph Scholes, was brought to the attention of the Parliamentary Joint Committee on Human Rights (JCHR, 2004), whose role it is to examine the potential human rights implications of public policy. The death of Joseph, the Joint Committee stated, highlighted 'successive failures within the criminal justice system in meeting the needs of a highly vulnerable children'. Its comments are lengthy, but they serve to highlight the fact that, despite government assurances to the contrary, the welfare of thousands of children is being jeopardised by the inappropriate use of custodial sentences:

> At the time of his arrest for involvement in a series of robberies – albeit peripherally – Joseph Scholes was depressed, had begun to self-harm and have periodic suicidal thoughts. Two weeks before his court appearance, he slashed his face with a knife over 30 times. Prior to sentencing, the trial judge was alerted to Joseph's vulnerability, his experience of sexual abuse and history of suicidal and self-harming behaviour. Despite this he was sentenced to a two-year detention and training order, although the judge stated that he wanted the warnings about Joseph's self-harming and history of sexual abuse 'most expressly drawn to the attention of the authorities'. Nevertheless, Joseph Scholes was placed in prison service custody rather than local authority secure accommodation. Just nine days into his time at Stoke Heath Joseph Scholes hanged himself from a sheet tied to the bars of the window in his cell, where he had been kept in virtual seclusion. (JCHR, 2004: 26)

Appalled at Joseph's death, the Joint Committee questioned whether 'imprisonment can ever be deemed to be in the best interests of the child' as defined by Article 3.1 of the Convention on the Rights of the Child. This states that: 'In all actions concerning children, whether undertaken by public or private social welfare institutions, courts of law, administrative authorities or legislative bodies, the best interests of the child shall be paramount' (Cunningham and Tomlinson, 2005: 264).

But does incarceration, as ministers suggest, succeed in deterring children from committing further offences? In other words, is the sacrifice of the welfare needs of child offenders in some sense 'justified' by its success in deterring and preventing future criminal behaviour? As was the case in the nineteenth century, all the available evidence indicates that the experience of imprisonment neither deters nor rehabilitates. In 1999 80 per cent of 14–17-year-olds discharged from prison were reconvicted within two years. That is not to say that children are resistant to the principle of rehabilitation. On the contrary, 91 per cent of girls and 89 per cent of boys in custody want to stop offending in the future. However, the retributive ethos of youth-offending institutions and the lack of rehabilitative support mitigate against 'reform'. For example, whilst the vast majority of children participating in *Juveniles in Custody* felt that finding a job was likely to be the one thing that stopped them re-offending, 68 per cent of boys and 56 per cent of girls said they had done nothing whilst detained that would help them obtain work on release (HM Inspectorate of Prisons, 2004: v). A recent

**Table 11.1**  *Average numbers of hours spent by juvenile prisoners in education*

| Year | Hours per week |
| --- | --- |
| 2000–1 | 8.32 |
| 2001–2 | 7.20 |
| 2002–3 | 6.77 |

*Source*: Home Affairs Select Committee, 2005: 96

Home Affairs Select Committee Report (2005) confirms the lacklustre nature of attempts at rehabilitation (see Table 11.1). It notes that the numbers of hours spent in education by juveniles falls well below *The Prison Rules'* requirement that all prisoners of compulsory school age be given education or training courses for at least 15 hours a week.

Education and training, the Select Committee argued, 'should form the cornerstone of the prison rehabilitation strategy for juvenile prisoners', and it deplored the government's failure to address this key issue. For the Howard League (2004), such findings represent 'a terminal indictment of a hugely wasteful system'. Children, it argues, 'should never be held in a prison – instead we should invest in the successful community based projects that help children change their lives and make amends for what they have done'.

Hitherto, though, ministers have shown a distinct reluctance to reduce the size of the juvenile prison population. Whether its reluctance to discard juvenile custodial sentences and embrace well-proven rehabilitative forms of juvenile justice is due to a genuine belief in the slogan 'prison works' or reflects its desire not to be seen as being 'soft' on 'juvenile miscreants' is not clear. With opinion polls telling ministers that crime and disorder is a significant concern amongst the electorate, political expediency is doubtlessly a significant factor. Irrespective of the consequences of custodial sentences, ministers clearly want to be seen as coming down 'hard' on what voters perceive to be 'morally culpable' juvenile offenders.

Overall New Labour's youth justice policies have shifted away from a 'welfare'-based' agenda to one framed around punishment and deterrence. In other words, the focus has moved from children's 'needs' to children's 'misdeeds', a shift encapsulated in Jack Straw's suggestion that 'the welfare needs of the young offender cannot outweigh the needs of the community to be protected from the adverse consequences of his or her offending behaviour' (cited in Smith, 2003: 59). For Hilton Dawson (2004), the growing failure to acknowledge the genuine welfare needs of youth offenders, and the social causes of crime, has been 'this government's failure'. As he argues, ministers 'cannot seriously argue that Every Child Matters', when they are responsible for locking up approximately 3000 children at a time in institutions that fail to meet 'any of the range of standards required for any other accommodation for children under the Children Act'. The government, he insists, should end custodial sentences for children, develop a genuinely inclusive, 'rights-based' youth justice strategy, and recognise that 'Children are children are children and every child actually does matter'.

## Refugee Children

A whole chapter in *Every Child Matters* was devoted to *Supporting Parents and Carers*. '*All children*', it began, 'deserve the chance to grow up in a loving, secure family'. 'The bond between the child and their parents is the most critical influence on a child's life', and the government would reinforce this by developing 'more and better universal services, *open to all families*, as and when they need them' (DfES, 2003: 39–40, our emphasis). As Williams (2004) notes, the Green Paper identifies the needs of a number of hitherto hidden and marginalised groups, including unaccompanied asylum-seeking children (who it describes as one of the groups in 'greatest need', DfES, 2003: 50). However, as with juvenile offenders, the needs of children of families seeking asylum are not mentioned, an omission noted by many respondents to the DfES's consultation exercise. Whilst supporting the notion underlying the title, that every child should indeed matter, in the absence of any mention of children of asylum seekers, many questioned whether this was, or would be the case:

> If . . . every child matters we would have expected further discussion of the specific needs of children of asylum seekers than occurs in the green paper . . . Such children ought to be considered since they stand a much higher risk of poverty-induced vulnerability than is the typical experience. (Child Poverty Action Group, 2003: 5–6)

Soon after the publication of *Every Child Matters*, the Home Office announced new legislative proposals on asylum and immigration. Like Labour's 1999 and 2002 Asylum Acts, they were predicated on the notion that the vast majority of asylum seekers were bogus, and that hasher systems of support needed to be put in place in order to combat 'what may be seen in many quarters as continuing evasions and exploitation of immigration and asylum controls at significant cost to the taxpayer' (Home Office, 2003c). Amongst the proposals were measures designed to coerce failed asylum-seeking families into leaving the country 'voluntarily', one of which envisaged removing all welfare support, including that given to families with children, from 'failed' asylum applicants deemed to be in a position to leave the UK. The Home Office's consultation document made it clear that in the event of assistance being withdrawn from failed asylum-seeking parents, local authorities would be prohibited from using Section 17 of the Children Act to support children. This obliges local authorities, wherever possible, to provide services for children *and their families*, with the aim of promoting the upbringing of children *in their families*. The proposal made explicit reference to the use of Section 20, which states that local authorities must provide accommodation for any child in need in the event of 'the person who has been caring for him being prevented (whether or not permanently, and for whatever reason) from providing him with suitable accommodation and care' (Bridge et al., 1990: 171). In short, it was envisaged that the children of those denied support and made destitute would be accommodated in local authority care.

The Home Office justified its proposals by claiming they were 'designed to remove the current incentive for families to delay removal as long as possible and so save money in support and legal costs' (Home Office, 2003a). In fact, sections of the press had been briefed about this specific proposal prior to the consultation process being announced. Then, reporters were told that voluntary return schemes for unsuccessful asylum applicants had failed and that a harsher, meaner approach was required. 'Having offered a bit of a carrot', one Home Office spokesperson commented, 'there is a need for a bit more stick' (cited in Cunningham and Tomlinson, 2005: 257). The Home Affairs Select Committee questioned the Home Office Minister, Beverley Hughes, on the proposals on 19th November 2003. Although she began by claiming it was 'not at all' the government's intention to make people destitute, her testimony offered little reassurance. David Winnick, one of the Select Committee's Labour MPs, asked whether 'it would be fair to describe the policy as "starve them out"?' Whilst Hughes denied this, when asked whether the government intended to deny families 'every form of support' and allow their children to be taken into care, she replied, 'Yes, that is what we are proposing' (cited in Cunningham and Tomlinson, 2005: 257). There was, she insisted, a 'need to eradicate the perverse incentives which lead failed asylum seeking families to refuse opportunities to leave voluntarily' (cited in Cunningham and Tomlinson, 2005: 257).

In her evidence, Hughes displayed no awareness of the real reasons why removals of failed asylum-seeking families are delayed. In fact, the vast majority of cancelled or deferred removals are for administrative reasons, allied to Home Office incompetence and *not* non-compliance. This was the cause of 71 per cent of removal deferrals/cancellations between November 2002 and October 2003. A further 10 per cent were due to flight cancellations by airlines and only 14 per cent resulted from a failure to comply (Thorpe and Young, 2003: 66). Hence, as the Refugee Children's Consortium (RCC) would subsequently state, in reality the proposal was not about 'voluntary' departure at all – it was a blunt instrument of coercion, designed to coerce families into leaving the country by plunging them into destitution and separating them from their children (Cunningham and Tomlinson, 2005). In short, the welfare needs of refugee children (it was estimated that up to 2000 may be removed from their parents as a result of the proposal) were being deliberately sacrificed in order to achieve the government's wider objective of controlling immigration. The Bishop of Southwark's suggestion, that the proposal had more than a hint of the 'social policy of the workhouse', was not far off the mark. Like the Poor Law, where part of the regime of humiliation was for children to be separated from parents, this proposal envisaged the use of the same 'pressure of the most painful kind' as a social lever in an attempt to ensure failed asylum seekers left the country 'voluntarily' (Cunningham and Tomlinson, 2005: 256). The government's proposals were eventually included in the Asylum and Immigration (Treatment of Claimants, etc.) Bill.

As we have shown elsewhere (Cunningham and Tomlinson, 2005), the reaction to the government's proposals was wholly negative. The Parliamentary Joint Commission on Human Rights questioned the legality of the government's use of children as 'pawns' in its attempts to control immigration. In 'using children and the threat of taking them into care as a deterrent or incentive to persuade adults to co-operate with the authorities', the government was, it argued, in direct contravention of the Article 3.1 of the UNCRC (Cunningham and Tomlinson, 2005: 264). The House of Commons Home Affairs Committee also criticised the proposals. Concerned they 'may be counterproductive', it recommended the government pursue a policy of swift and humane removal, rather than forcing children to suffer for their parents' actions. Child welfare professionals also condemned the proposal. 'In this country', commented Helen Dent, the Family Welfare Association's chief executive, 'we put children into care as a last resort and for their own protection.' It was, she insisted, 'inhuman to use our own version of tyranny and poverty by separating parents and children as a punishment' (Morris, 2003: 11).

The Home Secretary, David Blunkett (2003), answered the government's critics in the *Guardian*, declaring he 'did not come into politics to be the King Herod of the Labour party'. He was, though, unapologetic. His plans were 'necessary medicine', in the 'middle ground' of politics, and designed to counter the challenge of right-wing extremists rather than pander to them. Taking children into care would be a 'last resort', and a result not of government policy, but of the 'unreasonable behaviour of the parents'. 'Our obligations to the welfare of the child', Blunkett insisted, 'are paramount'.

This latter claim has not gone uncontested. By the time the Asylum Bill was published it was apparent that 'every child did not matter'. On 3 December 2003, Alison Harvey (2003: 21), chair of the Children's Refugee Consortium, an umbrella group consisting of 18 children's and refugee NGOs, wrote to *The Times* criticising the government's plans, claiming they not only contravened recommendations made in *Every Child Matters*, but also the best-interests principle set out in the Children Act 1989, the CRC and the European Convention on Human Rights (ECHR). 'The Government', she argued, 'tell us in its Green Paper on children at risk that every child matters.' 'Perhaps', she stated, 'someone should remind the Home Office.' The British Association of Social Workers (BASW) also vehemently opposed the measures:

> We are astounded that the Government can prepare a Green Paper aimed at raising outcomes for vulnerable and hitherto underachieving children with a title *Every Child Matters* that implies the inclusion of all children within its range of proposals and within a matter of weeks propose legislation that will exacerbate the difficulties already facing this particular disadvantaged group. (BASW, 2003)

Regardless of the decisions of adults it was 'fundamentally unjust to introduce legislation that will make children destitute' and force them into care. It was 'as if the government wishes to use children as a rod with which to implement its immigration policy' (ibid.).

---

**Activity 3**

*Go to the library or look on the internet and find out:*

- *What principles underpinned the 1989 United Nations Convention on the Rights of the Child?*
- *What are the principles incorporated in the 'Welfare Checklist' in part 1 of the Children Act 1989?*
- *To what extent are these principles adhered to in relation to the treatment of refugee children?*

---

The concerns expressed by those opposed to the government's proposals were, though, swept aside, and the Asylum and Immigration (Treatment of Claimants, etc.) Act received its Royal Assent at the end of July. Once again, it is difficult to gauge precisely why, despite the widespread concerns outlined above, the government decided to press ahead with its contentious proposals. As with its refusal to back down on the issue of juvenile custodial sentences, there can be little doubt that political expediency was a significant factor. Although in opposition Labour claimed it would have no truck with 'racist' immigration legislation, like its predecessors, this government has prided itself on its determination to be seen as 'tough' on 'asylum cheats', whatever the cost. Rather than countering the 'myths' that surround debates on asylum, drawing attention to the oppression and persecution that drive people to flee from their country of origin, government policy has thus far sought to appeal to those who, inaccurately, claim our asylum system is rife with abuse. Certainly, ministers seemed to revel in the controversy over its proposal to remove children of asylum seekers from their families, doubtlessly content at the 'hard-line' message their refusal to back down sent out to the electorate and potential asylum seekers. As Bill Morris, former General Secretary of the TUC argued, the sight of a Labour government 'thrashing around seeking to appease Middle England by attacking some of the weakest people on our shores' was not a pleasant one. 'Using children to blackmail their parents' was, as he insisted, 'plumbing the depths of morality' (cited in Cunningham and Tomlinson, 2005: 270).

It is quite clear that the government's approach towards children of asylum-seeking families enshrined in the 2004 Asylum Act was not influenced by a desire to meet their welfare needs, or ensure their human rights were acknowledged. On the contrary, in threatening children with destitution and possible removal from their families, the powers contained in the 2004 Asylum Act flew in the face of Britain's domestic and international human rights commitments. Moreover, and crucially for this discussion, the 2004 Act totally undermined the government's stated ambition to ensure that 'every child matters'. As Hilton Dawson argues, 'a Government which sets out to make the children of failed asylum seekers destitute cannot seriously argue that "Every Child Matters"' (Dawson, 2004). The Child Poverty Action Group agrees. Children of those seeking asylum, it argues, 'are, and ought to be treated as, precisely that, children', and simply because their right to remain in the UK remains unresolved 'should not take away from that simple fact' (CPAG, 2004: 5).

---

**Activity 4**

*What experiences might children of asylum-seeking families have to cope with?*

*To what extent have refugee children and their families been used to affect immigration control?*

*How are asylum-seeking families portrayed in the media? Why do you think this is?*

---

## Conclusion

Our broad sweep of child-related social policy has spanned three separate centuries, but some common themes have emerged. Perhaps the most consistent and pervasive of these has been a desire on the part of the state to use social policy relating to children – whether it be in the sphere of juvenile justice or asylum – to secure wider 'control'-orientated objectives. As we have seen, throughout the period under examination, a range of social policies, geared around 'control' rather than 'care', been introduced with the express purpose of modifying the behaviour of 'deviant' groups and their families, and securing acquiescence. For the most part, our historical discussion concentrated on juvenile justice. If space had permitted, we could also have discussed other aspects of social policy in the same context. For instance, the development of education policy has also been shaped historically more by social control concerns than humanitarian sentiment. In the words of James Kay-Shuttleworth, a nineteenth-century advocate of working-class schooling, public education was necessary in order to teach future workers 'sound economic opinions' and to induce them 'to leave undisturbed the control of commercial enterprises in the hands of the capitalists' (cited in Simon, 1960: 356–7).

Despite the limited focus of our historical analysis, it has hopefully served to undermine the commonly made claim that the problems facing society are relatively recent in origin. It is not possible, as some of the commentators cited at the beginning of this chapter seem to assume, to solve all our contemporary dilemmas by reverting back to some mythical golden age that never existed. What we hope it has also done is highlight the fact that long-standing social problems are unlikely to be solved by short-term populist solutions that trivialise their underlying complex causes. Hence, our historical approach can help us understand why the current government's strategy of detaining juvenile offenders is no more likely to have a 'reformative' influence on offending behaviour than did William Whitelaw's 'short sharp shocks' or, for that matter, the Parkhurst regime of 'less eligibility' in the mid-nineteenth century. Put simply, all previous experience suggests that retributive, custodial sentences have never 'reformed' child offenders, nor will they in the future.

We ended with an analysis of whether New Labour's child-related policies marked a break with previous 'controlling' strategies, and movement towards more progressive, welfare-focused interventions in children's lives. In particular, we tested the government's claims to be basing its policies on the principle that 'every child matters'. Our conclusion is that in the arenas of juvenile justice and asylum, social control and immigration control respectively have overridden New Labour's rhetorical emphasis on children's rights. In relation to juvenile justice, diversionist strategies, based on an acknowledgement of the wider structural determinants of crime, have been cast aside in favour of a populist 'retributive' approach of 'just deserts'. Meanwhile, the rights of refugee children have been severely undermined in an attempt by the government to pander to populist pressures to 'get a grip' of immigration control. Our fear is that the dominance of a political rhetoric that prioritises an individualised, aggressive and unmistakably punitive response to what are quite complex, structurally determined problems may serve primarily to stimulate a 'taste' in the public for control and punishment. As Brownlee (1998: 327) notes, 'Once excited, this desire can become insatiable.' Regarding juvenile justice, in seeking to satisfy expectations that more and more young criminals will be severely punished, the government may 'undercut the viability of any measure other than custody, as well as putting at risk other forms of social spending of a kind more likely to impact on the structural correlates of crime'. From this perspective, placing all the blame for juvenile offending on 'maladjusted individuals' and 'dysfunctional parenting' 'merely preserves the conditions under which a growing number of people turn to crime and, as a result, *managing* rather than reducing the offender population' (Brownlee, 1998: 331). Likewise, 'punishing' asylum seekers, by restricting the citizenship rights of refugees and their children, serves to reinforce popular myths about why people flee their countries of origin, and disguises the genuine, pressing reasons for why they are reluctant to return (Cunningham and Tomlinson, 2005).

What we have examined is a range of policies that are parts of an agenda of care, but underneath which lies an unswerving steel will of control, particularly focused towards marginalised groups of children. It seems clear that if the principles enshrined in *Every Child Matters* are to be realised, there needs to be a shifting culture within public policy towards one which genuinely promotes and supports *all* children's rights, and which locates the difficulties they face within wider social structures.

---

**Activity 5**

- *Can care and control ever be reconciled in welfare policy?*

---

**Further Reading**

Goldson, B., Lavalette, M. and McKechnie, J. (eds) (2002) *Children, Welfare and the State*. London: Sage.

Hayter, T. (2000) *Open Borders: the Case Against Immigration Controls*. London: Pluto Press.

Muncie, J. (2002) *Youth and Crime*, second edition. London: Sage.

Pearson, G. (1983) *Hooligan: a History of Respectable Fears*. London: Macmillan Press.

# TWELVE

# 'Demographic Time Bomb', or 'Apocalyptic Demography'

## *The Great Pensions Debate*
### *Stephen Cunningham*

---

**Outline Points**

- Population ageing and its implications for publicly funded pension schemes.
- The trajectory of pensions policy in the UK – demographically or ideologically driven?
- Pension reform under Conservative administrations.
- New Labour and a Third Way for pensions?
- The future: contributory pensions or a 'Citizen's Pension'?

---

## Introduction

Experts tell us that increased life expectancies and ageing populations will, in the near future, place an intolerable strain on the welfare states of advanced capitalist nations. Countries such as the United States, France, Germany and the United Kingdom (UK) are said to be facing a 'demographic time bomb' of unprecedented proportions, and immediate action must be taken if they are to avoid a 'meltdown' in their pension systems. According to one commentator, within 30 years developed countries will have to spend at least an extra 9 to 16 per cent of GDP simply to meet their old-age-benefit promises. Global ageing, it is argued, 'could trigger a crisis that engulfs the world economy'. 'This crisis', we are told 'may even threaten democracy itself' (Petersen, 1999: 46 and 56).

The implications of these changes for the UK seem clear. The risk is that in the relatively near future the UK will have too few workers to support the pension demands of an increasing elderly population. Some commentators have gone as far as to predict a 'generational war', as younger workers increasingly refuse to provide the funds necessary to support elderly populations. 'Anyone that doesn't think there's a big generational war coming', one analyst argues, 'must be on Prozac' (Kotlikoff, 2004, cited in BBC, 2004). This 'doomsday' scenario of young and old pitted against each other was the subject of a recent fictional 'docu-drama' on the UK's BBC2. Set in 2024, when the 'baby boomer' generation, currently in their forties and fifties, are starting to retire, the docu-drama depicted a 'rebellion' against the tax rises needed to pay the costs of supporting an increasingly ageing population. Young were pitted against old, families were split asunder, and a Foundation for the Rights of Future Generations was formed to fight for the 'right' of younger generations to abstain from financially supporting their elders in retirement. In one emotional scene, the Foundation's fictional leader, a character called Chet Tremmel, snarled that the young were 'not going to keep quiet when a band of pampered pensioners steal the future from us' (BBC, 2004).

Although it portrayed a fictional scenario, the stark warnings raised by the BBC's docu-drama – a future of protest, destruction and financial meltdown – will have struck a chord with the organisations, politicians and commentators who have for many years sought to draw attention to the looming global 'catastrophe' posed by changing demographics. Foremost among these 'sceptics' are the world's major financial institutions, the World Bank and the International Monetary Fund (IMF), both of which have long bemoaned the level of economic resources devoted to pensions by Western European nations. As early as 1994, a World Bank report, *Averting the Old Age Crisis*, warned of the future burgeoning costs of Europe's pension schemes. Universal publicly funded pensions, it cautioned, were unsustainable in the long term, and there was a need for a much 'greater reliance on personal savings and the active participation of the private financial sector in managing old age funds' (cited in Hutton, 1994: 15). A more recent World Bank report reiterated these concerns. It criticised European Union (EU) countries for devoting an average of 10.4 per cent of GDP to pension provision, when other 'affluent' non-EU OECD states such as Australia, Canada, the United States and New Zealand spend an average of only 5.3 per cent. 'If changes are not implemented into the current system of retirement income', the report concluded, 'a shrinking number of workers, especially younger workers, will be burdened with the responsibility of providing for an increasing number of elderly.' The report set out the World Bank's preferred solutions to the looming crisis: 'Clearly, major reforms are needed . . . The reform programme will need to combine measures to (1) delay retirement, (2) introduce changes in the benefit structure, and (3) diversify the sources of retirement income to better balance individuals' risks' (World Bank, 2003: vii). The World Bank's position is unequivocal. In order to avoid steep, unsustainable social security costs, EU governments should increase retirement ages, cut the value of publicly funded pensions, state unambiguously that they cannot and will not meet the welfare requirements of future pensioners, and make it clear that today's workers must take more responsibility for their own future financial needs. The post-war 'cradle to grave' settlements, whereby states accepted responsibility for the welfare of citizens, from birth and through old age, must therefore be 'reformed'. The alternative – intergenerational conflict and economic stagnation – is, we are told, too frightening to consider.

## Apocalyptic Demography?

However, as students of social policy, we need to be aware that the questions raised by the 'pensions timebomb' debate are not simply economic, or for that matter demographic. As Vincent (1995: 145) argues, debates over the most appropriate means of funding retirement incomes, like other aspects of social policy, are profoundly influenced and shaped by ideological principles. In this sense, it is important to acknowledge that the World Bank, the IMF and many of the other organisations, research bodies and politicians warning us of the dangers posed by a 'demographic timebomb' are not ideologically or politically neutral. Let us consider briefly the World Bank and IMF. Formed at the Bretton Woods Conference in 1944, with a remit to promote a new global economic order, these two institutions were initially influenced by Keynesian, 'social democratic' principles. However, with the rise of neo-liberalism in the 1980s, they were 'captured' by right-wing market fundamentalists. As Brazier (2004) notes, the World Bank and IMF now possess an almost quasi-religious adherence to the belief that untrammelled free markets can provide the solution to the world's economic and social problems. Their 'one size fits all' model of free-market reform continues to shape the advice given by both institutions to developing and developed countries, often with disastrous consequences. Even 'insiders' have criticised the ideologically loaded 'advice' given by these institutions. Joseph Stiglitz comments thus on his experiences as Chief Economist at the World Bank:

> Decisions were made on the basis of what seemed a curious blend of ideology and bad economics, dogma that sometimes seemed to be thinly veiling special interests. When crises hit, the IMF prescribed outmoded, inappropriate, if 'standard' solutions, without considering the effects they would have on the people told to follow these policies. Rarely did I see forecasts about what policies would do to poverty ... There was a single prescription. Alternative opinions were not sought. Open frank discussion was discouraged – there was no room for it. Ideology guided policy prescription and countries were expected to follow the IMF guidelines without debate. (2002: xiii–xiv)

The point is – and this is important to our discussion – the ideological bias of these institutions is rarely, if at all, mentioned in the reporting of their reports. With regard to the UK pensions debate, IMF and World Bank guidance on pensions and ageing is invariably portrayed as objective, authoritative and 'factual'. A largely uncritical media reports their 'findings' and recommendations, and little or no consideration is given to whether there is actually a 'crisis' that needs addressing. The question invariably posed is not, 'is there a problem', but rather, 'how can we cope with the imminent, looming catastrophe'? The voices of 'optimists', who argue that society is more than capable of meeting the financial needs of future retired workers, are swept aside by an overwhelmingly sceptical discourse.

'Optimists' point out that ageing populations are not a particularly new phenomenon. They note that Britain's population has been ageing right throughout the twentieth century, and although 'crises' relating to dependency ratios have been predicted throughout this period, they have never materialised. Mullan (2000: 74) argues that Britain 'coped with a tripling in the proportion of over-64s between 1911 and 1991' and 'in comparison a further 50 per cent rise over the next 50 years does not seem that onerous'. From this perspective, there is no demographic time bomb, nor will Britain's ageing population cause any insurmountable problems. The key to this argument is the acknowledgement that economic growth and growing tax revenues have historically been more than sufficient to ensure the increasing levels of resources needed to fund more costly retirement incomes: 'Historically modern societies double their wealth about every 25 years. This pace of expansion projected into the next half century dwarfs the extra cost for society from more elderly dependents' (Mullan, 2000: 9).

Other 'optimists' have linked the propagation of what they sometimes refer to as 'apocalyptic demography' in the UK to the rise of the neo-liberal right and its attempts to undermine state welfare. Thus, for Vincent (2003: 86), the notion that population ageing will create a demographic time bomb is a myth, constructed by neo-liberals, who share a particular agenda and specific way of seeing the world. Like the IMF and World Bank, the neo-liberal right in the UK has sought to undermine support for otherwise popular public pensions by creating a sense of inevitability and certainty that they will fail:

> If people believe the 'experts' who say that publicly sponsored PAYG systems cannot be sustained, they are more likely to act in ways that mean they are unsustainable in practice. Certainly in Britain and elsewhere in Europe the state pension is an extremely popular institution. To have it removed or curtailed creates massive opposition. Only by demoralising the population with the belief that it is demographically unsustainable has room for the private financiers been created and a mass pensions market formed. (Vincent, 2003 86)

Certainly, recent events in the UK and elsewhere in Europe point to the enduring popularity of publicly funded pensions. For example, in May 2003, in response to the French conservative government's attempts to curtail spending on public pensions, France was paralysed by a series of strikes that closed schools and halted planes, trains and buses right throughout the country. More than two million people marched through the streets carrying banners and shouting slogans against the French government's proposed cuts (Lichfield, 2003). Similar strikes brought Italy to a standstill in October 2003 and again in October 2004, in opposition to Silvio Berlusconi's right-wing Italian government's pensions reforms (Johnston, 2003). In both countries unions have argued that spurious demographic arguments have been used to justify cuts that are motivated by ideology rather than anxieties about ageing. Closer to home, the Trades Union Congress (TUC, 2005) called a national day of action in February 2005 in response to the Labour government's failure to acknowledge that everyone 'should be able to look forward to a secure income in retirement that provides a decent standard of living and allows full participation in society'. What these events illustrate is growing discontent over public pension residualisation, and, importantly for 'optimists' such as Vincent, the ideological functions of 'apocalyptic demography'. In short, it can act as a smokescreen, undermining support for pensions and disguising the ideologically based foundations underpinning neo-liberal reforms.

Despite the above qualifications, in the UK 'scepticism' about the future has dominated the policy debate. Is this scepticism justified? Raw statistical data for the UK does seem to lend support to IMF and World Bank claims that a demographic crisis is imminent. In 1950 the average 65-year-old UK male could expect to live for only another 12 years. Today, 65-year-old males can expect to live for a further 19 years, and this is expected to rise to 21.7 years by 2050 (female life expectancy is also increasing, although at a slightly slower rate). 'Optimists' have applauded these increases in life expectancy, seeing them as signs of improved, healthier standards of living. However, 'sceptics' have pointed out that when combined with current low birth rates (birth rates today are about 1.7 children per woman compared to 3 children per woman in the late 1960s), the UK will be faced with a doubling in the percentage of the population over 65 between now and 2050 (Pensions Commission, 2004: 33). Consequently, the ratio of 65+ year-olds to 20–64-year-olds (often referred to as the 'dependency ratio') is projected to increase from 27 per cent in 2004 to 48 per cent in 2050 (Pensions Commission, 2004: 3–4).

As already discussed, the idea that ageing populations necessarily lead to unsustainable fiscal burdens for pension schemes has been challenged. Despite this, since 1979, such demographic forecasts have been used by successive UK governments to justify a raft of policies designed to limit the 'burden' posed by the state's obligations to meet the financial needs of pensioners. For the most part, the discussion below examines these changes, and critically analyses the rationale advanced to support them.

---

### Activity 1

- *What ideological developments do 'optimists' link the relatively recent growth in 'apocalyptic demography' to?*
- *Why might neo-liberals be attracted to the ideas and arguments advanced by 'pessimists'?*

Randomly gather together a range of newspaper articles on pensions and population ageing (perhaps by utilising newspaper databases and other internet sources).

- *Place the articles into two piles, one containing material written from an 'Optimistic' perspective and one with material written from a 'Pessimistic' perspective.*
- *After doing this, assess the extent to which the media present us with a 'balanced' picture about the impact of ageing on public pensions.*

---

## The Residualisation of State Pensions – Demography or Ideology?

The non-means-tested basic state pension (BSP) is the benefit most people have in mind when they refer to the 'state pension'. Introduced in 1948, it constituted a key plank in Clement Atlee's Labour government's attempts to create a 'cradle to grave' welfare state. Unlike pensions systems that emerged in other European countries, which sought to provide retirees with relatively generous, income-related pensions, the UK's BSP was, and still is, a flat-rate benefit, with no links to previous earnings. Regarding the mechanics of funding, the BSP is what is known as a 'Pay As You Go' (PAYG) system, whereby the current generation of workers pay national insurance contributions and taxes to fund the BSP of today's pensioners. The PAYG nature of the BSP is the main reason 'sceptics', such as the producers of the BBC 'docu-drama' discussed above, are able to point to the prospect of a potential future 'generational war'. Just to reiterate, 'sceptics' believe that future generations of workers may break their 'generational contract' with their forebears, and refuse to accept the burden of supporting growing numbers of pensioners in an ageing society.

When Margaret Thatcher's Conservative government entered office in 1979 annual increases of the BSP were linked to increases in earnings or prices, whichever rose the highest, and as a result of improvements made by the previous Labour government, its value stood at a post-war peak of 19.8 per cent of average male earnings (Thane, 2000: 378). The Conservatives broke this earnings link in 1980 and consequently the value of the BSP has now fallen to approximately 16 per cent of average earnings (World Bank, 2003). Demographic arguments were at the forefront of the rationale advanced to account for this policy shift. Conservative ministers argued that the projected increase in the numbers of elderly people, together with the worsening dependency ratio, meant that maintaining the link between the value of the BSP and earnings was unaffordable. 'We have made it clear', argued Reg Prentice, then Social Security Minister, 'that we can no longer accept the present statutory provisions which, over a period, would result in pensions increasing by more than prices or earnings, regardless of the country's ability to provide the necessary resources' (Commons Hansard, Vol. 973, c. 1141). With Britain's projected ageing population, this 'would mean having an ever rising share of the national income going in national insurance contributions [and] that is a burden we simply cannot ask the working population to accept' (Commons Hansard, Vol. 976, c. 902).

'Optimists' argue that, in reality, demographics had little to do with the Conservative government's decision to break with the earnings link. Ministers, they insisted, were using 'apocalyptic demography' to justify their neo-liberal inspired ideological objectives of cutting taxation, reducing public expenditure and encouraging personal responsibility for welfare. The memoirs of David Donnison, the senior civil servant at the head of the Supplementary Benefits Commission when the incoming Conservative government came into office, confirm this may well have been the case. They show that ideology, rather than demographics, was responsible for the immediate and dramatic shift in direction that occurred within the Department for Health and Social Security (DHSS) after 1979. Within weeks of the Conservative victory, Donnison, an individual who believed passionately in the state's obligation to alleviate poverty, including pensioner poverty, felt like he was 'a voice from another world'. Incoming ministers dismissed the notion that social security could and should be used to help alleviate poverty, and contribute to the development of a more just, egalitarian society, outright. 'There was', he recalls, 'no more talk about the redistribution effects of government programmes.' 'The new team', Donnison lamented, 'had shed the burden of social conscience', believing that 'the most effective way of dealing with the poverty lobby was to tell it to go away.' Benefit cuts, the encouragement of individual responsibility for meeting retirement needs, and other 'explicitly reactionary steps', were the new order of the day. All this marked a decisive ideological break with the past. 'Previous Governments', Donnison noted, 'had made their cuts too, but always [reluctantly and] in fear of the storm of rage they would evoke from their Party and the pressure groups.' Not any more. In short, the residualisation of welfare, including pensions, had become a major plank of the Conservative government's neo-liberal strategy, and, according to 'optimists' it is in this context that we must interpret its decision to break with the earnings link. Demographic concerns, in reality, figured hardly, if at all. The ending of the earnings link was, as Donnison states, merely 'social security's main offering on the table of public sector cuts' (Donnison, 1982: 163–5).

## SERPS Reforms and the 'Pensions Misselling Scandal'

Implemented by the Labour government in 1978, SERPS (State Earnings Related Pension Scheme) represented an attempt to provide an earnings related 'top up' element to the BSP. Introduced at a period that is sometimes seen as a 'golden age' for pensions policy, it was initially calculated using the best 20 years of life-time earnings, and could deliver benefits on top of the BSP that were the equivalent of 25 per cent of pensionable earnings. SERPS contributions were somewhat more heavily loaded towards employers than workers, and the scheme allowed widows and widowers to inherit the whole of their spouse's additional pension (Phillipson, 1998: 70). Although there was a twenty-year 'run in' and existing pensioners and those just entering old age did not immediately benefit from SERPS, in the long term its effects were potentially substantial.

In 1985, the Conservative government announced it was intending to reform SERPS. Once again, there was much talk of a looming demographic crisis and possible financial meltdown of the national insurance scheme if state pensions, in this case SERPS, remained unreformed. In the words of the 1985 Green Paper, *Reform of Social Security*, it was time to 'accept that the full cost of SERPS cannot prudently be afforded and to begin now to make alternative arrangements'. 'It would', the Green Paper stated, 'be an abdication of responsibility to hand down obligations to our children which we believe they cannot fulfil' (1985: 18 and 24). However, for 'optimists', demographics provide us with only a partial understanding of its motives. True, the growing numbers of elderly predicted by the Green Paper were a certainty. However, the numbers who would be in work to support them was a matter of guesswork, involving notoriously unreliable estimates about future birth rates, levels of economic performance and the numbers of women likely to be employed. Aware of the flaws in the government's arguments, contemporary critics interpreted the proposed reforms as being driven by ideological concerns rather than demographic anxieties. For Weale (1985), the Green Paper represented 'the most sophisticated expression to date of the present Conservative Government's liberal theory of the state'. Certainly, ideological justifications for reform, which emphasise the moral virtues of shifting the burden of funding retirement incomes from the state to the individual, are not difficult to find in the Green Paper:

> the Government believe that social security must be designed to reinforce personal independence, rather than extend the power of the state; to widen, not restrict, people's opportunity to make their own choices; to encourage, not discourage, earning and saving. (Ibid.:18–19)

With hindsight, it now seems clear that the Conservative government's preferred option was to scrap SERPS, and to force individuals to make private provision for their own retirement needs over and above those met by the BSP.

However, due to the pension industry's inability to cope with the burden of providing earnings-related pensions for all, the government chose instead to residualise SERPS, cutting entitlements. Legislation was subsequently passed which reduced benefit entitlements from 25 per cent to 20 per cent of pensionable earnings, the entitlement basis was changed from the best twenty years of earnings to average lifetime earnings, and widows were in future only allowed to inherit 50 per cent of their spouses SERPS benefits. As a result of these changes, the projected costs of SERPS (together with the entitlements of future pensioners) were reduced by half.

The Green Paper also set out the government's vision for the future of pension provision in the UK, advocating a much greater role for the private sector. The state would continue to provide a limited degree of financial security in retirement via the BSP, but anything above this minimum would have to be provided by individuals themselves. There was, the government insisted, a need to 'move to a position in which additional pension provision derives from contributions by employers and employees to occupational and personal pension schemes rather than SERPS' (ibid.: 24).

Private personal pensions, though, were seen as the real panacea. These include the different kinds of personal pensions sold by banks, building societies and insurance companies. Traditionally popular among the self-employed, for whom occupational pensions have not been an option, the government argued they would offer 'consumers' more choice than monolithic state and occupational pension schemes. Subsequently, measures were introduced enabling individuals to transfer their SERPS and occupational pension funds to private personal pensions. Private pensions, the public were told, would be more responsive to diverse needs, allowing individuals to choose from a plethora of tailor-made packages better suited to their personal requirements. Moreover, competition between providers in a 'pensions marketplace' would bring efficiency gains and reduced administration costs, delivering better value for money. The government's ideological 'celebration' of the market meant that concerns about the complexity associated with exercising 'choice' in a pensions 'marketplace', and the possibility that private pension providers may wrongly advise individuals, were brushed aside. As Black and Nobles (1998) acknowledge, government advertising celebrated the new 'choice' unreservedly. Leaflets, television commercials and newspaper advertisements showed workers in chains gangs, straitjackets or locked in boxes. Advertisements announced the 'new freedom to choose your pension arrangements' and ended with the message 'the right pension for you is now yours by right' (cited in Black and Nobles, 1998: 796). At a time when the British electorate was being sold on the virtues of the private over the public – for example, in housing and industry – the Conservatives' reforms struck a chord. The prolonged stock-market boom of the 1980s and 1990s acted as an additional lure for people to take their pension plans into the private sector, as, of course, did doom-laden predictions about the state's inability to fund future pension commitments. For Vincent (1999), the impact of this final factor – 'apocalyptic demography' was crucial. Insecurity and doubt about the capacity of the state to deliver decent public pensions persuaded millions of individuals of the need to protect their own living standards in retirement. Subsequently, many took advantage of the availability of what appeared to be generous financial incentives introduced by the government to encourage individuals to move their SERPS and occupational pension contributions into private personal pensions. Indeed, if the effectiveness of this policy is to be gauged by the numbers transferring their SERPS and occupational pension funds to private personal pensions, then it proved successful beyond the government's wildest dreams. After 1988 more than five million people opted out of SERPS, and up to a further nine million were persuaded to leave their occupational pension schemes and take out private pension plans (Vincent, 1999). However, as Timmins argues, for those who quit their schemes one uncertainty soon replaced another:

> In place of doubts about whether the next generation would pay the taxes to provide this generation's pensions came the doubt about what their money purchase schemes would prove to be worth one, two or more decades hence; and whether future shareholders would allow the scale of dividends needed to fund the pensions that people now expected. (1996: 403)

It is now clear that millions of those who heeded the Conservative government's advice and changed their pensions were badly advised, as what has become known as the 'pensions misselling scandal' ensued. Basically, 'independent' financial advisers, most of whose salaries were commission based, inappropriately persuaded people to transfer their SERPS and occupational pension contributions into inferior private schemes. Bad advice, coupled with high administration costs and declining stock-market returns (upon which private pensions depend), meant that the promises of magnificent returns from private pensions proved to be hollow. Millions of people are now on course to be worse off as a result of transferring out of SERPS and opting for private provision. In 2003, the consumer magazine *Which* conducted a number of 'case studies', one of which estimated that a typical 50-year-old woman contracting out of SERPS into a private pension in 1989 will end up with just £817 per year instead of the £2029 she could have expected had she remained in. Ironically, the very same private pension providers who enthusiastically persuaded people to leave SERPS are now just as eagerly encouraging them to contract back in. Axa now says that 'no one should contract out' and that 'anyone who is currently contracted out should contract back in'. Another company, the HSBC, has recently contracted back in all its 51,000 personal pension customers after calculating that in virtually every case it was better for them to do so (Jones and Inman, 2004). Many of those opting out of occupational schemes and into private personal plans fared no better than those who chose to leave SERPS. Between April 1988 and June

2004, around 1.5 million people were persuaded, inappropriately, to transfer their occupational pensions funds into inferior private personal plans by commission sales staff. The overall sums involved are not small, with the Financial Services Authority, the pensions 'watchdog', estimating that the losses and compensation for those transferring out of occupational schemes could be upwards of £11 billion (Jones, 2002).

The private sector, then, has not proven to be the panacea that Conservative ministers claimed it to be. Indeed, according to Will Hutton (1995: 13), the government's promises constituted 'one of the greatest frauds perpetrated by a democratic government against its people in modern times'. The government's elevation of private pensions over public provision, he argues, constituted little more than an 'ideological attack' and was 'justified by a mishmash of dogma and a calculated misuse of statistics'. What, though, has the impact of these reforms been on the living standards of pensioners? What is clear is that UK pensioner incomes from state provision have fallen well behind those of their European counterparts. The UK system, including full BSP and SERPS entitlements, delivers to the average UK earner a replacement rate of less than 37 per cent of previous earnings in retirement, compared to 72 per cent in Sweden, 70 per cent in the Netherlands and 54 per cent in France. The UK system is even less generous than residual US social security, which delivers a gross replacement rate of 45 per cent (Pensions Commission, 2004: 58). Regarding the overall value of the BSP, in monetary terms, a single pensioner in receipt of their full BSP entitlement was £1570 worse off in 2002 than they would have been had the earnings link been retained. Pensioner couples were £2511.60 worse off (National Pensioners Convention, 2002). Clearly, such sums are not insignificant, and when coupled with other reduced levels of entitlement – for example, for SERPS – the consequences have been dire for many pensioners. Not surprisingly, research has consistently found pensioners to be one of the most socially excluded groups in Britain. In 1999/2000 33 per cent of single pensioners and 23 per cent of pensioner couples were living in poverty, defined as living below 50 per cent of median income after housing costs (Howard et al., 2001: 38). As illustrated by Table 12.1, these are considerably higher levels of pensioner poverty than those found in other European states.

Surveys conducted by pensioner groups serve to highlight the experience of poverty for UK pensioners. Help the Aged's 1999 Later Lifestyles survey discovered that half of those aged 80 or over lived on £80 or less per week. One in four worried about being unable to afford food, whilst two-thirds were concerned about paying clothing or heating bills. Regarding pensioners generally, half of those reliant on community care (for instance, meals on wheels, home care or nursing) had difficulties paying and a fifth had to stop using the services (Hall, 1999). A more recent survey in three electoral wards in Liverpool, Manchester and the London Borough of Newham confirms that few improvements have been made since 1999. This concluded that poverty, defined as an

**Table 12.1**  *Percentage of pensioners living in poverty in different European States*

| Country | Percentage |
| --- | --- |
| Denmark | 11.1 |
| Finland | 8.5 |
| France | 9.8 |
| Germany | 10.1 |
| Italy | 13.7 |
| Netherlands | 2.4 |
| Norway | 11.9 |
| Poland | 3.6 |
| Spain | 11.3 |
| Sweden | 7.7 |

*Source*: Luxembourg Income Study, 2004

inability to afford what the majority of the British population view as basic necessities, affects almost half of people aged 60 and over in deprived urban neighbourhoods. Almost half of the older people surveyed had gone without buying clothes in the previous year, 15 per cent had gone without buying food, and significant numbers had cut back on basic services such as fuel (Scharf et al., 2003).

## The Labour Government and Pensions Reform – Which Way?

There has been much debate within the social policy academic community over the precise direction of the Labour government's 'Third Way'. Tony Blair himself clearly feels his governments have pursued a distinctive, progressive agenda. For him, the Third Way is not simply 'Middle Way' – a pragmatic mishmash of neo-liberal and social democratic policies. It 'is not a third way between conservative and social democratic philosophy. It is social democracy renewed. It is a third way ... because it represents a third phase of post-war history – following the settlements of 1945 and 1979' (Blair, 2001: 10). Others have interpreted Blair's 'Third Way' more critically. Hobsbawm (1998: 4) has described it as 'Thatcherism in Trousers', while for Hall (1998: 14) 'the Blair project ... is still essentially framed by and moving on terrain defined by Thatcherism. Mrs Thatcher had a project. Blair's historic project is adjusting us to it.' This latter group of writers reject Labour's claim to be pursuing a distinctive 'Third Way', claiming that it has accepted key elements of the Conservative agenda. Which of these interpretations best explains the direction of pensions policy under Labour?

Certainly, prior to the General Election in 1997, there was little sign that Labour in government would pursue a broadly similar strategy to its Conservative predecessors. This is what its 1997 election manifesto said about Conservative pension reforms:

> For today's pensioners Conservative policies have created real poverty, growing inequality and widespread insecurity . . . Everyone is entitled to dignity in retirement. Under the Tories, the earnings link for state pensions has been ended, VAT has been imposed, SERPS has been undermined. (Labour Party, 1997: 7)

However, since May 1997 pensions policy has been characterised by a good degree of continuity, with Labour ministers, like previous Conservative ministers, emphasising the need to reign in overall public expenditure on pensions. For example, the government has consistently rejected calls from its own supporters to restore the earnings link with pensions. Whilst it never committed itself to re-establishing the link when in opposition, pensioners' groups, recalling a speech made by Gordon Brown in 1993, hoped that this was one initiative an incoming Labour government would press ahead with. Then, Brown had told the Labour Party Conference, 'I want to achieve what in 50 years of the welfare state has never been achieved. The end of the means test for our elderly people' (cited in Commons Hansard, 9 November 1999, c. 910). In their defence, Labour ministers claim that the cost of restoring the link would be too prohibitive. Increasing the BSP substantially, and linking future rises to earnings, would, ministers argue, mean that scarce resources would go to those who did not necessarily need them. Calls for across-the-board improvements in the BSP are, therefore, now rejected as wasteful, and the Labour government's pensions policy has been based on a strategy of targeting additional means tested benefits to the most needy. Critics accuse Labour of setting aside universal principles that have traditionally guided Labour administrations and of embracing 'selectivism' in the arena of pensions policy. In its defence, the government claims that targeting has enabled it to provide large increases in the value of means-tested support to the poorest pensioners. Certainly means-tested benefit rates have improved, so much so that by April 2002, a single pensioner claiming Income Support was £800 a year better off in real terms than in 1997. An equivalent pensioner couple was £1196 better off (DfWP, 2002: 4).

However, whilst the name of means-tested support for pensioners may have changed, the problems associated with this mode of delivering benefits remain. Theoretically, it provides a safety net, ensuring that no pensioners fall below the poverty line. However, the reality is that hundreds of thousands of pensioners – women and men – do not claim their means-tested support. Non-take-up of means-tested benefits among pensioners is not a new phenomenon. As early as 1965 Peter Townsend's and Brian Abel Smith's (1965) seminal study *The Poor and the Poorest* identified it as being the cause of much pensioner poverty in 1960s Britain. DfWP (2005: 19) statistics show that today little has changed. In 2002/03, between 26 and 37 per cent of pensioners eligible for what was then called the Minimum Income Guarantee (MIG) (means-tested Income Support for pensioners has since been renamed the Pension Credit) failed to claim their entitlement, saving the government between £800m and £1.520m. Just to put this into context, if we use this upper estimate for comparison, this is more than the total amount the government estimate was lost through social security fraud during the same year.

Stigma and complexity associated with claiming means-tested benefits are crucial factors in explaining high levels of non-take-up. Many pensioners are simply not aware of their entitlement. Others associate claiming with the intrusive, stigmatising means tests of the inter-war years, and they resent having to reveal detailed financial information in order to claim benefits that they feel they should be entitled to as a right. Between 1979 and 1997, Conservative ministers did little to remedy this situation. They saw non-take-up as non-problematic, indeed as something to be applauded. 'The claiming of benefit', argued Peter Lilley, the Conservative Social Security Secretary, 'is a matter of personal choice and there will always be those who choose not to make a claim' (cited in Commons Hansard, 28 November 1996, c. 503). Somewhat bizarrely, Lilley also claimed that if the government sought to identify non-claimants using DSS records, it may be in breach of confidentiality and in contravention of European human rights law (cited in Commons Hansard, 10 March 1998, c. 395). The current Labour government has done much more to encourage take-up, but as indicated above, stigma and complexity still deter hundreds of thousands from claiming. And as Goodman et al. (2003) note, if benefits are not taken up, then increases in entitlements, no matter how large, will not make a significant contribution to ending pensioner poverty. The evidence suggests that many of those failing to claim are the poorest pensioners and that hundreds of thousands are falling below this means-tested safety net and remaining in poverty due to missing out on their benefits (Goodman et al., 2003). Just to reiterate, the issue is not simply one of complexity or lack of awareness. Research shows that significant numbers of non-claimants are actually aware of their entitlements, but decline to claim because of the stigma associated with the process. A recent Department for Work and Pensions (DfWP) survey found that up to 5 per cent of non-claimants would still refuse to claim even if they received an extra £40 per week (cited in DfWP, 2005: 22). This has led some to argue that only effective way of getting additional resources to those pensioners who need them most is to increase the BSP and restore the earnings link. This is the preferred strategy of pensioner groups. Help the Aged (2002) call for the state pension to 'be raised immediately to a level that can be perceived objectively as decent', and then increases be linked to standards of living. The National Pensioners Convention (2002) agrees. The BSP, it argues, 'should be raised to the level of the MIG and the link with earnings should be restored for future upratings'.

---

### Activity 2

Download a Pensions Credit application form (together with the guidance notes) from the Department for Work and Pensions website www.dwp.gpv.uk. Once you have downloaded the form, read the guidance notes and try filling it in.

- *How 'accessible' are the guidance notes and the form? Are they easy to understand?*
- *How many different types of income are claimants required to declare? Why might older people resent providing such detailed financial information (perhaps try asking this question to parents and grandparents)?*
- *Assuming you manage to complete the form without giving up, how long did it take you?*
- *Whilst filling the form in, did you ask anybody for help or clarification?*
- *Do you think the complexity of the Pensions Credit form may prevent some vulnerable older people from claiming their entitlement?*

---

Hitherto, the government has rejected all calls for the earnings link to be restored. For some, its stated desire to target scarce resources to the most needy provides us with only a partial understanding of its reluctance to increase the value of the BSP and restore the earnings link. Vincent (2003: 89), for example, has questioned the ideological underpinnings of the Blairite 'Third Way'. Rather than being 'social democracy renewed', as Blair alleges, the Third Way, like neo-liberalism, 'seems to accept that there are severe limits on what the welfare state can provide in future'. Hence, whilst Labour's 1997 General Election Manifesto discussed the need to strike a more 'appropriate balance' of public and privately funded retirement incomes, the principal objective of pension reform remains essentially the same as under the Conservatives – to limit state provision to a 'poor' minority and to encourage self/private provision for the majority. To cite one recent government report, the role for the state is to 'target state resources on providing security for those who need it' (that is, poor pensioners), but to ensure that 'any further pensions reforms . . . look closely at encouraging individuals to save for themselves where they can' (DfWP, 2002). There can, in fact, be little doubt that the government intends the state to provide less and for individuals to save more. It openly admits that the intention is to reduce the proportion of total retirement income provided by the state from today's level of 60 per cent to 40 per cent by 2050. Public spending on pensions, it is envisaged, should decline as a share of GDP from 5.4 per cent to 4.5 per cent by 2050 (DSS, 1998: 8). In terms, then, of the overall direction of Labour's pension reforms, the evidence to date appears to support Jones and Novak's (1999) analysis of Labour's social security policies. Although the 'ideological veneer' surrounding reforms differs from previous Conservative governments, the trajectories of policy and practice have remained broadly the same. As with the Conservatives, private pensions – whether they are of the new 'stakeholder' variety, or more traditional personal pensions – have provided the key platform for Labour's reforms.

The rationale advanced to justify the shift from public to private has also been marked by a greater degree of continuity than it has change. Labour's policy documents on pensions reform also emphasise the 'problems' posed by the UK's ageing population. Pensions reform, one recent report noted, must be considered 'in the context of some key social and demographic issues', which pose 'serious threats' to public finances. The average age of the population, it warned, is due to increase from 39.2 to 44.2 years by 2040. There will be an increase of nearly 50 per cent of people over the retirement age, and the number of workers per pensioner will decrease from 2.5 to 1.8 people. There will, we were told, 'be fewer workers to support those in retirement' (DfWP, 2002: 1). The solution to the impending crisis is clear. The government needs 'to encourage people to take out private pension provision as part of its overall savings strategy, by making people more aware of the "need" to save' (DfWP, 2002: 12).

In the light of the 'misselling scandal' in the 1980s and 1990s, and the palpable failure of private schemes to match the outcomes of either SERPS or occupational pensions, the government's confidence in the capacity of private pensions to deliver decent incomes in retirement has been questioned. The reaction to the government's demographic claims has also been one of dismay. 'Optimists', such as Alan Walker, lament the fact that public debate about pensions continues to be filled 'by a demography of despair, which portrays population ageing not a triumph for civilisation, but something of an apocalypse' (cited in Dean, 2004: 4). There is, Vincent (2003: 89) agrees, 'some irony in the fact that the UK has among the lowest current and projected dependency ratios in the developed world, and a state insurance scheme in surplus, but persists in the view that the state should try and minimise its role in the provision of pensions'. In fact, numerous government-sponsored commissions of inquiry confirm that the UK is not facing a looming demographically induced financial meltdown. For example, the Royal Commission on Long-Term Care for the Elderly (1998) concluded that 'there is no demographic "timebomb"'. The UK, it argued, 'has already lived through its 'time bomb' earlier this century. The future is much more manageable.' Confirming Mullan's (2000) analysis, the Commission noted that the UK's elderly population has always grown, and society has proven to be more than capable of finding the additional necessary resources to fund retirement incomes. On this specific point, a recent House of Lords (2003) inquiry offers further encouragement. It points out that projected productivity gains mean that per capita income will more than double over the next half century, delivering more than enough revenue to cope with the UK's ageing population. 'We conclude', the inquiry's report stated, 'that population ageing does not pose a threat to the continued prosperity and growth of the United Kingdom economy; in this sense, therefore, there is no looming "crisis" of population ageing in the United Kingdom' (House of Lords, 2003: 15). More recently, statistical data in the first report of the Pensions Commission (2004: 61), whose role it is to assess the demographic 'challenges' facing the UK, lent further support to the 'optimists', case. Taking all the demographic trends into account – including the ageing population – it predicts that UK public spending on pensions is expected to *fall* as a proportion of GDP from 5.5 per cent to 4.4 per cent. Moreover, it reveals the parsimonious nature of UK public spending on pensions compared to our European counterparts. Whilst public pensions expenditure amounts to only 5.5 per cent of GDP here, the EU average is almost twice this, at 10.4 per cent. Regarding OECD states, only Korea and Australia spend a lower proportion of the GDP on state pensions than the UK, and the OECD believes that the UK will slip below these to become the lowest spender of all 21 OECD countries by 2050 (cited in Help the Aged, 2002). Even the World Bank, one of the strongest advocates of neo-liberal pension reforms, acknowledges the miserly nature of the UK's state pension provision means that future 'affordability' of public pensions should not be a major concern:

> State pensions [in the UK] are meagre – the maximum basic state pension (flat rate) was 16 per cent of the average wage in 1998. The combined replacement rate from the flat rate first tier and the earnings related second tier, currently 35–40 per cent, will decline if steps are not taken . . . [Public] pension expenditure is only 4 per cent of GDP. The main issues in Britain have to do with the well being of the elderly population and growing inequality among pensioners, not with the affordability of the pension system. (2003: 45)

However, the UK pensions policy debate continues to be dominated more by apocalyptic predictions about the 'unsustainable' nature of current levels of public expenditure than it does by concern over the economic and social well-being of retired pensioners. For example, despite acknowledging that UK public spending on pensions is forecast to *fall*, the bulk of the government's Pensions Commission's first report was devoted to discussing alarmist assumptions about the 'burdens' posed by ageing populations. If pensioners incomes were to improve, it warned ominously, society must choose between four options:

(i)   pensioners will become poorer relative to the rest of society; or
(ii)  taxes/NI contributions devoted to pensions must rise; or
(iii) the savings rate must rise; or
(iv)  average retirement ages must rise.

As the Pensions Policy Institute point out, whilst the Pensions Commission discussed in detail the potential of (iii) and (iv), it virtually ignored the case for (ii). There was little or no critical discussion about the current thrust of policy, and at no stage did the Pensions Commission question whether the government's aim to reduce the proportion of retirement income funded by the state from 60 per cent to 40 per cent was possible or desirable. Other crucial questions remained unanswered. There was little or no discussion of current and future levels of pensioner poverty, nor was consideration given to the feasibility of either improving the BSP or of creating a universal 'Citizen's Pension', based on residency status. As the Pensions Policy Institute note, both these policies have most support among current policy reform proposals and both appear 'possible, affordable and sustainable' (Pensions Policy Institute, 2005: 26).

## A Citizen's Pension?

Contrary to popular belief, the BSP is not available to UK pensioners as of 'right' when they retire. Unlike some other countries, where eligibility for state pensions *is* based on residence and citizenship status (for example, New Zealand), the UK's BSP is a *contributory benefit*, paid only to individuals who have made a requisite number of National Insurance (NI) contributions. The origins of today's BSP can be traced back to the principles for social security set out in the Beveridge Report, published in 1942. In this report, William Beveridge, the architect of the UK's post-war welfare state, proposed a NI scheme that gave 'Benefit in return for contributions, rather than free contributions from the state'. He was opposed to a 'Santa Clause' state, which appeared to give something for nothing, and in words that have some contemporary resonance, he argued that the individual 'should not be taught to regard the State as the dispenser of gifts for which no one needs to pay' (cited in Timmins, 1996: 58). NI contributions, paid through full-time work, would in future determine eligibility for unemployment benefits and pensions.

A few obvious, but important points are worthy of mention here. A state pension that is based on NI contributions from full-time paid employment is open to criticism on a number of grounds. Women, in particular, have found it difficult to balance the BSP's contributory requirements with the competing demands of family life, childrearing and insecure, part-time work. As Timmins (1996) notes, Beveridge shared the commonplace assumption that after the Second World War the vast majority of woman would return to the home to be housewives, and would not require access to NI-based benefits in their own right. 'On marriage', Beveridge argued, 'a woman gains a legal right to maintenance by her husband as a first line of defence against risks . . . she undertakes at the same time to perform vital unpaid service' (Beveridge Report, paragraph 108). As we now know, the assumptions that all women would marry, that marriage was 'for life', and that marriage guaranteed women economic security in old age have not stood the test of time. That world, if it ever existed, exists no more. There is clearly now a pressing need for women today to build up their own state pension entitlements. At present, a woman claiming her BSP (valued at £79.60 per week in 2005) at the current retirement age of 60 (though this will gradually be increased to 65 between 2010 and 2020) will only receive her full 100 per cent entitlement if she has made 39 years of NI contributions (after 2020 this will be 44 years, the same as the current requirement for men). If, as is often the case, women do not meet these stringent contributory conditions, their BSP is reduced on a pro-rata basis. Thus, a female pensioner retiring with

25 per cent of qualifying years will only receive 25 per cent of the full BSP – £19.90 per week. Women retiring with less than 25 per cent of the qualifying years receive no BSP, nor are they entitled to any refund of the NI contributions they have made (DWPs, 2004). Currently, 86 per cent of male and only 49 per cent of female pensioners receive a full BSP entitlement (DSS, 1998: 21).

Without wishing to state the obvious, caring responsibilities alone have prevented, and continue to preclude, women from accruing 39 years of NI contributions. Although partial mechanisms exist to compensate for caring tasks performed predominately by women, such as childrearing, these have long been recognised as inadequate. Hence, although Home Responsibility Protection (HRP), introduced in the 1970s, provides NI 'credits' for caring, the compensation it provides is less than total. The net effect of this is that 69 per cent of women aged 65–69 who do receive the BSP receive less than the full entitlement, compared to only 15 per cent of men (Pensions Commission, 2004: 268). A related point to note is that those earning below what is referred to as the Lower Earnings Limit (LEL), in 2005 £79 per week (£4,108 per year), do not pay any NI. As we know, for a host of reasons women are far more likely to be engaged in low-paid part-time work than men. One recent survey found that over the life cycle a 'typical' woman earns £250,000 less than a man (Ward, 2000). The fact is, many women are earning less than the LEL, do not pay NI contributions, and consequently do not accrue any BSP rights at all. In short, as Michelle Mitchell, Age Concern's head of public affairs argues, the BSP is 'rigid, inflexible and littered with obstacles for people with non-traditional working patterns – in particular women, carers and part-time workers' (Sylvester, 2004).

If you were not aware of the BSP's contributory conditions, you are not alone. A MORI opinion poll survey conducted for Age Concern (2002: 9–10) found that 41 per cent of adults had 'no idea' how many years of NI contributions were necessary to receive a full BSP. Only 2 per cent of men and 1 per cent of women guessed the correct amount of years.

---

### Activity 3

Try testing MORI's findings by asking your fellow students, friends and family about the nature of the UK's basic state pension.

- *Do they know what the current retirement ages are for the BSP?*
- *Do they know that the retirement ages for women and men are to be equalised. Have they any idea as to when this is due to take place?*
- *Are they aware their eligibility for the BSP is dependent on their NI contributory record and not their citizenship status?*
- *Do they know how many years' contributions are necessary in order to secure a full BSP?*

The National Consumer Council (NCC, 2004), a non-departmental, publicly funded body set up to safeguard the interests of consumers, has also drawn attention to the lack of understanding and complexity surrounding state pension entitlements. It is out of a recognition of the flaws of the UK's contributory-based BSP that in recent years the campaign for a 'Citizen's Pension', where everyone receives the same universal basic state pension as an entitlement of residency rather than work history, has gathered pace. Its advocates include the Liberal Democrats, the Scottish Nationalist Party and numerous campaign organisations, such as the National Association of Pensions Funds and the NCC. The recent House of Lords Select Committee on Economic Affairs Report, *Aspects of the Economics of An Ageing Population*, also advocated the introduction of a Citizen's Pension:

> Virtually all citizens make positive contributions to the economy and society through their paid and unpaid work in the period between the end of their formal education and their retirement. The Government's success in operating an active labour market policy to extend employment opportunities to all groups and ages within the population means that few people can now shirk their responsibility to contribute positively to the economic welfare of the country. Thus there seems little reason to operate a complex accounting system to track NI contributions and credits over each person's working life in order for them to qualify for a full or partial basic state pension . . . We therefore recommend that the basic state pension should be paid on the basis of citizenship rather than contribution record. (House of Lords, 2004: 37)

On the key question of affordability, the National Association of Pensions Funds (NAPF, 2004: 47) concludes that 'the UK could afford an immediate transition to a Citizen's Pension of £105 a week for each individual'. It believes that abolishing the complex and expensive system of administering current state benefits means that the costs of the Citizen's Pension up to 2030 could be met within existing taxation and NI levels. Whilst taxation may have to rise slightly after this date, the benefits of a Citizen's Pension in terms of 'adequacy, simplicity, inclusion, encouragement to save, efficiency and certainty' outweigh its relatively small future additional economic costs (NAPF, 2004: 1).

There now seems to be a political consensus that the contributory conditions inherent in the BSP mean that significant numbers of pensioners fail and will continue to fail to obtain a decent income in retirement. The BSP was, to quote David Willetts, the Conservative pensions spokesperson, 'designed for the days when men earned their pensions by work and women by marriage'. Ministers in the current Labour government also believe that the structural bias against women inherent in the BSP is a 'national scandal' (Helm, 2004). In the light of the BSP's manifest failure to adapt to take into account key social changes – for example, the growth in divorce rates, and women's changing role in the workplace – they could hardly do otherwise. Significantly, in 2004, the then Pensions Minister, Alan Johnson, expressed an interest in the development of a Citizen's Pension. However, whether this recognition will translate into effective, concrete action is not yet clear. The proposed Citizen's Pension is not without its opponents both within and outside government. Outside government, neo-liberals have questioned the morality and wisdom of breaking the link between contributing towards a pension and receiving it. It is quite right, they argue, that the state should seek to foster a sense of individual responsibility by tying what people get to what they pay in. In the words of one commentator, with a Citizen's Pension 'The feckless and the workshy would receive the same amount as those who worked all their adult lives' (Eastham, 2004). Within government, Gordon Brown, the principal architect of the complex maze of means-tested support for pensioners, has shown a distinct reluctance to alter the trajectory of pensions policy. The Chancellor's caution was reflected in the government's reaction to the House of Lord's Economic Affairs Committee's recommendations. Its response focused on the 'significant cost implications' of a Citizen's Pension, and reiterated the government's confidence in its 'selectivist' strategy of targeting benefits to the poorest pensioners (House of Lords, 2004: 29). More recently, Brown's November 2004 speech to the Confederation of British Industry rejected a more expansive role for the state in pensions policy. 'We are not suggesting', Brown insisted, 'that the state takes on additional responsibilities.' 'I can tell you', he continued, 'as I told my own political party conference – that I will resist demands from wherever they come, such as on linking pensions to earnings where this would put at risk the fiscal position today and in the long term. Such short-termism is not the best way forward.' As in the past, Brown invoked the prospect of a looming demographic catastrophe as justification for rejecting a greater role for the state. 'To imply that the burden of meeting the risks of the next generation should all be passed to the government', he argued, 'is simply a repetition of the problems that led us to fiscal problems in the past' (Brown, 2004).

---

**Activity 4**

- *What, if any, are the advantages of 'Citizen's Pensions' over contributory pension systems, such as the UK's BSP?*
- *What criticisms have been advanced against 'Citizen's Pensions'?*
- *Examine post-2005 proposals and policies for pension reform. Has the trajectory of pensions policy been influenced by 'optimistic' or 'pessimistic' interpretations of ageing?*
- *Finally, what does the direction of pension policy tell us about the ideological orientation of the governments concerned?*

---

## Conclusion

The prospects for progressive reform of the UK's public pension system are as yet unclear. Politicians have long been aware of the inadequacies of the BSP, yet instead of seeking to devise a more equitable, generous pension system that acknowledges changing family and employment patterns, governments have set about residualising state pensions still further, making them less attractive options not just for women, but for all pensioners. The important point for us to note is that demographic justifications have been at the forefront of these changes. For 'optimists', however, the danger to the UK's pension system lies not with changing demographics, but with the *political creation* of a self-fulfilling prophecy of despair and failure. 'Optimists' fear that if sufficient insecurity and doubt can be spread about the future of state pensions, the high levels of support they currently enjoy will be undermined. From this perspective then, the 'psuedo-scientific arguments' used by UK governments – Conservative and Labour – which seek to create the impression that the futures of state pensions are 'technical', 'demographic' issues rather than a political ones should be exposed for what they are – an ideological smokescreen. This is not to say that 'optimists' deny that the BSP should be reformed. As has been shown, it has its faults, and for the most part, these are acknowledged. What 'optimists' do argue, though, is that there is a choice – a *political* choice – for us as a society to make. Despite the 'doomsday scenario' depicted by the BBC docu-drama discussed at the beginning of this chapter, the evidence suggests that the future is not one circumscribed by a looming demographic crisis of epic proportions. Decent, universal, publicly funded pensions are both affordable and socially just. Hence, the state can and should accept greater responsibility for the financial well-being of older people and seek to develop the case for a *public* pensions strategy that will end pensioner poverty and dispense with the need for stigmatising, demoralising means tests. For advocates of a Citizen's Pension, any future provision should be based not on NI contributions, but on the recognition that all citizens make positive contributions to the economy and society through their paid and unpaid work.

---

### *Further Reading*

Mullan, P. (2000) *The Imaginary Time Bomb: Why an Ageing Population is Not a Social Problem*. London: Tauris and Co. Ltd.

Thane, P. (2000) *Old Age in English History: Past Experiences, Present Issues*. Oxford: Oxford University Press.

Timmins, N. (2001) *The Five Giants: a Biography of the Welfare State*. London: Fontana Proo.

Vincent, J. (1999) *Politics, Power and Old Age*. Buckingham: Open University Press.

Vincent, J. (2003) *Old Age*. London: Routledge.

# THIRTEEN

# Social Policy and the Politics of Food

## *Laura Penketh*

---

### Outline Points

- Food policy has become a high-profile and contested area of social and political debate.
- Neo-liberal policy initiatives have emphasised individual agency and choice at the expense of wider social and environmental concerns.
- The correlation between poverty, inequality, health and nutrition has been undermined.
- Marketisation and privatisation initiatives have led to the demise of state welfare provision associated with health and well-being.
- Corporate interests have disproportionate levels of power and influence in relation to food standards and public health legislation.

---

## Introduction

Barely a day goes by without the media in some way highlighting worries and fears associated with food and health. Newspaper articles discuss increasing health problems associated with food and nutrition, such as diabetes II and obesity, and TV programmes such as *Fit Club* follow celebrities as they attempt to lose weight and improve levels of fitness. There is also high-profile coverage around, for example, the quality of school dinners, the adulteration of food, the increasing lack of confidence in supermarkets and the exploitation of migrant labour within the food production industry.

This chapter examines these themes by looking at the development of food policy in contemporary Britain. It will examine why issues associated with food production, distribution and consumption have become a major focus of political debate. It will explore the extent to which economic, political and social developments have shaped debates, and how governments have responded in terms of legislative developments. In doing so, it will assess ideological perspectives which inform political action, and whose interests they serve. For example, are growing health problems associated with diet and nutrition a result of individual deficiency, or can they be explained more successfully in the context of growing socio-economic inequalities and the direction of government policy?

Historically, social policy analysis and writing have tended to ignore food and nutritional issues until relatively recently. Food and nutrition played a critical role in national well-being during and after the Second World War, and contributed to the measurement and lived experience of poverty. During the war government policy became directly interventionist with regard to the food supply, when the Ministry of Food was established to ensure adequate supplies for the British population during the blockade. Following the war, national food policy focused primarily on food production and restoration of national food security, but the government was reluctant to legislate in the field. Although the Ministry of Health did attempt a programme of education during and after the war, its position was one of benevolent paternalism as is evident in the comments of Douglas Jay, a Labour politician, who stated in 1939 that:

> Housewives as a whole cannot be trusted to buy all the right things where nutrition and health are concerned . . . for in the case of nutrition and health, just as in education the gentlemen of Whitehall really do know what is good for the people than the people know themselves. (Cited in Draper and Green, 2003: 57)

However, food and nutrition '. . . then largely disappeared from public and policy view, and scientific or social study, for much of the rest of the twentieth century' (Dowler, 2003: 143). Instead, food has been seen as an individualist affair, usually labelled under 'lifestyle' rather than being seen as a basic entitlement.

## Food Policy – Growing Areas of Concern

Food production, supply and consumption are now the subject of high-profile and highly charged debates amongst politicians, public health campaigners, nutritionists and scientists, and there has been a serious loss of public confidence in the safety of foods and in food safety policy-making institutions. This interest and concern has developed due to a growing concern that: 'In recent decades food policy in the UK has been malfunctioning across a number of . . . policy sectors including agriculture, health, environment, social and competition policy' (Barling et al., 2003: 1). There are concerns about, for example, the use of additives and pesticides, the development of genetically modified crops, growing levels of obesity amongst the population, and accompanying problems such as dental disease, mental performance, heart disease and diabetes. There is particular concern regarding high levels of fats and sugar in children's diets and a corresponding deficiency of nutrients and vitamins. Almost a third of all children are either obese or overweight, up 50 per cent since 1990. In the population as a whole, more than half are either overweight or obese (Lawrence, 2004). As, on average, obesity reduces life expectancy by nine years, the implications are serious.

Obesity is also contributing to increasing levels of 'type II' or 'late onset' diabetes, which was rare in the under-forties up to a decade ago. Now, the Chairman of the National Obesity Forum describes it as a time bomb just waiting to explode, and an epidemic that could cripple the NHS and the economy (Lawrence, 2004).

Some of the fiercest arguments put forward, particularly in relation to the changing diets and deteriorating health of children, are associated with the role of multinationals and advertisers in promoting and encouraging the intake of 'junk food'. Sales of snacks and sugary drinks overall are rising and, from 1998 to 2002, sales of snacks popular with children rose by 26 per cent. British youngsters consume 30 times the amount of soft drinks and 25 times the amount of confectionery that they did in 1950. Ninety-six per cent of children snack after school and 60 per cent of children eat crisps after school. In total, Britons eat more than ten billion bags of crisps a year, more than 150 packs per person per year and more than the rest of Europe put together (Lawrence, 2004a).

Changes in levels of exercise and physical activity are also issues that politicians and a range of other interested groups are attempting to address. Fewer children now walk or cycle to parks or green spaces or school, due mainly to dangerous levels of traffic on the roads. (Wheelwright, 2004), and currently in Britain just 40 per cent of men and 26 per cent of women take enough exercise (defined as 30 minutes of moderately intense physical activity on five or more days a week) (Revill, 2004).

---

**Activity 1**

*Why has food policy become a major area of debate and concern across British society in recent years?*

---

## Neo-Liberalism and Legislative Developments

In order to explain and make sense of the developments described above, and the intensity of political and social discourse associated with food policy in Britain today, it is necessary to critically explore the neo-liberal agenda that has informed British social policy over the past two decades.

Barling et al. state that:

> Contemporary food policy can . . . be placed within a dominant policy paradigm of national wealth creation through international competitiveness. Large food manufacturing industries and large farm producers are encouraged to compete successfully as export competitors in the neo-liberal trading system (notwithstanding the market distortions of the Common Agricultural Policy (CAP) and other national agricultural and food processing support mechanisms). (2003: 4)

The fact that policy developments associated with public health programmes and dietary change are pursued within the dominant paradigm which offers a privileged place to large corporate players in the food system undermines their progress and effectiveness.

As a result, political challenges and policy initiatives over the past decade or so have only reflected marginal and token reforms. For example, the food safety crises of the late 1980s led to the establishment of the Food Safety Directorate in 1989, but this development only gave the appearance of a separation of responsibilities for food safety from food production sponsorship. In 1991 a Consumer Panel was established, but there was no evidence that it engaged substantively with consumer concerns or had any effect on policy.

It was the announcement by the government on 20 March 1996 that Variant Creutzfeldt-Jakob disease (or vCJD) had emerged and was almost certainly caused by consuming BSE-contaminated food that led to a serious loss of public confidence in the safety of foods and food safety policy-making institutions, and instigated key institutional reforms in food policy. In 1999, the Food Standards Act was introduced, and in 2000 the Food Standards Agency (FSA) was established. In 2001, the Ministry of Agriculture, Fisheries and Food (MAFF) was abolished and its remaining functions, including environmental policy, were transferred to a new Department for Environment, Food and Rural Affairs (DEFRA).

The FSA took over responsibility for consumer protection and the public-health aspects of food policy. Its role was to protect the interests of consumers in relation to food, and its three core values were: to put the consumer first; be open and accessible; and be an independent voice. It was answerable to the Department of Health, indicating a separation of regulation from sponsorship, which had been a key feature of MAFF. Initially, it was proposed that the FSA would have responsibility for the entire food chain, but for reasons never explained, the government decided that MAFF would retain primary responsibility for veterinary and agricultural aspects of food policy. As a result, the FSA's responsibility only runs 'from the farm gate to the plate', rather than 'from the plough to the plate' (Millstone and van Zwanenberg, 2003: 47).

Yet, despite key reforms and legislative developments, there is no indication of a challenge to the dominant power relationships in the conventional food supply chain, and conventional notions of market efficiency and trade are accorded a higher priority than environmental protection. Economic sustainability is at the forefront of the policy agenda, and there is little recognition of a social dimension to the food supply chain. The rationale of the FSA remains rooted in the dominant paradigm. It has adopted a role as a defender of conventional agriculture and farming practices, and industrialised food manufacturing, as well as a consumerist, market-based approach to many issues of food safety (Barling et al., 2003). Despite claims that the FSA reflects a separation of regulation from sponsorship, it has to have regard for the costs and impact of regulations on the private sector, and has co-opted senior corporate staff to work on 'risk management'. Ministers had repeatedly asserted that once the FSA was in operation, food safety policy in the UK would be decided by democratically accountable ministers and not by unaccountable unelected officials. However, in practice this is not the case. Ministers, at most, apply a rubber stamp to the monolithic and prescriptive advice from the FSA Board (Millstone and van Zwanenberg, 2003).

In this respect, despite the laudable aims of the FSA regarding consumer protection, independence and accountability, the shift of responsibility in the regulatory burden from the public to the private sector and individuals has resulted in food retailers playing a central role in enforcing food standards.

More progressive developments that would incorporate environmental and social concerns stand in contradiction to neo-liberalism as a political doctrine which emphasises individual agency and choice, and whose social policy agenda is concerned with enhancing consumer freedom and choice. For neo-liberals, public health is viewed in the market terms of the needs of individual consumers rather than the needs of populations, and there is no legitimate role for the state to intervene in the food system.

Proposals to increase the role of the state and political influence in the area of food policy are often met with accusations from the libertarian right of 'nanny statism', the current code for unwelcome interference in personal freedom. Individuals are deemed to be responsible for their own actions, and health status is a matter of personal choice. In the past, the same arguments have been used to protest against, for example, laws against racism, the introduction of speed limits and the compulsory wearing of seat belts. All are seen as attacks on individual liberty.

This emphasis on individual choice and personal freedom has led to the promotion of developments such as nutrition education, food labels and dietary guidelines as policy instruments. These are posited on the notion that the informed individual is one able to make the right consumption choice.

---

**Activity 2**

*What have been the main legislative developments associated with food policy over the past decade or two?*

*To what extent has neo-liberal ideology informed and underpinned these developments?*

---

## Poverty, Inequality, Health and Nutrition

The limitations of market-based and individualistic policy initiatives are revealed most starkly in the context of socio-economic inequalities. In relation to food policy, those whose food access and nutritional status is compromised are usually poor and marginalised in society, and have little political clout. Nutritional conditions are notably worse for those in the lowest income groups and living in areas of multiple deprivations. For example, intake of fruit and vegetables is very low whilst intake of white bread, processed meats and sugar is very high. As a result nutrient intakes are often below reference levels. Over the last 15 years, vitamin C intake in the poorest fifth of families has declined by 23 per cent and vitamin A by 47 per cent. It is a well-established fact that the health status of adults and children in lower-economic groups is markedly lower, and mortality rates are higher, however social or economic status is measured (Dowler, 2003: 147).

Increases in poverty and inequality, and a growing divide between rich and poor, have had serious implications for the diets and health status of the poor and disadvantaged, particularly in America and Britain, whose governments pursue neo-liberal policy agendas which focus on individual responsibility rather than structural inequality.

A recent swathe of studies has revealed that America, once the home of the world's best-fed, longest-lived people, is now a divided nation made up of a rich elite and a large underclass of poor, ill-fed, often obese, men and women who are dying early. A man born in a poor area of Washington can have a life expectancy that is 40 years less than a woman in a prosperous neighbourhood only a few blocks away. Twenty years ago, America, the richest nation on the planet, led the world's longevity league. Today, however, American women rank 19th, while males can manage only 28th place, alongside men from Brunei. These figures are blamed by researchers on two key factors: obesity and inequality of health care (McKie, 2004). In terms of health inequalities, people die younger in Harlem than in Bangladesh.

In Britain, rising levels of poverty and inequality throw up similar findings. For example, male life expectancy in East Dorset, one of the healthiest places in Britain is 80.1 years, whilst in Glasgow it is 69.1 years. In the East End of Glasgow, with an average life expectancy of 63, men can expect to die 14 years earlier than the average Briton, living to the same ages as men in some developing countries, and on a par with males in Iraq and India (Revill and Hinscliff, 2004). This is believed to be the first decrease in life expectancy in Britain since the Second World War; in 1991 the average age of death was 65. It is no surprise that this area has the lowest average income in the country, at £17,170, and almost half of the children live in households with no working adults.

However, despite such evidence which starkly reveals the correlation between poverty, inequality, and mortality and morbidity rates, many politicians deny that deprivation and disadvantage are any barrier to eating healthily. This is reflected in a statement made by Lord Mackay of Ardbrecknish, the Minister of State,

Department of Social Security in 1996. During a debate on lone-parent benefit, he observed:

> My Lords, we do not believe there is any reason why people on Income Support should not be able to follow a normal healthy diet . . . people tend to eat different diets whatever their income. Some quite well-off people eat inadequate diets. Plenty of food is available at reasonable cost and people can thus maintain a reasonable and sensible diet. (Cited in Dowler, 2003: 155)

---

**Activity 3**

*How important is an understanding of poverty, health and inequality in debates surrounding the production, distribution and consumption of food?*

---

## Neo-Liberalism and the Local State – An Examination of School Meals Policies

As well as a tendency towards ignoring the links between structural inequality and food poverty, neo-liberal policies have, over the past two decades, further disadvantaged the poorest groups in society by attacking and undermining state initiatives that have focused on food and nutrition. The provision of school meals is a key example and a worthwhile case study.

The 1906 Education (Provision of Meals Act) was the first piece of legislation to make public provision for school meals, when Local Education Authorities were given the power to provide free or reduced-charge meals for those children who would otherwise be unable to profit from the education provided. However, the provision was extremely limited as meals were only available to children deemed by medical experts to be suffering from malnutrition and Local Authorities had discretionary powers. Also, much political motivation associated with school meals arose from concerns that high levels of malnutrition and under-nourishment were detrimental to the needs of industry and international competition. Hence, provision was influenced by concerns about national efficiency, and not from any humanitarian concern with the status of poor, sick and under-nourished children.

However, after the Second World War, the provision of school meals was influenced by the birth of the welfare state, and a recognition that state social provision had a role in ameliorating the inequalities in British society, and improving the lives of the poor and disadvantaged. Under the 1944 Education Act, Local Education Authorities were given the duty to provide school meals, reflecting a shift from a system providing some basic nutrients to the poor, to a regime offering school meals to all school children. This was to be a national system financed largely from central government funds, reflecting a social democratic commitment to universal and collective welfare provision. The Act warned that Britain should not dare risk under-educating its children in the areas of food, nutrition and diet. There was a recognition that inadequate nutrition impedes the cognitive development of children in ways that cause lasting damage, and clear nutritional guidelines were drawn up specifying precise proportions of various nutrients necessary for growing children.

However, the school meals policy agenda from the 1980s onwards reflected the neo-liberal ideological preoccupation with 'rolling back the state', and promoting an individualistic and moralistic policy agenda. There was no recognition of structural inequality, public expenditure was seen as wasteful and public provision as inefficient. It was in this context that the Thatcherite government introduced a range of policies which seriously impacted on the philosophy enshrined in post-war welfare developments.

The 1980 Education Act removed the duty of Local Education Authorities to provide school meals (except for those entitled to free school meals). Nutritional standards and fixed pricing systems were also removed. The 1986 Local Government Act introduced competitive tendering, which led to contracts for school meals provision being awarded to the caterer offering the cheapest price. Cash cafeterias were introduced where pupils could pick and choose foods they wanted. This was in line with government ideology, which saw such policy developments as increasing choice and efficiency and reducing waste. The 1986 Social Security Act removed the entitlement to free school meals from children whose families were receiving Family Credit. This was replaced by a notional amount of money paid in benefits, but penalised the children of parents who managed to find low-paid work. As a result, 400,000 children were no longer entitled to free meals. Entitlement was now limited to children whose families were receiving Income Support. Gone was the belief that every child, irrespective of income, should have access to a satisfying and nutritious meal during the school day (McMahon and Masch, 1999).

These legislative developments led to non-take-up of free school meals which became increasingly stigmatised. For example, some schools had separate queues; in others children had to wait until paying children had received their lunch. This type of stigmatisation was evident historically, before the advent of universal provision in the post-war period. In 1987 a 78-year-old pensioner wrote to the Child Poverty Action Group stating that: 'I still go hot all over when I hear the word 'free dinners'. We had a teacher who at 10 minutes to 12 would say "stand up free dinner girls" . . . I shall never forget the feeling of shame . . . I would rather have starved' (McMahon and Marsh, 1999).

The damaging and detrimental effects of deregulation and reduction in entitlement to school meals provoked great hostility from pressure groups such as the Child Poverty Action Group. Their concerns were upheld in figures which demonstrated that whereas in October 1979, 4.9 million children ate school meals (64 per cent), by October 1988, this had fallen to 2.8 million children

(47 per cent) (White et al., 1992, cited in Gustafsson, 2003: 130). The role of school meals in providing food and nutrition was reinforced by a survey carried out in 1999 by the Local Authority Caterers Association. This survey revealed that 22 per cent of parents relied on a school meal to provide a balanced diet, and 60 per cent believed that school meals played a vital role in their children's diet (McMahon and Marsh, 1999). The importance of free school meals in relation to health was also outlined in the Acheson Report (1998) on health inequalities.

By 1997, the school meals service had changed out of all recognition, and was, in reality, no longer a national service that could be an effective instrument for government policy. With figures in the 1980s and 1990s revealing that increasing numbers of children were living in poverty, school meals could have been a central feature of an anti-poverty strategy. Instead, the service was marginalised and standards left to the discretion of already squeezed Local Authority budgets. Also, delegated budgets for school meals were not ring-fenced, in effect allowing schools to spend the school meal budget in whatever way governors chose.

Attacks on state provision and the privatisation and marketisation of welfare provision have also impacted on school sports facilities. There has been increasing concern over the past decade regarding the lack of exercise that people take, and the impact on health and obesity. Here again, reductions in levels of exercise have been exacerbated by a policy agenda that has undermined sport and physical activity in schools and in local communities. Trends in schools towards introducing cafeterias and vending machines have been accompanied by, for example, the selling-off of playing fields. The Playing Fields Association cite a doubling in the number of applications to build on playing fields, from 625 in 1999/2000, to 1,325 in 2002/2003 (Wheelwright, 2004). In terms of Local Authority provision, Tim Gill of the Children's Play Council speaks of a vicious circle operating where cash-starved councils are allowing parks to become derelict. As a result, parents and children stop using them and they become increasingly unsafe. Rising insurance premiums and councils' anxieties about potential litigation have also pushed the cost of new playgrounds skywards.

Such developments reveal the damaging consequences for health and well-being when social provision is withdrawn or undermined. Yet governments over the past twenty years have persisted in prioritising individualistic and moralistic analyses despite facts, figures and statistics which point to the damage emanating from increasing inequality and attacks on state welfare services.

There is also much evidence that, despite political assertions about individual responsibility and prudent budgeting, in practice it is extremely difficult to live on state benefits or low wages for any length of time without getting into debt or cutting essential expenditure or both. Empirical qualitative studies have shown that people economise on food either by buying cheaper or different items, or by omitting meals altogether. Some survive by either borrowing food, or money for food.

As outlined earlier in the chapter, those living on low wages and state benefits cannot afford to purchase sufficient, appropriate food to meet healthy dietary guidelines or nutrient requirements laid down by government committees and experts because they have insufficient money. This point was reinforced by the statement from a doctor who has practised in the Shettleston area of Glasgow for the past 21 years. He was scathing about the government's lack of will to address the grinding poverty that blights so many of his patients' lives, stating: 'It's a bloody disgrace. It's not a medical problem. It's political. People here need to be given hope. They need job opportunites' (Revill and Hinscliff, 2004).

**Activity 4**

*What impact did marketisation and privatisation initiatives have on the ability of the local state to promote health and well-being?*

## The Increasing Power and Influence of Corporate Interests in the Field of Food Policy

The diets of the poor and their access to affordable and fresh produce have been further undermined over the past two decades as result of competitive pressures from major food retailers which have led to the closure of local shops, creating irreversible damage to towns and communities. During the last three decades, Britain has been transformed from what was described as a 'nation of shop-keepers', with innumerable small businesses, to a supermarket culture dominated by a handful of large retailers. The four giant supermarkets, Tesco, Asda, Sainsburys and Morrisons, now account for three-quarters of British grocery sales, exerting unprecedented control over what we eat and where we buy it. Tesco's share is over 27 per cent (25 per cent usually triggers a monopolies inquiry). The 'big four' abuse power and squeeze suppliers and competitors.

As Lawrence (2004b) states:

> Bill Grimsey the Chief Executive of the Big Food Group which owns Iceland shops said 'we can either act to curb monopolisation or allow choice to be dramatically reduced. If we fail to act, the affluent, could, in Grimsey's works find themselves with a choice of "Tesco, Tesco, Tesco" while the disadvantaged are left denied affordable access to good fresh food.

The increasing domination of supermarkets reveals the myth of choice that is often cited as justification for expansion. In effect, supermarkets have 'stitched up' the business of selling food. The mechanics of monopoly trading ensure that the major supermarkets can secure low prices and exclusive deals with suppliers, which puts a squeeze even on large retailers. For example, Londis, the cornershop chain, has admitted that it is cheaper to buy brands from Tesco and resell them, than to get items from wholesalers. 270 jobs are lost in a community each time a supermarket opens, and fifty small traders are forced out of business each week (Shabi, 2004). There are also wider social ramifications of supermarket expansion. In courting the car owner, they discriminate against those who depend on buses or lifts and struggle to reach supermarkets. Piachaud and Webb (1996) calculated that households on benefits would have to spend 25 per cent more of their income on food if they could not get to a large supermarket or street market (cited in Dowler, 2003: 149). Also, whereas local stores tend to stock local produce, which accounts for about 80 per cent of goods in urban independent shops, the supermarkets make only 1–2 per cent of turnover from local food providers (Shabi, 2004).

Consumer choice is terms of shopping around for the best price for a particular product is also a myth. People have no way of comparing prices in different stores over the range of what they buy, or of knowing which company is cheapest. Governments often justify these developments as creating choice. As Lawrence (2004b) observes: 'In reality, unprecedented choice comes down to agonising between 20 different boxes of over-processed cereal or 6 different thicknesses of loo paper.' In terms of low cost, loss leaders in the major retailers may keep a few items of produce cheap, but they now reel in the profits by selling non-food items such as drugs and electrical appliances. For example, Walmart's profits are five times higher in non-food sales than food sales, and retail analysts Verdict say that a massive £14.5 billion was spent on non-food items in supermarkets in 2000 (cited in Corporate Watch, 2004).

The government has failed to seriously address the growing power of major retailers and fast-food manufacturers in terms of market domination and associated social costs. This is not surprising given the undue influence that corporate interests have on government. For example, Terry Leahy, the chief executive of Tesco, sits on four government task forces; Archie Norman, former chief executive of Asda, was a key advisor to William Hague and a member of the shadow cabinet; and Tesco and Asda sponsored fringe meetings at the Labour Party Conference in 2003.

The British food industry has embarked on a huge lobbying campaign in Whitehall to see off growing pressure for regulation to tackle obesity and diet-related diseases. They have put all their efforts into convincing ministers that voluntary and industry-controlled measures are the most effective tools in dealing with public health issues. In 2003, the Food and Drink Federation, the food manufacturers' lobbying group had over 2000 contacts with ministers, MPs, MEPs, Lords and MSPs and special advisers. They often cite lifestyle choice to support their case. For example, Cadbury Trebor Bassett's customer-relations director stated that 'the thing that drives obesity is lifestyle and it is wrong to demonise confectionery' (Lawrence, 2004a).

The supermarket squeeze on food prices extends all the way to source. British farmers are seriously affected in trying to survive the price war between the four giants. To provide customers with the huge variety of inexpensive food that they promise, supermarkets ruthlessly exploit their effective monopoly as the biggest buyers of food. They can dictate how, where, when and for how much their food is produced, packaged, stored and delivered. Farmers are forced to invest a huge amount into meeting supermarket needs, and then can be dropped at a whim, wiping out their entire business and the businesses and rural communities that rely on them. One of the most shocking forms of exploitation is that farmers are frequently paid less than the cost of production for their goods. For example, it costs a small dairy farmer anything from 18p to 22p to produce a litre of milk. Until the Milk Marketing Board was abolished in 1994, they were being paid 24p per litre. Currently, farmers are being paid 19p per litre for what sells in the supermarket for 72p. In some cases the farm-gate price is so low, that even with subsidies farmers cannot cover their costs. Agricultural subsidies essentially go straight into supermarket profits (Corporate Watch, 2001).

The growing power of supermarkets has also impacted on workers' rights. As Tim Lang stated in a documentary by *Panorama* entitled 'Gangmasters', broadcast in June, 2000: 'cheap food tends to mean cheap labour and we need to start thinking a lot more about this as we encourage supermarkets to vie with each other over price wars.' MPs from the Environment, Food and Rural Affairs Select Committee (2003) contributed to this criticism when they observed:

> We are convinced that the dominant position of supermarkets in relation to their suppliers is a significant contributory factor in creating an environment where illegal activities by gangmasters can take root. Intense price competition and short timescales between orders and deliveries put great pressure on suppliers who have little opportunity or incentive to check the legality of the labour which helps them meet these orders. (Cited in Corporate Watch, 2001: 24)

## New Labour's White Paper on Public Health (2004)

New Labour's response to the many concerns, anxieties and criticisms regarding food policy articulated over the years culminated in the White Paper on public health which was unveiled by the Health Minister John Reid on the 16th November 2004. It covers obesity, binge drinking, smoking and sexually transmitted disease. However, it has already been described as lacking the boldness to seriously address a range of concerns. In relation to smoking, it falls short of bringing in a complete ban, despite evidence published in mid-November 2004 by the government's own independent Scientific Committee on Tobacco and Health which argued that a quarter of lung cancers were caused by second hand smoke, as were diseases such as childhood asthma and respiratory failure (Revill and Hinscliff, 2004). In relation to alcohol, the White Paper favours industry self-regulation and self-help. For example, the Portman group, which represents the drinks industry, started its own website to help consumers work out how much they could safely drink each week.

The White Paper's most concerted attempt to address problems associated with diet and disease involves a food-labelling scheme, where colours are given to foods according to their nutritional status. Red, orange and green labels are to be used, with red labels, for example, representing foods such as chocolate confectionery, doughnuts and fizzy drinks. Advertising of such foods on television will be prohibited.

The White Paper appear to have lost the opportunity to seriously address increasing health, social and environmental problems associated with food supply and consumption. There remains a strong emphasis on personal responsibility and the self-regulation of the food and drinks industry. Anna Coote, research fellow of the King's Fund think tank, argues that ministers are unnecessarily worried about pushing the public towards healthier living, even though voters have adapted remarkably well to controversial health measures such as drink-driving and vaccinations (Revill and Hinscliff, 2004). The government appears concerned with not upsetting the food and drink industry, and sections of the media who see any political intervention regarding food supply and consumption as interfering with personal freedom and undermining individual responsibility. In doing so, it ignores a burgeoning coalition of interests such as farmers, independent shops, environmental groups and trade unionists who want to see curbs on, for example, the powers of supermarkets and aggressive advertising to children.

There are serious consequences of not investing in social provision to tackle problems associated with diet and disease. For example, the Chief Medical Officer, Liam Donaldson, acknowledged that higher levels of physical activity amongst children were essential if they were to begin to tackle the effects of the obesity epidemic, and Paula Radcliffe advocated that every pupil in Britain should be able to enjoy at least two hours of sport a week at school by 2006. Yet, despite this being a moderate proposal, ministers have said that it is an impossible target to achieve. (Revill, 2004). Ministers have also recognised the great difficulty in providing a healthy and nutritious school dinner for 37p a day, yet have fallen short of recommending any new investment in school meals. The celebrity chef Jamie Oliver further raised the profile of the debate by speaking out against their poor quality in the press and on the television. He started a 'half a quid a kid' campaign, arguing that 50 pence isn't too much to ask if we care about what our children eat. Again the government responded with guidelines on the use of processed foods in schools, but no extra money.

More importantly, the White Paper fails to address the correlation between poor diet, poor health status and socio-economic status. As discussed earlier, in terms of food consumption there is a social chasm between the rich and poor, and obesity is much more prevalent in poorer parts of the country. Robert Beaglehole, Director of Chronic Diseases, Prevention and Health Promotion at the World Health Organization, recognises this link and the role of government in addressing it when he states:

> The availability of fruit and vegetables is socially patterned . . . government has a fundamental obligation to protect the health of its population. You can call it a nanny state if you like. I would say it is setting the conditions which allow individuals to make healthy choices. (Bosley, 2004)

## Activity 5

*Do corporate interests have disproportionate levels of influence on or undermine public health initiatives? What should governments do to regain control of the food policy agenda?*

## Conclusion

This chapter has examined the growing crises and conflicts associated with food production, supply and consumption. Although it has not been possible in a chapter of this length to cover in detail all aspects of the debate, key themes have been discussed.

Historically, governments have been reluctant to legislate in this field. However, since the 1980s, amidst growing food scares and increasing public concern regarding food safety, governments have been forced into taking action. The main catalyst for action was the BSE crisis of 1996, when it emerged that cattle were being fed the remains of dead sheep and cattle (and on occasions, in the United States, the corpses of cats and dogs purchased from animal shelters). Debates surrounding food safety began to dominate media coverage, and books such as Eric Schlosser's *Fast Food Nation* became bestsellers. These developments increased public awareness and concern regarding the food supply chain.

However, strategies to respond to crises regarding food have focused on personal choice and individual responsibility, reflecting neo-liberal concerns that the state should interfere as little as possible in regulating the food industry. Powerful corporate interests have argued that unhealthy eating is a lifestyle choice and that government intervention is indicative of 'nanny statism'. Their influence is reflected in New Labour's White Paper on Public Health (2004) which argues for industry self-regulation rather than promoting more punitive or radical initiatives to curb the powers of major food producers and retailers. *The Times* editorial of 17 November 2004 argued: 'This was an opportunity to focus on practical goals of particular benefit to children, and use the full force of the law to achieve them. Instead, it relies on websites, leaflets and cajolery.' More generally, deregulation over the past two decades and more has led to a serious decline in, for example, the provision of school meals. Children today do not have access to healthy and nutritious school meals. Instead, they are fed a diet of fast food and fizzy drinks in school cafeterias. Competition between schools has led to more and more children travelling to school by car, and curriculum initiatives have seen a decline in physical activity as part of school life.

It seems that the government has missed key opportunites to legislate in this field and respond to the growing concerns of parents, educators, doctors, and a range of other concerned professionals. Yet, unless a much more radical political approach to food policy is developed the prognosis is bleak. As Professor Philip James, an international authority on diet and obesity, has recently argued: 'If things continue as they are, the current generation of children will die before their parents, their arteries clogged by fatty plaque laid down by poor diets and indolent lifestyles' (cited in Revill and Hinscliff, 2004).

## Further Reading

Dowler, E. and Finer, C.J. (eds) (2002) *The Welfare of Food: Rights and Responsibilities in a Changing World*. Oxford: Blackwell.
Lawrence, F. (2004) *Not on the Label: What Really Goes Into the Food on your Plate*. London: Penguin.
Schlosser, E. (2001) *Fast Food Nation*. London: Penguin.

# FOURTEEN
# Wage Supplementation, Social Policy and the State
## *From the Old Poor Law to New Labour*
*Alan Pratt*

---

### Outline Points

- Within the labour market in Britain a large number of fully employed workers earn low wages and have at least one dependent child.
- The relationship between low wages, dependent children and family poverty.
- Wage supplementation as a policy response to the problems generated by the above relationship at three key moments in the history and development of British social policy.
- Wage supplementation, work incentives and labour market participation rates as an important issue in British social policy.
- Wage supplementation and its place in the consummation of a general vision of the 'good society'; from the 1834 Poor Law Report to the search for a 'progressive universalism'.

---

## Introduction

Wages in a capitalist labour market are determined by complex interactions between forces such as the scarcity value of labour, the bargaining power of trade unions and public policies like the national minimum wage. The presence of dependent children in families should have no direct role at all in this process since to include them would be to violate the nature of a free labour market. However it is axiomatic that low-paid workers with dependent children run a greater risk of experiencing poverty than those without children and will face greater demands on their wages than those without dependent children. This chapter is devoted to an examination of what has been one of the most controversial policy responses to this dilemma in the history of British social provision, the idea of paying direct cash subsidies to the wages of the low paid with a dependent child or children. In doing so it will touch on some of the most profound questions in the domain of social policy including:

- the responsibility on individuals to maintain themselves through their own efforts;
- that wages should reflect effort, productivity and responsibility;
- the importance of work incentives;
- the general characteristics of selective social provision.

To do this we will examine three key points of departure in British social policy: the practice of giving allowances-in-aid of wages under the 'Old' or pre-1834 Poor Law, probably best known as the Speenhamland system; the introduction of the Family Income Supplement in 1970/71; and, finally, the development of a large-scale system of tax credits by the New Labour government since 1997.

## Allowances-in-aid of Wages under the Old Poor Law

Between the Workhouse Test Act of 1723 and Gilbert's Act of 1782 English attitudes to poor relief changed. The 1723 Act tried to limit applications for relief by the able-bodied by making assistance conditional on entry into the workhouse while Gilbert's Act reserved the workhouse in newly formed parish unions for those who were unable to work such as the aged, sick and infirm. This paved the way for the spread of allowances in what was a more sympathetic attitude to the poor in the second half of the eighteenth century (Coates, 1958, 1960).

Although the poor law was legally defined by national legislation, like the Poor Law Act of 1601 and the Poor Law Amendment Act of 1834, it was for centuries administered and interpreted by local elites who were sensitive to the economic and social realities of their communities. A variety of traditions developed over time that reflected these local realities and the practice of giving allowances in aid of wages has been traced back to the early seventeenth century, but our specific concern is with the rapid spread of the allowance practice from the middle of the 1790s in the cereal-producing southern agricultural counties of England where agricultural labourers were faced with a major threat to their subsistence. They were more exposed than ever to rising bread prices while wages had become the largest part of total income as the profound changes associated with the rise of agrarian and industrial capitalism (such as enclosures of common land, loss of grazing rights and the decline of domestic crafts) reduced income and opportunities for food production. In 1794 the wheat harvest was 20 per cent below the average for the 1790s and was insufficient to meet the needs of a rural population whose diet was still dependent on the price and availability of wheat flour and bread. This situation was exacerbated by the severe winter of 1794–5 and it became obvious that the 1795 harvest would be inadequate. War and bad weather interrupted the trade in grain, and cereal prices rose rapidly.

The Berkshire magistrates were so concerned that they called a special meeting at the Pelican Inn in the parish of Speenhamland on 6 May 1795 to discuss their response to the crisis. After discussing a number of possibilities (including a minimum wage) they opted for a detailed 'bread scale' that determined the amount of any cash subsidy to be paid by the parish. This was a supplement to an earned wage with the amount of the payment governed by the current price of bread, and the total amount of the benefit depended on the number of a man's dependents (Marshall, 1968).

The decision to opt for a programme of wage subsidisation reflects the pragmatic outlook of local administrators born to older and more traditional forms of economic and social organisation that were being increasingly challenged by market capitalism. One of the major consequences of this conflict between the old and the new was that these older values and institutions were seen as barriers to the free flow of capital and labour. (Brundage, 2002: 30). While the apparent shift within the relief system towards 'providing social security for unemployed men and their families and subsidising the family income of those on low wages . . . was an affront to the moral, as well as economic sensibilities of a new generation which increasingly accepted the new philosophy we now know as "Classical Political Economy"' (Kidd, 1999: 19).

A powerful critique of existing legislation and practice developed, at the core of which was a fusion of classical political economy, Benthamism and Christian Economics which argued that public policy should limit itself to the relief of pauperism and not poverty. As Kidd says, the question was: 'how to relieve the genuinely indigent without discouraging self-reliance and demoralising the labourer?' (1999: 20) Some of the leading contemporary intellectuals became active protagonists in the debate and Bentham's proposals for rational administration in well-regulated workhouses attracted a group of influential followers while a narrow interpretation of Adam Smith's economic and moral philosophy, focusing on Smith's identification of the free market as an institution for the optimal allocation of scarce resources, was developed by disciples like David Ricardo and Nassau Senior into a plea for an unencumbered national free market in labour, one that might resolve the problem of a surplus population in the backward rural south of England. If we add Malthus' belief that existing poor-law practice encouraged a higher and unsupportable population to classical political economy's wages-fund theory (essentially the contention that there was only a fixed amount of resources available to pay labour and that poor relief came out of the same pot), by the end of the 1820s poor law reformers had developed an impressive case against existing practice. Christian Economics, with its linkage between market capitalism and spiritual growth added to an already potent brew. Outdoor relief in general and wage subsidisation in particular were the major targets of this critique. The case for reform was buttressed by what was regarded as good practice at local level and Nottinghamshire provided a number of influential figures of whom George Nichols, a devotee of Malthus and classical political economy, was the best known, all of which was a little ironic given that it was a relatively prosperous county, with limited and late experience of the allowance system and per-capita poor relief expenditure well below the English average.

Poor law expenditure varied in amount and direction in the first three decades of the nineteenth century, rising from £5.3 million in 1802–3 to £9.3 million in 1817–18 (reflecting the economic slump following the end of the war against Napoleon in 1815). The 1820s saw generally lower levels but then rose to £8.6 million in 1831–32 in the aftermath of the severe winter of 1829 and it was the disturbances that followed in the latter's wake that provided the major shock to political and social stability that significant poor law reform probably required. This arrived in 1830 in the form of 'the last great agricultural labourers' revolt' (Kidd, 1999: 25). The 'Captain Swing' riots began in the summer of 1830 in Kent and by the time they ended in the winter of 1831 they had affected well over 1400 parishes, mostly in the south and east of England. A precipitate decline in the living standards of the agricultural labourer following the harsh winter of 1829–30 had sparked the riots. More generous, traditional and less demeaning forms of poor relief were important features of the rioters' demands and although some magistrates responded sympathetically others favoured a harsher response: ultimately 19 men were executed and almost 500 were transported to Australia. (Brundage, 2002: 60)

Although savage, the governing class was also frightened and this fear was the catalyst for a determined push to change the poor law, especially when it became apparent that the riots had been concentrated in those areas where the allowance practice was concentrated. The legislative process began when Lord Brougham, the Lord Chancellor in Earl Grey's new coalition government, committed it to 'the consolidation and simplification of the existing Acts on the subject of the Poor-Laws', and in February 1832 the government announced its intention to set up a Royal Commission to investigate poor relief practice in England and Wales and to make recommendations for change.

The Royal Commission on the Poor Laws, 1832–34, has been widely condemned by historians for being biased in favour of a particular approach to reform, not surprising given that most of the nine commissioners, including people like Nassau Senior, were enthusiastic modernisers. Twenty-six Assistant Commissioners were also appointed to collect the data on which the final report was to be based. One of these was Edwin Chadwick who was to be promoted to the Commission itself in 1833. The investigation dealt mainly with the agricultural sector of the economy focusing on issues such as local employment practices and prospects, wage rates and seasonal employment patterns. Amongst other things, the Assistant Commissioners were instructed to investigate problems arising out of the allowance system and other evils. 10 per cent of the 15,500 parishes in England and Wales responded but the data they generated was questioned by contemporaries who claimed that the questionnaires had been designed to elicit answers that corresponded to the preconceived notions of the commissioners. Historians have tended to be even less charitable about the integrity of the investigation with typical judgements being that the report was 'brilliant, influential and wildly unhistorical' (Tawney 1938: 34) and 'wildly unstatistical' (Blaug, 1964: 243).

More recently Brundage has commented that the ambiguous wording of both questions and responses made it possible for Chadwick and Senior to construct a report 'that obscured the true complexity of poor relief practices and present a skewed picture of the prevalence of allowances in aid of wages' (2002: 65). The report made it appear that wage supplementation was common whereas it had largely disappeared in the 1820s. Kidd has described the Poor Law Report as a 'consistent polemic against the out-relief of the able-bodied male' (1999: 27) and has concluded that by abolishing all help to the poor (rather than the indigent) 'paupers would be transformed into independent labourers, surplus labour in the South would be dispersed and a national free market in labour encouraged' (Kidd, 1999: 27).

The 1834 Report provided the ideological and intellectual foundations of poor-relief policy well into the twentieth century and condemned the principle and practice of wage subsidisation in unequivocal terms:

> To suppose that the poor are the proper managers of their own concerns, that a man's wages ought to depend on his services, not upon his wants, that the earnings of the ordinary labourer are naturally equal to the support of an ordinary family, that the welfare of that family naturally depends on his conduct, that he is bound to exercise any sort of prudence or economy, that anything is to be hoped from voluntary charity, are views which many of those who have long resided in pauperised rural districts seem to reject as too absurd for formal refutation. (Checkland and Checkland, 1974: 139)

Moreover: 'Allowance-men will not work. It makes them idle, lazy, fraudulent and worthless, and depresses the wages of free labour' (ibid.: 146).

Generations of economic and social historians accepted the judgements of the 1834 Poor Law Report about the consequences of wage subsidisation and condemned the practice but these venerable opinions have been challenged by an approach pioneered by Blaug in the 1960s. He argues that in situations where wages were already below the biological minimum required for workers to work effectively (as was the case periodically with agricultural labourers): 'The amount of work put forth now depends on the wages paid rather than the other way around; lower wages would lower the consumption and hence the productivity of workers' (Blaug, 1963: 154). In this situation wage subsidisation raised consumption and hence productivity which in turn led on to further wage increases, this time justified in market terms by virtue of being rooted in greater productivity.

The Poor Law Report of 1834 recommended the abolition of all outdoor relief to the able-bodied and it became received wisdom that wages were something best left to the operation of the national labour market. For the state to subsidise directly the wages of low paid workers with dependent children would simply replicate the economic and moral evils identified by the 1834 Report. How and why this position was abandoned is the subject of the next section, which examines a programme that some regarded as Speenhamland's resurrection.

---

**Activity 1**

*Why do you think that supporters of classical political economy and other poor law reformers were opposed to the principles and practice of wage subsidisation?*

---

## Speenhamland revisited? The Introduction of Family Income Supplements

The manifesto on which the Conservative Party fought the general election in June 1970 was markedly different from every previous election since 1945. Although never as positively supportive of the economic and social policy developed in the 1940s as is sometimes imagined, Conservative governments from 1951–64 were relatively content to continue with a combination of full employment, economic growth, a mixed economy and rising public expenditure on welfare provision for as long as it was popular with the electorate (Fraser, 2000). 1970 changed all that and the vision of Conservatism developed by Edward Heath and his colleagues put clear and deep blue water between it and the Labour Party. The Conservative programme now offered the restoration of a freer (if not totally free) market as the dominant institution for the allocation of scarce resources, lower levels of direct taxes, and public expenditure as a smaller percentage of national income. In this way individuals' work incentives were to be restored and the entrepreneurial spirit revived.

The first public expression of the policy implications of this vision came on October 27 1970 when the government's public expenditure plans proclaimed an immediate and substantial cut in corporate taxation together with a reduction of 2.5 pence in the standard rate of income tax (the present basic rate) from its then level of slightly over 41 pence in the pound. All of this was consistent with the central strategy on which it had fought the recent election but the party was also committed to an increase in Family Allowances-with-clawback as its short-term answer to family poverty pending the development of a workable system of negative income tax, its preferred long-term solution. Clawback was a technique introduced in the last two years of the previous Labour government and justified as a civilised and acceptable form of selectivity (Pratt, 1976). It involved a reduction in the value of the child-tax allowances of those who paid income tax at the standard rate and above so that the only people to benefit from the increase in Family Allowances were those who paid no taxes, or were taxed at rates below the standard rate. The Conservative Party had been opposed to clawback and only accepted it reluctantly when its search for a workable system of negative income tax ran into difficulties.

Given this general ideological orientation and specific policy pledge it was doubly surprising that the statement declared the government's intention to introduce a cash supplement to the earnings of the poorest of the working poor who worked full time and had at least one dependent child. This not only broke an election promise but also violated what had been one of the enduring ortho-doxies of British social policy since 1834, that to supplement the wages of the low-paid full-time worker with child dependents was an act of folly. It was entirely consistent with the spirit of 1834 that people in full-time work could not claim social assistance because of the full-time work prohibition, and if unemployed their benefit was limited to their earnings when last in full-time employment through an administrative device known as the wage-stop, even though their resources might be less than their needs as defined in the nation's social assistance scale rates. How and why did the Conservative Party accomplish such a dramatic volte-face in only a few months?

The Conservative Party has always denied any responsibility for the invention of the Family Income Supplement (FIS) and has insisted that it was a civil service plan that had been presented to the previous Labour government. Jim Callaghan, Chancellor of the Exchequer until his replacement by Roy Jenkins after the devaluation crisis in late 1967, had presented it to the Cabinet as an alternative to what eventually became Family Allowances-with-clawback but the proposal was rejected after it was leaked to a number of trade union leaders who objected to what they regarded as the re-introduction of the Speenhamland principle (Pratt, 1976). Confirmation of the civil service's parentage can be found in some comments made by Richard Crossman (Secretary of State for Health and Social Services in the first years of the Wilson government) during his contribution to the Second Reading Debate on the FIS Bill on 10 November 1970: 'It is no secret that this scheme is an old friend of ours. Many a person has put it up to us and said: why not do it?' (Hansard, 1970, Vol. 806, Col. 253).

FIS provided a cash supplement worth 50 per cent of the difference between actual earnings and a 'prescribed amount' appropriate to the claimant's family size and structure; in effect an additional marginal tax rate of 50 per cent. At an estimated cost of £8 million a year, significantly less than the £183 million annual gross expenditure entailed by the election promise of an increase in Family Allowances-with-clawback, it must have been attractive to a government whose *raison d'être* was reductions in public expenditure and cuts in direct taxation. The Secretary of State argued that the government had been prevented from honouring its Family Allowance commitment because the actions of the previous Labour government had reduced the scope for further use of the claw-back technique. Significantly, the government only budgeted for a maximum 80 per cent take-up rate.

Parliamentary response to the Family Income Supplement Bill was generally critical and references to Speenhamland abounded. The most rigorous critique from a classical liberal perspective was made by Enoch Powell and its analysis would have graced the 1834 Poor Law Report itself. Powell drew on the experience of the years between 1795 and 1835 to warn of the grave dangers of wage supple-mentation. Although the poor law reformers were harsh and unimaginative men:

... at least they re-established a principle, a principle from which this Bill decisively departs. It is the principle that it is an act of fateful consequence to pay relief – cash supplementation of income – to persons in full-time employment; that it is something which is bound profoundly to distort the wage system and to frustrate the ambition, which seems to me to be almost indissociable from the idea of a free society – that a man should receive as near as may be the full value of his work in cash. Sooner or later, and I fear it may be later, we shall have to return to that principle. (Hansard, Vol. 806, Cols 264–5)

Despite ministers' protestations that other benefits also provided targeted help to the working poor, Powell was surely correct in his assertion that FIS was a decisive new step, because for the first time since the 1834 Poor Law Amendment Act a government was proposing to pay cash subsidies to the earnings of the low-paid in full-time employment with one or more dependent children *and to them alone*. FIS *was* a historic break with the past.

Opponents of means-testing had already developed a formidable critique of targeting in which administrative complexity, stigmatisation of claimants and poor take-up rates were all important features but Powell's fears that FIS might damage the integrity of the wage system and work incentives matched what became the most damaging element of opponents' attack on FIS: the poverty trap. This concept first appeared in the late 1960s and by the early 1970s it had become a sophisticated theoretical analysis of the interrelationship between benefits and taxation and how this might impact on the income of the working poor. It was soon established that a rise in earnings for low-paid workers could, because of their increased liability to higher income taxation and National Insurance contributions, together with a loss of entitlement to a range of income-related benefits, lead to effective marginal tax rates well in excess of 100 per cent. As qualification for FIS was a passport to other benefits, without the necessity of making separate applications for these benefits, any increase in take-up was bound to increase the severity of the poverty trap, with all that this implied for work incentives (Pratt, 1976).

If its critics were right, and FIS was analogous to Speenhamland, then the Conservative government was vulnerable to the charge that FIS was a major threat to the work incentives of the very poor given that its economic and social policy was based on the overriding imperative of restoring incentives by cutting the marginal rate of direct taxes. Perhaps surprisingly, the government showed little concern for the incentives of the working poor as Sir Keith Joseph, the Secretary of State for Health and Social Services, demonstrated during the Committee Stage of the FIS Bill:

In most cases we do not have to worry about their motivation. They are proving in the clearest possible way their desire to work. If it is a question of enabling them to receive more from supplementary benefit by abating their work for two hours a week, who in the Committee would grudge them? (Hansard, 1970, Vol. 806, Col. 1144)

Although the government was willing to accept the existence of a theoretical case for the poverty trap, in the real world it didn't exist. What was to become the stock response to this charge, until FIS was abolished in the social security review of 1986 and replaced by a very similar programme, Family Credit, was given by Paul Dean, on 26 January 1972. Claims that thousands of families would be worse off after a pay rise were hypothetical, and any possible disincentive effects would be mitigated because income was tested over different periods for the various means-tested benefits and there would be a time-lag before an increase in earnings affected benefit entitlement or amount. Once awarded FIS ran for six months (later 12) regardless of any subsequent rise in earnings. Take-up rates never reached the 80 per cent level the government had budgeted for, with a peak of around 75 per cent if lower value amounts are excluded.

Throughout the life of the Heath government, which ended in the aftermath of the miners' strike in 1974, the Labour Party had consistently opposed FIS, largely because of its contribution to the poverty trap, and had promised to repeal it. In the first two years of the new Labour government this intent was constantly reiterated as it sought to implement its 1975 Child Benefit legislation. The International Monetary Fund imposed its demands for public expenditure cuts during the financial crisis of 1976 and Labour ministers suddenly discovered hitherto unexpected virtues in FIS, while the full introduction of the Child Benefit programme was delayed amidst a political storm. FIS was defended in exactly the same terms as it had been by the previous government, and the poverty trap dismissed as a statistical and theoretical abstraction. Labour lost the 1979 election decisively and when it returned to office in 1997 it would have a radically different approach to the whole question of the place of wage subsidisation in modern social policy.

---

**Activity 2**

*Why do you think the Conservative government in 1970, whose entire economic and social policy depended in large part on the restoration and improvement of work incentives, introduced the Family Income Supplement scheme?*

---

## New Labour, Tax Credits and the Search for a 'Progressive Universalism'

Unlike the Labour Party, Labour governments have not been averse to means-tested social provision and have, from time to time, made important additions to the range of such benefits, but when in opposition the party has always favoured universalism, as it did from 1979 to 1997. For example the 1989 policy review said that: 'We want to reduce the need for means-tested benefits by providing insurance benefits as of right', while Gordon Brown told the 1993 Party Conference that he wanted 'the next Labour government to achieve what . . . has never been achieved. The end of the means test for our elderly people' (in Collins and Wicks 2003: 50). In contrast, since 1997 the Labour government has made selective tax credits the policy mechanism of choice in its drive to eliminate child poverty and make work always worth more than non-working. Under Gordon Brown at the Treasury means-testing has achieved a victory 'now so complete that it is rarely noted how remarkable it is' as more people have been brought within the scope of selective or targeted provision than ever before (ibid.).

Tax credits are a means-tested benefit delivered through the tax system or the pay packet that enables the government to pay in one sum what might otherwise have required separate claims and separate benefits and they have transferred very large amounts of cash support to the earned incomes of low-paid families with a dependent child or children. Brown has said of his tax-credit strategy that: 'Our approach helps all and is at the same time progressive – a progressive universalism . . . as we build a fully modern tax and benefit system under which for the first time the taxman can give money as well as receive it' (quoted in Collins and Wicks, 2003: 50).

Collins and Wicks describe progressive universalism as *neither* means-testing *nor* universalism but both at the same time, and pose the rhetorical question: 'Could there be anything more third way? A universal base to the welfare state but resources targeted at the least well off. And, into the bargain, the claim that this is a step towards the goal of an integrated tax and benefit system' (ibid.). Thus described, progressive universalism may or may not be quintessentially third way but it is not unlike the earlier claims made for clawback. Moreover, it also bears a startling similarity to Richard Titmuss's attempted resolution of the conflicting claims of selectivity and universality in a very famous essay in *Commitment to Welfare*, first published in 1968:

> The challenge that faces us is not the choice between universalist and selective social ser-
> vices. The real challenge resides in the question: what particular infrastructure of univer-
> salist services is needed in order to provide a framework of values and opportunity bases
> within and around which can be developed socially acceptable services aiming to dis-
> criminate positively, with the minimum risk of stigma in favour of those whose needs are
> greatest. (1976: 135)

For Collins and Wicks, a proper understanding of Labour's use of tax credits as a means of targeting resources on lower earners with dependent children can only be achieved if they are rooted in two of the government's most important social policy ambitions: to eradicate child poverty, and always to make work more profitable than non-working. This understanding also needs to be informed by an appreciation of the fact that both the means-tested tax credits and the universal Child Benefit have been rising sharply in value, in marked contrast to 1979–1997 (Collins and Wicks, 2003: 50).

## Activity 3

*What do you understand by the term 'progressive universalism'?*

## The Introduction of Tax Credits

Successive governments have struggled to devise delivery systems that can actually give most help to those whose needs are greatest without incurring the high administrative costs, low take-up rates and risk of stigma commonly associated with targeting, and the greater integration of the tax and benefit system has long been the holy grail of British social policy. These objectives are easily expressed but difficult to accomplish, and on one level the tax credit can be seen as only the most recent in a quite lengthy list of initiatives, except that on this occasion the aspiration has become a reality, one involving several billion pounds of public spending.

The Working Families Tax Credit (WFTC) was the first time a benefit had been administered through the tax system and paid through the pay packet. Inspired by Bill Clinton's earned income tax credit for low-wage earners, the WFTC was a benefit for people in low-paid work who had dependent children. It guaranteed a minimum income of £200 a week for families with a full-time earner. At the same time the Childcare Tax Credit (CCTC) was introduced which provided 70 per cent of childcare costs incurred up to £150 a week and was payable to those eligible for the WFTC. 2001 saw the Children's Tax Credit worth up to £442 per child (Brewer 2003).

It is likely that the government only intended these reforms as an interim measure and in April 2003 it introduced a more radical set of policies. These included the abolition of:

- the Children's Tax Credit, which had been reducing the income tax bills of some five million families since its introduction in April 2001 and was now to be subsumed in a new Child Tax Credit from April 2003.
- The Working Families Tax Credit (WFTC), which had been providing financial help for 1.34 million low-paid families with dependent children working 16 or more hours a week and was to be subsumed in the Child Tax Credit and the new Working Tax Credit (WTC) from April 2003.
- The Childcare Tax Credit (CCTC), which had been subsidising the eligible childcare costs of 167,000 families that received the WFTC and was to be subsumed within the WTC from April 2003.
- Child allowances and the family premium in income support (IS) or income-related Jobseeker's Allowance (JSA), which had been providing extra money to 1.18 million families with dependent children claiming IS or income-related JSA, and were to be subsumed within the CTC from April 2004.

- Child additions to some National Insurance benefits that had provided extra money to about 170,000 families with dependent children. These additions were to be abolished for new claimants only so that existing beneficiaries would not lose out although it represents a long-run cut in the generosity of these benefits. (Brewer, 2003)

The Working Families Tax Credit and the Children's Tax Credit have been fused into a new benefit, the Child Tax Credit (CTC), designed to simplify the system of financial support for children providing income-related support to the main carer and which, when fully operational, will represent the majority of government financial support for children. The most novel feature of these reforms is the Working Tax Credit that for the first time in modern British social policy extends the principle of wage supplementation to include in-work support to couples and individuals in low-paid work who have no children. As a consequence of these changes there has been a reduction in the number of sources of financial support for families with dependent children from four to two, Child Benefit and the Child Tax Credit (Brewer, 2003: 1–5).

Limitations of space preclude a lengthy discussion of the nature and details of the current form of the tax credits aimed at families, so the following sections are limited to their general character.

### The Child Tax Credit

In 2003–4 the Child Tax Credit consists of two elements:

- A family component of £545 per year (approximately £10–45 a week), doubled in the financial year of the child's birth.
- £1,445 per year for each dependent child (approximately £27–75 a week, and higher for disabled children).

Families with gross incomes below £13,230 are entitled to the full amount, but for incomes above this amount entitlement to the per-child element is subject to a withdrawal rate of 37p in the pound. Entitlement to the family component is retained up to an annual income of £50,000 but for annual incomes above this figure the family element is reduced by 6.7p in the pound. Around 90 per cent of families with children are entitled to some Child Tax Credit with around 50 per cent entitled to both elements and 40 per cent to the family element only and the government has promised to increase the per-child element in family credit at least in line with the growth in average earnings (Brewer, 2003).

### The Working Tax Credit

The details of the Working Tax Credit for 2003–4 are as follows:

- Single people with no dependent children are entitled to £1,525 per year (approximately £29–30 a week).
- Couples with or without children and lone parents are entitled to a credit of £3,025 a year (some £58.15 a week).

- There is a bonus of £620 per annum (£11.90 a week) for those working 30 hours a week or more.
- Families with children where all adults are working, caring or disabled are entitled to receive help with the costs of childcare. This works in the same way as the Childcare Tax Credit under the former WFTC and pays 70 per cent of approved childcare costs below a maximum of £135 a week for those with one child under 16 and £200 for others.
- There are extra amounts for some adults with disabilities and for people over 50 who are returning to work.
- Families with children must work at least 16 hours a week to qualify and those without children must work at least 30 hours, and will therefore always be entitled to the bonus for working full-time.

Families on incomes below £5,060 are entitled to the full amount of the Working Tax Credit. Above this figure entitlement is reduced at the rate of 37p in the pound. Treasury estimates put the cost of the new tax credits at £2.7 billion in 2003–4 and £2.6 billion in 2004–5. The government estimates that £13 billion of the total support of £21.2 billion paid in respect of dependent children in 2003 will be delivered through the tax credit system. Of the 7 million families with children in Great Britain approximately 4.1 million will gain from the new arrangements and 300,000 will lose, with the gains declining as income rises, 'fully in keeping with the pattern of Labour's reforms to date' (Brewer, 2003: 11).

The take-up rate for the WFTC has been estimated at 62–65 per cent, lower than the 72 per cent for Family Credit achieved in the summer of 1999, its last year of operation. As with FIS and Family Credit, non-claimants of WFTC would only have qualified for small payments, which nonetheless saved the government £1.4 billion in 2000–1. The government's estimate is that 90 per cent of the target population will claim the Child Tax Credit, about 5.75 million of families with dependent children, implying that 775,000 of eligible families with children will not. If previous experience is repeated the amounts not claimed are likely to be small. Brewer's estimate of take-up for the Working Tax Credit for people without children is as low as 50 per cent and could be below 50 per cent (Brewer, 2003).

Although improving work incentives is not the main aim of the new tax credits for families with children there will be some impact on labour market behaviour. Compared with previous tax and benefit systems low-income families with children will generally get higher incomes both in and out of work although most of these changes are only small in magnitude. The effective tax rates of about a third of parents, including those not working, will change. About 1.6 million will face higher marginal tax rates, mostly people who earned too much to claim WFTC but who now find themselves on the first taper of the Child Tax Credit. In contrast about 2.4 million will see their effective marginal tax rates fall because the credits will be assessed against gross income, which is of particular advantage to those people who earn too little to pay basic rate income tax. Moreover, the old Children's Tax Credit had a withdrawal rate based on the income of the higher earner in a two-earner family and this has given way to the new arrangements in respect of the Child Tax Credit where the withdrawal rate is based on joint income. Couples with a joint income that places them on the second taper are both now faced with an increase in their effective marginal tax rate of 6.7 per cent points. Overall about 600,000 individuals are faced with this higher marginal tax rate compared with 400,000 under the Children's Tax Credit.

In contrast, the government did intend that the Working Tax Credit should improve work incentives for all low-income households by reducing both the poverty and unemployment traps but Brewer is sceptical of these claims and maintains that the impact of the Working Tax Credit on the unemployment trap will be very mixed, similar to that of the WFTC, and that if all those entitled to the benefit claim it then approximately 800,000 people without children would see their marginal tax rate increase, with only 50,000 experiencing a fall: 'Overall the number of adults without children facing marginal deduction rates between 50 per cent and 70 per cent would increase by 490,000' (Brewer, 2003: 12).

---

**Activity 4**

*Try to get hold of application forms for the Child Tax Credit and the Working Tax Credit. How user-friendly are they and how long does it take to complete them?*

---

## Conclusions

Is it possible to establish any elements of continuity and change in this brief analysis of wage subsidisation over two centuries, given that we are talking about societies at very different stages of development? The 1834 reformers regarded allowances-in-aid of wages as a real obstacle to the creation of a national market in labour and they were equally convinced that they did great damage to work incentives and the integrity of the wages system. The 1834 report and legislation were hugely influential in helping to create a set of attitudes that still resonates today in the wider culture but, perhaps, has lost some of its grip on policy makers.

A good example of this from our consideration of FIS and New Labour's ambitious programme of tax credits is that, with the single exception of the Working Tax Credit which had an overt intent to improve the work incentives of the childless low paid, especially for those working 30 hours a week or more, neither the Conservative nor Labour Parties showed any concern that their policies might have a disincentive effect. The only incentives to concern the Conservatives were those of middle-to-high earners and businessmen whose ambition, creativity and enterprise were deemed essential to economic salvation. New Labour's policies do seem to be driven by a genuine desire to ameliorate and, ultimately, abolish child poverty and always to make work a more attractive proposition than non-work. The latter element in this twin-track approach appears to have less to do with work incentives than an affirmation of its ideology of rights and duties that has placed the obligation to work if at all possible at the heart of the government's social vision. As a consequence of its espousal of generous means-tested tax credits it has pushed the poverty trap much higher up the income scale and many more people have been drawn into its (hypothetical?) embrace. But, as Collins and Wicks have recently suggested, 'Better a trap high up the scale where the marginal impact of every extra pound is less than at the bottom where every pound really counts' (2003: 52).

We have already alluded to New Labour's ideology of rights with obligations and it seems appropriate to leave the final word with Collins and Wicks on a possible future for the British welfare state in the conditions of currently existing capitalism. Thus:

> Perhaps a distinctive conception of a conditional welfare state is emerging. No longer a method for allocating resources tied to unconditional entitlement, but instead a corrective against capitalism, a huge leviathan for the mitigation, indeed eradication of poverty. No longer grants as of citizenship right, but conditional: today on income, tomorrow, perhaps increasingly, on behaviour too. (2003: 55)

---

### Further Reading

Brewer, M. (2003) *The New Tax Credits.* Institute for Fiscal Studies Briefing Note, No. 35.

Brewer, M. and Shepherd, A. (2004) *Has Labour Made Work Pay?* York: Joseph Rowntree Foundation.

Brundage, A. (2002) *The English Poor Laws, 1700–1930.* Basingstoke: Palgrave.

Collins, P. and Wicks, R. (2003) 'Special Report on Means Tests and Tax Credits', *Prospect*, May: 50–5.

# FIFTEEN

# New Labour and the Management of Welfare

*Gerry Mooney*

---

### Outline Points

- Continuities and change between New Labour and the Conservatives.
- The key elements of New Labour's programme of welfare 'reform'.
- The third way as applied to welfare and social policy.
- Private Finance Initiative (PFI) and Public Private Partnerships (PPPs).
- The extent to which a new welfare 'settlement' is in the making under New Labour.

---

## Introduction

This chapter explores some of the central components in New Labour's ongoing programme of 'reforming' the welfare state and the provision of public services in the UK. Since coming to power in 1997, Labour has presented the 'modernisation' of the welfare state as one of its key political objectives. Indeed, in government Labour has proved to be just as enthusiastic about welfare 'reform' as the Conservatives were during their eighteen years of rule between 1979 and 1997. Central to the Conservative approach was an attack on 'welfarism', the idea that welfare creates a 'dependency' culture and an 'undeserving underclass' of the poor (see Jones and Novak, 1999). However, this was combined with an assault on state-welfare provision as unproductive, inefficient, ineffective, bureaucratic and primarily serving the interests of the professional groups involved in its delivery. This anti-public sectorism paved the way for the opening-up of welfare provision to competition from a range of statutory, voluntary and corporate agencies. 'Rolling back the state' and reducing the costs of welfare provision were pivotal elements of the Conservative approach to welfare, often couched in a language that heralded greater 'choice' for consumers of health, education and housing.

By the mid-1990s such shifts in welfare delivery had led to a diminishing of the scale and significance of state provision while enhancing the role of the private sector (that is delivery by for-profit organisations). But 'the private' was also celebrated in another way: individual and family responsibility for care and support also became a Conservative mantra. Taken together this stress on both senses of private helped to significantly alter the landscape of welfare delivery during the 1980s and 1990s.

Welfare reform, or 'modernisation', continues to be on the agenda of many governments in the Western world. Growing demand for welfare provision, not least across Western Europe and in North America, reflects rising unemployment, the growth and spread of labour market flexibility with its attendant problems of low wages and irregular earnings, shifts in family and household formation together with other demographic changes and new patterns of migration. Alongside this there appears to be less willingness on the part of many governments to resource sufficiently publicly provided welfare to meet these new demands as they pursue policies of no tax increases and minimising non-wage labour costs in the drive to attain competitiveness and attract investment. As governments have sought to reduce the 'costs of welfare' and control public expenditure, new opportunities have been provided for corporate organisations to become more involved in provision. What are termed the 'modernisation' of welfare delivery and the reform of welfare states have become central political platforms of governments in many countries.

This chapter considers the extent to which a new welfare settlement has emerged based upon Conservative and New Labour policies around the increasing use of the market (and non-statutory sectors) as a means of delivering welfare and public services, especially in health, housing and education. As leading New Labour architect Peter Mandelson once put it: 'New Labour's mission is to move forward from where Margaret Thatcher left off, rather than dismantle every single thing she did' (quoted in Mandelson and Liddle, 1996: 1).

How far is this reflected in New Labour's programme of welfare state 'modernisation'? Certainly New Labour has adopted many of the premises of neo-liberalism, as well as the language and rhetoric of the market: choice, competition, performance, targets, customers/consumers, and performance-related pay. But has a new 'welfare consensus' emerged in which non-state forms of provision, cost control, managerialism and individual responsibilities are the key elements? Labour has continued to open up important areas of public sector provision to the market – far surpassing that undertaken by the Conservatives during the 1980s and 1990s. The market now enjoys unparalleled opportunities for involvement and for profit maximisation. For critics of New Labour's policies in this field, from trade unions through to a diverse range of campaigning and community groups, the government is following the Conservatives in seeking to 'privatise' the welfare state (see Monbiot, 2000; Whitfield, 2001; Ferguson, et al., 2002; Farnsworth, 2004).

Before proceeding any further something should be said about the term 'privatisation' itself. As one would expect there is no universal agreement as to what this means as it carries considerable ideological and political baggage. It is a term that is banded about both by critics of welfare reform, as well as those who seek to embrace and support such reform by denying that any privatisation is taking place. In a narrow sense privatisation can refer simply to the replacement of public sector service delivery by a private firm or non-statutory agency. More generally, and this is the sense used in this chapter, privatisation is taken to signify a process through which the private sector (the market) is provided with an opportunity to take on a more extensive role in the financing, operation and management of health, housing, education and welfare services which may or may not include wholesale replacement of public provision. Privatisation then, is part and parcel of wider attempts to reformulate and reconstruct the public sector in ways that increasingly blur the boundaries between public and private.

In the next section the legacy of Conservative welfare reform and the development of New Labour's approach is discussed.

## From New Right to New Labour: the Conservative Inheritance

While direct use of privately provided social welfare services remains limited and outside the reach of the majority of people in Britain, the last two decades of the twentieth century witnessed a significant shift away from state welfare provision towards a greater role for the market. This took a number of diverse forms: a shift in the welfare 'mix' in which public sector provision was diminished or steadily replaced by both voluntary and for-profit agencies. That this was uneven across the public sector does not detract from the major inroads that were made in the marketisation of the public sector. For the Conservatives policies such as Right to Buy, introduced under the 1980 Housing Act, the Assisted Places Scheme brought in under the 1980 Education Act, and tax relief for private pensions and private health care insurance, would reduce welfare dependency while opportunities for the exercise of individual choice would be maximised.

Increased 'welfare pluralism' had become the order of the day by the early 1990s. This was accompanied by a gradual though widespread introduction of management and business strategies for coordinating welfare delivery. One of the most significant examples of this was in the distinction between provider and purchasing roles that became so central to Conservative reforms for the NHS in the 1980s and 1990s. This allowed for the mimicking of competition between the different components of the internal, or 'quasi', market. Additionally new providers were encouraged to bid for contracts, particularly in the field of social care where there has been a proliferation of private sector nursing and care establishments in recent decades, or for the running of schools, prisons, and so on.

An important element of the Conservative approach to welfare was to transform those state agencies that remained significant providers (such as social work/services) into more 'business-like organisations'. Through this it was argued more efficient forms of delivery could be developed, offering better 'value for money'. Contracting out services and Compulsory Competitive Tendering (CCT) opened up important sectors of local government to the market, while in many areas driving down the costs of labour and eroding conditions of employment. Key to this was the claim that 'more and better' management was the route to a more cost-effective welfare system.

The growth of managerialism in the public sector during the 1980s and 1990s has been well documented (see Clarke et al., 1994; Clarke and Newman, 1997; Clarke et al., 2001; Newman, 2001). Public services in both Britain and the United States were, in the language of New Right critics, lacking 'proper management'. Managerialism as an ideology became established as the means through which public sector agencies would become more effective service providers. Importantly, while this was to lead to a significant growth in the numbers of public sector managers, all members of the organisation were to become infused with the managerialist rhetoric and language: clients were now customers, public services were now businesses with mission statements, objectives and contracts. All workers were to behave differently as a result. Social workers would become, for instance, care managers. Budget control, cost effectiveness and efficiency were now the key by-words. Through improved management, therefore, 'more could be had for less'. Taken together these changes have, as has been noted, led to major shifts in welfare delivery and in the prevailing view about the role of the welfare state. There is an ongoing debate as to whether these changes led to the 'end of the welfare state' or represented the restructuring of an otherwise 'resilient' welfare system. While opposition remains to all forms of what has generally been termed 'privatisation', a number of past critics of Conservative welfare reforms, particularly in the Parliamentary Labour Party, have now embraced many of the changes previously introduced, as well as now themselves operating within discourses that see managerialism as the key method of achieving particular goals – and any 'problems' in the delivery of welfare and public services constructed as managerial issues.

However, it is important to distinguish between rhetoric and reality. We cannot simply take a New Right (or indeed a New Labour) perspective on what was achieved during the period of Tory rule without question. One of the first points to make in relation to this is that despite claims that a more cost-effective welfare system had been introduced, Conservative policies had little impact on overall public expenditure on welfare spending in general. As Burchardt and Hills point out, welfare spending accounted for a higher percentage of government spending towards the end of the Conservative period in government compared to 1979, despite all their attempts to reduce it (Burchardt and Hills, 1999). As the Conservatives sought to shift the costs of welfare further on to the poor and disadvantaged, through changes in taxation and the benefits system, this served only to increase the numbers who were in need of state support. This was further exacerbated by policies that sought to achieve wage discipline through mass unemployment. Further, although a key goal of the Conservative agenda was to 'roll back the state', this was not achieved in any simple way. Indeed in relation to income maintenance and social security (not to mention policing strategies and immigration policies) the state became even more interventionist and oppressive. In any case 'roll back' was hindered by opposition and by the growing awareness, even among Conservative politicians and policy makers, that cherished welfare institutions such as the NHS would have to remain largely as public sector organisations, not least for reasons of electoral support.

The Conservatives, then, were able to introduce major changes in relation to health and welfare, albeit ones that were partial, uneven, ambiguous and, at times, contradictory. However, they did succeed to a significant extent in securing legitimation for the role of the market in the delivery of heartland social and welfare services, and in the role of management in securing cost effectiveness. More importantly for the purposes of this chapter, they also created a new culture around welfare which New Labour was to embrace.

Much has already been written about the New Labour political project, and its approach to welfare and the welfare state (see, for example, Anderson and Mann, 1998; Clarke and Newman, 1998; Driver and Martell, 1998; Jones and Novak, 1999; Powell, 1999, 2002; Clarke, et al., 2001; Ferguson, et al., 2002). One of the key themes to have emerged in the ongoing debates about the basis of the New Labour ideology is the extent to which it is founded upon ground already secured by the New Right. In other words, how much continuity or difference is there between New Labour and the New Right/Conservatives, or indeed 'Old Labour'? There are a number of different threads in this debate about New Labour's project, if indeed it is possible to talk of a single, coherent project at all. These include the concern with New Labour's apparent pragmatism and emphasis on style and presentation; its reassertion of the social and communal over the rampant individualism of neo-liberalism; the support for European notions of 'social exclusion' and its close relationship with the Clinton administration in the United States which has been influential on Labour policies, particularly in relation to welfare to work. In addition to this controversy there is New Labour's own story about its political trajectory and how it seeks to transcend the 'old differences' between Left and Right in constructing a 'Third Way' in British politics. Blair contrasts the political commitments of Old Labour/the Left, as pro-state and anti-market, with the pro-market and anti-state position of the Right (Blair, 1998b). For Blair and for New Labour's leading theoretician Anthony Giddens, these represent two 'failed pasts', based upon the state or the market or, to borrow the language of the 1998 Green Paper on Health, *Our Healthier Nation* (Secretary of State for Health, 1998), 'nanny state engineering' on the one hand, and 'individual victim blaming' on the other. Between these two sharply polarised positions, it is claimed, a new pragmatic and modern approach to politics can be developed. But before considering the key elements of this Third Way, it is useful to explore some of the key shifts in Labour thinking since the late 1980s.

In its 1997 General Election Manifesto, the Labour Party committed itself to keeping within Tory spending limits for at least the initial two–three years of any period in government. The Manifesto clearly signalled Labour's desire to distance itself from the 'old' 'tax and spend' policies that it was so closely associated with in the past. Blair expressed this as follows:

> I want a country in which people get on, do well, make a success of their lives . . . We need more successful entrepreneurs, not fewer of them. But these life chances should be for all the people. And I want a society in which ambition and compassion are seen as partners not opposites – where we value public service as well as material wealth . . . but we must recognise also that the policies of 1997 cannot be those of 1947 or 1967. (Labour Party, 1997: 2)

Elsewhere in the Manifesto there were further signs of the general approach New Labour would take to public spending:

> New Labour will be wise spenders, not long spenders. We will work in partnership with the private sector to achieve our goals. We will ask about public spending the first question that a manager in any company would ask – can existing resources be used more effectively to meet our priorities? And because efficiency and value for money are central, ministers will be required to save before they spend. Save to invest is our approach, not tax and spend. (Labour Party, 1997: 12)

The seeds of New Labour's thinking were all too evident long before the publication of the 1997 Manifesto. During the Conservatives second period of office, between 1983 and 1987, Labour had been anti-market and was clearly opposed to privatisation in any shape or form. But under Neil Kinnock in the late 1980s there were already signs of a major shift in the party's approach. This reached new heights in the early 1990s under the leadership of John Smith. The party's 1992 Manifesto, for instance, interpreted the role of the government as one of supporting the market as opposed to replacing it through direct provision. Elsewhere Smith's Commission on Social Justice signalled support in principle for the private funding of services, as well as a commitment to developing a 'partnership' between the public and private sector. The market, it was argued, could be harnessed to the pursuit of social justice. Thus 'the ethics of community and the dynamics of a market economy' could be combined (Commission on Social Justice, 1994: 95). The Commission also appeared to accept other important tenets of New Right thinking by accepting that greater levels of inequality were inevitable and that welfare spending was a drain on resources. The Commission on Social Justice marks how far Labour had retreated from its previous position in defence of the 1945 welfare state. With Blair there were to be further major shifts in Labour ideology: one of the most cherished elements of Labour's constitution, Clause 4, which committed the party to public ownership and state control, was revised, providing a clear indication of the party's growing willingness to embrace a neo-liberal market agenda. Not only did Blair and other Labour leaders spend considerable time wooing the business lobby and corporate leaders, but they also provided opportunities for business and management consultants to work on redrafting party policy.

This brings us back to the issue of the Third Way. This has already received considerable attention (see Blair, 1998b; Giddens, 1998, 2000; Le Grand, 1998; Glennerster, 1999; Lavalette and Mooney, 1999; Rose, 1999; Newman, 2001). The intention here is to consider its main features as they impinge on New Labour's approach to reforming the welfare state. The Third Way represents the clearest attempt to provide New Labour with an intellectual basis (see Giddens, 1998, 2000). For Giddens, the Third Way provides a 'framework of thinking and policy making that seeks to adapt social democracy to a world that has changed fundamentally over the past two or three decades' (1998: 26).

What links the Third Way and the approach outlined in the 1997 Manifesto is a shared view of a changing world. To quote Blair again, 'the policies of 1997 cannot be those of 1947 or 1967'. So just what has changed according to this perspective? New Labour shares with the US Democrats a view of the world shaped by globalisation – one where the inexorable forces of the global market render the nation state unable to moderate its effects except in the most limited of ways. A world in which mobile capital is taken as given. In this new globalised world, competition is the order of the day. In order to achieve global competitiveness and to enhance Britain's economic performance, flexible labour markets are to be encouraged as well as the reskilling and education of a new workforce to cope with the requirements of 'knowledge' – and 'information' – based employment. However, the drive for economic competitiveness also requires a far-reaching programme of 'national renewal', a key element of which is the modernisation of major institutions, such as the welfare state, local government and the role of the state itself.

For proponents of the Third Way there are other changes that make this new approach to politics both necessary and feasible. These include increasing individualism and detraditionalisation along with the pursuit of self-fulfilment. Related to these is what Giddens refers to as the decline in collectivism, reflected in the decreasing salience of class politics (see Lavalette and Mooney, 1999: 35).

'Modernisation' is, therefore, central to the overall goal of economic competitiveness and in this respect welfare plays an important role. Welfare strategies that enhance competitiveness, such as Welfare to Work, are to be welcomed. In his speech to the Trades Union Congress in 1997, Blair claimed that there were two crucial elements in the process of modernisation:

> The first is to create an economy fully attuned to a new global market; one that combines enterprise and flexibility with harnessing the creative potential of all our people. The second is to fashion a modern welfare state, where we maintain high levels of social inclusion based on values of community and social justice, but where the role of government changes so it is not necessary to provide all social provision, and fund all social provision but to organise and regulate it most efficiently and fairly. (1997a)

Only through the Third Way for social and welfare policy could Britain build a 'twenty-first century' welfare system. Against critics who have attacked his plans as bringing about the end of the welfare state he claimed that New Labour:

> is not dismantling welfare, leaving it simply as a low-grade safety net for the destitute; nor keeping it unreformed and under performing; but reforming it on the basis of a new contract between citizen and state, where we keep a welfare state from which we all benefit, but on terms that are fair and clear. (1998b: v)

Both these comments imply a fundamental re-thinking of the role of the state in general, and in relation to welfare provision in particular. The Third Way approach questions the extent to which services should be provided by the state and emphasises instead the contribution that non-state agencies can make, albeit in 'partnership' with the state. This is an issue to which we return. What emerges from this though is the idea that the state takes on an enabling role, rather than the role of mass provider that characterised the social democratic state. As Giddens put it: 'Investment in human capital wherever possible, rather than direct provision of economic maintenance. In place of the welfare state we should put the social investment state, operating in the context of a positive welfare society' (1998: 117). In this regard Blair and other architects of the Third Way project have much in common with both Thatcher and Major. Thus the state is to be harnessed in the drive for global competitiveness. In place of a role as large-scale provider, myriad partners and providers will be steered from the centre through regular audits, inspections and appraisal systems conducted by a range of elected and non-elected governmental agencies. For Blair:

> Governments . . . now need to learn new skills: working in partnership with the private and voluntary sector; sharing responsibility and devolving power . . . answering to a much more demanding public . . . In the key public services, the third way is about money for modernisation – new investment of £40 billion over the next three years driving reform and higher standards . . . In all areas, monitoring and inspection are playing a key role, as an incentive to higher standards and as a means of determining appropriate levels of intervention. (1998b: 7 and 16)

The further managerialisation of welfare, and local government in particular, with the introduction of competitive practices and the stress on partnerships, undermines the traditional role of local state agencies in service delivery. For New Labour, however, these methods will ensure value for money, efficiency, flexibility and responsiveness among service providers

Although Labour is keen to downplay the role of the state, and emphasise instead monitoring and regulation, this itself reflects centralising and controlling tendencies in government. Moreover, in important ways the power of the state has been extended, in, for example, initiatives like the 1998 Crime and Disorder Act. The government has extended processes of criminalisation through curfews, parenting orders and the forced removal of the homeless from the streets of some towns and cities. The stress on combating crime and 'disorder' reflects the moral authoritarianism at the heart of New Labour and signifies the greater disciplinary involvement of the state. In this respect Jones and Novak argue that the state is not being 'rolled-back', rather it is being 're-tooled' (Jones and Novak, 1999: Chapter 5) – arguably evidenced by the ever increasing links between criminal justice policies and 'other' social polices under New Labour.

The Third Way is presented by Labour as something that is 'new' and distinctively 'modern', distinct from 'Old Labour' methods of service delivery on the one hand, and the rampaging market of neo-liberalism on the other. The Third Way is offered above all as a project of 'modernisation'. This is, as Clarke and Newman argue (1998), crucial for New Labour's political project of constructing a new relationship between the state, market and civil society. Rose asks some important questions about the notion of modernisation:

> This is the appeal to 'modernisation' as if it in itself provided the guidelines for the justification and the rationale for specific policy and organisational changes: become modern or face the destiny of the obsolete – the scrap heap of history. But what is it to be modern? Have we ever been modern? Why should we want to be modern? (1999: 471)

The idea of a Third Way has been widely criticised (see, for example, Jones and Novak, 1999; Rose, 1999). There is little that is novel about the idea of a Third Way itself, while it can be argued that Labour has always sought to tread a path between the state on the one hand and the market on the other (Ferguson, et al., 2002). It is an extremely slippery notion, reflecting as it does a diverse range of ideological traditions. However, the Third Way represents an acceptance that the market is the most effective way of organising economic activity, albeit with some role for the state as regulator. Through this there is an attempt to marry for-profit services with a never to be defined elusive 'public interest'. For Jones and Novak:

> In the third way capitalism is not challenged: rather it is embraced. New Labour's acceptance of the market differs little from that of the new right, echoing its predecessor's claim that 'there is no alternative'. . . The global market is seen as the final and unchallengeable arbiter in economic – and ultimately in social – life. But the market is not only accepted as setting the agenda and imposing constraints which national governments are powerless to resist. It is also embraced as the main provider. (1999: 181)

The question of the distinctiveness of the New Labour project remains the subject of ongoing debate and argument. We have seen that for some critics the New Labour approach represents the wholesale acceptance of the market as the best method of delivering services, in tune with a neo-liberal agenda. However, there are important signs that this is not simply the continuation of the neo-liberal agenda of the Conservatives. Blair has argued that 'social-ism' is something worth pursuing (Blair, 1998a) and the desire for social justice is presented as a key element in New Labour's discourse, though this appears to be secondary to the goal of limiting public expenditure. However, New Labour has sought to tie the pursuit of social justice and social inclusion to economic growth and competitiveness. In this respect modernisation has an important social element with support for the market and the 'entrepreneurial' ideal, closely interwoven with a language of equal opportunity, as opposed to equality per se, partnership, responsibility and community. Further, Blair and other leading Labour politicians have been keen to stress New Labour's pragmatism – transcending the 'old' ideological battles between Left and Right – by refusing to make a judgement about the relative merits of the state or the market. This is tied up in New Labour's catchphrase, 'what counts is what works' (Labour Party, 1997: 4).

There are important continuities between the New Labour project and that of the Conservatives. But there are also significant differences, notably in the greater emphasis given to 'the social' and the recognition, against Thatcher, that there is something called 'society'. However, there are also significant contradictions in this project, primarily in relation to the goal of integrating the pursuit of social justice with the drive for economic competitiveness.

In this section key elements of New Labour's general political agenda have been considered. In the discussion that follows we explore how this approach is directly reflected in its social and welfare policy, focusing on health, housing and education.

---

**Activity 1**

*What are the key elements of New Labour's Third Way approach to social policy and in what ways are these distinctive from the policies of both Old Labour and the Conservatives?*

---

## New Labour in Power: 'Modernising' the Welfare State?

> Reform is a vital part of rediscovering a true national purpose, part of a bigger picture in which our country is a model of a 21st century developed nation: with sound, stable economic management; dynamism and enterprise in business; the best educated and creative nation in the world; and a welfare state that promotes our aims and achievements. But we should not forget why reform is right, and why, whatever the concerns over individual benefits, most people know it is right. Above all, the system must change because the world has changed, beyond the recognition of Beveridge's generation . . . We need a system designed not for yesterday, but for today. (Blair, quoted in IPPR, 1998: iii–iv)

As we have seen, in the 1997 Election Manifesto Labour was at pains to stress that the days of 'tax and spend' had gone and in its place the key objective was reforming and modernising the welfare state: a 'modern' welfare state for a 'modern world' as Blair put it. Towards the end of the previous section it was noted that New Labour's project combined a mix of continuity with and divergence from the neo-liberal agenda of the Conservatives. This is clearly evident in the 1997 Manifesto. On the one hand there was a commitment to keep to Conservative public spending plans and to avoid increases in income tax. In the first Queen's Speech made within weeks of the General Election, Blair claimed that 'we have reached the limit of the public's willingness simply to fund an unreformed welfare system through ever higher taxes and spending'. However, there would be a one-off 'windfall' tax on the privatised utilities that would generate upwards of £3.5 billion to fund the New Deal for Employment ('welfare to work'). Elsewhere there was a commitment to reducing NHS waiting lists, an issue that would return to haunt Labour in its first four years in power. The NHS itself would be reformed with the abolition of the internal market, though the purchaser/provider split (now designated as commissioning and service management) would remain, along with devolved budgetary responsibility. In education the Conservatives' Assisted Places Scheme was to be abolished but there were to be new opportunities for the private sector to become involved through the Education Action Zones programme and in the direct management of schools.

In Local Government CCT was to be replaced by 'Best Value'. Local authorities were now required to introduce strategies that stressed objective setting, performance management, partnership, consultation and service improvement. However, marketisation and competition were to remain as key elements of this approach and, as with the Conservatives, there was a continuing emphasis on value for money, efficiency and effectiveness. In this renewed stress on managerialist approaches, the language of efficiency, benchmarking and, a goal that New Labour was to continually stress, quality were to become important ideas. Additionally outcomes were emphasised rather than the relative merits of the public or private sector in delivering services, in line with Third Way thinking.

Another feature of New Labour's discourse was the prominence accorded to 'partnerships'. This is reflected across the policy spectrum: there are partnerships in delivering health care, education programmes, housing, in social work, youth policy and urban regeneration among others. Once more it is important to note that such a concern with 'partnership' is hardly new, particularly in relation to urban social policy and urban regeneration programmes. However, under New Labour it has been given renewed vigour. One of the obvious attractions for the Blair government is that partnership can take a number of different forms. Public Private Partnerships (PPPs) – the new name for the Private Finance Initiative (PFI) – are attractive as they work to blur the distinction between public and private. 'Partners' would work together to ensure projects were well managed and targets met, with the threat of regular inspection and audit by government agencies.

These developments were part and parcel of welfare 'reform'. 'Reform' had become something of a mantra among leading Labour politicians and policy makers, with the modernisation of the £90 billion per annum welfare system a key target. In the 1997 General Election campaign Labour had, after all, constructed itself as 'the party of welfare reform'. We have already noted the role that the discourse of modernisation has played in New Labour's political agenda. But it is important to acknowledge once again that there is little that is new in the desire for 'modernisation'. The rhetoric of modernisation has been an appealing discourse for successive governments, albeit mobilised in different ways in different periods.

The extension of managerialism and the increased role for the private sector in delivering public services were crucial elements of New Labour's platform as we have seen. These were accompanied by two key 'flagship' policies: Welfare to Work and the Social Exclusion Unit (see Levitas, 1998; Jones and Novak, 1999; Lavalette and Mooney, 1999; Fergusson, 2004). The task of modernising welfare was given to Frank Field, along with the grandiose title Minster for Welfare Reform, who was charged with 'thinking the unthinkable' about welfare reform (Secretary of State for Social Security and Minister for Welfare Reform, 1998). For Field this would involve combining public and private provision wherever possible. 'Modernisation', then, was directly tied to marketisation.

---

**Activity 2**

*What role does the discourse of 'modernisation' play in New Labour's political project?*

---

## PFI/PPP under New Labour

PFI was one of the most contentious strategies through which the Conservatives sought to promote the role of the market in the provision of public services. Although the seeds of PFI were evident in the late 1980s, it was introduced in the 1992 Budget Speech as a way of encouraging the private sector to invest in public infrastructure, such as new roads and hospitals. At its simplest private funding would be used to construct and manage facilities that would then be leased back by the public sector. Guarantees are made to the firms involved that they will be reimbursed in some way. One obvious attraction for the Conservatives was that it provided an opportunity for the increasing use of private sector management techniques in the delivery of public goods and services. More importantly it also appeared to address the need for improved public services without resorting to increased taxation – or escalating the public sector borrowing requirement. Indeed there is a great deal of political expediency involved in PFI schemes. They offer political advantages today while the costs are borne in the future.

Many Labour politicians had opposed PFI under the Conservatives but by 1997 support for PFI/PPP had become a central element of New Labour policy and in any case it was increasingly being adopted by hard-pressed Labour councils who were searching for capital funds for large-scale public projects. By early 2000, over £16 billion of PFI projects had been organised by the government which has enthusiastically embraced PFI as a means of delivering its promises of improved public services, new hospitals, better transport links and a wide range of schemes across the range of public services, without resorting to increased taxation. The Treasury Financial Statement and Budget Report in July 1997 stated that:

> The Government sees productive public/private partnerships as being key to delivering high quality public services that offer the taxpayer value for money . . . Effort will be focused where it will achieve results, cutting costs for the public and private sectors alike . . . The Government is committed to make PFI work where appropriate.

Elsewhere in the same Report ex-Paymaster General Geoffrey Robinson was to claim that:

> The success of PFI is vital for Britain. Our infrastructure is dangerously run down. Our schools and transport networks are seriously neglected and all too often our urban environment has been allowed to deteriorate. In an age of tight public spending, value for money public/private partnerships will be at the heart of a much-needed renewal of our public services. (Treasury Taskforce on Private Finance, 1997)

Value for money was a repeated message used to present PFI in a positive guise. There were already widespread concerns about PFI following well-publicised cases where PFI was shown to be a very costly way of providing public services and infrastructure. One of the most notorious examples of this was the Skye Road bridge project. This was a type of PFI scheme that allowed for the private sector to charge users, thereby securing a return on investment – and a healthy profit for the financers and operators, The Bank of America. Originally quoted at £10.5m, the final cost to the public of this one bridge (with the highest tolls in Western Europe) is around £128m (see Monbiot, 2000). However, it is in relation to the NHS where some of the strongest criticisms of PFI have been voiced. For Health Services Trade Unions and organisations such as the British Medical Association, PFI means little more than 'Profits from Illness'. Labour is extremely sensitive to its position in relation to the NHS. It has historically portrayed itself as 'the party of the NHS' and argued in opposition that it would save the NHS from the legacy of Conservative under-funding. It has increasingly looked to PFI to build new hospitals and to finance other health-related projects. Since the early 1990s most major capital projects in the NHS have been through PFI/PPP schemes of one kind or another. The private sector is not only involved in building but in a range of activities, from the designing of new hospitals through to running them, which are then leased back to the NHS for periods of up to 60 years. A whole industry of advisers, consultants, financers, brokers, managers, and so on has built up around PFI in the NHS. In 2002 the CBI argued that the government should create more opportunities for private firms to be involved in the delivery of health care and in England Alan Milburn, then Secretary of State for Health, was quick to respond by announcing that private health-care firms could bid to take over the running of 'failing' hospitals (Pollock, 2003). In 2003 the government (in Westminster) announced its proposals to establish 'foundation hospitals' in England and Wales. These would operate as semi-independent organisations within the NHS, with a much more explicit private-sector ethos allowing them to offer pay incentives and locally arranged terms and conditions of employment. Such proposals have generated much opposition with critics claiming that the result will be the creation of a two-tier hospital/ health care service with foundation hospitals luring the best staff and enjoying far greater resources.

These health 'reforms' have been pursued much more vigorously in England than in Scotland where the foundation hospital trust idea has not been adopted. While there is some sign of post-devolutionary divergence here, in other respects across the UK the increasing use of PFI/PPP and the attendant spread of manage-rialist discourses is all too evident. Not only has PFI/PPP been attacked for its higher costs but for many critics the whole PFI ethos is founded on the belief that 'private is better'. PFI is presented as the 'best option' against the public sector where there are in-built negative assumptions. Further, PFI has also resulted in cut-backs in services and, importantly, deteriorating conditions of employment for many thousands of public sector workers who become effectively 'privatised'.

## The End of Council Housing?

On coming to power in 1997, Labour inherited a housing environment that was markedly different from when it was last in power in 1979. In 1981 council housing accounted for 30 per cent of all housing in Britain, but by 1996 this had declined to 19 per cent. Over the same period owner occupation increased from 56 per cent to 67 per cent. From its opposition to the Conservatives' Right to Buy policy in the early 1980s, Labour now appears to have accepted many of the policy prescriptions of the Conservatives in relation to social housing (see Cowan and Marsh, 2001; Lund, 2002; Stirling and Smith, 2003). One particular shift in its approach is in relation to the provision of public sector housing itself. Once more Labour has embraced the market as the means through which demand for more and better housing will be addressed. To quote the then English Housing Minister, Hilary Armstrong:

> Our overriding aim is to make the housing market work for all the people. If the housing market worked perfectly there would be no need or rationale for government interven-tion but the free market cannot accommodate the needs and aspirations of all. Government

must intervene – but that intervention must be limited and strategic, empowering and enabling, not centralising and controlling. [New Labour] will make no preference between public or private sectors . . . I have no ideological objection with the transfer of local authority housing. If it works, and it is what tenants want, transfer may be an appropriate option. What matters is what works. (1998: 3–4)

The limited role provided here for the state is very much in line with both previous Conservative policies and Third Way thinking. While Armstrong has sought to emphasise that she is in line with New Labour's pragmatism by singing the 'what matters is what works' song, New Labour has gone further than the Conservatives in favouring the demunicipalisation of housing stock, and its transfer to a plethora of partnerships, cooperatives and housing associations, along with the transfer of management responsibilities. Once more this transfer has been couched in terms of promoting 'community ownership', choice, self-reliance and responsibility. According to the National Campaign to Defend Council Housing, between 1997 and 2000 over 140,000 homes were removed from the public sector housing stock through transfer schemes, more than the Conservatives achieved during their last decade in office (National Campaign to Defend Council Housing, 2000). On 24, January 2000, the *Guardian* ran with the headline 'Prescott plans to abolish council housing' as the Housing Green Paper was published announcing proposals to transfer up to 200,000 more council houses each year for the next decade.

The Scottish Executive has earmarked £300 million for the creation of new Housing Partnerships that would see the transfer of stock from the public sector. Here the desire of New Labour, both in the Scottish Parliament and at local authority level, to offload as much of socially rented housing as possible is all the more significant given the historic importance of this sector in the Scottish housing market. In both Scotland and England these moves signal a comprehensive break with one of the central elements of the Beveridgean welfare state. But they are not without opposition as across Britain local tenants' groups and public-sector trades unions have organised to successfully defeat the transfer plans of a number of local authorities, notably in 2002 in England's largest council housing landlord, Birmingham.

## Marketising Education?

New Labour has placed considerable importance on 'modernising' Britain's education sector. It has closely linked education and employment/employability in its eagerness to increase Britain's capacity to compete effectively in the global marketplace. In the government's enthusiasm to promote the 'knowledge economy', education plays a significant role. The relationship between education and the economy extends to adopting business and managerial practices in the delivery of education and in the running of schools and other educational institutions. Labour's distrust of local education authorities is evidenced by the commitment of the then Education Minister (for England) David Blunkett to making PPPs (in education) attractive to the private sector (Blunkett, 1997), through the Education Action Zones (EAZs) programme. For Blunkett, EAZs represent 'the beginning of an entirely new way of delivering the education service. It is about partnership based on success rather than outdated dogma on either side' (quoted in Gewirtz, 1999: 23). For New Labour, EAZs would address problems of under-funding (though few additional resources are available) while tackling social exclusion in the localities concerned, through strategies such as those to reduce truancy rates. But it was clear from the outset that the private sector would have a considerable role in running the zones (Whitfield, 1999). Parental choice remains, as do league tables detailing each school's performance, and there may also be some academic selection and marketisation (Gewirtz, 1999: 148). For both Gewirtz and Whitfield, through EAZs the way is open for a full privatisation of school education. In what Whitfield refers to as the 'commodification and mar-ketisation of education', the opportunities for business are immense. Arguably in recent years we have seen an emerging 'edubusiness' sector take shape with the government promoting much closer business–education linkages (see Farnsworth, 2004: 97). While PPP/PFI has become the preferred method of new school build-ing and of refurbishment, the increasing penetration of the market into the edu-cation sector extends far beyond this to businesses running schools and influencing and shaping the curriculum.

---

**Activity 3**

*What are the common features of New Labour's policies in relation to health, housing and education?*

---

## New Labour's Social Policy: a New Welfare Settlement?

In education, housing and the health service, as in other public services, there is an ongoing struggle between two competing discourses: the New Labour-sanctioned view that the increasing use of the private sector in the delivery of public services is to be welcomed as more cost effective and efficient while deliv-ering better quality services, and the position being adopted by an increasing number of trade unions, professional organisations and user groups, and indeed among a growing number of Labour voters, that despite the rhetoric of 'reform' and 'modernisation' the government has continued to privatise large swathes of the public sector leading to deteriorating services and worsening conditions for public sector workers. As pointed out above, Labour committed itself to remain within Conservative spending plans for the first three years in office. This resulted in a further reduction in public spending, estimated by the *Guardian* to be at its lowest for 40 years at 39.4 per cent of GDP. It says much about Labour's attitude to the public sector when it can be claimed that 'Thatcher was more lavish than Labour' (*Guardian*, 25 August 1999). A succession of public outcries about the lack of funding in education and the NHS in particular forced the government to act. However, the indication is that Labour is only partially prepared to redress funding shortfalls. In its much heralded Spending Review and new NHS Plan in 2000, for example, the government promised £13 billion for the NHS in a five-year reform plan. In its 2002 Spending Review there were also real-term increases in finding for key areas of the welfare state. But as Parry shows, while in 2002–3 social expenditure increased to 40.2 per cent of GDP, this is only where it was under the last year of Conservative rule in 1996–7 (Parry, 2003: 38).

In these plans, however, once more there are clear signs that Labour is increasingly looking to the private sector, as well as to PPP/PFI, to help deliver its plans. Along with promises of public sector investment, there was a continuing commitment to 'reform' which now included a more market-led public sector labour market with greater 'flexibility' and local pay and working agreements being advocated against the national collective bargaining agreements which had largely dominated in the public sector in recent decades. Increasingly under New Labour it is those remaining often lowly paid public workers who are finding themselves paying the real costs of welfare state and public sector 'modernisation' and 'reform' (see Newman and Mooney, 2004).

While Labour has continued to portray itself as the party of public services and of the welfare state it has, at times almost by stealth, gone much further than the Conservatives in removing from the public sector what remains of local authority housing, an increasing number of schools and other previously publicly run organisations such as National Air Traffic Control. Where there is an opportunity, it would appear, Labour is committed to providing the private sector with all the encouragement it needs to get involved in delivering public services. The following comments from Gordon Brown and Tony Blair display the government's fondness for the private sector:

> Through the Private Finance Initiative, the private sector is able to bring a wide range of managerial, commercial and creative skills to the provision of public services, offering potentially huge benefits for the Government. We are keen to see the Private Finance Initiative and other public/private partnerships succeed in delivering the necessary investment the country needs, on terms it can afford. (Gordon Brown, quoted in Treasury Taskforce on Private Finance, 1997)

In July 1999 Blair informed the British Venture Capitalist Association that: 'One of the things I would like to do, as well as stimulating more entrepreneurship in the private sector, is to get a bit of it into the public sector as well, (*Guardian*, 7 July 1999). In the same speech he also attacked Britain's public sector workers for being deeply resistant to change. Identified by Blair as one of the key 'forces of conservatism' in the country, leading Labour politicians have not been slow in criticising public sector workers for failing to embrace modernisation and reform. Teachers, for long a target of the Conservatives, have continued to be denounced by sections of the government for their opposition to EAZs and a number of other educational policies being adopted by the government. One important sign of the government's attitude to public sector workers has been its refusal to fund pay increases that would see the public sector regaining some of the ground lost in comparison with private sector pay awards during the 1980s and 1990s. In its 1997 Manifesto Labour committed itself to a policy of public sector pay restraint and this has been a recurring theme of government pronouncements in the period since. Further, it has presented Performance Related Pay (PRP) as a key element of its reform of the public sector. Plans for the introduction of PRP are well advanced in education while in other sectors the government has made it clear that it wishes to abolish national pay bargaining.

The increasing involvement of business in the delivery of public services has for the government brought with it badly needed managerial and financial skills. For many workers it has brought changes in working practices and employment status, at times mounting to little more than the effective casualisation of work. In addition there have been major job losses in the public sector in recent years, with the promise of more to follow.

This leads to the question of whether Labour's 'reforms' are creating a new welfare settlement. There is no one simple answer to this. There are signs that Labour is seeking to continue with Conservative policies – not to mention attitudes – in relation to the public sector. But it has also gone further than the Tories in extending managerialism and privatisation across the public sector. Labour has, albeit in the language of the Third Way, interpreted the role of the state as enabler, not the provider of services, in line with the approach adopted by the Conservatives. However, once again it is important to highlight that this does not mean that the state has 'gone away', as we can observe in its oppressive attitude to policing and refugees – more that Labour has continued with the Tory project to reconstruct the public sector in a more limited way but one that opens up new opportunities for the market (see Hughes et al., 1998). New Labour have travelled far from the commitment to the welfare state that was characteristic of what is now defined as 'Old Labour'. There is now a stress on individual and family responsibility and a downplaying of rights to public goods and services.

Despite the competing ideological influences in the New Labour project, like the Conservatives before them they have stressed that 'there is no alternative' to the market. Where they diverge is in the Labour view that public services, and social welfare in particular, can be harnessed to the drive of creating a 'modern, dynamic, economy'. How many would now accept without question that what remains of the public sector is 'safe in New Labour's hands'?

**Activity 4**

*What signs are there that a new welfare settlement has emerged around New Labour's social policy agenda?*

**Further Reading**

Ferguson, I., Lavalette, M. and Mooney, G. (2002) *Rethinking Welfare*. London: Sage.

Newman, J. (2001) *Modernising Governance*. London: Sage.

Powell, M. (ed.) (2002) *Evaluating New Labour's Welfare Reforms*. Bristol: The Policy Press.

# SIXTEEN
# Globalisation and Social Policy
*Michael Lavalette*

---

### Outline Points

- Globalisation is a contested concept.
- 'Economic globalisation' is often equated with a neo-liberal political project where 'prescription' and 'description' often get confused.
- 'Strong', neo-liberal globalisation assumes the weakening of the nation state and the necessity of a deregulated capitalist world. The prospects for social legislation and state welfare on this perspective are weak.
- There is considerable evidence to show that things are not as bleak as the neo-liberal prognosis would suggest and that welfare states are 'resilient'.
- The last few years have witnessed the growth of a global movement of protest against the consequences of neo-liberal globalisation (and war).

---

## Introduction

The term 'globalisation' has become one of the most used (and possibly abused) economic, social and political concepts of recent times. As Ellwood notes, the concept is used by:

> Environmentalists, human rights advocates, trade unionists, Third world farmers and citizens' groups who decry it at meetings of the world's power elite[s] . . . At the same time economists and business journalists churn out shelves of hefty tomes praising 'globalisation' as an 'historical inevitability'. (2001: 8)

In the media, within politics, and in academic discourse there is an increasingly common assertion that 'globalisation' is having a profound impact on our lives.

But there are a number of important questions that need to be considered. Where and when did the concept of globalisation develop? What does 'globalisation' mean? And, can, and should, globalisation be resisted? This chapter will look at these questions and try to plot a way through what is often a complex debate. In doing so it will try to answer a final question: does globalisation mean the end of the welfare state?

---

**Activity 1**

*Write an initial list of what you think globalisation means and what, in the modern world, has been affected by globalising pressures.*

---

## Globalisation: the History of a Concept

The notion that we live within a global world system is not new. Within classical Marxism there has always been a recognition that capitalism is an internationally integrated system – a 'totality' (see Chapter 4). Indeed this is one of the distinguishing features of classical Marxism in contradistinction to a variety of forms of Stalinism, social democracy and various Third World nationalisms which all (traditionally) emphasised the possibility of independent, national economic development and social transformations.

Similarly within sociology, the 'world system' theories of writers like Gunder Frank (1969), Emmanuel (1972) and Wallerstein (1974) emphasised the systemic nature of a globally integrated capitalism that generated 'dependency' via 'unequal exchange' relationships between north (or metropolitan states) and south (or peripheral or satellite states). While within social theory, the Weberian-influenced tradition of 'historical sociology' took global themes (particularly military competition) as one of the key factors of social development (Skocpol, 1979; Mann, 1986, 1993), while still emphasising 'local', subjective factors that shaped state formations.

Yet in the post-war era, in both academic and activist circles, these perspectives remained minority currents. The dominant accounts of the world within social theory emphasised the ability of nations states to control capital and promote their own road to social betterment. This was the era of what we might call 'state managed capitalism' (Callinicos, 1999).

However, by the 1990s, the concept of globalisation started to be used more widely in academic and activist circles. The concept seemed to emphasise the uncontrollability of modern capitalism – and hence it reflected the growing disillusionment of many former 'national-reformers' that their project was over:

neo-liberalism was dominant and the various 'alternative economic strategies' (and within this expansion of state welfare) of left social democrats and communists now represented an impossible dream.

As it came to be used, the concept of globalisation suggested that the world was being drawn closer together – or 'enmeshed' in the words of many globalisation theorists – with difference and diversity being squeezed by the unfettered development of market forces. The general background to this process – the rise in popularity of the globalisation concept – was a number of economic and political events and crises that shaped the world in the 1970s and 1980s. Let us look at these factors in turn.

### Economic Factors

Economically, the early 1970s witnessed the end of the long post-war boom. The post-war boom was an unprecedented period of economic growth. From about 1948 to the early 1970s the world economy expanded with relatively slow but steady growth rates, leading many commentators to conclude that the crisis-ridden nature of capitalism was a myth – or that, at the very least, 'Keynesian' economic management by national governments could control the crisis tendencies of capitalism (Crosland, 1956). In other words, astute government planning, management and intervention in the economy could sustain and improve national economic growth – which, through appropriate welfare policies, could bring improved living standards to all. If there were short-term difficulties, these were 'local' affairs, requiring adjustment of national policy by national government.

Over this period economic growth rates were spectacular. For example:

> [In America] Gross national product grew until it was three times as great in 1970 as it had been in 1940; German industrial output grew five-fold from the (depressed) level of 1949; French output four-fold. Even the miserable, long declining British economy was producing about twice as much at the end of the long boom as at the beginning. . . . Japan . . . [had] a thirteen-fold increase in its industrial output . . . Russia's economy likewise grew, until it . . . was about seven times as high in the mid-1970s as in the mid-1940s. (Harman, 1984: 74)

Of course, there was unevenness in this process. Industrialisation in India, China, across Africa and in many Latin American countries, for example, brought huge social costs for the majority and vast wealth for the few amongst the urban elites. For the rich there was the development (and fulfilment) of 'sophisticated' Western tastes; for the poor, often living in shanty-towns as 'marginal' workers, there was completely inadequate social infrastructures and poor or non-existent health, education and welfare systems. Nevertheless, despite this unevenness, 'Humanity [at the end of the boom] was producing wealth on a scale that had only been dreamed of previously' (Harman, 1984: 75).

By the end of the 1960s, however, the system was showing signs of slowing down. In 1970–1 there was a short recession that hit nearly all the major economies at once. There was then a sharp co-ordinated boom during 1972 and 1973 before a major recession got under way in late 1973 – a recession the likes of which had not been witnessed for 35 years. Across the globe both inflation and unemployment grew. The Keynesian economic orthodoxies of state economic management no longer fitted. Although there was a brief and weak 'stagflationary' recovery in the second half of the 1970s, there was a further recession in 1979. Recovery in the mid-1980s (on the back of what was termed the 'bubble economy' that saw policies put in place to deliberately raise the value of property and shares) was brought to a halt by recession in 1990 – and so it has continued up to the present. Over the last thirty years the system internationally has been marked by successive waves of brief boom, followed by slump. While it is certainly the case that these boom/slump cycles have impacted differently on various parts of the world economy (hitting the poorest, the weakest and least industrialised sectors most severely), they have been international in nature, emphasising the global integration of modern capitalism.

### Political Factors

The second set of events promoting the concept of globalisation was a number of political developments that occurred in the 1980s. First, in 1979 and 1980 Margaret Thatcher in Britain and Ronald Reagan in the US were elected to office. Reagan, with Thatcher in tow, took a more confrontational stance towards the USSR, leading to an intensification of the nuclear arms race. Both sides in the Cold War now had the capability to destroy the planet – and its population – several times over. In this atmosphere it was clear that the world was becoming smaller in the sense that international, or geo-political, confrontations threatened nuclear holocaust that would destroy all humanity. In response, disarmament campaigns across the globe were born or renewed.

At the same time there was a growing 'environmental consciousness' – a recognition that the increase in the production and emission of greenhouse gases, principally carbon dioxide, and the destruction of, for example, the Amazonian rainforest, were creating problems of global warming that again threatened the population across the world. Various movements were born, and in some parts of the world Green Parties established a presence in national and local politics.

Thus we witnessed the growth of a number of global social issue movements that were a response to the social, environmental and political problems of modern capitalism. Now social movements with a global orientation – and even organisation – are not new. The trade union movement, for example, has a well-established international structure. Neither are globally linked protest movements particularly novel – the various movements of the late 1960s had a variety of both formal and informal links with each other across national borders. But the 'novelty' of these movements came from the claim that these were new, non-class movements motivated by a global humanitarian or global citizenship agenda and that, furthermore, the movements could only be successful if their demands were met globally (i.e. the destruction of all nuclear weapons because nuclear war anywhere would kill us all; by establishing international binding agreements, regulations and standards to protect the environment, etc.).

### 1989 and the 'End of History'

The final element that promoted the globalisation concept were the revolutionary events of 1989 in what used to be called the Eastern Bloc. The revolutions of 1989 were, in many respects, a vindication of those theories that express the belief that ordinary people can shape their world by expressing their collective power in direct action. But for some theorists on the Left the revolutions marked the end of the 'socialist project' (though there were very many socialists and Marxists who rejected the notion that the East European societies had anything in common with socialism) (see Callinicos, 1991).

The collapse of what some referred to as 'really existing socialism' seemed to indicate, to many on the 'old Left', that capitalism had won the great ideological confrontation of the twentieth century. This was a theme taken up by the popularisation of the right-wing philosopher Francis Fukuyama's (1992) article 'The End of History' (written a few months before the collapse of the Berlin Wall). In the aftermath, sections of the liberal Left intelligentsia moved to some form of accommodation with Western liberal-democratic capitalism – viewing it as the best system achievable. The author Salman Rushdie, for example, claimed: 'we may be heading towards a world in which there will be no real alternative to the liberal-capitalist social model' (1990: 109). While on the Left, authors like Communist Party member Eric Hobsbawm (1990) and 'New Left' writer and academic Fred Halliday (1990) interpreted the events as the final defeat for socialism and the victory for capitalism.

If this was the perception on much of the Left, then the response of politicians and writers on the Right can only be described as gloating. Margaret Thatcher announced the 1980s as the decade that finally marked the end of socialism. While US President George Bush (the elder) declared the establishment of a 'New World Order' of peace, stability and economic expansion under the guise of a US-led United Nations.

The reality of course, was more complicated. In fact the early 1990s seemed to mark a period of New World *Dis*order with a whole series of wars and economic crises shaping the 1990s and the early years of the twenty-first century (see Ferguson et al., 2002). But this not withstanding, it was this context – the claimed establishment of a New World Order, of the victory of capitalism and the collapse of what was, for many left wing academics and writers, 'really existing socialism', the series of global economic booms and slumps that has wracked the world since the 1970s, and the growth of a number of globally orientated social movements – that gave birth to notions of globalisation.

From the very beginning therefore the globalisation concept reflected real political and economic developments within the world system, but did so in a way that was imbued with pessimistic notions of the unrivalled and untrammelled power of large multinational corporations and businesses, of the lack of any systemic alternative to capitalism and the absence of any agency capable of resisting free-market policies and politics. Although more recently the concept has been re-enthused with a spirit of rebellion – of a global resistance to global capitalism – it is the earlier conceptions that have framed the debate on the impact of globalisation on our lives.

---

**Activity 2**

*What factors – political, economic, technological – led to the growth of 'globalisation'?*

---

## Defining Globalisation

So what is globalisation? In the literature it is possible to identify three dominant sets of ideas or concerns that underpin the concept of globalisation. First, globalisation is used to refer to the ways in which the world is said to be shrinking socially and culturally. Second, it is used to denote an array of economic changes that are shaping the modern world. For some writers these changes are 'inevitable', but for others they are a set of political and economic ideas – the neo-liberal agenda of the major international financial institutions and most powerful nation states across the globe, sometimes termed the 'Washington Consensus'. Third, the concept is occasionally used in discussion of more 'traditional' political questions – specifically the extent to which we are witnessing (or should be establishing) global forms of regulation and governance.

### Global Culture

The first way the term globalisation is used is as a shorthand to emphasise the fact that the world is said to be 'shrinking'. For example, providing you have the resources, it is now far easier to move across the globe to holiday or conduct business in various far-flung and exotic locations. At the same time there are increasing levels of migration both voluntary and forced between countries (and, of course, a range of political barriers put in place to stop some people's movements) (Stalker, 2001). The growth in communications and media-related industries, reflected in the rapid growth of the Internet and of satellite broadcasting, is seen as leading to 'global homogenisation', what Barbar (1996) calls the creation of a 'McWorld', with an increasingly uniform and dominant commercial culture:

Disney films, Barbie dolls, Nike trainers, fast-food outlets and hip-hop music can be found everywhere. As Ellwood notes, these symbols of the 'corporate-driven, American-style youth culture attract millions of converts from the *bidonvilles* of Abidjan, Côte d'Ivoire, to the wealthy suburbs of Sydney' (2001: 9).

Now some of these notions of 'homogenisation' may overstate the case – indeed the fusion of various cultures, foods, forms of music, literature and the arts is much more positive in many respects than the concept of homogeneity suggests (and indeed many 'local' cultural forms are more resistant to these types of globalising pressures than this concept allows). But clearly there are trends producing similar cultural forms across the globe and these reflect the spread of market capitalism, waged labour, urbanisation and, importantly, resistance to these pressures within cultural production.

### Economic Globalisation

The second way in which globalisation is used is to refer to 'economic globalisation'. This is the most common usage of the globalisation concept in political and socio-economic discourse and, given the implications that are often claimed to follow from this form of globalisation, it is also the most important.

Asserted in its 'strongest' form, economic globalisation claims that the world economy has entered a new stage marked by the growing internationalisation of production and marketing. To be successful companies have to become multinational companies (MNCs) or transnational corporations (TNCs), organise production on an international scale and, in the process, ignore national borders. To use the language, these companies become 'footloose', which means they are no longer attached to any particular nation and will move their production bases anywhere across the globe – to wherever labour is cheapest and the state most accommodating. By so doing, the corporations can escape control by any one nation state and avoid significant opposition (or sideline such opposition) from nationally based popular movements and trade unions.

In this scenario all that states and governments can do is de-regulate their economies, keep taxation rates low and their labour markets flexible and cheap as part of a strategy to attract multinational companies.

The social policy outcomes are far from sanguine. As Yeates notes, in 'strong' versions of globalization:

> Governments . . . [come] 'under siege' from global capital and its institutional allies and . . . [have] no choice but to pursue social and economic policies that are compatible with the 'realities' of globalization and the 'needs' of the international business classes. Globalization . . . undermine[s] 'mature' welfare states, particularly those with comprehensive state provision, and stall[s] their development elsewhere. (2001: 2)

The consequence, so it is claimed, is that we are starting to witness 'welfare convergence' around a broadly neo-liberal model of state activity and welfare provision. Here is Geyer summarising this process:

It does not matter whether the national institutional contexts are conservative or social democratic, if the welfare state is conservative, liberal or social democratic, or if a leftist or rightist party is in power, the constraints have become so extreme that only market-orientated welfare-state structures will be allowed. (1998: 77)

In other words, states become marginalised and find their space for national policy development – or for real policy choices – constrained and determined by the new global market. Here, party politics is increasingly irrelevant because all governments, no matter the party in power, have to act in the same way to attract multinational investment.

In terms of social legislation and social policy, globalisation means a 'race to the bottom'. States must cut public and social services and welfare states must be 'retrenched'. Within national labour markets the dominant themes are labour-market flexibility and deregulation, while a low-wage economy becomes the only option available in a competitive world economy. In these circumstances, trade unions must be marginalised – even by 'trade union friendly' governments – because effective trade unions which defend workers' rights and conditions at work become a barrier to economic growth. All that is left is for states to become 'enablers' – to create the conditions that will attract inward investment. As Taylor-Gooby puts it: 'welfare states are all driven in the same direction by the imperatives of international competition' (1997: 171).

On the 'strong' version of globalisation, therefore, the future looks bleak for the majority who will find their standard of living forced down and state social and welfare services undermined.

But how accurate is this version of globalisation? Some of the key themes associated with globalisation are highly contested. For Hirst and Thompson (1996) the extent of internationalisation is exaggerated – and neither is it particularly unique. They look at the period from the end of the nineteenth century to the beginning of the First World War and note that between 1870 and 1913 world trade grew by 900 per cent – at an average rate of 3.4 per cent per year. This is about the same as the growth rate of international trade today, but below the 'high point' of international trade (during the post-war boom of 1950–1973) when annual growth was just under 10 per cent per annum. Their conclusion is that there is nothing particularly novel in the extent of international trade flows that the world is witnessing in the present period.

Supporters of the globalisation thesis today make much of the 'global mobility of financial markets'. The ability of financiers to transfer large sums in and out of stock markets and the 'disciplining effect' this has on governments (forcing them to follow broadly neo-liberal policies). But Hirst and Thompson note that the end of the nineteenth century was also marked by the enormous growth in the world financial system – which was based on the unrestricted flow of gold from country to country. The breakdown in the Gold Standard in the inter-war period coincided with economic recession and a decline in international trade. It was the establishment of the Bretton Woods system at the end of the

Second World War that marked an attempt by the most powerful governments in the world to control the world economy. The breakdown of this system in the early 1970s allowed currencies to 'float' in value in relation to each other. But this process is not really a 'free market' as governments and their central banks exert enormous influence buying and selling currencies. Again the 'novelty' that is suggested in the present situation is open to question.

The claim that multinationals are free to move easily across the globe is also not as straightforward as is often asserted. There are, of course, multinationals who move their production bases to wherever labour is cheaper. As Sheridan and McCoombes note:

> Even semi-developed countries like Brazil and the Philippines are being spurned by the transnationals as they search for even cheaper labour and even lower rates of taxation. Over the past decade or so, Nike . . . has flitted from the US to South Korea, to Indonesia and now to Vietnam in a never ending quest for cheaper labour, lower production costs and higher profits. (2000: 49)

But this common picture can be overstated. Multinational companies are actually part of large integrated 'industrial complexes'. They require guarantees about the availability of raw materials, the suitability of an appropriate power supply, the quality and reliability of component manufacturers, the availability of good quality transport networks to get goods to and from the market. The company will also have spent years forging relationships with other local businesses, and the local, regional and national state (which may see them obtaining preferential contracts). Of course none of this means they will not move, but moving requires appropriate planning and is a potentially risky activity (and risk is something capitalist enterprises try to avoid). Moving is certainly not something that is done lightly, on a whim, and is not as easy as the phrase 'footloose' suggests.

Finally, the theorists of globalisation tend to suggest that the globalisation process is undermining the ability of states to shape the world, their economies and their regulatory regimes. Yet states remain vital economic and military players in the present era.

On the economic plane, states continue to provide large contracts for companies and centralised state policy direction is essential to enable companies to both plan and maximise their accumulation strategies. States are also key players in the process of securing contracts for 'their' multinationals in dealings with overseas governments. Take, for example, the case of British Aerospace:

> British Aerospace was returned to the private sector in 1981 and 1985. But the umbilical cord linking BAe's business in turnover terms is generated by the defence side . . . The overseas sales are inextricably linked with government policy. Out of BAe's turnover of £5.6 billion in 1988, it could be inferred that perhaps just £1 billion could be described as generated independently of the British government. (Quoted in Harman, 1991: 38)

These specific figures may be slightly dated, but they do emphasise the fact (which continues to be relevant) that large multinationals rely on 'their' states to help secure lucrative contracts. So, more recently, CorpWatch note that one of America's biggest companies (Boeing) is reliant on state support and contracts: 'America's largest exporter, Boeing is . . . the Pentagon's second largest contractor, eclipsed only by Lockheed Martin. In 2003 Boeing landed over $27 billion in contracts from the Department of Defense' (2004a). The links between the US state and the company are perhaps best described as 'cosy':

> Boeing . . . has a lot of well-connected people looking out for its interests. John Shalikashvili, retired Chairman of the Joint Chiefs of Staff is on the Boeing board. Former Deputy Secretary of Defense, Rudy de Leon heads up Boeing's Washington office. . . . Former Ambassador Thomas Pickering, Boeing's senior vice president for international relations, uses his forty years of experience to generate business for Boeing with foreign governments and corporations. Richard Perle, former Chairman and current member of the Pentagon's Defense Policy Board, is another important Boeing ally within the corridors of power. Two other Defense Policy Board members also work as consultants for Boeing: the Air Force's General Ronald Fogelman and former Navy Admiral David Jeremiah. (Ibid.)

And it's not just Boeing whose interests are 'looked after' by the US government. Lockhead gets similar treatment: 'Lockheed Martin gets $105 from each U.S. taxpayer and $228 from each U.S. household. In 2002 the company was effectively taxed at 7.7 per cent compared to an average tax rate for individuals of 21–33 per cent' (CorpWatch, 2004b).

But states are not just major economic players, they continue to exert a huge military-political role. The last few years we have witnessed US and British intervention into Afghanistan and Iraq, with devastating consequences for ordinary people living in these countries. But these wars were as much about economic and geo-political interests than they were about 'freedom from terror' (Ali, 2003). For the 'neo-cons' at the heart of the US state, these wars were about the interests of US capitalism. As Callinicos notes:

> Economically the US practices a version of the imperialism of free trade on which Victorian Britain relied, using its politico-military power to ensure that world markets are sufficiently open to allow its capital and commodities to flow relatively freely. (2003b: 106)

Without diverting into an analysis of the ongoing wars in the Middle-East, the very least that can be said is that we do not seem to be in a period where states no longer matter or that 'national interests' are being undermined by an integrated global capitalism.

None of these criticisms of economic globalisation suggest there have been no changes to the world economy. Rather they suggest that there is nothing inevitable about the social and political consequences of such developments, which takes us to the heart of one of the problems we have assessing 'globalisation': the concept has become intimately wrapped up in a political project, namely advocacy of neo-liberalism on a global scale. Here advocates of neo-liberal globalisation confuse what neo-classical economics asserts 'ought' to happen within the world economy with a reality that is quite different.

### Global Governance

The third way that globalisation is used is to refer to moves towards global forms of 'governance'. Governance is an analytical term that refers to the various relationships of power and regulation, the forms of authority and the interconnected networks that are utilised and shape a particular approach to governing. In theory 'governance' can be used to refer to all and any form of government – they all use particular forms of governance – but in present discourse it is used to refer to changes in government roles and activities which are a consequence of assumed economic and social transformations in the global era. Here is Rhodes's definition: 'Governance signifies a change in the meaning of government, referring to a *new* process of governing; or a *changed* condition of ordered rule; or the *new* method by which society is governed' (1997: 46). So theories of governance are derived from assumed changes in the global economic system. It is assumed that globalisation means that the state can no longer manage or control capitalism 'in the old way' and therefore can no longer function as an adequate instrument for social reform and improvement. Yet, as noted above, some of these more extreme claims – about the inevitable consequences of economic globalisation – are open to question and thus the basic premise of theories of modern governance may be flawed.

For some theorists of governance, globalisation has meant that the functions of the state have been 'hollowed out'. In this scenario the 'power of the state' has moved in two directions. First, power has shifted 'outwards' to international financial markets, global companies and supra-national state organisations and bodies like the European Union and the World Bank, World Trade Organization and International Monetary Fund. Secondly, some power has shifted downwards to regional bodies and large cities (such as the Scottish Parliament in Britain, or to London with its Mayoral Office). These regional powers can act 'flexibly' and dynamically to attract inward investment. The consequence is that 'big government' has shrunk in size and been fragmented. The consequence is that 'Globalisation, internal devolution within states and the growth of supra-national bodies challenge the capacity of nation states to control their environment' (Newman, 2001: 13).

In this climate neo-liberal theorists and policy makers have argued that capitalism has undergone such a profound transformation in its mode of operation that the basis for state intervention, the mixed economy, nationalisation and the provision of public services, has been undermined. In particular it is argued that the nation state is now relatively impotent in the face of the forces of 'globalisation'. They advocate a minimalist state with deregulated labour markets, privatised welfare provision with the state's role reduced to a mere 'enabler' of economic expansion based around 'free-market principles'.

For some theorists on the Left a similar analysis has led to radically different conclusions. For Deacon et al. (1997) or Monbiot (2003) the necessary solution is to move towards some form of 'global regulation'. For these writers the power of the multinationals has become so great that it is necessary to control their activities through global social clauses or global forms of governance (through reform of the United Nations).

Deacon et al. (1997) argue that there is a need for a global social policy that includes a commitment to 'global social redistribution, global social regulation, and global social provision and/or empowerment'. The means of achieving this, they claim, are:

1   regulating global competition;
2   making the Bretton Woods institutions more accountable;
3   reforming the United Nations;
4   strengthening global political, legal and social rights;
5   empowering international civil society.

Monbiot (2003) calls for a 'global democratic revolution' which includes: (i) democratisation of the UN; (ii) the establishment of a global parliament; (iii) the scrapping of the World Bank, the International Monetary Fund and the World Trade Organization and their replacement with an International Clearing Union; and (iv) the creation of a new International Trading Organisation.

Both Deacon and Monbiot clearly emphasise that the international nature of modern capitalism and the international nature of socio-economic problems, require international solutions – the era of state managed capitalism is over. But noting this does not mean that either the solutions posed by Deacon (1997) and Monbiot (2003) are valid, or that the new internationalised world means that states are now helpless to deal with social problems.

First, let's look at the proposed solutions, in particular the notion that the UN is potentially a useful tool or organ to regulate international capitalism. The problem, for advocates of this type of solution is that they often confuse what they would like the UN to be – a benign, democratic assembly for all nations – with its reality. The UN is not an assembly of equals. It was constructed in the immediate post-Second World War period to protect the power of the most powerful imperialist states. Within the UN it is the Security Council that has real authority, and within this body the 'permanent members', comprising the most powerful military regimes from the Cold War era (USA, Britain, France, USSR (now Russia) and China. Even here, the reliance of China and Russia on both aid and economic agreements has meant that real decision-making is left to what are now often referred to as the 'permanent three'. The prospect of the permanent members relinquishing their power is – to say the least – remote.

Without such reform of the UN, the international social policy agenda is embodied within a series of conventions, recommendations and policy initiatives that member states can choose to sign up to (though there is no mechanism to force them to sign up to such international agreements). Neither are there sufficient penalties for countries who fail to meet agreed targets (of poverty reduction, for example) or who simply sign the conventions as 'social policy blueprints' with little concern for implementation, as International Labour Office researcher Guy Standing (1982) has argued often happens.

An equally important point to make is that while capitalism is now more internationalised than it has ever been, and long-term solutions, including systemic alternatives, to the problems and inequalities generated by capitalism will need to have an international focus, this does not mean that states in the present are powerless, that they cannot shape their societies or that they cannot provide welfare for their citizens.

---

**Activity 3**

*What do you think is meant by:*

1 *describing multinational companies as 'footloose'?*
2 *the term 'governance'?*

*What is meant by the phrase 'the race to the bottom' (with regard to social legislation?*

---

## Globalisation and the Fate of Welfare Systems

On the 'strong', or neo-liberal, interpretations of economic globalisation, the prospects for welfare are bleak. Even erstwhile supporters of state welfarism are often pessimistic about the future. In the early 1990s Ramesh Mishra, a long-time advocate of a fully 'integrated welfare state' (i.e. a comprehensive system of state welfare provision), wrote that:

> The pre-eminence of the economic sphere means that not only full employment but also universality can no longer be seen as sacrosanct in the modern world . . . once we bid farewell to full employment as well as to universality, the 'welfare state' as a distinct phase in the evolution of social policy in the West will have come to an end. (1993. 36)

Similarly, long-term left-wing critic of state welfare provision Peter Leonard wrote that:

> The old ideas which ruled the modern welfare state – universality, full employment, increasing inequality – are proclaimed to be a hindrance to survival. They are castigated

as ideas which have outlived their usefulness: they are no longer appropriate to the conditions of a global capitalist economy where investment, production, labour and consumption are all characterised by flexibility, transience and uncertainty. (1997: 113)

Leonard believes that these developments have undermined the basis of state welfare (and more generally of social democratic reforms). He suggests that the necessity to pursue 'competitive taxation policies' requires governments to cut the social wage and reduce public expenditure. The result is (inevitably) privatisation of state services and provision and increasing marketisation in welfare delivery. Leonard sums the process up in a neat phrase. He suggests that regardless of the particular ideological commitments of governments they increasingly find themselves with no choice – they are either 'enthusiastic welfare dismantlers' (like the Thatcher governments in Britain, for example) or 'reluctant welfare dismantlers' (the service-cutting social democratic and labourist governments of France and Spain in the 1990s, for example). 'Enthusiastically' or 'reluctantly' governments will dismantle welfare: 'There Is No Alternative'.

Concerned at the potential impact of economic globalisation on welfare, Mishra (1999) undertook a study to assess its actual impact. He identified seven propositions regarding the implications of 'globalisation logic' on welfare. These were that globalisation:

1 undermines the ability of governments to pursue the objectives of full-employment and economic growth through reflationary policies;
2 leads to increasing inequality and a downward shift in wages and working conditions;
3 exerts downwards pressure on 'systems of social protection and social expenditure' by prioritising reduction in tax and government debt reduction within state policy;
4 undermines notions of 'social solidarity' and social protection by increasing inequality;
5 undermines tripartism and shifts the balance of power from organised labour to states and capital;
6 constrains policy by excluding 'left-of-centre' approaches;
7 will increasingly lead to conflict between the economic logic of globalisation; and the 'logic' of national community and democratic politics. (1999: 13)

After extensive cross-national study his conclusions were that there was substantial evidence to support propositions 1, 4 and 5. There are, in other words, increasing trends towards neo-liberal labour market strategies, growing inequality within countries and marginalisation of trade unions. All important findings but ones that suggest that there is an increasingly neo-liberal politics at the heart of many governments – not that such policies are the inevitable outcome of economic globalisation.

As for the other propositions, his conclusion is that there is not a lot of evidence to support them. On proposition 2 he notes that in Germany, for example, 'A dynamic, competitive economy is apparently quite compatible with a well-regulated labour market, centralised collective bargaining, high wages, good working conditions and strong, entrenched workers' rights' (1999: 95).

In terms of proposition 3 he notes that there is a wide variation in tax levels across OECD countries. He suggests many countries have found it exceptionally difficult to cut social expenditure (partly because of the political opposition it generates). His final conclusion is that there is nothing inevitable about welfare retrenchment as a consequence of economic globalisation, a finding supported by Yeates (2001) who notes the significant degree of 'resilience' shown by welfare systems in the face of the globalisation onslaught.

Taylor-Gooby (1997) suggests that the evidence points to the fact that nation states continue to play a major role in generating divergent responses to 'economic globalisation'. Esping-Andersen (1996) argues that diversity continues to be a remarkable feature of forms of welfare delivery in contrasting nation states. All of which leads Mishra (1999) to suggest that it is really only in the 'Anglo-American' regimes that the neo-liberal globalisation agenda has been pursued.

The conclusion of a variety of comparative welfare studies, therefore, suggests that there is nothing 'inevitable' about welfare retrenchment in the 'globalisation era'. Rather what we have is an ideological drive by some governments and major international financial institutions to promote a particular form of globalisation: this is a political project to reshape the world in line with neo-liberal perspectives about how the world *should* operate, a *prescription* of how the world should be rather than a *description* of how the world is.

---

**Activity 4**

*What does it mean to suggest that too often 'prescription' and 'description' get confused in debates over the impact of globalisation?*

---

## Globalisation and Global Resistance: By Way of a Conclusion

If this assessment is correct – that what we are facing is a political project rather than an inevitable economic and predetermined 'fact' – then a key question must be 'how can it be resisted?'

There is not the space to explore this fully but it would be remiss of any chapter on 'globalisation' to ignore the development in recent years of the global social movement to resist neo-liberal globalisation. This movement was born on the streets of Seattle in November and December 1999 at the protests against the World Trade Organization Third Ministerial. The global justice or anti-capitalist movement then grew at a series of spectacular protests over the following year – Prague,

Stockholm, Barcelona and Genoa, to name but four. The slogan of the movement was that 'Another World Is Possible' and central to the demands for this 'other world' were a whole series of basic welfare demands (see, for example, Callinicos, 2003a; George, 2004). As we entered 2002 the movement grew to encapsulate the movement against the threat of war in the Middle East and produced three of the biggest demonstrations in British history.

The anti-capitalist movement is a truly global movement. It has co-ordinated several days of international protest. Its intellectuals are drawn from the global north and the global south. Its forums (the World, European and Asian Social Forums) that meet annually are massive celebrations of diversity and opposition to the consequences of neo-liberal economics. It is perhaps here, in a 'people's globalisation', that the seed-bed of an 'other world' which prioritises the welfare needs of all will start to take shape.

---

### Further Reading

Callinicos, A. (2003) *An Anti-Capitalist Manifesto*. Cambridge: Polity.
Ferguson, I., Lavalette, M. and Whitmore, E. (2005) *Globalization, Global Justice and Social Work*. London: Routledge.
Yeates, N. (2001) *Globalization and Social Policy*. London: Sage.

# Bibliography

Abbott, E. and Bompass, K. (1943) *The Woman Citizen and Social Security: A Criticism of the Proposals of the Beveridge Report as they Affect Women*. Keighley: Wadsworth and Co.

Abel-Smith, B. and Townsend, P. (1965) *The Poor and the Poorest*. London: George Bell and Sons.

Adonis, A. and Pollard, S. (1997) *A Class Act: The Myth of Britain's Classless Society*. Harmondsworth: Penguin.

Age Concern (2002) *Attitudes Towards Income in Retirement: Research Study Conducted for Age Concern*. London: MORI.

al Yafai, F. (2004) 'Anti-Muslim bias on the rise', *Guardian*, 16 December.

Alcock, C., Payne, S. and Sullivan, M. (2000) *Introducing Social Policy*. London: Prentice Hall.

Alcock, P., Erskine, A. and May, M. (1998) *The Student's Companion to Social Policy*. Oxford: Blackwell.

Ali, T. (ed.) (2000) *Masters of the Universe?* London: Verso.

Anderson, P. and Mann, N. (1998) *Safety First: The Making of New Labour*. London: Granta.

Anonymous (2004) 'Prison scandal: Children in jail', *Independent*, 11 August: 4.

Appadurai, A. (1996) *Modernity at Large: Cultural Dimensions of Globalization*. Minneapolis: University of Minnesota Press.

Arber, S. and Ginn, J. (1991) *Gender and Later Life*. London: Sage.

Arber, S. and Ginn, J. (eds) (1995) *Connecting Gender and Ageing: A Sociological Approach*. Buckingham: Open University Press.

Arensberg, C.M. and Kimball, S.T. (1940) *Family and Community in Ireland*. Cambridge, MA: Harvard University Press.

Ariés, P. (1962) *Centuries of Children*. Edinburgh: J. and J. Gray.

Armstrong, H. (1998) 'Speech to the Annual Conference of the Chartered Institute of Housing', Harrogate, June.

Atkin, K. (1998) 'Ageing in multi-racial Britain: demography, policy and practice', in M. Bernard and J. Phillips (eds), *The Social Policy of Old Age*. London: Centre for Policy on Ageing.

Atkinson, D. and Elliott, L. (1999) 'Reflating Keynes: a different view of the crisis', *International Socialism*, 82.

Axford, B. (2000) 'Globalization', in G. Browning, A. Halcli and F. Webster (eds), *Understanding Contemporary Society: Theories of the Present*. London: Sage.

Aziz, R. (1992) 'Feminism and the challenge of racism: deviance or difference?', in H. Cowley and S. Himmelweit (eds), *Knowing Women*. Oxford: Polity.

Bacon, R.W. and Eltis, W.A. (1976) *Britain's Economic Problem: Too Few Producers*. London: Macmillan.

Baldock, J. et al. (eds) (1999) *Social Policy*. Oxford: Oxford University Press.

Bandalli, S. (2000) 'Children, responsibility and the new youth justice', in B. Goldston (ed.), *The New Youth Justice*. Lyme Regis: Russell House Publishing.

Barbar, B. (1996) *McWorld* New York: Ballantine.

Barker, M. and Beezer, A. (1983) 'The language of racism – an examination of Lord Scarman's report on the Brixton riots', *International Socialism*, 18.

Barling, D. Lang, T. and Caraher, M (2003) 'Joined up food policy? The trials of governance, public policy and the food system', in E. Dowler and C.J. Finer (eds), *The Welfare of Food: Rights and Responsibilities in a Changing World*. Oxford: Blackwell

Barlow, A., Bowley, M. and Butler, G. (1999) *Advising Gay and Lesbian Clients: A Guide For Lawyers*. London: Butterworth.

Barrett, M. and McIntosh, M. (1980) 'The 'family wage': some problems for socialists and feminists', *Capital and Class*, 11.

Barrett, M. and McIntosh, M. (1985) *The Anti-Social Family*. London: Verso.

Barrett, M. and Phillips, A. (eds) (1992) *Destabilizing Theory: Contemporary Feminist Debates*. Cambridge: Polity Press.

Barry, B. (1975) 'Review of "Anarchy, State and Utopia"', *Political Theory*, 3: 330–3.

Bart, P. (1971) 'Depression in middle-aged women', in V. Cornick and B. Moran (eds), *Women in Sexist Society*. New York: Basic Books.

Bartlett, W., Roberts, J.A. and Le Grand, J.A. (1998) *Revolution in Social Policy: Quasi-market Reforms in the 1990s*. Bristol: Policy Press.

Bas, N. (2004) 'Exposing Sweatshops': www.corpwatch.org/article.php?list=type&type=108

BASW (2003) *Briefing: Asylum and Immigration (Treatment of Claimants) Bill*. London: BASW.

Bauman, Z. (1993) *Postmodern Ethics*. Oxford: Blackwell.

BBC (2004) 'If . . . the Generations Fall Out', Internet reference: downloaded 20/04/04

Becker, S. (1997) *Responding to Poverty*. London: Longman.

Beechey, V. (1985) 'Familial ideology', in V. Beechey and J. Donald (eds), *Subjectivity and Social Relations*. Milton Keynes: Open University Press.

Bennett, F. (1993) *Social Insurance. Reform or Abolition?* Commission on Social Justice, Vol. 1. London: IPPR.

Bergmark, A., Thorslund, M. and Lindberg, E. (2000) 'Beyond benevolence – solidarity and welfare state transition in Sweden', *International Journal of Social Welfare*, 9(4): 238–49.

Berman, M. (1982) *All That is Solid Melts Into Air: The Experience of Modernity*. London: Verso.

Berman, M. (1999) *Adventures in Marxism*, London: Verso.

Bernard, J. (1973) *The Future of Marriage*. New York: Souvenir Press.

Bernstein, E. (1909) *Evolutionary Socialism*, trans. E.C. Harvey. London: ILP.

Beveridge, W. (1942) *Social Insurance and Allied Services*, Cm. 6404. London: HMSO.

Biggs, S. (1990/91) 'Consumers, case management and inspection: obscuring social deprivation and need?', *Critical Social Policy*, 10 (30): 23–8.

Bircham, E. and Charlton, J. (2001) *Anti-capitalism: A Guide to the Movement*. London: Bookmans.

Black, J. and Nobles, R. (1998) 'Personal pensions misselling: the causes and lessons of regulatory failure', *Modern Law Review*, 61 (6), November: 789–820.

Black, M. and Coward, R. (1981) 'Linguistic, social and sexual relations', *Screen Education*, 39, Summer.

Blackburn, R. (1997) *The Making of New World Slavery*. London: Verso.

Blair, T. (1996) *New Britain: My Vision of a Young Country*. London: Fourth Estate.

Blair, T. (1997a) 'The modernisation of Britain', speech to the Trades Union Congress.

Blair, T. (1997b) Speech at the Aylesbury estate, Southwark, 2 June: www.open.gov.uk/co/seu.more. html/speech by the prime minister.

Blair, T. (1997c) Speech at Stockwell Park School, Lambeth, 8 December: www.open.gov.uk/co/seu. more.html/speech by the prime minister.

Blair, T. (1998a) *New Britain: My Vision of a Young Country*. London: Fourth Estate.

Blair, T. (1998b) *The Third Way*. London: The Fabian Society.

Blair, T. (1998c) Foreword to *New Ambitions For Our Country: A New Contract For Welfare*, Cm. 3805, Department of Social Security. London: Stationery Office.

Blair, T. (1999a) 'Beveridge revisited: a welfare state for the twenty-first century', in R. Walker (ed.), *Ending Child Poverty: Popular Welfare for the Twenty-first Century*. Bristol: Policy Press.

Blair, T. (1999b) Speech to Labour Party Conference, September.

Blair, T. (2001) 'The Third Way: Phase Two', *Prospect*, March, 61.

Blakemore, K. and Boneham, M. (1994) *Age, Race and Ethnicity*. Buckingham: Open University Press.

Blaug, M. (1963) 'The myth of the old Poor Law and the making of the new', *Journal of Economic History*, 23.

Blaug, M. (1964) 'The Poor Law re-examined', *Journal of Economic History*, 24 (2): 229–45.

Blaug, M. (1986) *Great Economists before Keynes: An Introduction to the Lives and Work of One Hundred Great Economists of the Past*. Brighton: Wheatsheaf.

Bloch, A. and Schuster, L. (2002) 'Asylum and welfare: contemporary debates', *Critical Social Policy*, 22 (3): 393–414.

Blocker, H.G. and Smith, E.H. (1980) *John Rawls's Theory of Justice: An Introduction*. Columbus, Ohio: Ohio University Press.

Blumenfeld, W. and Raymond, D. (1993) *Looking at Gay and Lesbian Life*. Boston: Beacon Press.

Blunkett, D. (1997) *PPP's Key to Tackling Crumbling Schools*. London: Department for Education and Employment, Press Release 152/97, 23 June.

Blunkett, D. (2003) 'I am not King Herod', *Guardian*, 27 November.

Booth, C. (1904) *Life and Labour of the People in London*. London: Macmillan.

Bosanquet, N. (1983) *After the New Right*. London: Heinemann.

Bosley, S. (2004) 'Sick to our stomachs', *Guardian*, 25 September.

Boulding, K.E. (1967) 'The boundaries of social policy', *Social Work*, 12 (1).

Bowden, B. (2003) 'The perils of global citizenship', *Citizenship Studies*, 7 (3).

Bowles, S. and Gintis, H. (1976) *Schooling in Capitalist America*. London: Routledge.

Bradley, H. (2000) 'Social inequalities: coming to terms with complexity', in G. Browning, A. Halcli, and F. Webster, (eds), *Understanding Contemporary Society: Theories of the Present*. London: Sage.

Bradshaw, J. and Wakeman, I. (1972) 'The poverty trap up-dated', *The Political Quarterly*, 43: 459–69.

Brazier, C. (2004) 'The power and the folly: unelected, unapproachable, indefensible', *New Internationalist*, 365, March.

Brecher, J. (1997) *Strike*, rev. edn. Boston, MA: South End Press.

Brewer, M. (2003) *The New Tax Credits*, London: Institute for Fiscal Studies Briefing Note, No. 35.

Bridge, J., Bridge, S. and Luke, S. (1990) *Blackstone's Guide to the Children Act 1989*. London: Blackstone Press Ltd.

Briggs, A. (1969) 'The Welfare State in Historical Perspective', in C. Schottland (ed.), *The Welfare State*. New York: Harper and Row.

Bright, M. (2000) 'Youth jails "must be closed" ', *Guardian*, 19 November.

Bright, M. (2004) 'Failure to sack "racist" prison staff condemned', *Guardian*, 26 September.

Bristow, J. and Wilson, A. (eds) (1993) *Activating Theory: Lesbian, Gay, Bisexual Politics*. London: Lawrence and Wishart.

British Association of Social Workers (2004) 'Notice to Members: Asylum and Immigration (Treatment of Claimants, etc.) Bill 2004', Internet reference: www. basw.co.uk/articles.php?articleId= 179&page=1. Downloaded 1 August 2004.

Broadie, A. (ed.) (1997) *The Scottish Enlightenment: An Anthology*. Edinburgh: Canongate.

Brodie, J. (2002) 'Citizenship and solidarity: reflections on the Canadian way', *Citizenship Studies*, 6 (4): 377–94.

Brody, H. (1973) *Inishkillance: Change and Decline in the West of Ireland*. London: Allen Lane.

Bromley, C. (2003) 'Has Britain become immune to inequality?', in A. Park, J. Curtice, K. Thomson, L. Jarvis and C. Bromley (eds), *British Social Attitudes 20th Report: Continuity and Change over Two Decades*. London: Sage.

Brown, C. (1984) *Black and White Britain: The Third PSI Survey*. London: Heinemann.

Brown, G. (2004) Speech by the Chancellor of the Exchequer Gordon Brown at the CBI annual conference in Birmingham, 9 November, Internet reference: www.hm-treasury.gov.uk/newsroom_ and_speeches/press/2004/press_88_04.cfm, Downloaded 24 February 2005.

Brown, M. (1983) 'The development of social administration', in M. Loney, D. Boswell and J. Clarke (eds), *Social Policy and Social Welfare*. Buckingham: Open University Press.

Brown, P. (1996) 'Modernism, post-modernism and sociological theory', *Sociology Review*, 5 (2).

Browning, G., Halcli, A. and Webster, F. (2000) 'Theory, theorists and themes: a user's guide to understanding the present', in G. Browning, A. Halcli and F. Webster (eds), *Understanding Contemporary Society: Theories of the Present*. London: Sage.

Brownlee, I. (1998) 'New Labour: New penology. Punitive rhetoric and the limits of managerialism in criminal justice policy', *Journal of Law and Society*, 25: 3.

Bruegal, I. and Kean, H. (1995) 'The movement of municipal feminism', *Critical Social Policy*, 44/45.

Brundage, A. (2002) *The English Poor Laws, 1700–1930*. Basingstoke: Palgrave.

Buckler, S. and Dolowitz, D. (2000) 'New Labour's ideology: a reply to Michael Freeden', *Political Quarterly*, February: 102–9.

Bull, D. (ed.) (1971) *Family Poverty*. London: Duckworth.

Bunting, M. (2004) 'A job is not enough', *Guardian*, 11 October.

Burchardt, T. and Hills, J. (1999) 'Public expenditure and the public/private mix', in M. Powell (ed.), *New Labour, New Welfare State?* Bristol: Policy Press.

Burgess, S. and Propper, C. (1999) 'Poverty in Britain', in P. Gregg and J. Wadsworth (eds), *The State of Working Britain*. Manchester: Manchester University Press.

Burr, V. (2003) *Social Constructionism*. London: Routledge.

Burrows, R. and Loader, B. (eds) (1994) *Towards a Post-Fordist Welfare State?* London: Routledge.

Bury, M. (1988) 'Arguments about ageing, long life and its consequences', in N. Wells and C. Freer (eds), *The Ageing Population: Burden or Challenge?* London: Macmillan.

Bury, M. and Holme, A. (1991) *Life after Ninety*. London: Routledge.

Butler, J. (1990) *Gender Trouble: Feminism and the Subversion of Identity*. London: Routledge.

Byne, W. (1994) 'The biological evidence challenged', *Scientific American*, May: 50–5.

Bytheway, B. (1995) *Ageism*. Buckingham: Open University Press.

Callinicos, A. (1983) *The Revolutionary Ideas of Karl Marx*. London: Bookmarks.

Callinicos, A. (1989) *Against Postmodernism*. Cambridge: Polity Press.

Callinicos, A. (1991) *The Revenge of History: Marxism and the East European Revolution*. Cambridge: Polity.

Callinicos, A. (1993) *Race and Class*. London: Bookmarks.

Callinicos, A. (1999) *Social Theory: A Historical Introduction*. Oxford: Polity Press.

Callinicos, A. (2000) *Equality*. Cambridge: Polity.

Callinicos, A. (2003a) *An Anti-Capitalist Manifesto*. Cambridge: Polity.

Callinicos, A. (2003b) *The New Mandarins of American Power*. Cambridge: Polity.

Campbell, B. (1984) *Wigan Pier Revisited: Poverty and Politics in the 80s*. London: Virago.

Campbell, B. (1987) *The Iron Ladies: Why Do Women Vote Tory?* London: Virago.

Carby, H.V. (1982) 'White women listen! Black feminism and the boundaries of sisterhood', in *The Empire Strikes Back*. London: Hutchinson in association with the Centre for Contemporary Cultural Studies, University of Birmingham.

Carvel, J. (2000) 'Basics denied to 2m children, *Guardian*, 11 September.

Carvel, J. (2004a) 'Census shows Muslim's plight' *Guardian*, 12 October.

Carvel, J. (2004b) 'Britain violates rights of child says UN', *Guardian*, 29 November: 1.

Carvel, J. (2004c) 'Super-rich have doubled their money under Labour', *Guardian*, 8 December.

CCETSW (1991) *Rules and Requirements for the Diploma in Social Work (Paper 30)*, 2nd edn. London: CCETSW.

Chambers, R. (1994) 'Poverty and livelihood: whose reality counts?', United Nations Stockholm Round Table on Global Change.

Chancellor of the Exchequer (1976) *Public Expenditure to 1979–80*, Cm. 6393. London: HMSO.

Charlton, J. (2000) 'Class struggle and the origins of state welfare reform', in M. Lavalette, and G. Mooney (eds), *Class Struggle and Social Welfare*. London: Routledge.

Charlton, J. (2000) 'Talking Seattle', *International Socialism*, 2 (86): 3–18.

Checkland, S.G. and Checkland, E.O.A. (1974) *The Poor Law Report of 1834*. London: Pelican Classics.

Cheetham, J. (1987) 'Racism in practice', *Social Work Today*, 27 September.

Child Poverty Action Group (2003) *Ensuring that Every Child Matters: Policy Briefing*, CPAG, Internet Reference: www.cpag.org.uk/info/briefings_policy/

Child Poverty Action Group (2004) *Poverty: The Facts, A Summary*. London: CPAG.

Chiozza Money, L.G. (1910) *Riches and Poverty*. London: Methuen.

Chodorow, N. (1978) *The Reproduction of Mothering*. London: University of California Press.

Clarke, J. (1996) 'After social work?', in N. Parton (ed.), *Social Theory, Social Change and Social Work*. London: Routledge.

Clarke, J. (1998) 'Consumerism', in G. Hughes (ed.), *Imagining Welfare Futures*. London: Routledge/ Open University.

Clarke, J. (2004) *Changing Welfare, Changing States*. London: Sage.

Clarke, J. and Newman, J. (1997) *The Managerial State*. London: Sage.

Clarke, J. and Newman, J. (1998) 'A modern British people? New Labour and welfare reform', paper for Discourse Analysis and Social Research Conference, Copenhagen, September.

Clarke, J., Cochrane, A. and McLaughlin, E. (eds) (1994) *Managing Social Policy*. London: Sage.

Clarke, J., Gewirtz, S. and McLaughlin, E. (eds) (2001) *Reinventing the Welfare State: From New Right to New Labour*. London: Sage.

Clegg, S. and Gough, R. (2000) 'The struggle for abortion rights', in M. Lavalette, and G. Mooney, (eds), *Class Struggle and Social Welfare*. London: Routledge.

Cloke, C. and Davies, M. (eds) (1995) *Participation and Empowerment in Child Protection*. Chichester: Wiley/NSPCC.

Coates, A. (1958) 'Changing attitudes to Labour in the mid-eighteenth century', *Economic History Review*, XI (1): 35–51.

Coates, A. (1960) 'Economic thought and Poor Law Policy in the eighteenth century', *Economic History Review*, XIII (1): 39–51.

Cohen, S., Humphries, B. and Mynott, E. (2002) *From Immigration Controls to Welfare Controls*. London: Routledge.

Collard, D. (1971) 'The case for universal benefits', in D. Bull (ed.), *Family Poverty*. London: Duckworth.

Collins, P. and Wicks, R. (2003) 'Special report on means tests and tax credits', *Prospect*, May: 50–55.

Commission on Social Justice, Staff Paper (1993) 'Making sense of benefits', *Commission on Social Justice*, Vol. 2. London: IPPR.

Commission on Social Justice (1994) *Strategies for National Renewal*. London: Vintage/IPPR.

Conservative Political Centre (1950) *One Nation*. London: CPR.

Cook, D. (1998) 'Racism, immigration policy and welfare policing: the case of the Asylum and Immigration Act', in M. Lavalette, L. Penketh and C. Jones (eds), *Anti-Racism and Social Welfare*. Aldershot: Ashgate.

Coote, A. (1999) 'The helmsman and the cattle prod', in A. Gamble and T. Wright (eds), 'The new social democracy', *Supplement to the Political Quarterly*. Oxford: Blackwell.

Corporate Watch (2001) *What's Wrong with Supermarkets*. Oxford: Corporate Watch.

CorpWatch (2004a) 'War Profiteers: Boeing': www.corpwatch.org/article.php?list=type&type=10

CorpWatch (2004b) 'War Profiteers: Lockheed Martin' www.corpwatch.org/

Cowan, D. and Marsh, A. (2001) 'New Labour, same old Tory housing policy?', *Modern Law Review*, 64: 2.

Creighton, C. (1980) 'Family, property and relations of production in western Europe', *Economy and Society*, 9.

Creighton, C. (1985) 'The family and capitalism in Marxist theory', in M. Shaw (ed.), *Marxist Sociology Revisited*. Basingstoke: Macmillan.

Crook, S. (1990) 'The end of radical social theory? Notes on radicalism, modernism and postmodernism', in R. Boyne and A. Rattansi (eds), *Postmodernism and Society*. London: Macmillan

Crosland, A. (1956) *The Future of Socialism*. London: Jonathan Cape.

Crosland, A. (1974a) *Socialism Now and Other Essays*. London: Jonathan Cape.

Crosland, A. (1974b) *,The Teacher of Sociology*. London: Jonathan Cape.

Crouch, C. (1999) 'The parabola of working class politics', *Supplement to the Political Quarterly*. Oxford: Blackwell.

Crowley, H. and Himmelweit, S. (eds) (1992) *Knowing Women*. Oxford: Polity.

Cunningham, H. (1995) *Children and Childhood in Western Society Since 1500*. London: Longman.

Cunningham, S. and Tomlinson, K. (2005) 'Starve them out: Does every child really matter?', *Critical Social Policy*, 25: 2.

Dalley, G. (1996) *Ideologies of Caring: Rethinking Community and Collectivism*, 2nd edn. Basingstoke: Macmillan.

Daly, M. (1978) *Gyn/Ecology: The Metaethics of Radical Feminism*. Boston: Beacon Press.

Daly, M. (1994) 'A matter of dependency: gender in British income maintenance provision', *Sociology*, 28 (3). Exeter: BSAP.

Dammer, S. (2000) 'The Clyde rent wars: The Clydebank rent strike of the 1920s', in M. Lavalette and G. Mooney (eds), *Class Struggle and Social Welfare*. London: Routledge.

Dammer, S. (1980) 'Housing, class and state', in J. Melling, (ed), *Housing, State and Social Policy*. London: Croom Helm.

Danos, J. and Gibelin, M. (1986) *June '36: Class Struggle and the Popular Front in France*. London, Bookmarks.

Danson, M., Fleming, I., Gilmore, K., Sternberg, A. and Whittam, G. (2000) *Glasgow City Council Proposed Housing Stock Transfer: Final Report*. Glasgow: Unison Scotland.

Davies, B. with Reddin, M. (1978) *Universality, Selectivity and Effectiveness in Social Policy*. London: Heinemann.

Davis, A. (1991) 'Hazardous lives – social work in the 1980s: a view from the left', in M. Loney, B. Bocock, J. Clarke, A. Cochrane, P. Graham and M. Wilson, (eds), *The State or the Market*. London: Sage.

Dawson, H. (2004) Speech on youth justice, 27 January, Internet Reference: www.hiltondawson. fsnet.co.uk/press_r/youthjusticespeech.htm. Downloaded 1st March 2005.

Deacon, A. (1996) 'Welfare and character', in *Stakeholder Welfare*. London: Institute for Economic Affairs.

Deacon, A. (2000) 'Learning from the US? The influence of American ideas upon "New Labour" thinking on welfare reform', *Policy and Politics*, 18 (1).

Deacon, A. (2002) *Perspectives on Welfare: Ideas, Ideologies and Policy Debates*. Buckingham: Open University Press.

Deacon, B. with Hulse, M. and Stubbs, P. (1997) *Global Social Policy*. London: Sage.

Dean, M. (2004) Growing older in the 21st century, London, ESRC. Internet Reference: www.esrc. ac.uk/esrccontent/DownloadDocs/GO_in_the_21st_century.pdf. Downloaded 24 February 2005.

Denham, J. (2004) 'The fairness code', *Prospect*. June: 28–33.

Department for Education and Skills (2003) *Every Child Matters*, Cm 5860. London, DfES, Internet reference: www.dfes.gov.uk/everychildmatters/pdfs/EveryChildMatters.pdf. Downloaded 1 August 2004.

Department for Education and Skills (2004) *Summary of the Children Act 2004*. London, DfES, Internet Reference: www.everychildmatters.gov.uk/_content/ documents/5750–DfES-Sum%20of% 20CA2004.pdf. Downloaded 1 March 2005.

Department for Education and Skills (2005) *Children Act and Reports*, Internet Reference: www.dfes.gov.uk/ publications/childrenactreport/. Downloaded 1 March 2005

Department for Work and Pensions (2002) *Memoranda Submitted to the House of Commons DfWP Committee Report on the Future of UK Pensions*, Internet reference: www.parliament.the-stationery-office.co.uk/cm200203/cmselect/cmworpen/cmworpen.htm. Downloaded 17 February 2005.

Department for Work and Pensions (2004) *State Pensions: Your Guide*, Internet reference: www.thepensionservice.gov.uk/pdf/pms/pm2–apr04.pdf

Department for Work and Pensions (2005) *Income Related Benefits: Estimates of Take-Up*. London: DfWP.

Department of Health (1997) *The New NHS: Modern, Dependable*. London: The Stationery Office.

Department of Health (1998) *Modernising Social Services*. London: The Stationery Office.

Department of Health and Social Security (Dec 1985a) *Programme for Action*, Cm. 9691. London: HMSO.

Department of Health and Social Security (1985b) *Reform of Social Security*, Vol. 1, Cm. 9517; Vol. 2, *Programme for Change*, Cm. 9518; Vol. 3, *Background Papers*, Cm. 9519. London: HMSO.

Department of Social Security (1998a) *A New Contract for Welfare: Partnership in Pensions*, Cm. 4179. London: The Stationery Office.

Department of Social Security (1998b) *Households Below Average Income: A Statistical Analysis, 1979–1995/96.* London: The Stationery Office.

Department of Social Security (1998c) *New Ambitions for our Country: A New Contract for Welfare,* Cm 3805. London: HMSO.

Department of Social Security (1999) *Opportunity for All: Tackling Poverty and Social Exclusion.* London: Department of Social Security.

Department of Social Security (2000) *Opportunity for All: One Year On,* (second annual report). London: HMSO.

Dinnerstein, D. (1976) *The Rocking of the Cradle and the Ruling of the World,* second rev. edn in 1987. London: The Women's Press.

Divine, D. (1991) 'The value of anti-racism in social work education and training', in CCETSW (eds), *Northern Curriculum Development Project.* London: CCETSW.

Docherty, T. (ed.) (1993) *Postmodernism: A Reader.* Hemel Hempstead: Harvester Wheatsheaf.

Donnison, D. (1982) *The Politics of Poverty.* Oxford: Martin Robertson.

Donovan, C., Heaphy, B. and Weeks, J. (1999a) 'Everyday experiments: narratives of non-heterosexual relationships', in E. Silva and C. Smart (eds), *The New Family?* London: Sage.

Donovan, C., Heaphy, B. and Weeks, J. (1999b) 'Partners by choice: equality, power and commitment in non-heterosexual relationships', in G. Allan (ed.), *The Sociology of the Family: A Reader.* Oxford: Blackwell.

Donzelot, J. (1980) *The Policing of Families.* London: Hutchinson.

Dowler, E. (2003) 'Food and poverty in Britain: rights and responsibilities', in E. Dowler and C.J. Finer (eds) *The Welfare of Food: Rights and Responsibilities in a Changing World.* Oxford: Blackwell.

Dowler, E. and Finer, C. J. (eds) (2003) The Welfare of Food: Rights and Responsibilities in a Changing World. Oxford: Blackwell.

Downs, A. (1957) *An Economic Theory of Democracy.* London: Harper and Row.

Doyal, L. (1985) 'Women and the National Health Service: the carers and the careless', in E. Lewin and V. Olesen (eds), *Women's Health and Healing.* London: Tavistock.

Doyal, L. and Gough, I. (1991) *A Theory of Human Need.* Basingstoke: Macmillan.

Drakeford, M. and McCarthy, K. (2000) 'Parents' responsibility and the new youth justice', in B. Goldston (ed.), *The New Youth Justice.* Lyme Regis: Russell House Publishing.

Draper, A. and Green, J. (2003) 'Food safety and consumers: constructions of choice and risk', in E. Dowler and C.J. Finer (eds), *The Welfare of Food: Rights and Responsibilities in a Changing World.* Oxford: Blackwell.

Driver, S. and Martell, L. (1998) *New Labour: Politics After Thatcherism.* Cambridge: Polity.

Duberman, M. (1991) *Hidden from History.* London: Penguin.

Durham, M. (1991) *Sex and Politics: The Family and Morality in the Thatcher Years.* London: Macmillan.

Dwyer, P. (2002) 'Making sense of social citizenship: some user views on welfare rights and responsibilities'. *Critical Social Policy,* 22 (2).

Dyson, A.E. and Lovelock, J. (eds) (1975) *Education and Democracy.* London: Routledge and Kegan Paul.

Eastham, P. (2004) 'Benefits maze may be swept away to give same pension for all', *Daily Mail,* 31 December.

Eichenbaum, L. and Orbach, S. (1982) *Outside In, Inside Out.* Harmondsworth: Penguin.

Eisenstein, H. (1984) *Contemporary Feminist Thought.* London: Unwin.

Elliot, L. (2004) 'Labour fails to stop widening of income gap', *Guardian,* 24 June.

Elliott, L., Denny, C. and White, M. (2000) 'Poverty gap hits labour boasts, *Guardian,* 14 July.

Ellwood, W. (2001) *The No-Nonsense Guide to Globalization.* London: Verso.

Emmanuel, A. (1972) *Unequal Exchange: a Study of the Imperialism of Trade.* London: New Left Books.

Engels, F. (1845/1976) *The Condition of the Working Class in England.* London: Lawrence and Wishart.

Engels, F. (1848/1978) *The Origins of the Family: Private Property and the State.* Beijing: Foreign Languages Press.

Espada, J.S. (1996) *Social Citizenship Rights: A Critique of F. A. Hayek and Raymond Plant.* Basingstoke: Macmillan.

Esping-Andersen, G. (1990) *The Three Worlds of Welfare Capitalism.* Oxford: Polity Press.

Esping-Andersen, G. (1996) *Welfare States In Transition.* London: Sage.

Estes, C. (1979) *The Aging Enterprise*. San Francisco, CA: Jossey Bass.

Evans, D. (1993) *Sexual Citizenship: The Material Construction of Sexualities*. London: Routledge.

Falkingham, J. (1989) 'Dependency and ageing in Britain; a re-examination of the evidence', *Journal of Social Policy*, 18 (2): 211–33.

Falkingham, J. and Victor, C. (1991) 'The myth of the woopie? Incomes, the elderly and targeting the elderly', *Ageing and Society*, 11 (4): 471–93.

Farnsworth, K. (2004) *Corporate Power and Social Policy in a Global Economy*. Bristol: The Policy Press.

Farrelly, P. and Morgan, O. (2001) 'Supermarkets abuse power' *Observer*, 1 October.

Faulks, K. (2000) *Citizenship*. London: Routledge.

Fennell, G., Phillipson C. and Evers, H. (1988) *The Sociology of Old Age*. Stony Stratford: Open University Press.

Ferguson, I. (1994) 'Containing the crisis: crime and the Tories', *International Socialism*, 62.

Ferguson, I. and Lavalette, M. (1999) 'Postmodernism, Marxism and social work', *European Journal of Social Work*, 2 (1): 27–40.

Ferguson, I., Lavalette, M. and Mooney, G. (2002) *Rethinking Welfare: a Critical Perspective*. London: Sage.

Fergusson, R. (2004) 'Remaking the relations of work and welfare', in G. Mooney (ed.), *Work: Personal Lives and Social Policy*. Bristol: The Policy Press.

Field, F. (1998) Beveridge Memorial Lecture, 18 February: www.dss.gov.uk/hq/press/speeches/ff18298.htm. Accessed 19/02/98.

Field, F. (2000) 'Pay off the oldest ones', *Guardian*, 26 May.

Field, F. and Piachaud, D. (1982) *Poverty and Politics*. London: Heinemann.

Finch, J. (1988) 'Whose responsibility? Women and the future of family care', in J. Allen, M. Wicks, J. Finch and D. Leat (eds), *Informal Care Tomorrow*. London: Policy Studies Institute.

Finch, J. and Groves, D. (1983) *A Labour of Love: Women, Work and Caring*. London: Routledge and Kegan Paul.

Finkelhor, D. (1983) 'Common features of family abuse', in D. Finkelhor, R.J. Gelles, G.T. Hotaling and M. Straus (eds), *The Dark Side of Families*. London: Sage.

Finlayson, A. (1999) 'Third way theory', in A. Gamble and T. Wright (eds), 'The New Social Democracy', *Supplement to the Political Quarterly*. Oxford: Blackwell.

Firestone, S. (1970) *The Dialetic of Sex: The Case for Feminist Revolution*. New York: Bantam Books.

Fitzpatrick, T. (2001) *Welfare Theory*. Basingstoke: Palgrave.

*Forbes* (2004) The *Forbes* Rich list 2004: www.woopidoo.com/reviews/news/ forbes-rich-list 2004.htm

Foucault, M. (1967) *Madness and Civilisation*. New York: Pantheon Books.

Foucault, M. (1977) *Discipline and Punish*. London: Penguin.

Foucault, M. (1978) *The History of Sexuality*, Vol. 1, trans. R. Hurley. Harmondsworth: Penguin.

Foucault, M. (1981) *The History of Sexuality, I,* Harmondsworth: Penguin.

Foucault, M. (2001) *Madness and Civilisation*. London: Routledge.

Frank, A.G (1969) *Capitalism and Underdevelopment in Latin America*, (rev. ed.) London: Modern Reader Paperbacks.

Franklin, B. (ed.) (1995) *Handbook of Children's Rights*. London: Routledge.

Franks, S. (1999) *Having None of It. Women, Men and the Future of Work*. London: Granta.

Fraser, D. (2000) 'The post-war consensus: a debate not long enough?', *Parliamentary Affairs*, 53.

Fraser, N. (1998) 'From redistribution to recognition? Dilemmas of justice in a "Post-socialist" age', in C. Willett (ed.), *Theorising Multiculturalism: A Guide to the Current Debate*. Oxford: Blackwell.

Freeden, M. (1999) 'True blood or false genealogy: New Labour and British social democratic thought', *Political Quarterly*, 70: 151–165.

Freud, S. (1905) 'Three essays on the theory of sexuality', in *On Sexuality* (1976) (PFL 7). Harmondsworth: Penguin.

Friedan, B. (1963) *The Feminine Mystique*. Harmondsworth: Penguin.

Fries, J.F. (1980) 'Aging, natural death and the compression of morbidity', *New England Journal of Medicine,* 303: 130–6.

Fries, J.F. (1989) 'The compression of morbidity: near or far?', *Milbank Quarterly*, 67 (2): 208–32.

Frow E. and Frow, R. (1970) *The Half-Time System in Education*. Manchester: E.J. Moxton.

Fryer, P. (1984) *Staying Power: The History of Black People in Britain*. London: Pluto.

Fryer, P. (1988) *Black People in the British Empire*. London: Pluto.

Fukuyama, F. (1992) *The End of History and the Last Man*. London: Hamish Hamilton.

Gaffney, D. and Pollock, A.M. (1998) *Putting a Price on the PFI: The Illusionist Economics of the PFI*. London: Unison.

Gamble, A. (1987) 'The weakening of social democracy', in *Politics and Welfare in Contemporary Britain*, in M. Loney, et al. (eds), *The State or the Market*. London: Sage.

Gamble, A. (1996) *Hayek: The Iron Cage of Liberty*. Cambridge: Polity Press.

Gavron, H. (1966) *The Captive Wife: Conflicts of Housebound Wives*. Harmondsworth: Penguin.

Gee, E.M. 'Misconceptions and misapprehensions about population ageing', *International Journal of Epidemiology*, 31: 750–3.

Geiger, T. (1979) *Welfare and Efficiency*. London: Macmillan.

Gelissen, J. (2000) 'Popular support for institutionalised solidarity: a comparison between European welfare states', *International Journal of Social Welfare*, 9 (4): 285–300.

*General Household Survey* (1996) (Social Service Division, OPCS). London: HMSO.

George, H. (1979) [1879] *Progress and Poverty*. London: Hogarth Press.

George, S. (1999) *The Lugano Report*. London: Pluto.

George, S. (2004) *Another World is Possible If*. Cambridge: Verso.

George, V. (1998) 'Political ideology, globalisation and welfare futures in Europe', *Journal of Social Policy*, 27 (1): 17–36.

George, V. and Wilding, P. (1994) *Welfare and Ideology*. London: Harvester Wheatsheaf.

Gewirtz, S. (1999) 'Education action zones', in H. Dean and R. Woods (eds), *Social Policy Review*, 11. Luton: University of Luton/Social Policy Association.

Geyer, R. (1998) 'Globalisation and the (non-) defence of the welfare state', *West European Politics*, 21 (3).

Giddens, A. (1990) *The Consequences of Modernity*. Cambridge: Polity Press.

Giddens, A. (1998) *The Third Way: The Renewal of Social Democracy*. Oxford: Polity Press.

Giddens, A. (2000) *The Third Way and Its Critics*. Cambridge: Polity.

Gil, D. (1973) *Unravelling Social Policy*. New York: Schenkman.

Gilbert, B.B. (1970) *British Social Policy 1914–1939*. London: Batsford.

Gilligan, C. (1982) *In a Different Voice: Psychological Theory and Women's Development*. London: Harvard University Press.

Ginsborg, P. (1990) *A History of Contemporary Italy*. Harmondsworth: Penguin.

Ginsburg, N. (1992) *Social Divisions of Welfare*. London: Sage.

Gittins, D. (1985) *The Family in Question*. London: Macmillan.

Glasgow City Council (2000) 'Project 2002: Glasgow's secondary school public/private partnership:' www.glasgow.gov.uk

Glennerster, H. (1999) 'A third way?', in H. Dean and R. Woods (eds), *Social Policy Review*, 11. Luton: University of Luton/Social Policy Association.

Goldson, B. (2000) 'Wither diversion? Interventionism and the new youth justice', in B. Goldston (ed.), *The New Youth Justice*. Lyme Regis: Russell House Publishing.

Goldson, B. (2003) 'Approaches to youth crime', www.nacro.org.uk/safersociety/approachyouth. htm

Golombok, S. and Tasker, F. (1994) 'Children in lesbian and gay families: theories and evidence', *Annual Review of Sex Research*, 4: 3–100.

Golombok, S. and Tasker, F. (1996) 'Do parents influence the sexual orientation of their children? Findings from a longitudinal study of lesbian families', *Developmental Psychology*, 32 (1): 1–9.

Goodhart, D. (2004) 'Too diverse?', *Prospect*, February: 30–7.

Goodman, A. Myck, M. and Shephard, A. (2003) *Sharing in the Nation's Prosperity? Pensioner Poverty in Britain*. London: Institute for Fiscal Studies.

Gore, C. (1998) 'Inequality, ethnicity and educational achievement', in M. Lavalette, L. Penketh and C. Jones (eds), *Anti-Racism and Social Welfare*. Aldershot: Ashgate.

Gough, I. (1979) *The Political Economy of the Welfare State*. Basingstoke: Macmillan.

Gould, A (1993) *Capitalist Welfare Systems*. London: Longman.

Graham, H. (1987) 'Being poor: perceptions and coping strategies of lone mothers', in J. Brannen and G. Wilson (eds), *Give and Take in Families*. London: Allen and Unwin.

Gray, J. (1993) *Beyond the New Right*. London: Routledge.

Gray, J. (1994) 'On the edge of the abyss', *Guardian*, 18 July.

Green, H. (1988) *Informal Carers*. OPCS Series GHS, No. 15, Supplement A. London: HMSO.

Grmek, M. (1990) *History of AIDS: Emergence and Origin of a Modern Pandemic*, trans. Russell C. Maulitz and Jacalyn Duffin. Princeton, NJ: Princeton University Press.

Gunter, R. (1967) Untitled article, *Sunday Times*, 19 August.

Gustafsson, V. (2003) 'School meals policy: the problem with governing children' in E. Dowler and C.J. Finer (eds), *The Welfare of Food: Rights and Responsibilities in a Changing World*. Oxford: Blackwell.

Habermas, J. (1987) *The Philosophical Discourse of Modernity*. Cambridge: Polity.

Habermas, J. (1996) *Between Facts and Norms*. Cambridge: Polity Press.

Haliday, F. (1975) *A Political History of Japanese Capitalism*. London: Monthly Review Press.

Hall, S. (1979) 'The work of representation', in S. Hall, (ed.), *'Representation: Cultural Representations and Signifying Practices'*. London: Sage in association with the Open University.

Hall, S. (1984) 'The rise of the representative/interventionist state', in G. McLennan et al. (eds), *State and Society in Contemporary Britain*. Oxford: Polity Press.

Hall, S. (1998) 'The great moving nowhere show', *Marxism Today*, Nov.–Dec.: 9–14.

Hall, S. (1999) 'Half over-80s exist on £80 a week or less', *Guardian*, 5 October: 10.

Hall, S. (2001) 'Foucault, power, knowledge and discourse' in S. Wetherall et al. (eds) *Discourse Theory and Practice*. London: Sage.

Hall, S. and Jacques, M. (eds) (1989) *New Times*. London: Lawrence and Wishart.

Halliday, F. (1990) 'The end of the cold war', *New Left Review*, 180.

Hamer, D. and Copeland P. (1994) *The Science of Desire: The Search for the Gay Gene and the Biology of Behavior*. New York: Simon and Schuster.

Hammarberg, T. (1995) 'Preface', in B. Franklin (ed.), *The Handbook of Children's Rights*. London: Routledge.

Hammond, J.L. and Hammond, B. (1917) *The Town Labourer: The New Civilisation*. London: Longmans and Co.

Hammond, J.L. and Hammond, B. (1941) *The Town Labourer 1760–1832*. London: Longman.

Harman, C. (1984) *Explaining the Crisis*. London: Bookmarks.

Harman, C. (1991) 'State and Capital', *International Socialism*, 51.

Harman, C. (1996) 'Globalisation: a critique of a new orthodoxy', *International Socialism*,

Harman, C. (1999) *A People's History of the World*. London: Bookmarks.

Harman, C. (2000) 'Anti-capitalism: theory and practice', *International Socialism*, 88.

Harman, C. (2001) 'Beyond the boom', *International Socialism*, 90.

Harris, J. (1972) *Unemployment and Politics: A Study in English Social Policy 1886–1914*. Oxford: Oxford University Press.

Harris, J. (2003) *The Social Work Business*. London: Routledge.

Harris, R. with Seldon, A. (1963/1965) *Choice in Welfare*. London: IEA.

Hartmann, H. (1979) 'The unhappy marriage of Marxism and Feminism – towards a more progressive union', *Capital and Class*.

Harvey, A. (2003) 'Child policy on asylum seekers', *The Times*, 3 December.

Harvey, D. (1989) *The Condition of Postmodernity*. Oxford: Blackwell.

Harvey, D. (1996) 'Globalisation in question', *Rethinking Marxism*, 8 (4): 1–17.

Hassan, R. (2000) 'Riots and urban unrest in Britain in the 1980s and 1990s', in M. Lavalette and G. Mooney (eds), *Class Struggle and Social Welfare*. London: Routledge.

Hay, J.R. (1975) *The Origins of the Liberal Welfare Reforms 1906–1914*. Basingstoke: Macmillan.

Hayek, F.A. (1944) *The Road to Serfdom*. London: Routledge and Kegan Paul.

Hayek, F.A. (1976a) *Law, Legislation and Liberty, vol. 1: Rules and Social Order*. London: Routledge.

Hayek, F.A. (1976b) *Law, Legislation and Liberty, vol. 2: The Mirage of Social Justice*. London: Routledge.

Hayek, F.A. (1976c) *Law, Legislation and Liberty, vol. 3: The Political Order of a Free People*. London: Routledge.

Hayek, F.A. (ed.) (1963) *Capitalism and the Historians: A Defence of the Early Factory System*. Chicago: University of Chicago Press.

Healey, E. and Mason, A. (1994) *Stonewall 25: The Making of The Lesbian and Gay Community in Britain*. London: Virago.

Health Matters (2000) 'Globalisation and Health': www.healthmatters.org.uk.

Heller, A. (1974) *The Theory of Need in Marx*. London: Allison and Busby.

Helm, S. (2000) 'It's easier to work than to mother', *New Statesman*, 19 May.

Helm, T. (2004) 'Tories to End Women's Pension Bias', *Daily Telegraph*, 13 December: 2.

Help the Aged (2002) 'Memoranda Submitted to the House of Commons DfWP Committee Report on the Future of UK Pensions', Internet reference: www.publications.parliament.uk/pa/cm200203/cmselect/cmworpen/92–III/92m40.htm. Downloaded 21 February 2005.

Her Majesty's Inspectorate of Prisons (2004) *Juveniles in Custody*. London: Home Office.

Her Majesty's Treasury (1999) *The Modernisation of Britain's Tax and Benefit System, Number Four: Tackling Poverty and Extending Opportunity*. London: HM Treasury.

Her Majesty's Treasury (2000) *Prudent for a Purpose: Working for a Stronger and Fairer Britain: Financial Statement and Budget Report*. London: Stationery Office.

Herman, A. (2001) *The Scottish Enlightenment: The Scots' Invention of the Modern World*. London: Fourth Estate.

Heron, E. and Dwyer, P. (1999) 'Doing the right thing: Labour's attempt to forge a new welfare deal between the individual and the state', *Social Policy and Administration*, 33 (1).

Hillyard, P. and Watson, S. (1996) 'Postmodern social policy: a contradiction in terms?', *Journal of Social Policy*, 25 (3).

Hirsch, F. (1977) *The Social Limits to Growth*. London: Routledge and Kegan Paul.

Hirst, P. and Thompson, G. (1996) *Globalization in Question: The International Economy and the Possibilities of Governance*. Cambridge: Polity Press.

Hinscliff, G. (2004) '£7,000 pay gap hits ethnic minorities' *Observer*, 21 November.

HMSO (1994) *Social Trends*, 24. London: HMSO.

Hobhouse, L.T. (1893) *The Labour Movement*. London: Harvester.

Hobhouse, L.T. (1974) [1911] *Liberalism*. New York: Galaxy Books.

Hobsbawm, E. (1969) *Industry and Empire*. Harmondsworth: Penguin.

Hobsbawm, E. (1977) *The Age of Capital 1840–1875*. London: Sphere.

Hobsbawm, E (1990) 'Waking from history's great dream', *Independent on Sunday*, 4 February.

Hobsbawm, E. (1998) 'The death of liberalism', *Marxism Today*, Nov.–Dec.: 4–8.

Hobson, D. (1999) *The National Wealth: Who Gets What in Britain*. London: HarperCollins.

Holdsworth, A. (1988) *Out of the Doll's House*. London: BBC Publications.

Holt, J. (1974) *Escape From Childhood*. Harmondsworth: Penguin.

Home Affairs Select Committee (2005) *Rehabilitation of Prisoners: First Report of Session 2005/2005*. London: The Stationery Office.

Home Office (1997a) *No More Excuses: A New Approach to Tackling Youth Crime in England and Wales*, Cm 3809. London, HMSO.

Home Office (1997b) *Young Prisoners: A Thematic Review by HM Chief Inspector of Prisons for England and Wales – Thematic Report*. London: HMSO.

Home Office (2003a) 'Clearing the Decks for Tough New Asylum Measures', Home Office press release, 24 October, Internet reference: http://www.homeoffice.gov.uk/n_story.asp?item_id=657

Home Office (2003b) *Youth Justice: The Next Steps*. London, HMSO.

Home Office (2003c) *New Legislative Proposals on Asylum Reform, Consultation Letter*. London: Home Office.

Home Office (2005) *Strength in Diversity, Towards a Community Cohesion and Race Equality Strategy: A Summary of Reponses to the Consultation*. London: HMSO.

hooks, b. (1984) *Feminist Theory: From Margin to Center*. Boston, MA: South End Press.

Horne, L., Rights of Women (ed.) *Valued Families: The Lesbian Mothers' Legal Handbook*. London: The Women's Press.

Houghton, D. (1967) 'Paying for the social services', *Occasional Paper*, 16. London: Institute of Economic Affairs.

House of Lords (2003) 'Select Committee on Economic Affairs: aspects of the economics of an ageing population', London, HMSO, HL Paper 179–I, Internet reference: www.publications.parliament.uk/pa/ld200203/ldselect/ldeconaf/179/179.pdf. Downloaded 21 February 2005.

House of Lords (2004) 'Government response to the Select Committee on Economic Affairs: aspects of the economics of an ageing population', London, HMSO, HL Paper 179–I, Internet reference: www.publications.parliament.uk/pa/ld200304/ldselect/ldeconaf/129/129.pdf. Downloaded 21 February 2005.

Howard, M., Garnham, A. Fimister, G. and Veit-Wilson, J. (2001*) Poverty: The Facts*, 4th edn. London: CPAG. www.childpoverty.org.uk/info/briefings_policy/Every%20child%20matters_04.doc.Downloaded 1 August 2004.

Hughes, G., Clarke, J., Lewis, G. and Mooney, G. (1998) 'Reinventing the public?', in G. Hughes (ed.), *Imagining Welfare Futures*. London: Routledge.

Humphries, S. (1981) *Hooligans or Rebels? An Oral History of Working Class Childhood and Youth 1889–1939*. Oxford: Basil Blackwell.

Hurt, J. (1984) 'Reformatory and industrial schools before 1933', *History of Education*, 13 (1).

Husband, C. (1980) 'Culture, context and practice: racism in social work', in R. Bailey and M. Brake (eds), *Radical Social Work*. London: Edward Arnold.

Husband, C. (1991) 'Race, conflictual politics and anti-racist social work: lessons from the past for action in the 1990s', in Northern Curriculum Development Project (ed.), *Setting the Context for Change*. London: CCETSW.

Hutt, W.H. (1963) 'The factory system of the early nineteenth century' in F.A. Hayek (ed.), *Capitalism and the Historians: A Defence of the Early Factory System*. Chicago: University of Chicago Press.

Hutton, W. (1994) 'Ageing population threatens global crisis', *Guardian*, 4 October.

Hutton, W. (1995a) *The State We're In*. London: Jonathan Cape.

Hutton, W. (1995b) *Why They Want to Put Down Older Generation, Guardian*, 6 February 6: 13.

Hyde, H.M. (1970) *The Love that Dared Not Speak its Name: A Candid History of Homosexuality*. Boston, MA: Little Brown.

Institute for Public Policy Research (1993) 'Making sense of benefits', Staff Paper, Vol. 2. London: IPPR.

International Confederation of Free Trade Unions (2005) 'Global Unions Campaign: Get Involved to Stop Child Labour': www.icftu.org/focus.asp?Issue = childlabour&Language=EN

IPPR (1998) *Leading the Way: A New Vision for Local Government*. London: Institute for Public Policy Research.

Jayasuriya, K. (2000) 'Capability, freedom and new social democracy', in A. Gamble and T. Wright (eds), 'The new social democracy', *Supplement to the Political Quarterly*, 71 (3). Oxford: Blackwell.

Jeffreys, S. (1986) *The Spinster and Her Enemies*. London: Pandora Press.

Jeffreys, S. (1990) *Anti-Climax*. London: The Women's Press.

Jenkins, R. and Solomos, J. (1989) *Racism and Equal Opportunity Policies in the 1980s*, 2nd edn. Cambridge: Cambridge University Press.

Johnson, J. and Slater, R. (eds) (1993) *Ageing and Later Life*. London: Sage.

Johnson, N. (1990) *Reconstructing the Welfare State*. London: Harvester Wheatsheaf.

Johnson, P. (1999) 'Inequality, redistribution and living standards in Britain since 1945', in H. Fawcett and R. Lowe (eds), *Welfare Policy in Britain: The Road from 1945*. Basingstoke: Macmillan.

Johnson, P. and Falkingham, J. (1992) *Ageing and Economic Welfare*. London: Sage.

Johnston, B. (2003) 'Italy hit by pensions strike', *Daily Telegraph*, 25 October: 20.

Joint Committee on Human Rights (2004) *Deaths in Custody: Third Report of 2004/2005*. London: The Stationery Office.

Jones, C. (1998) 'Setting the context: race, class and social violence', in M. Lavalette, L. Penketh and C. Jones (eds), *Anti-Racism and Social Welfare*. Aldershot: Ashgate.

Jones, C. and Novak, T. (1999) *Poverty, Welfare and the Disciplinary State*. London: Routledge.

Jones, C. and Novak, T. (2000) 'Class struggle, self-help and popular welfare', in M. Lavalette, and G. Mooney (eds), *Class Struggle and Social Welfare*. London: Routledge.

Jones, H. and MacGregor, S. (eds) (1998) *Social Issues and Party Politics*. London: Routledge.

Jones, R. and Inman, P. (2004) 'What happened to your glowing future?', in *Guardian*, Jobs & Money Supplement, 12 June: 2.

Joseph, K. and Sumption, J. (1979) *Equality*. London: John Murray.

Kavanagh, D. (1990) *Thatcherism and British Politics. The End of Consensus?*, 2nd edn. Oxford: Oxford University Press.

Kearns, K. (1997) 'Social democratic perspectives on the welfare state', in M. Lavalette and A. Pratt (eds), *Social Policy: A Conceptual and Theoretical Introduction*. London: Sage.

Kelly, E. (1988) *Surviving Sexual Violence*. Cambridge: Polity Press.

Kelly, P. (1998) 'Contractarian social justice: an overview of some contemporary debates', in D. Boucher and P. Kelly (eds), *Social Justice from Hume to Walzer*. London: Routledge.

Kemp, P.A. (1999) 'Making the market work? New Labour and the housing question', in H. Dean and R. Woods (eds), *Social Policy Review*, 11. Luton: University of Luton/Social Policy Association.

Keynes, J.M. (1936) *The General Theory of Employment, Interest and Money*. London: Macmillan.

Kidd, A. (1999) *State, Society and the Poor in Nineteenth Century England*. Basingstoke: Macmillan.

King, D.S. (1987) *The New Right: Politics, Markets and Citizenship*. London: Macmillan.

Kingston, P (2004): 'Criminal Waste', *Guardian*, 14 September.

Klein, N. (2000) *No Logo*. London: Flamingo.

Kley, R. (1994) *Hayek's Social and Political Thought*. Oxford: Clarendon Press.

Kumar, K. (1995) *From Post-Industrial to Post-Modern Society: New Theories of the Contemporary World*. Oxford: Blackwell.

Kymlicka, W. (1994) *Multicultural Citizenship: A Liberal Theory of Minority Rights*. Oxford: Clarendon Press.

Labour Party (1945) *Let Us Face the Future*. London: Labour Party.

Labour Party (1974) *Let Us Work Together – Labour's Way out of the Crisis*. London: Labour Party.

Labour Party (1997) *New Labour: Because Britain Deserves Better*. London: Labour Party.

Lang, T. (1997 'Going public: food campaiging during the 1980s and early 1990s', in D. Smith (ed.), *Nutrition in Britain, Science, Scientists and Politics in the Twentieth Century*. London and New York: Routledge.

Lansdown, G. (1995) 'Children's rights to participation: a critique', in C. Cloke and M. Davies (eds), *Participation and Empowerment in Child Protection*. Chichester: Wiley/NSPCC.

Lash, S. and Urry, J. (1987) *The End of Organised Capitalism*. Cambridge: Polity.

Latham, M. (1998) *Civilising Global Capital*. Sydney: Allen and Unwin.

Lavalette, M. and Mooney, G. (1999) 'New Labour, new moralism: the welfare politics and ideology of New Labour under Blair', *International Socialism*, 85: 27–47.

Lavalette, M. and Mooney, G. (eds) (2000) *Class Struggle and Social Welfare*. London: Routledge.

Lavalette, M. and Pratt, A (eds) (2001) *Social Policy: A Conceptual and Theoretical Introduction*, 2nd edn. London: Sage.

Law, I. (1998) 'Sharpening the conceptual tools – racial and ethnic inequalities in housing policy', in M. Lavalette, L. Penketh and C. Jones (eds), *Anti-Racism and Social Welfare*. Aldershot: Ashgate.

Lawrence, J (2004) 'Diabetes "catastrophe" means twice as many will suffer from it by 2000', *Independent*, 7 October.

Lawrence, F. (2004a) 'Crunch time for crisps', *Guardian*, 19 May.

Lawrence, F. (2004b) 'The myth of choice', *Guardian*, 15 June.

Lawrence, F. and Evans, R. (2004) 'Food firms go all the way to no. 10 in fight over what we eat', *Guardian*, 26 May.

Le Grand, J. (1998) 'The third way begins with CORA', *New Statesman*, 6 March.

Lees, D. (1967) 'Poor families and fiscal reform', in *Lloyds Bank Review*, October.

Lee-Tweweek, G. (1998) 'Women, resistance and care: an ethnographic study of nursing auxiliary work', *Work, Employment and Society*, 11 (1).

Leonard, P. (1997) *Postmodern Welfare: Reconstructing an Emancipatory Project*. London: Sage.

Lerner, G. (1979) *The Majority Finds its Past: Placing Women in History*. New York: Oxford University Press.

Levay, S. (1993) *The Sexual Brain*. Cambridge, MA: MIT Publishing.

Levitas, R. (1998) *The Inclusive Society: Social Exclusion and New Labour*. Basingstoke: Macmillan.

Levitas, R. (2004) 'Let's hear it for humpty. Social exclusion, the third way and cultural capital', *Cultural Trends*, 50 (13): 2.

Lewis, G and Phoenix, A. (2004) ' "Race", "Ethnicity" and Identity' in K. Woodward, (ed.), *Questioning Identity*. London: Routledge.

Lewis, G. (2000) 'Coming apart at the seams: the crises of the welfare state', in G. Hughes, and G. Lewis, (eds), *Unsettling Welfare*. London: Routledge in association with the Open University.

Lewis, G., Gerwirtz, S. and Clarke, J. (2000) *Rethinking Social Policy*. London: Sage.

Lewis, G. et al. (eds) (2000) *Rethinking Social Policy*. London: Sage in association with the Open University.

Lewis, J. (1992) *Women in Britain since 1945*. Oxford: Blackwell.

Lewis, J. (1993) *Women and Social Policies in Europe, Work, Family and the State*. London: Edward Elgar Publishing.

Lewis, J. and Meredith, B. (1988) *Daughters who Care: Daughters Caring for Mothers at Home*. London: Routledge.

Lichfield, J. (2003) 'French protest: France paralysed as two million strike over pension reform', *Independent*, 14 May: 11.

Linebaugh, P. (1991) *The London Hanged*. Harmondsworth: Penguin.

Lister, R. (1990) 'Women, economic dependency and citizenship', *Journal of Social Policy*, 19 (4): 445–68.

Lister, R. (2000) 'Gender and the analysis of social policy', in G. Lewis et al. (eds), *Rethinking Social Policy*. London: Sage in association with the Open University.

Lister, R. (2003a) 'Investing in the citizen workers of the future: transformations in citizenship and the state under New Labour', *Social Policy and Administration*, 37 (5): 427–43.

Lister, R. (2003b) *Citizenship. Feminist Perspectives*. Basingstoke: Palgrave, Macmillan.

Lister, R., Smith, N., Middleton, S. and Cox, L. (2003) 'Young people talk about citizenship: empirical perspectives on theoretical and political debates', *Citizenship Studies*, 7 (2): 235–53.

Livia, A. and Hall, K. (1997) *Queerly Phrased: Language, Gender and Sexuality*. Oxford: OUP.

Lloyd-George, D. (1909) *The New Liberalism: Speeches by the Right Hon. David Lloyd George*. London: Daily News.

Local Government Association (2004) *Children Bill and Every Child Matters: Next Steps*. London: LGA.

Logan, J. (1996) *Confronting Prejudice*. London: Arena.

Loney, M., Bocock, R. Clarke, J., Cochrane A., Graham, P. and Wilson, M. (eds) (1991) *The State or the Market. Politics and Welfare in Contemporary Britain*. London: Sage.

Lorde, A. (1984) *Sister Outsider: Essays and Speeches*. New York: The Crossing Press.

Lowe, R. (1990) 'The Second World War, consensus and the foundation of the welfare state', *Twentieth Century British History*, 1 (2).

Lowe, R. (1993) *The Welfare State in Britain since 1945*. London: Macmillan.

Lund, B. (2002) 'Safe as houses? Housing policy under New Labour', in M. Powell (ed.), *Evaluating New Labour's Welfare Reforms*. Bristol: The Policy Press.

Luxembourg Income Study (2004) *Relative Poverty Rates for the Total Population, Children and the Elderly*, Internet reference: lisproject.org/keyfigures/povertytable.htm.

Lyotard, J.F. (1984) *The Postmodern Condition: A Report on Knowledge*. Manchester: Manchester University Press.

MacDonagh, O. (1958) 'The nineteenth-century revolution in government: a reappraisal', *Historical Journal*, 1 (1).

Macfarlane, L.J. (1998) *Socialism, Social Ownership and Social Justice*. Basingstoke: Macmillan.

Mack, J. and Lansley S. (1985) *Poor Britain*. London: Allen and Unwin.

MacLeod, H. and Saraga, E. (1988) 'Challenging the orthodoxy: towards a feminist theory and practice', *Feminist Review*, 28: 16–25.

MacLeod, I. and Powell, E. (1952) *The Social Services: Needs and Means*. London: Conservative Political Centre (updated by Powell, 1954).

Maclure, J.S. (1968) *Educational Documents: England and Wales 1816–1967*. London: Methuen.

Madrick, J. (1997) *The End of Affluence*. New York: Random House.

Mahamadallie, H. (2002) 'Racism myths and realities', *International Socialism*, Summer, 95.

Mandelson, P. (1997) *Labour's Next Steps: Tackling Social Exclusion*. London: Fabian Society.

Mandelson, P. and Liddle, R. (1996) *The Blair Revolution*. London: Faber and Faber.

Mann, M. (1986) *Sources of Social Power, Vol. 1*. Cambridge: Cambridge University Press.

Mann, M. (1987) 'Ruling class strategies and citizenship', *Sociology*, 21 (3): 339–54.

Mann, M. (1993) *Sources of Social Power, Vol. 2. The Rise of Classes and Nation States*. Cambridge: Cambridge University Press.

Marfleet, P. (1999) 'Nationalism and internationalism in the new Europe', *International Socialism*, 84.

Marquand, D. (1967) 'Change gear', *Socialist Commentary*, October.

Marquand, D. (1987) *The Unprincipled Society*. Fontana: London.

Marquand, D. (1996) 'Moralists and hedonists', in D. Marquand and A. Seldon (eds), *The Ideas that Shaped Post-War Britain*. London: Fontana.

Marquand, D. and Seldon, A. (eds) (1996) *The Ideas that Shaped Post-War Britain*. London: Fontana.

Marshall, J.D. (1968) *The Old Poor Law, 1795–1834*. Basingstoke: Macmillan.

Marshall, T.H. (1950) *Citizenship and Social Class*. Cambridge: Cambridge University Press.

Marshall, T.H. (1975) *Social Policy in the Twentieth Century*. London: Hutchinson (1st edn 1965).

Marshall, T.H. (1981) *The Right to Welfare*. London: Heinemann.

Marx, K. and Engels, F. (1848/1998) 'The manifesto of the Communist Party' (Communist Manifesto), in *Marx and Engels Classics in Politics*. London: ElecBook.

Mason, D. (2000) *Race and Ethnicity in Modern Britain*, 2nd edn. Oxford: Oxford University Press.

May, M. (1973) 'Innocence and experience: the evolution of the concept of juvenile delinquency in the mid-nineteenth century', *Victorian Studies*, September.

McGregor, O. (1957) 'Sociology and welfare', *Sociological Review Monograph*, 4.

McIntosh, M. (1998) 'Dependency culture? Welfare women and work', *Radical Philosophy*, 91, September/October: 5.

McKie, R. (2004) 'Lifespan crisis hits supersize America', *Guardian*, 18 September.

McKnight, A., Glennerster, H. and Lupton, R. (2005) 'Education, education, education . . . : an assessment of Labour's success in tackling education inequalities', in J. Hills and K. Stewart (eds), *A More Equal Society? New Labour, Poverty, Inequality and Exclusion*. Bristol: Policy Press.

McLaughlin, E. (1994) 'Flexibility in work and benefits', *Commission on Social Justice*, Vol. II., London: IPPR.

McLean, U. (1989 ) *Dependent Territories: The Frail Elderly and Community Care*. London: NPHT.

McMahon, W. and Marsh, T. (1999) *Filling the Gap: Free School Meals, Nutrition and Poverty*. London: Child Poverty Action Group.

Meacher, M. (1972) 'The malaise of the low-paid worker', in J. Hughes and R. Moore (eds), *A Special Case: Social Justice and the Miners*. London: Penguin.

Meade, C. (1989) *The Thoughts of Betty Spital*. Harmondsworth: Penguin.

Micklewright, J. and Stewart, K. (2000) 'Child well-being and social cohesion: is the UK the oddball in Europe?', in *New Economy*, March.

Middlemas, K. (1980) *Politics in Industrial Society*. London: Macmillan.

Miles, R. (1982), *Racism and Migrant Labour*. London: Routledge.

Miles, R. (1989) *Racism*. London: RKP.

Miles, R. (1993) *Racism After Race Relations*. London: Routledge.

Miles, R. and Phizacklea, A. (1984) *White Man's Country*. London: Pluto.

Miles, R. and Phizacklea, A. (eds) (1979) *Racism and Political Action in Britain*. London: RKP.

Miliband, R (1972) *Parliamentary Socialism*. London: Merlin.

Miliband, R. (1989) *Divided Societies: Class Struggle in Contemporary Capitalism*. Oxford: Oxford University Press.

Millar, J. and Gendinning, C. (1987) *Women and Poverty in Britain*. Brighton: Wheatsheaf.

Miller, D. (1999) *Principles of Justice*. Cambridge, MA: Harvard University Press.

Millett, K. (1971) *Sexual Politics*. New York: Avon Books.

Millstone, E. and van Zwanenberg, P. (2003) 'The evolution of food safety policy-making institutions', in E. Dowler and C.J. Finer (eds), *The Welfare of Food (Rights and Responsibilities in a Changing World)*. Oxford: Blackwell.

Minford, P. (1987) 'The role of the social services: a view from the new right' in M. Loney, R. Bocock, J. Clarke, A. Cochrane, P. Graham and M. Wilson (eds), *The State and the Market: Politics and Welfare in Contemporary Britain*. London: Sage.

Ministry of Pensions and National Insurance (1966) *The Economic Circumstances of Retirement Pensioners*. London: HMSO.

Minkler, M. and Estes, C. (eds) (1984) *Readings in the Political Economy of Aging*. New York: Baywood.

Minkler, M. and Estes, C. (eds) (1998) *Critical Gerontology: Perspectives from Political and Moral Economy*. New York: Baywood.

Mishra, R. (1984) *The Welfare State in Crisis*. London: Harvester Wheatsheaf.

Mishra, R (1993) 'Social policy in a post-modern world' in C. Jones (ed.), *New Perspectives on the Welfare State in Europe*. London: Routledge.

Mishra, R (1999) *Globalisation and the Welfare State*. Cheltenham: Edward Elgar.

Mitchell, J. (1974) *Psychoanalysis and Feminism*. Harmondsworth: Penguin.

Monbiot, G. (2000) *The Captive State*. London: Macmillan.

Monbiot, G. (2003) *The Age of Consent*. Basingstoke: Macmillan.

Money, L.G.C. (1905) *Riches and Poverty*. London: Methuen.

Mooney, G. (2000) 'Class and social policy', in G. Lewis, S. Gewirtz and J. Clarke (eds), *Rethinking Social Policy*. London: Open University/Sage.

Mooney, G. (ed.) (2004) *Work: Personal Lives and Social Policy*. Bristol: The Policy Press.

Moore, Barington, Jnr (1973) *Lord and Peasant in the Making of the Modern World*. Hemel Hempstead: Harvester.

Moore, S. (2000) 'Child Incarceration and the New Youth Justice', in Goldston, B. (ed.), *The New Youth Justice*. Lyme Regis: Russell House Publishing.

Morris, J. (1991) *Pride and Prejudice: A Personal Politics of Disability*. London: Women's Press.

Morris, N. (2003), 'The Queen's Speech: Asylum', *Independent*, 27 November: 11.

Mullan, P. (2000) *The Imaginary Time Bomb: Why an Ageing Population is Not a Social Problem*, London: Tauris and Co. Ltd.

Muncie, J. (1984) *The Trouble With Kids Today: Youth and Crime in Post-War Britain*. London: Hutchinson.

Muncie, J. (1990a) 'Failure never matters: detention centres and the politics of deterrence', in *Critical Social Policy*, 28, Summer.

Muncie, J. (1990b) 'Juvenile delinquency', in R. Dallos and E. McLaughlin (eds), *Social Problems and the Family*. London: Sage.

Muncie, J. (1998) 'Give 'em what they deserve: the young offender and youth justice policy', in M. Langan (ed.), *Welfare: Needs, Rights and Risks*. London: Routledge.

Muncie, J. (1999) 'Institutionalized intolerance: youth justice and the 1998 Crime and Disorder Act', *Critical Social Policy*, 19: 2.

Muncie, J. and McLaughlin, E. (1993) 'Juvenile delinquency' in R. Dallos and E. McLaughlin (eds), *Social Problems and the Family*. Milton Keynes: Open University Press.

Murphy, M. and Harty, S. (2003) 'Post-sovereign citizenship', *Citizenship Studies*, 7 (2): 181–97.

Murray, C. (1990) *The Emerging British Underclass*. London: Institute of Economic Affairs.

Murray, C. (1994) *Underclass: The Crisis Deepens*: London: Institute of Economic Affairs.

Myrdal, G. (1972) 'The place of values in social policy', *Journal of Social Policy*, 1 (1).

National Association of Pension Funds (2004) *Towards a Citizens Pension*. London: NAPF, Internet reference: www.napf.co.uk/publications/Downloads/PolicyPapers/SectionL/citizens_pension_report. pdf. Downloaded 24 February 2005.

National Campaign to Defend Council Housing (2000) *Defend Council Housing*: www.defend councilhousing.org.uk/

National Consumer Council (2004) *Retirement Realities: Shocked and Struggling*. London: National Consumer Council, internet reference: www.ncc.org.uk/moneymatters/retirement_realities.pdf. Downloaded 23 February 2005.

National Pensioners Convention (1998) *Pensions, Not Poor Relief.* London: NPC.

National Pensioners Convention (1999) *Pensions: Who Pays?* London: NPC.

National Pensioners Convention (2002a) 'Memoranda submitted to the House of Commons DfWP Committee Report on the Future of UK Pensions', Internet reference: www.publications.parliament.uk/pa/cm200203/cmselect/cmworpen/92–III/92m41.htm. Downloaded 21 February 2005.

National Pensioners Convention (2002b) *NPC Briefing No. 27: Facts and Figures.* London: NPC.

New Internationalist (2004) *Country Profile – Mexico*, November.

Newburn, T. (1995) *Crime and Criminal Justice Policy.* London: Longman.

Newman, J. (2001) *Modernising Governance: New Labour, Policy and Society.* London: Sage.

Newman, J. and Mooney, G. (2004) 'Managing personal lives: Doing "welfare work"', in G. Mooney (ed.), *Work: Personal Lives and Social Policy.* Bristol: The Policy Press.

Norris, C. (2000) 'Post-modernism: a guide for the perplexed', in G. Browning, A. Halcli and F. Webster (eds), *Understanding Contemporary Society: Theories of the Present.* London: Sage.

Norton-Taylor, R. (1999) *The Colour of Justice.* London: Oberon.

Novak, T. (1988) *Poverty and the State.* Milton Keynes: Open University Press.

Nozick, R. (1974) *Anarchy, State and Utopia.* London: Blackwell.

Oakley, A. (1974) *The Sociology of Housework.* London: Martin Robertson.

O'Brien, M. and Penna, S. (1998) *Theorising Welfare: Enlightenment and Modern Society.* London: Sage.

Office of Fair Trading (1997) *Inquiry into Pensions.* London: OFT.

Oliver, M. and Barnes, C. (1998) *Disabled People and Social Policy: From Exclusion to Inclusion.* London: Longman.

Owen, D. (1967) 'Change gear', *Socialist Commentary*, October.

Page, R. (1984) *Stigma.* London: Routledge and Kegan Paul.

Page, R.M. (1996) *Altruism and the British Welfare State*, Aldershot: Avebury.

Pahl, J. (1965) *Private Violence and Public Policy.* London: Routledge and Kegan Paul.

Pahl, J. (1985) *Private Violence and Public Policy*, 2nd edn. London: Routledge.

Palier, B. and Sykes, R. (2001) 'Challenges and change: issues and perspectives in the analysis of globalization and the European welfare states', in R. Sykes, B. Palier and P. Prior, *Globalization and European Welfare States.* Basingstoke: Palgrave.

Palmer, A. (1993) *Less Equal than Others.* London: Stonewall.

Parker, J. (1998) *Citizenship, Work and Welfare: Searching for the Good Society.* Basingstoke: MacMillan.

Parkinson, M. (1998) *Combating Social Exclusion: Lessons From Area-Based Programmes in Europe.* Bristol: Policy Press.

Parry, R. (2003) 'Invest and reform: Spending review 2002 and its control regime', in C. Bochel, N. Ellison and M. Powell (eds), *Social Policy Review 15.* Bristol: The Policy Press/SPA.

Parton, N. (1994) 'Problematics of governance: (post) modernity and social work', *British Journal of Social Work*, 24 (1): 9–32.

Parton, N. (ed.) (1996) *Social Theory, Social Change and Social Work.* London: Routledge.

Parton, N. and Marshall, W. (1998) 'Postmodernism and discourse approaches to social work', in R. Adams, L. Dominelli and M. Payne (eds), *Social Work: Themes, Issues and Critical Debates.* Basingstoke: Macmillan.

Pascall, G. (1986) *Social Policy: A Feminist Analysis.* London: Tavistock.

Pateman, C. (1988) *The Sexual Contract.* Cambridge: Polity.

Pateman, C. (1992) 'The patriarchal welfare state', in L. McDowell and R. Pringle (eds), *Defining Women, Social Institutions and Gender Division.* Oxford: Polity.

Payne, S. (1991) *Women, Health and Poverty: an Introduction.* Hemel Hempstead: Harvester Wheatsheaf.

Pearson, G. (1981) *Hooligan: a History of Respectable Fears.* London: Macmillan.

Pearson, G. (1983) *Hooligan: a History of Respectable Fears.* London: Macmillan.

Pease, B. and Fook, J. (1999) *Transforming Social Work Practice.* London: Routledge.

Pelling, H. (1993) *A Short History of the Labour Party.* Basingstoke: Macmillan.

Penketh, L. (1998) 'Anti-racist policies and practice: the case of CCETSWs Paper 30', in M. Lavalette, L. Penketh and C. Jones (eds), *Anti-Racism and Social Welfare.* Aldershot: Ashgate.

Penketh, L. (2000) *Tackling Institutional Racism*. Bristol: Policy Press.

Penketh, L. and Ali, Y. (1997) 'Racism and social welfare', in M. Lavalette and Alan Pratt (eds), *Social Policy: A Conceptual and Theoretical Introduction*. London: Sage.

Penna, S. and O'Brien, M. (1996) 'Postmodernism and social policy: a small step forwards?', *Journal of Social Policy*, 25 (1): 39–61.

Pensions Commission (2004) *Pensions: Challenges and Choices: The First Report of the Pensions Commission*. London: HMSO.

Pensions Policy Institute (2005) 'Submission from the Pensions Policy Institute in response to the Pensions Commission's first report', London, PPI, Internet reference: www.pensionspolicyinstitute. org.uk/uploadeddocuments/PPI_ Pensions_ Commission_Response_January_2005.pdf. Downloaded 21 February 2005.

Petersen, P. (1999) 'Gray Dawn: the Global Ageing Crisis', *Foreign Affairs*. 78: 42–55.

Phelan, S. (ed.) (1997) *Playing With Fire: Queer Politics, Queer Theories*. London: Routledge.

Phillips, A. (1999) *Which Equalities Matter?* Cambridge: Polity.

Phillips, M. (1997) 'Workfare for lone mothers: a solution to the wrong problem', in A. Deacon (ed.), *From Welfare to Work*. London: Institute of Economic Affairs.

Phillips, M. (2002) 'Hypocrisy, crude gimmicks and the truth about feckless parents', *Daily Mail*, 29 April 2002.

Phillips, T. (2004) 'Genteel xenophobia is as bad as any other kind', *Guardian*, 16 February.

Phillipson, C. (1982) *Capitalism and the Construction of Old Age*. London: Macmillan.

Phillipson, C. (1998) *Reconstructing Old Age*. London: Sage.

Phillipson, C. and Walker, A. (1986) *Ageing and Social Policy: A Critical Assessment*. Aldershot: Gower.

Phoenix, A. (2000) 'Constructing gendered and racialised identities: young men, masculinities and educational policy', in G. Lewis et al. (ed.). *Rethinking Social Policy*. London: Sage in association with the Open University.

Piachaud, D. (1971) 'Poverty and taxation', *The Political Quarterly*, January–March.

Piachaud, D. (1987) 'Problems in the definition and measurement of poverty', *Journal of Social Policy*, 16 (2).

Piachaud, D. and Webb, J. (1996) 'The price of food: missing out on mass consumption', *Suntory and Toyota International Centre for Economics and Related Disciplines*. London: LSE.

Pierson, C. (1991) *Beyond the Welfare State*. Cambridge: Polity.

Pilgrim, D. (2000) 'The real problem for postmodernism', *Journal of Family Therapy*, 22: 6–23.

Pinchbeck, I. and Hewitt, M. (1973) *Children in English Society, Volume II*. London: Routledge and Kegan Paul.

Pinker, R. (1971) *Social Theory and Social Policy*. London: Heinemann.

Pinker, R. (1999) 'Social work and adoption: a case of mistaken identities', in T. Philpot (ed.), *Political Correctness and Social Work*. London: IEA.

Plant, R. (1985) *Equality, Markets and the State*, Fabian Trust 495. London: Fabian Society.

Plant, R. (1990) 'The New Right and social policy: a critique', in M. Manning and C. Ungerson (eds), *Social Policy Review* 1989/90. London: Longman.

Plant, R. (1991) *Modern Political Thought*, London: Blackwell.

Plewis, I. (2000) 'Educational inequalities and educational action zones', in C. Pantazis and D. Gordon (eds), *Tackling Inequalities*. Bristol: Polity.

Plummer, K. (ed.) (1981) *The Making of the Modern Homosexual*. London: Hutchinson.

Pollock, A. (2003) 'Foundation hospitals will kill the NHS', *Guardian*, 7 May.

Pollock, A., Price, D. and Dunnigan, M. (2000) *Deficits Before Patients*. London: University College London.

Pope, R., Pratt, A. and Hoyle, B. (1986) *Social Welfare in Britain, 1885–1985*. Beckenham: Croom Helm.

Popper, K. (1945/2002) *The Open Society and its Enemies*, Vols 1 and 2. London: Routledge.

Powell, E. (1970) *House of Commons Hansard*, 806: 264–5.

Powell, M. (ed.) (1999) *New Labour, New Welfare State?* Bristol: Policy Press.

Powell, M. (2002a) 'The hidden history of social citizenship', *Citizenship Studies*, 6 (3).

Powell, M. (ed.) (2002b) *Evaluating New Labour's Welfare Reforms*. Bristol: The Policy Press.

Powell, V. (2000) 'Fears for future of Section 28 repeal', *Gay Times*, 258, March: 37–8.

Pratt, A. (1976) 'The Family Income Supplement: Origins and Issues', MA thesis, University of Salford.

Pratt, A. (1988) 'The Labour Party, family income support policy, and the labour market, 1940–79', PhD thesis, University of Bradford.

Pringle, R. and Watson, S. (1992) 'Women's interests and the post-structuralist state', in M. Barrett, and A. Phillips (eds), *De-establishing Theory*. Cambridge: Polity.

Radzinowicz, L. and Hood, R. (1986) *A History of English Criminal Law and its Administration from 1750, Vol. 5: The Emergence of Penal Policy*. London: Stevens.

Rafkin, L. (1990) *Different Mothers: Sons and Daughters of Lesbians Talk about their Lives*. Pittsburgh, PA: Cleis Press.

Ramdin, R. (1987) *The Making of the Black Working Class in Britain*. Aldershot: Gower.

Ransome, P. (1999) *Sociology and the Future of Work*. Aldershot: Ashgate.

Rapp, R. (1979) 'Household and family', in R. Rapp, R. Ross and R. Bridenthal, 'Examining family history', *Feminist Studies*, 181, Spring.

Rawls, J. (1971) *A Theory of Justice*. Oxford: Oxford University Press.

Reisman, D. (1977) *Richard Titmuss: Welfare and Society*. London: Heinemann.

Rendall, J. (1985) *The Origins of Modern Feminism: Women in Britain, France and the United States, 1780–1860*. London and Basingstoke: Macmillan.

Renelagh, J. (1991) *Thatcher's People*. London: Fontana.

Revill, J (2004a) 'Last chance to make us all healthier', *Observer*, 14 November.

Revill, J. (2004b) 'How fat became the big issue', *Observer*, 30 May.

Revill, J and Hinscliff, G. (2004) 'Her health, her cash, her life: Is it anyone else's business?' *Observer*, 14 November.

Rhodes, R.A.W. (1997) *Understanding Governance*. Buckingham: Open University Press.

Rich, A. (1977) *Of Women Born: Motherhood as Experience and Institution*. London: Virago (first published New York, Norton, 1976).

Rich, A. (1980) 'Compulsory heterosexuality and the lesbian existence', *Signs*, 5 (4), Summer: 389–417.

Richardson, D. (1993) *Women, Motherhood and Childhood*. London: Macmillan.

Rights of Women Custody Group (1984) *Lesbian Mothers' Legal Handbook*. London: Women's Press.

Ringen, S. (1986) *The Possibility of Politics: A Study in the Political Economy of the Welfare State*. Oxford: Clarendon.

Ritzer, G. (1993) *The McDonaldization of Society: an Investigation into the Changing Character of Contemporary Social Life*. California: Pine Forge Press.

Robb, B. (1967) *Sans Everything: a Case to Answer*. London: Nelson.

Roberts, D. (1969) *The Victorian Origins of the British Welfare State*. London: Archon Books.

Robertson, R. (1993) *Globalization: Social Theory and Global Culture*. London: Sage.

Robins, K. (1997) 'What is globalisation?', *Sociology Review*, 6 (3): 2.

Rodger, J. (2000) *From a Welfare State to a Welfare Society*. Basingstoke: Macmillan.

Roemer, J.E. (1996) *Theories of Distributive Justice*. London: Harvard University Press.

Rogers, A. (1993) 'Back to the workhouse?', *International Socialism*, 59.

Rogers, A., Pilgrim, D.and Lacey, R. (1993) *Experiencing Psychiatry*. Basingstoke: Macmillan.

Room, G. (ed.) (1995) *Beyond the Threshold*. Bristol: Polity Press.

Rose, M. (1971) *The English Poor Laws 1780–1930*. David and Charles: Newton Abbott.

Rose, N. (1999) 'Inventiveness in politics', *Economy and Society*, 28 (3): 467–93.

Rosenau, P.M. (1992) *Post-Modernism and the Social Sciences: Insights, Inroads and Intrusions*. Princeton, NJ: Princeton University Press.

Rowbotham, S. (1969) *Women's Liberation and the New Politics*. Pamphlet. London.

Rowbotham, S. (1974) *Hidden from History: Three Hundred Years of Women's Oppression and the Fight Against It*. London: Pluto Press.

Rowbotham, S. (1989) *The Past is Before Us: Feminism in Action since the 1960s*. Harmondsworth: Penguin.

Rowntree, B.S. (1901) *Poverty: a Study of Town Life*. London: Macmillan.

Rowntree, B.S. and Lavers, G.R. (1951) *Poverty and the Welfare State*. London: Longmans.

Royal Commission on Long-Term Care for the Elderly (1998) *With Respect to Old Age: Long-Term Care – Rights and Responsibilities*, London, HMSO, Cm 4912–I, Internet reference: www.archive.official-documents.co.uk/document/cm41/4192/4192–02.htm#3. Downloaded 21 February 2005.

Ruddick, S. (1980) 'Maternal thinking', *Feminist Studies*, 6 (2): 342–67

Runnymede Trust (2000) *Report of the Commission on the Future of Multi-Ethnic Britain*: www.runnymedetrust.org/projects/meb/report.html Accessed 17/02/05.

Rushdie, S. (1990) 'Is nothing Sacred?' *Granta*, 31.

Russell, D. (1983) 'Instances and prevalence of intrafamilial and extrafamilial sexual abuse of female children', *Child Abuse and Neglect*, 7: 133–46.

Rutherford, A. (1999) 'The new political consensus on youth justice in Britain', in G.L. McDowell and J.S. Smith (eds), *Juvenile Delinquency in the United States and the United Kingdom*. London: Macmillan.

Saffron, L. (1996) *What About the Children? Sons and Daughters of Lesbian and Gay Parents Talk About Their Lives*. London: Cassell.

Sanchez, P and Swaminathan, M.S. (2005) 'Cutting World Poverty in Half', *Science*, Vol. 307, 21 January: www.earthinstitute.columbia.edu/news/ 2005/cutting_world_hunger_science_mag.pdf

Sapsford, R. and Abbott, P. (1988) 'The body politic, health, family and society', in *Family, Gender and Welfare*. Milton Keynes: Open University Press.

Saraga, E. (1993) 'The abuse of children', in R. Dallos and E. McLaughlin (eds), *Social Problems and the Family*. London: Sage.

Sassoon, D. (1996) *One Hundred Years of Socialism: The West European Left in the Twentieth Century*. London: I.B. Tauris.

Saville, J. (1983/1954) 'The welfare state: an historical approach', in *The New Reasoner* (reprinted as 'The Origins of the Welfare State' in M. Loney, D. Boswell and J. Clarke (eds), (1983) *Social Policy and Social Welfare*. Milton Keynes: Open University Press.

Sayer, D. (1983) *Marx's Method*. London: Harvester Wheatsheaf.

Scarman, Lord (1981) *The Scarman Report: The Brixton Disorders*. Harmondsworth: Penguin.

Scharf, T., Phillipson, C., Smith, A.E. and Kingston, P. (2003) *Older People in Deprived Neighbourhoods: Social Exclusion and Quality of Life in Old Age*. London: ESRC.

Schumpeter, J.A. (1943/1976) *Capitalism, Socialism and Democracy*. London: George Allen and Unwin.

Scottish Office (1999a) *Investing in Modernisation – An Agenda for Scotland's Housing*. Edinburgh: The Stationery Office.

Scottish Office (1999b) *Social Exclusion in Scotland*. Edinburgh: The Stationery Office.

Scraton, P. (ed.) (1997) *Childhood in Crisis*. London: UCL Press.

Scruton, R. (2004) *The Need for Nations*. London: Civitas.

Searle, G.R. (1971) *The Quest for National Efficiency*. London: Basil Blackwell.

Secretary of State for Health (1998) *Our Healthier Nation: a Contract for Health*, Cm. 3852. London: The Stationery Office.

Secretary of State for Social Security and Minister for Welfare Reform (1998) *A New Contract for Welfare: New Ambitions for our Country*, Cm. 3805. London: The Stationery Office.

Segal, L. (1987) *Is the Future Female? Troubled Thoughts on Contemporary Feminism*. London: Virago.

Segal, L. (1993) 'A feminist looks at the family', in M. Wetherell, R. Dallos and D. Miell (eds), *Interactions and Identities*. Milton Keynes: The Open University.

Segal, L. (1999) *Why Feminism?* Cambridge: Polity.

Seldon, A. (1967) 'Taxation and welfare', *Research Monograph*, 14. London: IEA.

Seldon, A. (1977) *Charge*. London: Temple Smith.

Self, P. (1993) *Government by the Market? The Politics of Public Choice*. London: Macmillan.

Self, P. (2000) *Rolling Back the Market Economic Dogma and Political Choice*. London: Macmillan.

Senior, N. (1865) *Historical and Philosophical Essays*. London: Longman Green.

Shabi, R. (2004) 'The price isn't right' *Guardian*, 26 January.

Sheridan, T. and McCoombes, A. (2000) *Imagine: a Socialist Vision for the 21st Century*. Edinburgh: Rebel Inc.

Shin, D.M. (2000) 'Economic policy and social policy: policy linkages in an era of globalisation', *International Journal of Social Welfare*, 9: 17–30.

Shrimsley, R. (1996) 'Cook tells Labour not to forget the poor', *Daily Telegraph*, 18 April.

Simon, B. (1960) *Studies in the History of Education 1780–1870*. London: Lawrence and Wishart.

Simon, B. (1965) *Education and the Labour Movement 1870–1920*, London: Lawrence and Wishart.

Simon, B. (1986) 'The Education Act: A Conservative Measure?', *in History of Education*, Vol. 15, No 1.

Sivanandan, A. (1981) 'From resistance to rebellion: Asian and Afro-Caribbean struggles in Britain', *Race and Class*, 23 (2–3).

Sivanandan, A. (1982) 'Waiting for Scarman', *Race and Class*, 23 (2–3).

Sivanandan, A. (1991) 'Black struggles against racism', in Northern Curriculum Development Project (ed.), *Setting the Context for Change*. London: CCETSW.

Skeggs, B. (1997) *Formations of Class and Gender*. London: Sage.

Skeggs, B. (2004) *Class, Self and Culture*. London: Routledge.

Skellington, R. and Morris, P. (1992) *'Race' in Britain Today*. London: Sage.

Skocpol, T. (1979) *States and Social Revolutions*. Cambridge: Cambridge University Press.

Smith, C. and White, S. (1997) 'Parton, Howe and postmodernity: a critical comment on mistaken identity', *British Journal of Social Work*, 27 (2): 275–95.

Smith, R. (2003) *Youth Justice: Ideas, Policy and Practice*. Cullompton: Willan Publishing.

Smith, S. (1994) 'Mistaken identity – or can identity politics liberate the oppressed?', *International Socialism*, 62: 3–50.

Smith, S. (1999) 'The trickle up effect', *Socialist Review*, November.

Social Security Consortium (1986) *Of Little Benefit: a Critical Guide to the Social Security Act*. London: SSC.

Social Trends (2000) *Social Trends 30*, edited by J. Matheson and C. Summerfield. London: The Stationery Office.

Socialist Worker (2005) 'Ending world poverty: an unequal world', 12 February (issue 1938).

Spencer, S. (2000) 'Making race equality count: measuring progress towards race equality', *New Economy*, 7 (1), March: 35–41.

Spybey, T. (1998) 'Globalisation or imperialism?', *Sociology Review*, 7 (3): 29–33.

Stalker, P. (2001) *The No-Nonsense Guide to International Migration*. London: Verso.

Standing, G. (1982) 'State policy and child labour: accumulation versus legitimation', *Development and Change*, 13.

Stedman-Jones, G. (1971) *Outcast London: A Study of the Relationship Between Classes in Victorian Society*. Oxford: Oxford University Press.

Stiglitz, J. (2002) *Globalization and its Discontents*. London: Penguin.

Stirk, P.M.R. (2000) *Critical Theory, Politics and Society*. London: Pinter.

Stirling, T. and Smith, R. (2003) 'A matter of choice? Policy divergence in access to social housing post-devolution', *Housing Studies*, 18: 2.

Sullivan, M. (1992) *The Politics of Social Policy*. Hemel Hempstead: Harvester Wheatsheaf.

Summerskill, B. (2000) 'Adoption drive set to target more gay parents', *Observer*, 1 October.

*Sunday Times* (2004) '*Sunday Times* Rich List 2004': www.timesonline.co.uk/section/0,,2108,00.html

Swift, J. (1726) *Gulliver's Travels*. London: Motte.

Sylvester, R. (2004) 'Women to benefit from citizens pension plan', *Daily Telegraph*, 4 December.

Tambini, D. (2001) 'Post-national citizenship', *Ethnic and Racial Studies*, 24 (2): 195–217.

Tansey, G. (2003) 'Patenting our food future intellectual property rights in the global food system', in E. Dowler and C.J. Finer (eds), *The Welfare of Food: Rights and Responsibilities in a Changing World*. Oxford: Blackwell.

Tasker, F. and Golombok, S. (1997) *Growing Up in a Lesbian Family – Effects on Child Development*. London: Guilford Press.

Tattersall, M. (1997) 'From punk to pastiche: are Oasis postmodernists?', in *Sociology Review*, 6 (3): 20–3.

Tawney, R. (1951) *Equality*, 2nd edn. London: Unwin Books.

Tawney, R.H. (1938) *Religion and the Rise of Capitalism*. London: Penguin.

Taylor, D. (1996) *Critical Social Policy*. London: Sage.

Taylor-Gooby, P. (1994) 'Postmodernism and social policy: a great leap backwards', *Journal of Social Policy*, 23 (3).

Taylor-Gooby, P. (1997) 'In defence of second-best theory: state, class and capital in social policy', Journal of Social Policy, 26 (2).

Taylor-Gooby, P. (2002) 'The silver age of the welfare state: perspectives on resilience', *Journal of Social Policy*, 31 (4).

Thane, P. (2000) *Old Age in English History: Past Experiences, Present Issues*. Oxford: Oxford University Press.

Thom, D. (1986) 'The 1944 Education Act: the 'art of the possible?', in H.L. Smith, (ed.), *War and Social Change: British Society in the Second World War*. Manchester: Manchester University Press.

Thomas, K. (1976) 'Age and authority in early modern England', *Proceedings of the British Academy*, 62: 205–48.

Thompson, E.P. (1968) *The Making of the English Working Class*. Harmondsworth: Penguin.

Thompson, E.P. (1991) *Customs in Common*. Harmondsworth: Penguin.

Thompson, N. (1996) *Political Economy and the Labour Party*. London: UCL Press.

Thompson, P., Itzin, C. and Abendstern, M. (1990) *I Don't Feel Old*. Oxford: Oxford University Press.

Thompson, S. and Hoggett, P. (1996) 'Universalism, selectivism and particularism', *Critical Social Policy*, 46: 211–43.

Thomson, R. (1993) 'Unholy alliances: the recent politics of sex education', in J. Bristow and A. Wilson (eds), *Activating Theory*. London: Lawrence and Wishart.

Thorpe, A. and Young, R. (2003) 'Asylum and Immigration: the 2003 Bill', House of Commons Library Research Paper 03/88, 11 December.

Timmins, N. (1996) *The Five Giants: a Biography of the Welfare State*. London: HarperCollins.

Tinker, A. (1996) *Older People in Modern Society*, 4th edn. London: Longman.

Titmuss, R.M. (1950) *Problems of Social Policy*. London: HMSO.

Titmuss, R.M. (1955) 'Pension systems and population change', *Political Quarterly*, 26 (2): 152–66, reprinted in R.M. Titmuss (1958) *Essays on The Welfare State*. London: Allen and Unwin.

Titmuss, R.M. (1962) *Income Distribution and Social Change*. London: George Allen and Unwin.

Titmuss, R.M. (1974) *Social Policy*. London: Allen and Unwin.

Titmuss, R.M.(1976) *Commitment to Welfare*. London: George Allen and Unwin (first published 1968).

Tomlinson, J. (1997) *Democratic Socialism and Economic Policy: the Attlee Years, 1945–1951*. Cambridge: Cambridge University Press.

Tout, K. (1989) *Ageing in Developing Countries*. Oxford: Oxford University Press.

Townsend, P. (1962) *The Last Refuge*. London: Routledge and Kegan Paul.

Townsend, P. (1972) 'Selectivity: a nation divided', in *Sociology and Social Policy*. London: Penguin.

Townsend, P. (1979) *Poverty in the United Kingdom*. Harmondsworth: Penguin.

Townsend, P. (1981) 'The structured dependency of the elderly: the creation of social policy in the twentieth century', *Ageing and Society*, 1 (1): 5–28.

Townsend, P. (1985) 'A sociological approach to measuring poverty: a rejoinder to Professor Anartya Sen', *Oxford Economic Papers* 37 (4): 649–58.

Townsend, P. (1987) 'Deprivation', *Journal of Social Policy*, 16 (2): 125–46.

Townsend, P. and Abel Smith, B. (1965) *The Poor and the Poorest*. London: Bell & Sons.

Townsend, P., Davidson, N. and Whitehead, M. (1988) *Poverty in the United Kingdom*. Harmondsworth: Penguin.

Toynbee, P. (2000a) 'Give them hope', *Guardian*, 24 November.

Toynbee, P. (2000b) 'Pensioner power', *Guardian*, 26 May.

Toynbee, P. (2004) 'Why isn't New Labour proud to be the nation's nanny?', *Guardian*, 17 November.

Tran, M. (2005) 'World failing to meet millennium goals', *Guardian*, 17 January.

Travis, A. (2004) 'European Union list prompts human rights fears', *Guardian*, 27 September.

Treasury Taskforce on Private Finance (1997) *Partnerships for Prosperity: the Private Finance Initiative*. London: HM Treasury.

Troyna, B. (1992) 'Can you see the join? A historical analysis of multicultural and anti-racist education policies', in D. Gill, B. Mayor and M. Blair (eds), *Racism and Education – Structures and Strategies*. London: Sage.

Troyna, B. and Hatcher, R. (1992) 'Racist incidents in school: a framework for analysis', in D. Gill, B. Mayor and M. Blair (eds), *Racism and Education – Structures and Strategies*. London: Sage.

TUC (1998) 'Economic inequality and benefit levels', Internet reference: www.tuc.org.uk/vbuilding/tuc/brouse/brouse.exe

TUC (2005) 'Pay up for Pensions', Internet reference: www.tuc.org.uk/theme/index.cfm?theme=oink. Downloaded 14 February 2005.

Turner, B. (1990) 'Outline of a theory of citizenship', *Sociology*, 24 (2): 189–217.

Twigg, J. (1997) 'Deconstructing the "social bath": help with bathing at home for older and disabled people', *Journal of Social Policy*, 26 (2): 211–32.

Twigg, J. (2000) 'Social policy and the body', in G. Lewis, S. Gewirtz and J. Clarke (eds), *Rethinking Social Policy*. London: Sage.

Twigg, J. (2002) 'The body in social policy: mapping a territory' *Journal of Social Policy*, 31, (3).

UKPHA (2000) *Report: Newsletter of the UK Public Health Association*, 4, Summer.

Ungerson, C. (ed.) (1990) *Gender and Caring: Work and Welfare in Britain and Scandinavia*. Hemel Hempstead: Harvester Wheatsheaf.

Unison (1999) *Report of the Unison Working Group on PFI*. London: Unison.

Unison (2000) *Local Government PFI Newsletter*, 5: http://www.unison.org.uk/

United Nations (1989) *Convention on the Rights of the Child*. Geneva: United Nations.

United Nations Development Program (1999) *Human Development Report*. New York: UNDP.

United Nations Development Program (2003) *Millennium Development Goals: a Compact Amongst Nations to End Human Poverty*: www.hdr.undp.org/reports/global/2003/

van Oorschot, W. (2000) 'Who should get what and why? On deservingness criteria and the conditionality of solidarity among the public', *Policy and Politics*, 28 (1): 33–48.

Vandenbroucke, F. (1999) 'European social democracy: convergence, divisions and shared questions', in A. Gamble, and T. Wright (eds), *The New Social Democracy – Supplement to the Political Quarterly*. Oxford: Blackwell.

Veit-Wilson, J. (1992) 'Muddle or mendacity? The Beveridge Committee and the poverty line', *Journal of Social Policy*, 21 (3): 269–303.

Victor, C. (1991) *Health and Health Care in Later Life*. Buckingham: Open University Press.

Vincent, J. (1995) *Inequality and Old Age*. London: University College Press.

Vincent, J. (1999) *Politics, Power and Old Age*. Buckingham: Open University Press.

Vincent, J. (2003) *Old Age*. London: Routledge.

Walby, S. (1988) 'Gender politics and social theory', *Sociology*, 22 (2): 215–32.

Walby, S. (1994) 'Is citizenship gendered?', *Sociology*, 28 (2, 3): 79–395.

Walker, A. (1980) 'The social creation of poverty and dependency in old age', *Journal of Social Policy*, 9 (1): 45–75.

Walker, A. (1981) 'Towards a political economy of old age', *Ageing and Society*, 1 (1): 73–94.

Walker, A. and Walker, C. (eds) (1998) *Britain Divided*. London: Child Poverty Action Group.

Walker, A. and Maltby, T. (1997) *Ageing Europe*. Buckingham: Open University Press.

Walkowitz, J. (1980) *Prostitution in Victorian Society: Women, Class and State*. Cambridge: Cambridge University Press.

Wallerstein, I. (1974) *The Modern World System*. New York: Academic Press.

Walvin, J. (1982) *A Child's World: a Social History of English Childhood 1800–1914*. Harmondsworth: Penguin.

Walzer, M. (1983) *Spheres of Justice*. Oxford: Martin Robertson.

Ward, L. (2000) 'Typical woman earns £250,000 less than a man', *Guardian*, 21 February: 5.

Warland, B. (ed.) (1992) *Inversions*. London: Open Letters.

Warnes, A. (ed.) (1982) *Geographical Perspectives on the Elderly*. Chichester: John Wiley.

Watney, S. (1987) *Policing Desire: Pornography, AIDS and the Media*. London: Methuen/Comedia.

Watson, S. (2000) 'Foucault and the study of social policy', in G. Lewis, S. Gewirtz and J. Clarke (eds), *Rethinking Social Policy*. London: Open University/Sage.

Weale, A. (1985) 'Mr Fowler's psychology', *Political Quarterly*, 56 (4).

Webb, S. and Webb, B. (1913) 'What is socialism?', *New Statesman*, 10 May.

Webster, G.G. (1986) 'Putting father back at the head of the table', Press Conference Speech, 14 March.

Weeks, J. (1977) *Coming Out: Homosexual Politics in Britain from the Nineteenth Century to the Present*. London: Quartet.

Weeks, J. (1981) *Sex, Politics and Society: the Regulation of Sexuality since 1800*. London: Longman.

Weeks, J. (1985) *Sexuality and its Discontents*. London: Routledge.

Weiner, M.J. (1994) *Reconstructing the Criminal – Culture, Law and Policy in England 1830–1914*, Cambridge: Cambridge University Press.

Wenger, G.C. (1990) 'Elderly carers: the need for appropriate interventions', *Ageing and Society*, 10 (2): 197–219.

Wheelwright, J. (2004) 'Streets of fear', in *Guardian*, 26 May.

Wheen, F. (1999) *Karl Marx*. London: Fourth Estate.

White, M. (2000) 'Poor lost ground in Labour's first years', *Guardian*, 13 April.

White, S. (1999) 'Rights and responsibilities: a social democratic perspective', in A. Gamble and T. Wright (eds), *The New Social Democracy – Supplement to the Political Quarterly*. Oxford: Blackwell.

Whitfield, D. (1999) 'Private finance initiative: the commodification and marketisation of education', *Education and Social Justice*, 1 (2): 2–13.

Whitfield, D. (2001) *Public Services and Corporate Welfare*. London: Pluto.

Wicks, M. (1991) 'Family matters and public policy', in M. Loney, R. Bocock, J. Clarke, A. Cochrane, P. Graham and M. Wilson (eds), *The State or the Market. Politics and Welfare in Contemporary Britain*. London: Sage.

Widdowson, B. (2004) 'Retiring lives: old age, work and welfare', in G. Mooney (ed.), *Work, Personal Lives and Social Policy*. Bristol: Policy Press in association with the Open University.

Wilding, P. (1997) 'Globalization, regionalism and social policy', *Social Policy and Administration*, 31 (4): 410–28.

Williams, F. (1989) *Social Policy: a Critical Introduction*. Cambridge: Cambridge University Press.

Williams, F. (1992) 'Somewhere over the rainbow: universality and diversity in social policy', in N. Manning and R. Page (eds), *Social Policy Review*, 4. London: SPA.

Williams, W. (1985) 'Redefining institutional racism', *Ethnic and Racial Studies*, 8 (3).

Williams, Z. (2004) 'Prisons', *Guardian*, 24 September.

Wilson, A. (2001) 'Social policy and homosexuality' in M. Lavalette, and A. Pratt, (eds), *Social Policy: a Conceptual and Theoretical Introduction*, 2nd edn. London: Sage.

Wilson, E. (1989) 'In a different way', in K. Grieve (ed.), *Balancing Acts: On Being a Mother*. London: Virago.

Wilson, G. (1997) 'A postmodern approach to structured dependency theory', *Journal of Social Policy*, 3: 341–50.

Wilson, G. (2000) *Understanding Old Age: Critical and Global Perspectives*. London: Sage.

Wintour, P. and White, M. (2005) 'Citizens' pension plan to lift nearly million out of poverty', *Guardian*, 29 January.

Wolfe, A. and Klausen, J. (2000) 'Other People', *Prospect*, December, pp. 28–33.

Wolff, R. (1977) *Understanding Rawls*. Princeton, NJ: Princeton University Press,

Woodroffe, J. and Ellis-Jones, M. (2000) *States of Unrest* (World Development Report): www.wdm.org.uk/cambriefs/DEBT/unrest.htm

Woodward, K. (1997) 'Motherhood: identities, meanings and myths', in K. Woodward. (ed.), *Identity and Difference*. London: Sage.

Woodward, K. (1999) 'Representing reproduction; reproducing representation', in G. Kirkup, L. Janes, F. Hovendon and K. Woodward (eds), *The Useful Cyborg*. London: Routledge.

Woodward, K. (2002) 'Up close and personal: the changing face of intimacy', in S. Pile, and T. Jordan, (eds), *Social Change*. Oxford: Blackwell.

World Bank (2003) *Pension Reform in Europe: Process and Progress*. Washington, DC: World Bank.

World Bank (2004) 'World development indicators 2004': www.worldbank.org/data/wdi2004/index.htm

Wright, E.O. (1979) *Class Crisis and the State*. London: Verso.

Yeates, N. (2001) *Globalization and Social Policy*. London: Sage.

Yllö, K. and Bograd, M. (eds) (1988) *Feminist Perspectives on Wife Abuse*. London: Sage.

Young, I.M. (1990) *Justice and the Politics of Difference*. Chichester: Princeton University Press.

Younge, G. (2005) 'We can choose our identity but sometimes it also chooses us', *Guardian*, 21 January.

# Index

# Index